Napoleon's Campaign
in Poland
1806-1807

Napoleon's Campaign in Poland
1806-1807

F. Loraine Petre

LEONAUR

Napoleon's Campaign in Poland 1806-1807
by F. Loraine Petre

Leonaur is an imprint of Oakpast Ltd

Material original to this edition and
presentation of text in this form
copyright © 2009 Oakpast Ltd

ISBN: 978-1-84677-928-2 (hardcover)
ISBN: 978-1-84677-927-5 (softcover)

http://www.leonaur.com

Publisher's Notes

Contents

PART 5: THE FINAL TRIUMPH—
HEILSBURG, FRIEDLAND & TILSIT

Preface

This volume owes its inception to the difficulty experienced by its author in finding, in English, any satisfactory history of a campaign which he felt could not be less interesting than its predecessors of Austerlitz and Jena. There is, it is true, an outline of it in Alison's History of Europe; but that is hardly sufficient for the student of military history, and there is no good general map attached to it. Sir Robert Wilson's account of it is not available in every library, and it is not very accurate in many respects. The English text-books on military history, as a rule, scarcely allude to the campaign. The brief sketch of it in Adams's *Great Campaigns* is, unfortunately, marred by inaccuracies and misprints.

In French, the best history of the campaign is contained in vols. xvii-xix. of Comte Mathieu Dumas' admirable *Précis des Evénements Militaires*, etc. It was, however, written at a time (1826) when many sources of information, now easily accessible, were closed to most writers.

Thiers' *Histoire du Consulat et de l'Empire* is not more reliable in regard to 1806-7 than it is in the case of Waterloo. The memoirs of Rapp, Savary, de Fezensac, Masséna, Marbot, and Baron de Comeau do not profess to be histories of the wars in which the writers were engaged, except in so far as the operations came within their personal cognisance. Probably the best history of the campaign in Poland is that of General von Hoepfner, published in 1855, and based upon Prussian and, to some extent, on Russian and French official documents. The work is fully illustrated by numerous excellent maps and plans. As far as can be ascertained, this book has not been translated from the German. Nor has the diary of Carl von Plotho, which is a good account of such parts of the campaign as came under the writer's view.

In Russian, there is a history by Danilewski, which the present writer has been prevented from quoting, except where it is referred to by Hoepfner, owing to his ignorance of the language in which it is written.

A list of the published works, and the unpublished documents, which the author has consulted is appended to this preface. He takes this opportunity of acknowledging the great courtesy and assistance which he received from the officials of the Historical Section of the General Staff of the French Army, in his search for information in their admirably kept and arranged records. Thanks to these records, it has been found possible to clear up, beyond all reasonable doubt, many disputed and obscure points. Amongst these are the question whether Napoleon intended to storm the village of Eylau on the 7th February, 1807; the course of events in the village of Schloditten during the night of the 8th February; the exact extent of Ney's disobedience in pushing towards Koenigsberg in January, 1807; and the history of the famous captured despatch to Bernadotte, of the 31st January. References to documents supporting these conclusions are made in the footnotes, which, it is hoped, will be found to give chapter and verse for almost every disputable or doubtful statement in the text.

Is the campaign worth the attention of the military student? It is hoped that a perusal of this history of it may show that it is so. The campaign in Poland was the first occasion on which Napoleon found himself pitted against Russia as his principal opponent; for, before it commenced, Prussia, as a military power, had been practically obliterated. The small corps which she was able to put into the field, in support of Russia, covered itself, and Lestocq its leader, with glory, and was able, on one memorable occasion at least, to play an all-important part. Still its numbers were too small to render it more than a secondary factor in the great events of the war.

The glamour of the campaigns of Austerlitz and Jena has eclipsed that of their successor. Yet Napoleon's great scheme for the destruction of Bennigsen in February, 1807, though it failed, largely in consequence of the capture of a single despatch, is hardly inferior, as a strategic combination, to the marches upon Ulm and Jena. As a tactician, he perhaps never exhibited to greater advantage his appreciation of the features of a battlefield than at Friedland. Modern weapons have, no doubt, rendered the interest of the tactics of 1807 merely academic; but it is not so with the strategy. So long as campaigns are conducted on the surface of the earth, the principles of strategy which have guided Alexander, Caesar, Turenne, Marlborough, Frederick, Wellington, Napoleon, and every other great general of the past, will hold equally good. If ever the perfection of aerial navigation should introduce a third dimension into the operations of war, a new theory of strategy, as well as of tactics, may become necessary; unless, indeed, war should then become so destructive as to be impossible.

In organising his armies, his supplies, his finances, and his lines of communication, Napoleon never surpassed his efforts in 1806 and 1807. It is of the military aspect of the war in Poland that this history mainly treats. The politics of the time are dealt with only in so far as they directly affected the course of military events. The campaign marks the zenith of Napoleon's power in Europe. In the beginning of October, 1806, he still had to oppose him three great powers—Prussia, Russia, and England. By July, 1807, one only was left—England. Europe had her chance, in the three eventful years 1805-7, of throwing off the yoke of the tyrant. The campaign of 1807 is the record of her failure. Had its issue been different, Leipzig and Waterloo might have been anticipated by several years. Napoleon's military talents had, in 1805 and 1806, shone forth in their greatest glory, his army had scarcely begun to decline or to be composed largely of allies. Was it likely that the next campaign would show any falling off in either respect?

Another fact which adds interest to the campaign is that in it Napoleon first had a foretaste of the difficulties of campaigning in winter in Northern Europe. Even in 1806 he considered the campaign he was entering on to be the greatest enterprise he had ever undertaken. He had yet to learn the value of the Russian troops. It is impossible to doubt that he stored up in his memory all the trials of 1807 when he was preparing for his fatal enterprise of 1812. His enormous preparations for the invasion of Russia, in the latter year, show how he had learnt to appreciate the difficulties of his task. It was only at Moscow that his troubles of 1807 seem to have faded from his recollection.

A few words on the maps attached to this volume. They have been prepared with great care from many sources. The requisites of a good map for the study of a campaign, the writer thinks, are (1) that it should show the name of every place mentioned in the text, and (2) that it should not be encumbered or confused by names not alluded to. With these requirements, save in the omission of a very few unimportant villages, it is believed the maps comply.

If his work succeeds in attracting some attention to an episode in Napoleon's military career which seems hitherto to have been unduly neglected, the writer's object will have been attained.

F. L. P.
27, Gledrow Gardens
London, S.W.
17th September, 1901

Note on the Third Edition

This edition, as regards the text, differs from its predecessors only by a few typographical and other unimportant corrections. The illustrations are the most marked feature of change. As in the author's Napoleon's Conquest of Prussia, 1806, the great majority are reproductions of engravings in the collection of Mr. A. M. Broadley, of the Knapp, Bridport, who has kindly allowed Mr. Lane to utilise them. The photograph of Eylau, in March, 1901, was taken for the author from the Landsberg road. When compared with the frontispiece, it shows that the church is new just as it was on the day of the battle. It also has the advantage of showing the scene covered with snow as it was this day 100 years ago.

F. L. P.

8th February, 1907

Part 1

The Situation and the Contending Armies

CHAPTER 1

The State of Europe

Shortly after the tragic death of the Duc d'Enghien, on the 21st March, 1804, Napoleon, then first consul for life, took measures to induce the French senate to propose his elevation to the Imperial dignity. With the senate he found no difficulty. On the 18th May, that subservient body declared him Emperor of the French. With regard to his wish to make the title hereditary, he had recourse to a plebiscite, the result of which was an overwhelming majority in his favour. On the 2nd December, 1804, he was crowned, or rather crowned himself, amidst a scene of unrivalled pomp, surrounded by a brilliant court and by the marshals whom he had recently appointed. The Pope himself had been induced, or compelled, to attend the ceremony and confer his benediction on the new sovereign.

If this revival of the sovereignty was received with resignation, rather than with enthusiasm, by the bulk of the populace, such was not the case with the army. It was by his matchless military talents, and by the brilliant victories to which he had so often led the soldiers of the republic, that Napoleon had became their idol and, with them at his back, had risen from a humble lieutenant of artillery to be the greatest personality in France and in Europe.

It was as much by the necessity for retaining the favour of the army as by his own boundless ambition, and his schemes for an universal empire, that the Emperor was impelled to enter upon a continued career of conquest. His designs he cloaked by pretended overtures to England, with whom he had been again at war since May, 1803. He neither believed nor hoped that peace would follow, but the negotiations served to reveal to him the existence of an alliance between England and Russia. Austria too, he knew, was labouring to repair the losses she had suffered in recent campaigns. Prussia, confident in the strength of an army which was believed to be as invincible as those of the great Frederick, was bent on playing her own game rather than that of Europe generally. She offered a splendid opportunity for the exercise of the diplomatic talents of Talleyrand and his master who soon saw that, by judicious treatment, she could be kept out of the field, until it was too late for her to enter it with powerful allies.

Whether Napoleon really ever intended seriously to attempt the invasion of England or not, his avowed intentions enabled him to train, on his northern coasts, the finest army he ever commanded. At that distance, his preparations were far removed from the view of Austria, who little thought that an army collected at a point so remote from her frontier could be used against her with such rapidity and deadly effect as it presently was.

At the same time, the Emperor was busy strengthening himself on his continental frontier. Holland, soon to be erected into a monarchy for bestowal on his brother Louis, was brought under French control. The Italian republic was induced to declare Napoleon king of Italy.

It was now time for him to precipitate matters. His coronation at Milan with the iron crown of Lombardy, the incorporation of the republics of Genoa and Lucca, as well as other northern Italian states, his military celebration on the field of Marengo, were so many insults calculated to excite the anger and the fear of Austria. It was on Austria that the Emperor had resolved to fall first. In August, 1805, that power joined the coalition of England and Russia. To them was added Sweden. Prussia alone, refusing to join them, allowed herself to be led astray by the bait of Hanover which she coveted, and which Napoleon insidiously dangled before her greedy eyes. He had already occupied it in pursuance of his war with England. On his south-western frontier, his alliance with Spain and Portugal left him free from anxiety.

In the end of July, 1805, Sir R. Calder's naval action convinced Napoleon that all hope of an invasion of England was, for the present, at an end. He had no longer any motive for delaying his meditated attack on Austria.

That power, which had long seen that war was inevitable sooner or later, hoping to steal a march on her wakeful adversary whilst he was occupied with his schemes for the invasion of England, moved, early in September, into Bavaria, a state allied to France. In doing so she, notwithstanding her previous experience of him, underrated Napoleon and, moreover, moved at least two months before she could expect the arrival of the Russian army advancing to her assistance. The Emperor's decision to hurl upon Austria the army of England was taken at once. Every necessary order for the march from Boulogne to the Danube had already been prepared. It was executed with unparalleled rapidity and exactness. On the 10th October, the unhappy Austrian general Mack, surrounded in Ulm by the French, capitulated with 30,000 men, all that remained under his command of the 80,000 with whom he had invaded Bavaria six weeks before. The very next day, Napoleon's power at sea was for ever destroyed by Nelson at Trafalgar. A few days later, the Austrian forces in Italy, under the Archduke Charles, were compelled to retreat before Masséna in the hope of covering Vienna, now threatened by Napoleon's advance. Negotiations for an armistice failed, owing to Napoleon's excessive demands.

Prussia had, at last, come to a sense of the false position she was occupying. She attempted no resistance to the invasion of Hanover, now almost entirely clear of French soldiers, by the allied troops of Russia, Sweden, and England. The Prussian cabinet had taken offence at the violation of Anspach territory, by the march through it of French troops on their way to the Danube. So strong was the feeling against France that Duroc, Napoleon's ambassador, left Berlin whilst the King and the Tsar, who had arrived there, solemnly swore to rearrange Europe on the lines of the treaty of Luneville. Haugwitz was despatched to inform Napoleon of this intention and, in the event of its non-acceptance by him, to declare war against him on the part of Prussia. On the 15th December, Prussia had decided on a course which, if she had followed it two months earlier, placed as she was on the flank of the line of march from Boulogne to the Danube, would have frustrated the Emperor's whole plan. Whilst she was making up her mind to an honest course, Napoleon had entered Vienna, had moved to Brünn, and had finally, on the anniversary of his coronation, inflicted on the Austrians and their Russian allies the decisive defeat of Austerlitz. Haugwitz, arriving at the French headquarters with the Prussian ultimatum in his pocket, was put off till after the impending battle. Its result caused him to take a very different course, to suppress the ultimatum, the terms of which Napoleon could guess, to offer Prussia's congratulations on the victory, and to conclude a disgraceful treaty by which his master bartered the honour of Prussia for the cession of Hanover.

Austria defeated, not crushed, agreed to the terms of the treaty of Presburg, to cede territory to Italy and to Bavaria, to pay an indemnity, to recognise the recent changes in Italy, and the elevation of Bavaria and Wurtemberg from electorates to kingdoms.

Everything prospered for Napoleon. The allied invaders withdrew from Hanover; Naples, attacked by the French, shortly came under the rule of Joseph Buonaparte.

Having disposed, for the time being, of Austria, the Emperor turned upon Prussia. He had always intended to do so; her perfidious conduct had rendered him more determined than ever to destroy her. He could not trust her, even had he wished to. Prussia had embroiled herself with England by accepting from Napoleon the cession of Hanover. Under pretext of defending his new ally against Great Britain, he heaped insults on her, the last being the creation of the Confederation of the Rhine as a standing threat against her, and a great base for French operations, whether against Prussia or against Austria.

After Austerlitz, the Russian troops had retired; but the Tsar had not been a party to the negotiations at Presburg, and his hand was still free. Negotiations between Napoleon and Russia and England, during the early months of 1806, broke down. Prussia had been lashed to fury by the discovery that Napoleon had attempted to bribe England with Hanover, which he had so recently ceded to Prussia.

Wishing to strike her before succour could reach her from distant Russia, the Emperor anticipated her ultimatum by marching against her towards the Elbe.

The ultimatum reached Napoleon on the 7th October, 1806; seven days later the Prussian army had been destroyed at the fatal double battle of Jena and Auerstädt. The broken remnants were pursued to the Baltic by Soult, Murat, Bernadotte, and Lannes. Blücher was driven northwards to the Danish frontier, where he surrendered with the last of his force. Magdeburg, with a large garrison, capitulated to Ney on the 8th November; Hanover was occupied by an army under Louis Buonaparte from Holland; Saxony, detached from the Prussian alliance, was eventually attached (12th December) to that of Napoleon. The Saxon Elector's alliance was cemented by his promotion to a kingdom. No considerable organised hostile force remained to confront the Emperor west of the Oder. A small fraction, all that remained to the King of the Prussian army, alone succeeded in retiring to the Vistula and East Prussia. The Russians were still far off to the east of the Vistula when, on the 26th October, 1806, Napoleon, preceded on the 24th by Davout, the victor of Auerstädt, entered Berlin in triumph.

In less than a year he had disastrously defeated Austria, had forced the Russian army to retreat, and had absolutely broken the power of Prussia. In all Europe there remained but two substantial bulwarks against the tide of French aggression—Russia and England.

Against the latter, at sea, the Emperor, since the battle of Trafalgar, had been powerless. To ruin her, as he thought possible, in her commerce, he, on the 21st November, issued from Berlin his famous decree declaring the British islands in a state of blockade and all English subjects, who might be found in the countries under his control, prisoners of war. British merchandise in those countries was confiscated, and all entry of English vessels into continental ports was prohibited. Much as has been said against the Berlin decree, it must always be remembered that it recited some principles, such as the necessity for a blockade being efficient in order to be valid, which have since been accepted by most of the civilised powers. Napoleon did not pretend to carry out these principles. His argument was that, as Britain refused to admit them, she must be compelled to do so by other methods.

Napoleon's position at Berlin was this. He was in effective occupation of the whole of Northern Europe as far as Berlin, his rear was safe owing to his alliance with Spain and Portugal. In front of him, at a great distance still, were the armies of Russia which had, in the first instance, been designed only to support, as auxiliaries, the great army of Prussia, now destroyed. Henceforth they were to bear the whole brunt of Napoleon's onslaught.

His right flank, as he advanced against the Russians, would be threatened by Austria, who, humiliated and sorely wounded by the previous year's campaign, was yet far from being a negligible quantity. Her finances were crippled, but, if she threw in her lot with England and Russia, she might well hope for pecuniary assistance from the former[1] The Archduke Charles was reorganising the army, and had already collected a considerable force in Bohemia and Silesia.

If Austria should, however, decide to renew the struggle, she would still have to reckon with the army which Napoleon maintained in Northern Italy after the conquest of Naples.[2] That army, as it was

---

1. Austria's position was analogous to that which had been occupied by Prussia in the preceding year. By throwing her weight into the scale against the Emperor, if she could not entirely prevent his farther advance for the time being, she could, at any rate, most seriously embarrass him. On the other hard, she felt that a renewal of the war so soon, in violation of the truly of Presburg, would justly expose her to the charge of perfidy, whilst, if defeated again, she could expect nothing short of annihilation at the hands of the incensed Napoleon. To assist Prussia she could hardly feel bound, looking to the selfish and treacherous policy pursued by the North German kingdom in 1805, when Austria was herself in such dire distress. For that conduct the debacle of Jena seemed to Austria little more than a just retribution. The interests of Europe called Austria again to the breach. She was not unselfish, or farseeing enough to expose herself to the awful risk.

2. This army was entirely separate from that guarding the Neapolitan kingdom.

drained of the best French troops for employment in Germany, consisted, no doubt, largely of inferior troops. Nevertheless, it was a power to be considered, and Austria would be bound to defend her southern frontiers with at least 80,000 or 100,000 men.

Napoleon's left flank in Germany, and his rear in France, were, now that the control of the sea had passed to England, open to a descent by the English, the Swedes, and the Russians, on the coasts of France, Holland, and Germany. The Swedes held a footing on the German shore in Stralsund and Swedish Pomerania. It was hardly likely at any time that a descent would be attempted in France; it became more and more unlikely, as the Emperor succeeded in his advance towards Russia. The utmost expeditionary force which Napoleon considered England capable of landing was about 25,000 men.[3] The attempt on Holland, in 1799, by England and Russia, had not had an encouraging success. The danger to the French left and rear was distinctly less than was to be apprehended from a renewal of the war by Austria. The fear of this last eventuality hung perpetually, during the wars of 1806-7, like the sword of Damocles, over the head of Napoleon.[4] His correspondence teems with references to the subject, and much of the negotiations which he carried on, during the latter part of the campaign, was mainly with a view to avoid giving offence to Austria, whose mediation had been offered. On the 26th October[5] he inquires, through his ambassador at Vienna, as to the truth of reports that the Archduke Charles was collecting 80,000 men at Prague. If so, a remonstrance is to be addressed to the Austrian Court, which is to be told that such measures are unnecessary for maintenance of the neutrality promised by it. On the 4th November,[6] he writes to Eugène Beauharnais, explaining how he intends to place at the disposal of the Viceroy 60,000 men, including Marmont's corps in Dalmatia. That, he thinks, should suffice to detain 100,000 Austrian troops on the southern frontier, should that power sufficiently recover from its alarm at the fate of Prussia to assume a hostile attitude. Eugène is to be ready to take the field on the 1st December. To his brother Joseph the Emperor writes, on

3. *Corr.* 12,135.
4. Austria defended her armaments partly on the ground of fear of a fresh French invasion. "Austria took the opportunity to allege fears for her neutrality; as if we had not enough to do with the winter and the Muscovite, she pretended to think that we should pass the gorges of her mountains" (*Savary*, iii. 2).
5. *Corr.* 11,088.
6. *Corr.* 11,172.
7. *Corr.* 11,173

the same date, in similar terms,[7] remarking that Austria appears to be arming under pretext of assuring her safety as a neutral. On the 7th November,[8] he again desires that the Emperor of Austria be informed that his neutrality only is required, not his active alliance, but that Napoleon cannot view with equanimity the collection of 60,000 or 80,000 men on his flank, or regard such action as evincing a genuine desire to maintain neutrality. On the 14th March, 1807,[9] he writes that he already has 80,000 men in Italy, and hopes shortly to have 90,000. This should fully occupy 120,000 Austrians. He would really prefer the alliance of Russia to that of Austria, but with the latter he wants peace. On the 19th and 20th of the same month[10] he instructs Talleyrand to inform Austria that her conduct has necessitated the increase which he is making to his forces, and to say, unofficially, that Austrian mediation can be considered only on condition of her abstention from arming. He adds that he suspects Russia of endeavouring to draw Austria into the coalition. On the 9th April[11] he calls Talleyrand's attention to a suspicious correspondence between the Russian general Essen and the Austrian cordon on the Gallician frontier. On the 16th[12] he agrees to accept the offer of mediation tendered by the Austrian Emperor. On the 30th May[13] he writes to Brune, now commanding the army of observation in Germany, pointing out that, should Austria move, that marshal would be able to meet her with 60,000 men of his own army, reinforced by 20,000 Poles and 20,000 men, under Jerome Buonaparte, in Silesia.

These references suffice to show how constantly Napoleon was harassed by the dread of an Austrian intervention, and the means by which he sought to prevent or defeat it.

He saw, from Berlin, in front of him the Russian armies—now preparing to meet him as his principal adversary. He felt that, until he could gain over or crush the great Northern power, he could never hope for success in his contest against Great Britain. He would probably have preferred to gain Russia to his side without having to embark on an expedition against her which he himself described as the greatest project which he had ever undertaken.[14] He told Talleyrand, as has just been mentioned, that he would prefer the alliance of Russia

8. *Corr.* 11,194.
9. *Corr.* 12,028.
10. *Corr.* 12,028, and 12,098.
11. *Corr.* 12,333.
12. *Corr.* 12,391.
13. *Corr.* 12,704.
14. *Corr.* 11,292. Letter to Lacuée, dated 22nd November, 1806.

to that of Austria. But the former power had been too honourable in her adherence to her engagements to give much hope of her detachment from them, until she had been beaten in the field.

To embarrass her to the utmost, Napoleon sought, successfully, to embroil her with Turkey. He incited Persia also to wage war on her rear. Russia, unfortunately for Europe and herself, fell into the trap; at a time when every available man should have been at liberty to fight against Napoleon, she hampered herself by the detachment of a large army against the Turks.

Throughout the war with the French, the necessity for carrying on this subsidiary war with Turkey was a serious drain on Russian resources, whilst the assistance which Napoleon gave, through Marmont in Dalmatia, to Turkey in no way weakened his power in Germany or Italy.[15] He promised many things to the Sultan; in the end, he deserted the ally who had served him to such good purpose.

Before closing this brief account of the general political situation in Europe towards the close of 1806, a few words must be said on the subject of Poland.

The three partitions, in the latter half of the preceding century, of the Polish kingdom, had finally resulted in the acquisition by the three partitioning powers of the following shares:[16]

	Square leagues	Population
Russia	23,247	5,764,398
Prussia	6,707	2,596,389
Austria	8,296 3	600,000

The recollection of their former independence, and the hope of its recovery, were strong in the hearts of the Polish people, especially in those of the nobles. They felt that from the three powers which had absorbed them they had no hope. The advent of Napoleon, the effacement of Prussia in the late campaign, and the defeat of Austria in 1805, afforded them grounds of expectation.

No sooner had Napoleon's armies commenced their eastward progress from Berlin than he was besieged with deputations and pe-

---

15. Napoleon (or rather Jomini, *Vie de Napoleon*, ii. 336) at one time estimated Michelson's army on the Danube at 80,000, which was certainly in excess of its real strength. Two divisions were presently withdrawn for employment in Poland, and Berthier, writing on the 29th of January, 1807, to Marmont, puts the Russian army of Moldavia at 30,000 (*Arch. Hist.*, Berthier's correspondence). The prevention of such a number from joining the Russian army in front of him was of the greatest advantage to the Emperor.
16. *Wilson*, p. 67, note.

titions from the Poles, setting forth their hopes and urging him to reconstitute the monarchy.[17]

His position in regard to this question was extremely delicate. It was certain that, whatever differences might exist between Russia, Prussia, and Austria on other subjects, they would be unanimous in their opposition to any proposal for the undoing of the partitions of Poland. Prussia's feelings, in her present abased condition, he could afford to disregard. Austria he could not treat in the same way, for her neutrality was all important to him in his advance against Russia. The latter power he was anxious, when he should have defeated her, to bind to his own side in the struggle against England. When, therefore, the Austrian Cabinet, in reply to his remonstrances on the subject of its assembly of troops in Gallicia, urged the danger of insurrectionary movements in Prussian Poland extending to Gallicia, Napoleon agreed not to allow his incitements of the Poles to be extended to the Austrian portion.[18] At the same time, he sounded that Government on a proposal that it should cede to him its share of Poland in exchange for Prussian territory in Silesia, which had been wrested by Frederick the Great from Maria Theresa.[19] The bait was tempting. To his own honour, and the advantage of Europe, the Emperor of Austria avoided the snare which was designed to embroil him with Prussia.

For the reasons which have above been stated, Napoleon also resolved not to irritate Russia by inciting the Poles subject to her to insurrection, and he, throughout the campaign, restricted his operations in this sense to the Prussian share of Poland.

To the deputations which approached him at Berlin and at Warsaw, he replied vaguely, "France has never recognised the different partitions of Poland; nevertheless, I cannot proclaim your independence until you have decided to defend your rights as a nation with arms

---

17. De Fezensac (p. 125) says that Lannes and Augereau, marching to the left of Posen, found the Polish country-folk far less enthusiastic for revolt against Prussia, and that the movement was mainly supported by the nobles.

18. To Baron de Comeau the Emperor said, "Poland! so much the worse for them! They have allowed themselves to be partitioned. They are no longer a nation, they have no public spirit. The nobles are too much, the people too little. It is a dead body to which life must be restored before making anything of it. I will make soldiers and officers of them; afterwards I will see. I shall take Prussia's portion. I shall have Posen and Warsaw, but I will not touch Cracow, Gallicia, or Wilna" (Comeau, 281).

19. Corr, 11,339. Instructing Andreossy, his new Ambassador at Vienna, the Emperor says he wishes to force nothing; but if Austria would be inclined to exchange Gallicia for part of Silesia, he is ready to treat, either openly or secretly. This was early in December, 1806.

in your hands by every sort of sacrifice, even that of life. You have been reproached with having, in your continued civil dissensions, lost sight of the interests of your country. Instructed by your misfortunes, reunite yourselves and prove to the world that one spirit animates the whole Polish nation."[20]

According to de Fezensac, Napoleon was furious with Murat for forwarding one petition from Warsaw, in which it was prayed that the Polish kingdom might be reconstituted under a French general. The Emperor discerned in it the handiwork of his ambitious brother-in-law, and that he was, doubtless, the French general suggested.[21]

The Emperor's replies, whilst making no definite promises, were sufficiently encouraging to assure to him the moral and material support of the Poles in the ensuing campaign, and to deprive Prussia of all hope of recruiting her shattered army by voluntary enlistment in Poland. It was, however, most desirable for the Emperor to support the Poles, in their resistance to Prussia, by occupying their territory, especially Warsaw, their ancient capital, and by conferring on their representatives at least a nominal share in the administration of the country.

As soon, therefore, as he was in possession of Warsaw, he constituted a provisional government of seven of the chief nobles. The country was parcelled off into six departments, the boundaries of which were already known.[22] The branches of justice, the interior, finance, war, and police, were assigned to separate members of the government, which voted by majority and was empowered, on the report of the departmental director, to pass necessary laws and orders.[23] In West Prussia, Napoleon had already organised his own government, placing at the head of the civil departments Daru, and at that of the military Clarke.[24]

---

20. *Corr.* 11,279, dated 19th November 1806.

21. *De Fezensac*, p. 125.

22. Warsaw, Posen, Kalisch, Bromberg, Plock, Bialystok.

23. *Corr.* 11,630, decree of 14th January, 1807.

24. West Prussia was divided into four departments, having their capitals at Berlin, Custrin, Stettin, and Magdeburg. The existing local administrative officers were generally retained, but the Emperor appointed his own men to the general financial control, and for the collection of the contributions with which the towns and states had been assessed (*Savary*, iii. 3). Napoleon was not seriously troubled by disturbances in Germany. His hold on the country was too firm, and the strength of the army of occupation too great, to encourage insurrection. The Hessian troops, from which he thought trouble might arise, were got out of the way in Holland, France and Naples (*Savary*, iii. 2). An attempted insurrection in Hesse Cassel, the Elector of which had been deprived by Napoleon of his territories, was put down in a manner calculated to discourage any further outbreaks.

Silesia was yet unconquered, and its great fortresses remained to be subdued.

Such, briefly, was the situation of Europe in November, 1806. Napoleon, holding all the territory of France, Italy, Holland, and Northern Germany up to the Oder, was in possession of immense resources in men, money, and material. His rear was safe from the direction of Spain, and the garrison left in France was ample to repel any descent likely to be made by England on her coasts. Austria was a danger to his right flank; but, lying, as she did, between the French armies in Germany, and in Northern Italy, and crippled by her recent disasters, she could only intervene at great risk to herself. Sweden was only dangerous as the ally of England, in the event of a descent by sea on the Dutch or German coasts. Turkey was in active alliance with the French.

CHAPTER 2

The Armies and the Leaders

THE FRENCH ARMY

It has already been said that the army which Napoleon led against Austria in the autumn of 1805 was the finest he ever commanded. From that year commenced its decline, slow at first, more rapid as the youth of the country was exhausted by his overdrafts. It was in 1805 that he first drew upon the resources of the future, by calling out, before their time, the conscripts of 1806. They, however, formed no part of the army which fought at Ulm and at Austerlitz. As in 1805, so in 1806, Napoleon overdrew his account by calling out, nearly a year before their time, the conscripts of 1807. At this period the conscription was expected to yield annually about 80,000 recruits. There would thus be in the French army, when the advance against the Russian armies commenced, 80,000 recruits called out and trained a year before their proper time of service, and shortly afterwards 80,000 more also anticipated by nearly a year, and only commencing their training.[1]

Even the recruits of the conscription of 1806 were not, apparently, provided with uniforms by the 22nd November; Napoleon on that date had to urge the completion of their equipment, as well as that of the conscripts of 1807.[2] He proposed to call to the front the recruits of 1806, now fairly trained, though he would be prepared to leave 20,000 in reserve for the present. That would give him 60,000 for the front.[3]

He recognised, as has been related already, that the advance against Russia was the greatest enterprise he had ever, so far, entered upon.[4] Operating at so great a distance, he would necessarily require forces

---

1. Napoleon called for the conscripts of 1807, in January of that year, instead of September. *Corr.* 11,282, dated 21st November, to Senate.
2. *Corr.* 11,291.
3. *Corr.* 11,292, to Lacuée, dated 22 November, 1806.
4. *Corr.* 11,292, as above.

far in excess of those which had sufficed for the destruction of Prussia. To provide these additional men, he now employed various methods. He had to think not only of the army at the actual scene of operations, but also of that to be maintained in Italy as a threat to Austria on her southern border, of forces to repel any attempt from the sea on the Dutch or German coasts, and, finally, of the troops necessary to protect the ports of France against a possible descent.

The last was the least important; for a descent on the French coast by England was not probable and, if undertaken, would not be likely to be made in great force.

Napoleon calculated that early in December he had in Germany, with the Grand Army, 1400 companies of infantry averaging 123 men each.[5] He had 61 regiments; each regiment, as a rule, consisted of 3 battalions, one of which was left in France as a depot. But a few regiments had 4 battalions, 3 on service and one in depot. Of these he had 18 in Germany. He designed to increase the companies to 140 men each, which would give a total of nearly 200,000 for the infantry in Germany.

The cavalry regiments he proposed to raise to 5 squadrons of 200 sabres each.[6]

Kellerman, who was in charge of the depots on the eastern frontier of France and in Western Germany, was ordered to send to the front 8,000 or 10,000 conscripts, whom he would have collected by the 15th November.[7]

Irrespective of these, he was to form eight provisional battalions, of which the nucleus was to be one company sent back from each of eight 3rd battalions serving with the Grand Army. To this nucleus were to be added conscripts who had only undergone eight or ten days' training, who would be then sent to continue their training with the provisional battalions at Magdeburg or Cassel. As their training progressed, they were to be formed into companies, then into battalions, finally into provisional regiments for the march to the front. As they marched their training continued. Men who were left behind, sick or footsore, by one provisional battalion, at any of the halting-stages, were gathered up by the next to pass.[8] As these battalions passed through the principal places

---

5. *Corr.* 11,478, to Lacuée.
6. *Corr.* 11,238, dated 12th November, 1806.
7. *Corr.* 11,146, dated 2nd November, 1806.
8. Kellerman's report of his proceedings as commander of the Army of Reserve is a document full of interest. He says that at first he was left with only enough officers and non-commissioned officers to carry on the (continued on next page)

such as Wurtzburg, Erfurt, Wittenberg, and Spandau, they were required to be inspected by the local commandant, who reported on them to headquarters. Thus Napoleon had a continuous series of reports, enabling him to keep his eye on the progress of his recruits who were sent forward under officers from the depots.

On arrival at the front, the provisional regiments were again broken up for distribution, according to requirements, to the various corps and regiments.[9]

For the defence of the French ports Cambacérès was directed to raise 9000 National Guards in the departments of the Somme and the Lower Seine.[10] These were to join the reserve in Paris, standing ready for movement to any part of the coast that might be threatened. There

---

(from previous page) administration, and the men were nothing but sick, wounded, and convalescents. He was dependent on the conscripts of 1806, who began to reach him in October. He considered that in one month he could turn out a fair soldier, understanding his musket, how to use it, take it to pieces, to put it together, and exercised first with blank cartridge, then at target practice. He complains bitterly of his difficulties with clothing and transport contractors. For instance, the 28th regiment marched from France with its baggage, but reached Kellerman several months before it. As he despatched each detachment of 150 infantry or 50 cavalry, another was ready to follow it closely. During the whole campaign he despatched 20 provisional regiments of infantry, and 11 of cavalry, numbering 50,683 men, and 7112 horses. As the regiments were sent off, there was such a dearth of officers that the marshal had to promote, subject to the Emperor's confirmation, many non-commissioned officers.

Amongst his many troubles were sore backs among the horses, the result of neglect. He proposes to cashier one sub-lieutenant who produced 32 horses with sore backs out of a detachment of 47.

Besides these troops, Kellerman formed Mortier's corps at Mayence, and the Legion of the North at Landau. The latter corps exercised him much, as it was to be, under the Emperor's orders, composed of deserters from the enemy-largely Poles. It had, owing to the neglect of contractors, to be sent off almost without clothes and supplies. Yet, though, as was not unnatural, there were many desertions from it, the Legion did good service before Danzig.

Kellerman also organised several corps of gendarmes, artillery, etc. Altogether, he says, there passed the Rhine at Mayence and Wesel, as reinforcements for the Grand Army, 152,456 men, and 19,306 horses, of which 73,624 men, and 9559 Horses were from the Army of Reserve. These numbers of course do not include the troops marching from Italy, Switzerland, and Holland, or the German contingents (Kellerman's report, *Arch. Hist.*).

9. "The bad method," says Von der Goltz, "of reinforcing armies by new units, instead of by fresh drafts, bringing the old ones up to their normal numbers, has long since been discarded by all great armies" (*Nation in Arms*, p. 378). Napoleon, it will be observed, followed generally the principles here advocated.

10. *Corr.* 11,130. To Cambacérès, 31st October, 1806.

were in Paris three regular regiments for this purpose. Two of them were replaced by these National Guards, and moved towards the front in Poland. Napoleon later remarks[11] that 40,000 men will be available in the 3rd battalions left in France. 3000 National Guards were mobilised at Bordeaux.[12] From Brittany he drew to the front two regiments. To compensate for these, he sent there 6000 conscripts of 1805 and 4000 of 1807. He also raised 5000 men amongst the shipbuilders and artificers of the ports, who were thrown out of employ owing to the British supremacy at sea.[13]

The regiment of "vélites" of the Guard, not having been found to fulfil the objects for which it was intended, he proposed to form into a regiment of fusiliers of the guard 1500 or 1600 strong,[14] which was to leave Paris for Berlin on the 12th December.[15]

To his brother Louis he wrote[16] that he should expect him to provide at least 20,000 Dutch troops for the Grand Army, the number, if possible, to be raised to 25,000 in the spring. Three days earlier[17] he had ordered Louis to occupy Hanover with three French regiments and 7000 or 8000 Dutch troops.

He was even willing to accept the offer of a Breton gentleman to raise 500 or 600 volunteers, though he stipulated that they should not be men who would be otherwise taken by the conscription.[18] He directed the raising of regiments in Switzerland.[19] For the armament of regiments to be raised amongst the Poles, large numbers of muskets were sent to Davout for delivery to Dombrowski, who was charged with their organisation.[20] For a large cavalry force in the great plains of Poland Napoleon at once recognised the necessity. He was anxious to hurry up as many horsemen as possible before he should meet the Russians. He had already decided on adding a fifth squadron to his cavalry regiments, bringing them nominally to a strength of 1000

---

11. *Corr.* 11,262. To Cambacérès, 16 November, 1806.

12. *Corr.* 11,066, dated 24th October, 1806.

13. *Corr.* 11,477, 15th December, 1806, to Dejean, and *Corr.* 11.479 of the same date to Admiral Decrés.

14. *Corr.* 11,292, dated 22nd November, 1806, to Lacuée.

15. *Corr.* 11,330, dated 30th November, 1806, to Junot.

16. *Corr.* 11,192, dated 7th November, 1806.

17. *Corr.* 11,171, dated 4th November, 1806.

18. *Corr.* 11, 164, dated 4th November, 1806.

19. *Corr.* 11,237, dated 12th November, and 11,302, dated 24th November.

20. *Corr.* 11,237, dated 12th November, and 11,258, dated 14th November, to Davout. The latter dispatch remarks that 6 battalions might be expected from Posen and 12 more from Warsaw, should it rise against the Prussians.

each, though he did not expect them to appear in the field with more than 700 sabres. He writes to Dejean that altogether he has 60,000 or 70,000 cavalry in different parts of Europe, and that he believes there are still 10,000 in the depots in France.[21] On the 5th January, 1807, he calculates there should be with the Grand Army 24 regiments of dragoons and cuirassiers, 18 of chasseurs, 9 of hussars, making 51,000 men, at the nominal strength of 1000 per regiment. They would not, however, amount to more than 36,000 actually present. A few days earlier he had said he expected reinforcements of 16,000 cavalry during the year.[22] So urgent was the need for cavalry that he ordered Kellerman to send the men forward in batches of even 15 or 16, as they were collected. Cavalry was not required to any great extent in Italy. The south was too mountainous for it, the north too much intersected with canals and vineyards. Therefore, on the 4th November, 1806, he writes to Joseph that he has taken 8 French cavalry regiments from the army of Northern Italy, trusting to Joseph's replacing them with 8 out of 12 regiments which he had in Naples.

The army in Northern Italy was to be reinforced by 20,000 men from France in the beginning of December.[23] From Spain the Emperor directed Talleyrand to demand 10,000 infantry and 4000 cavalry, and the 6000 Spaniards in Italy were ordered to march up to Germany.[24]

Such were the principal methods by which the Emperor increased his armies in preparation for his first advance against the Russians. In the spring he was compelled to make still further demands on the military strength of France. They will be described later in their proper chronological order.

He was able by the end of November to count on 80,000 men towards Warsaw, whilst another 80,000 were following in second line.

Napoleon evinced, at all times, extraordinary care for the measures to be taken to provide for the sustenance of his armies. Certainly he did not adhere to any fixed system, but took the means of nourishing his hosts just wherever he found them. He knew how, by promising high payment, by his dexterous treatment of authorities and communities, as well as by threats and brute force, to furnish himself with supplies, even in exhausted districts. . . . But, before all things, he was a master of organis-

---

21. *Corr.* 11,556, to Dejean.
22. *Corr.* 11,554, to Dejean.
23. *Corr.* 11,172, to Eugène Beauharnais, dated 4th November, 1806.
24. *Corr.* 11,476, dated 15th December, 1806, to Talleyrand.

ing his lines of rear communication; and purchases, transport, requisitions, and compulsory provisioning by the population, all contributed to fill his soldiers' bellies.[25]

As soon as he found himself supreme in Prussia and the allied states, the Emperor proceeded to impose enormous war contributions on them all, especially on rich cities such as Hamburg. The total sum exceeded 160 millions of francs (£6,400,000).[26] A great proportion of this sum he could not hope to realise in cash. What he did was to levy supplies of various sorts from the cities and states. These were nominally on payment; the value was met, not in cash, but by a credit against the demand for war contribution.

Wherever there was a great local manufacture of articles required for an army, it was utilised in this way: uniforms were made up at Hamburg and Magdeburg, Leipzig and Berlin, saddles at Berlin and elsewhere, boots at numerous centres. If it is true that an army marches on its belly, Napoleon equally recognised the care required for its feet. Scarcely a day passes on which there is not some letter or order from him dealing with the supply of boots, the construction of bakeries, and the means of forwarding bread to the armies. No detail was below his notice. "Every detachment," he writes, "coming from Paris or Boulogne should start, each man with a pair of shoes, besides two pairs in his knapsack. At Mayence they will receive another pair to replace that worn on the march. At Magdeburg they will receive a new pair to replace that worn on the march from Mayence to Magdeburg, so that every man may reach his corps with a pair of shoes on his feet and a pair in his knapsack."[27] Notwithstanding all

---

25. Von der Goltz, *The Nation in Arms*, p. 354.
26. The contributions varied from 25 millions of francs in the case of Saxony (which was subsequently modified by his alliance with that state) to 100,000 francs in the case of the smallest states (see *Corr.* 11,010, decree dated 15th October, 1806, the day after the battle of Jena). By the same decree, all English merchandise in the northern cities, in whatsoever hands it might be, was declared forfeit to the use of the French army. The sums given here as contributions, do not include the ordinary financial resources of the countries which were applied by the French to their own uses. Altogether, there passed into Napoleon's hands, in money and goods collected from Germany, more than 560 millions of francs (£22,400,000), whilst the net cost of the war against Prussia and Russia was put at only 213 millions (see summary of Daru's report, *Dumas*, xix. 489). Truly, in this instance, war was made to support itself.
27. *Corr.* 11,413. During the campaign there were supplied to the army, from first to last, 587,008 pairs of shoes, 16,948 of boots, and 37,386 of gaiters, all made up in Germany, besides 397,000 pairs of shoes sent from France (summary of Daru's report, *Dumas*, xix. 490).

this care for their food, their clothing and their boots, the French troops were often in dire distress for all three.

Napoleon, writing to Soult, for instance, on the 27th February, 1807, remarks that the Russians appear to be "like us," and not to have eaten for several days.

The difficulty, even under much more favourable circumstances, of keeping men properly shod and clothed is illustrated by Von der Goltz: "In December, 1870, some German soldiers might have been seen plodding along the miry roads, in the depth of winter, barefoot, whilst many had only wooden shoes and linen trousers." There were some weak German companies with so many as forty shoeless men. Every sort of garment was utilised, with the exception of the ominous French red breeches, the possible consequences of wearing which were obvious (*Nation in Arms*, pp. 375-376). De Fezensac (132) says that, in the winter of 1806-7, the French soldiers were living mainly on what they could find in the country, as the arrival of supplies was delayed by the horrible weather and the state of the roads.

The following quaint little note, written by Lasalle on the back of a despatch from Milhaud to Murat as it passed through his quarters, speaks volumes. It is in the daily correspondence, 5th December, 1806, in the *Archives Historiques*. "*A force de cris et de menaces, j'ai obtenu un pain et une dame-jeanne de vin que je suis trop heureux d'offrir à vôtre Altesse. Notre noble hôte est un ladre qui nous laissera mourir de faim.*" Figure the shortness of supplies when a general commanding a cavalry division has no hesitation in offering, as an acceptable gift to the Emperor's brother-in-law, a loaf of bread and a bottle of wine! What, too, must have been the feelings of the unfortunate despatch-bearer, unexpectedly burdened with this precious and fragile load! Envy of the good things he was carrying, and anxiety lest breakage of the bottle should draw upon him the wrath of Murat, perhaps divided his sentiments equally.

For his sick and wounded the Emperor was equally solicitous. The provision of hospital and ambulance arrangements became more and more difficult as the armies advanced into a country where the roads were atrocious and local means of transport very scarce. The numbers, both of sick and wounded, to be dealt with were very great; the supply of hospital attendants and surgeons was deficient, especially at the advanced hospitals. Nevertheless, by the end of January, 1807, no less than 21 hospitals were open in Warsaw alone, with more than 10,000 occupants who had been brought back, on foot in the case of those slightly wounded or suffering from trifling ailments, on carts or sledges in the more serious cases. The pressure was still greater after the battle of Eylau. Hospitals were opened at Bromberg, Marienburg, Marienwerder, Elbing, and other places. To relieve the hospitals in Poland, later on, many wounded and sick, who could bear the journey, were transferred to Breslau and other places in Silesia, where spacious barracks afforded excellent accommodation. So great were the preparations made that though, on the 30th June, 1807, there were 27,376 men in hospital, it was calculated that there was still available accommodation for nearly 30,000 men. From the 1st October, 1806, to the 31st October, 1808, over 421,000[28] cases of sickness or wounds occurred, with 32,000 deaths. The average stay in hospital was 29 days. It may be taken, therefore, that during this period the mean number in hospital was somewhere about 16,500; at times it was very much higher.[29] These figures do not include the enemy's sick and wounded prisoners, or those of the allied troops, who ranged, during the period November, 1806, to July, 1807, from one twelfth to one seventh of the number of French. For the service of the hospitals, the resources of the conquered countries were fully utilised, as they were in the case of supplies, clothing, boots, and saddlery. The captured Prussian tents were cut up, partly for bandages, partly for shirts, and partly for mattresses. Napoleon's army carried no tents. If cantonments were out of the question, they bivouacked in the open, whatever the weather. Great numbers of cavalry and artillery horses, captured from the Prussians, were pressed into the French service. The cavalry from Italy and France were marched to Germany on foot, and there remounted at the great cavalry depot which Napoleon established at Potsdam. Altogether he raised 40,555 horses in the conquered territories.[30]

Into the finance of the war this work cannot enter, beyond the remarks above, in footnote.

The army was organised in corps, by no means of even strength, rarely reaching the modern standard of 30,000 men. The only corps which generally approached this figure were the 1st, 3rd, 4th, and 10th.

In addition to the corps of all arms, there were two cavalry reserves—the first under Murat, nearly 10,000 strong at the end of

28. The number sounds enormous, yet it is worth remembering that in 1870 (with, of course, a much larger army), the Germans had 400,000 sick, and 100,000 wounded (*Nation in Arms*, p. 331).
29. For this brief account of the hospitals, see abstract of Daru's report at end of vol. xix., Dumas. The number of wounded out of the total in hospitals was 47, and of fever cases 105 out of every 190. The largest number in hospital was, in June 1807, 27,376.
30. Daru's report, Dumas, end of vol. xix.

November, 1806.[31] The second, under Bessières, only existed during the first phase of the campaign. It was broken up before Eylau. The artillery was armed with a good gun, as guns were at that date. Both it and the cavalry drew their remounts largely from the captured Prussian troops and from the horses found in the country.

The rank and file of the army was but little, if at all, past its best. In the earlier part of the campaign, its youngest men were the conscripts of 1806 who had, owing to their premature enrolment, already undergone a year's training. Many of the troops had been with Napoleon in his earlier campaigns and in Egypt, very many had been at Ulm and Austerlitz, the majority had just emerged from the brilliant campaign of Jena. They were now preparing for a renewed war against fresh enemies; the hardest task that an army can undertake.[32] Even these hardened and enthusiastic warriors contemplated with dread the prospect of a fresh winter campaign in an inhospitable and difficult country, and Napoleon was often remonstrated with, as he rode alongside of his men, for insisting on their advance into Poland.[33] To such complaints he would reply with the rough jests which his veterans loved to hear from him, and with promises to give them rest as soon as he possibly could. In action, the infantry was still splendid, and did not as yet require to be formed in deep columns of many battalions, such as was Macdonald's at Wagram, three years later.

The cavalry were excellent and well mounted, though, in the latter respect, they fell short of many of the Russian cavalry regiments. The artillery was highly trained and invariably made good practice.

Of the French soldier generally, Jomini makes Napoleon say, "My soldiers are as brave as it is possible to be, but they argue too much. If

---

31. *Corr.* 11,305, to Murat, dated 24th November, 1806. It comprised

Beaumont's and Klein's dragoons	4800
Decker's dragoons	1200
Nansouty's brigade	2400
Milhaud's brigade	800
Total	9200

32. "The most difficult task that can be imposed upon an army is to enter on a second campaign, against fresh enemies, immediately after one in which its moral energies have been partially consumed. Fortunate as Napoleon's operations against the Prussians and the Saxons in the autumn of 1806 had been, they all the same came to a standstill when, in the winter, he encountered the Russians and the corps of General von Lestocq, which had not preciously been in action" (*Nation in Arms*, p. 335).

33. "Our soldiers were less satisfied; they showed a lively repugnance to cross the Vistula. Misery, the winter, the bad weather, had inspired them with an extreme aversion for this country" (*Rapp*, p. 118).

they had the impassable firmness and the docility of the Russians the world would not be great enough for me. The French soldiers love their country too much to act the part of the Macedonians."[34]

To the chief generals a separate section will be devoted; but there are many regimental, brigade, and divisional commanders whom it will be impossible to notice separately. Several of them rose to the highest rank. Generally speaking, the officers and non-commissioned officers were of excellent quality and great experience in war.

The discipline of the army was certainly not such as would be approved at the present time, either in the case of the officers or in that of the men. De Fezensac mentions[35] that Marchand changed the cantonments of his division three times without vouchsafing any information to Ney, the commander of the corps Marauding, chiefly in search of food, was common amongst the men. Even Thiers puts the number of men "absent" after Eylau at 60,000.

THE RUSSIAN ARMY

Of the Russian army of 1806[36] we have an account by Sir Robert Wilson, avowedly written with a favourable bias. Still, being written by an eye-witness, at a time when England was at war with Russia, it sums reasonable to accept it as, on the whole, correct, at any rate as regards facts.

The infantry consisted of men between the ages of 18 and 40, generally of small stature, but endowed with considerable physical strength and inured to hardships of all sorts. They could bear the stress of the worst weather, and, at the same time, could subsist on the scantiest fare. The keynote to their character was implicit obedience to superior authority and absolute reliance on it. This submissive obedience was not corrected by intelligence in the interpretation of orders. Whatever commands he received, the Russian soldier would do his best to carry out. It mattered not to him that, in the meanwhile, circumstances had so changed as to render the orders incapable of execution. Once he had received them, and until they were cancelled by their authority, it was his sole aim to perform them. The lengths to which his sense

---

34. *Vie de Napoleon,* ii. 434. This work is in the form of a narrative supposed to be addressed by the spirit of Napoleon in the next world to an audience of all the great commanders who preceded him. The words quoted here Napoleon is made to represent as used by himself to a connoisseur. They would, therefore, appear to have been His own actual views.
35. *Souvenirs Militaires,* p. 139.
36. For this account of the Russian army, see chiefly *Wilson,* pp. 1–70.

of duty, in this respect, would carry him are well illustrated by the account given by Marbot of the battle of Golymin. He describes how a stray body of Russians, hoping to conceal, by their silence, their nationality from the French who surrounded them in the darkness, restrained their cries. Neither the excitement of action, nor the agony of wounds, could draw from them the slightest sound. The wounded and the dying fell and lay in perfect silence; to their opponents it seemed as if they were firing at shadows.[37]

The courage of men who could do such deeds was unquestionable; their intelligence was of a very different order. Absolutely uneducated, they fought like animals rather than like intelligent beings. The idea of seeking cover was foreign to their nature and disdained by their courage. Death had no terrors for them, no carnage appalled them. The one thing which they could ill brook was a continued retreat. In such circumstances only did their feelings express themselves in murmurs, so audible as, at times, to compel their commanders to stand and fight when retreat was the wiser course.

Their powers of marching were marvellous. For days at a time they would march regularly every night and yet fight all day with the very minimum of rest and food. Even the terrible night of the 7th-8th February, spent without shelter and without food, exposed to the full rigour of almost arctic weather, with the scantiest clothing and almost without boots, failed to damp their ardour for the awful battle which was to succeed it.

The Russian soldier could be trained to march and drill with precision and rapidity, to fight steadily in square or column; but he was lost under circumstances where separation from his companions, and perhaps from his officers, required the exercise of that individual intelligence and that natural aptitude for war which has always characterised the French soldier. Their uniforms were bad in quality of material, and they were armed with a musket so heavy and cumbersome that the supplies of arms received from England, not being sufficient for all, were reserved as a reward for meritorious men. When it is remembered how clumsy a weapon was the "Brown Bess" of those days, it is possible to form some conception of the burden which must have been imposed by the carriage and use of the Russian musket.

The troops fought in 1807 in a country whence the terror of war and famine had driven every inhabitant who could by any possibility quit it. In their flight the peasants carried with them all that was portable. What they had to leave behind they had done their best to bury

37. *Marbot*. Available in a three volume Leonaur edition.

beyond the reach of the approaching armies. With a commissariat of the most wretched description, unable often to supply any food, the sufferings from hunger of the Russian soldiery are easier to imagine than to describe. They could live only on what was provided by their own diligence in unearthing and robbing the hidden stores of the inhabitants. Long habituation to the plainest and scantiest food could alone enable an army, under such circumstances, to maintain life and strength. Yet the Russians were always ready and able to fight with undiminished fury and obstinacy.

The army was recruited on no fixed principle. A certain number of men being required, the magistrates selected the best of the young men up to that limit. Their pay was infinitesimal—about half a guinea a year.

As might be expected, the arm in the use of which they excelled was the bayonet. Their generally superior physique gave them an advantage over the French in personal combat. With the bayonet, Sir R. Wilson considers that the British alone could dispute the supremacy of the Russian.

The Russian soldier's sense of moral obligations was that of the barbarian. His religion was mixed with superstition, but he was not a bigot. His sovereign he invested with an almost godlike supremacy, and, whilst his untold privations at times overcame his sense of discipline in regard to his officers, nothing could diminish his reverence for the Tsar, the father of his people. A curious story is told by Sir R. Wilson, illustrative of this trait in the character of the Russian soldier. At a time when privation had driven many Russians, as well as French, to form bands marauding in search of food, a party of Russian officers, prisoners on parole, accompanied by some French officers, was marching towards Warsaw. Falling in with a body of Russian marauders, commanded by a sergeant, the French officers were, in spite of the protest of their Russian companions, massacred. Then came the turn of the Russians. As honourable men, they refused to listen to the demand of the soldiers that they should break their parole and return to the army at the head of their captors. They were told that their country's right to their allegiance over-rode all obligations of honour towards their enemy. They still refused, and were thereupon done to death, with the exception of one officer who, left for dead, eventually recovered and escaped to tell the story. Yet the soldiers who could commit an atrocity such as this, would share their last crust with a starving peasant whose all had begin unearthed and robbed.

The Light Infantry (Jägers), recruited mainly in Siberia, were superior as marksmen to the line regiments. The Imperial Guard was a picked body of about 17,000 men, of magnificent physique, far superior in this respect do Napoleon's guard, and even to the corresponding Prussian force.[38] The Russian regular cavalry had the great advantage over their enemies of being mounted on horses, "matchless," says Sir R. Wilson, "for an union of sire, strength, activity, and hardiness; whilst formed with the bulk of the British cart horse, they have so much blood as never to be coarse, and withal are so supple as naturally to adapt themselves to the *manége*, and receive the highest degree of dressing."

When the Guard cavalry proceeded from St. Petersburg to the front, the 700 miles was accomplished, as far as Riga, at the rate of 50 miles a day, the men riding in wagons. For the remainder of the journey the horses were ridden 35 miles a day. Yet they reached their destination in the finest condition. The hardships which the Russian cavalry underwent, in a snow-covered country, were beyond bounds. Forage, save the old thatch stripped from the roofs, was unprocurable, and shelter, of course, was unknown.

As a horseman, the Russian regular cavalryman had no experience, except in the schools. He was not born to the use of horses, and he had to learn both how to ride and how to care for them. Yet the Russian cavalry distinguished itself throughout the campaign and was often victorious over the French with all its training. They had no great cavalry leader, no one who knew when to use them to the greatest advantage.[39]

If good horses were a great advantage to the cavalry, they were still more so to the artillery, which had to drag its guns through the new element of mud, which Napoleon alleged he had discovered in Poland.

The Russian guns, according to Sir R. Wilson, were good—better, apparently, than the infantry musket. The carriage was strong, without being heavy, the harness and tackle of the best quality. The horses were small, but powerful and well bred. The ordinary teams were four for the light guns, and eight or ten for the 12-pounders. With these teams, guns were forced through drifts of soft snow deep enough to cover

---

38. Jomini puts into Napoleon's mouth these words, "I saw at Tilsit a regiment of Russian guards; and I have not forgotten the sensation which I felt at its appearance. Many only saw in it a disagreeable stiffness. I have never loved armies of automatons, I required soldiers of intelligence; however, I was surprised at the precision and assurance of this infantry. I understood that an army so well disciplined and of such extraordinary firmness would be the first in the world if, to these qualities, it united a little of the electric enthusiasm of the French." The words were, perhaps, not used by Napoleon himself, but the criticism, as that of Jomini, is valuable.

39. The cavalry, which had been very inferior under Suvarow, had been vastly improved since his time (Jomini, *Vie de Napoleon*, ii, ?36, note).

them, and, at Friedland, they were first got across a ford so deep that the horses were almost swimming, and then up a nearly perpendicular bank. The drivers, gunners, and non-commissioned officers were good, but the officers were often ignorant of their arm. The number of guns was excessive; at Eylau, there were 460 on the battlefield, which gives nearly 6 per 1000 men. This great number was at times a disadvantage, and delayed the movements of the army. Before Eylau, Bennigsen had to send his heavy artillery by a circuitous route, to avoid encumbering his columns. The possibility of its capture, whilst detached, was a cause of serious anxiety to him.

The comparatively small number of guns lost in the campaign (the numbers were greatly exaggerated by Napoleon) speaks volumes for the exertions of men and horses. Some 70 or 80 guns had to be abandoned in deep mud, during the retirement to Pultusk and Golymin, in December. The French were not more successful at that time in carrying along their guns; but, as they were advancing, they were able to recover those they left behind, whilst the Russian guns necessarily fell into the enemy's hands, when abandoned in retreat.

In addition to their regular cavalry, the Russians depended largely on their Cossacks. This irregular cavalry, mounted on "very little ill-conditioned but well-bred horses,"[40] was, throughout, a terror to the French. Against the heavy cavalry they could not, in ordinary circumstances, stand; but at Eylau, when the French cuirassiers, exhausted and with blown horses, encountered, after passing through the Russian infantry, the fresh and fearless Cossacks, they went down before them and suffered terribly. At the outposts, when the armies were in cantonments, these hardy warriors, inured, like their horses, from their birth to hardships of all sorts, were a continual thorn in the side of the French light cavalry, whose training and previous experience had failed to fit them or their horses to bear the starvation and cold, which the Cossacks felt but little. Platow, the Ataman of the Cossacks, had immense personal influence with them, and it was only necessary for him to dismount and appeal to them in order to steady them against overwhelming odds. Accustomed from childhood to the use of the lance, the Cossack was more than a match for the horseman armed only with a sword, or for any but a very expert lancer.

The last class of troops employed by Russia consisted of 1500 *baskiers*, clad in chain mail, and armed with bows and arrows. These men appeared on the field at the close of the campaign. They were, of course, useless, and merely excited the derision of Napoleon.

40. *Wilson*, p. 27.

The officers who led the infantry of the Tsar were not worthy, as a rule, of the magnificent raw material which they should have been able to mould into shape. The lower grades were especially ill qualified. Scarcely better educated than their ignorant men, they could neither inspire respect nor teach an art of which they knew nothing. Poorly paid, and looked down upon by the officers of the cavalry and the Guard, the position of an infantry officer had no attractions for the upper classes. The Guard, on the other hand, was commanded mainly by men of these classes, and even the ordinary cavalry officers were of a better class than those of the infantry. There was no scientific class of native officers for the artillery. The pick of the officers of the whole army were foreigners; but they were too few, and too much confined to the more important commands, to have much influence in leavening the native mass. Gambling was very prevalent, and the Russian officers were much inclined to indolence, generally preferring to drive rather than ride or walk.

The staff was clogged with red tape, and overburdened with reports, which had to be submitted by every officer, down to the commandant of a Cossack outpost. With all this reporting, there was no real method such as prevailed in Napoleon's army.[41] Leaders of ability were lamentably scarce; the commissariat was wretched; the treasury was exhausted; without money, magazines and transport could not be organised, even if there had been any one with the ability required to do so. At first, as the army was advancing, it was possible to live on the country; but its never very great resources were soon exhausted by the passage and return of two great armies, and then the existence, even of the French army, became precarious; for the Russian, life became possible at all only owing to the hardihood and patience of its men.

The hospital and medical arrangements were, if possible, worse than the commissariat and transport. The medical officers, uneducated and wretchedly paid, were worse than useless. Platow, when asked by the Tsar if he would have an increase to his medical staff, then consisting of a single officer, replied, "God and your Majesty forbid; the fire of the enemy is not half so fatal as one drug."[42]

---

41. Napoleon was not a stickler for rigid adherence to set forms of report. He required reports of the operations of the various corps in a campaign, yet he accepted documents varying so widely as Davout's elaborate report and the skeleton reports of Ney and Murat. Ney's report is a mere *"journal de marche,"* giving the positions of his troops on each day; Murat's is much the same. Lannes' appears never to have been written—perhaps in consequence of his death at Essling in 1809.
42. *Wilson*, p. 53.

What was good in the medical arrangements at Koenigsberg was supplied by Prussia. At the battle of Friedland, for the first time, some attempt was made to succour the Russian wounded on the field. What more pathetic picture can there be of the suffering of the Russian soldiery than these words of one of them who forced himself into the presence of the Tsar? "For nine months I and my comrades have endured, without a murmur, all the ills of the most severe campaign. We wished to serve our Emperor faithfully, and not augment his difficulties. I call God to witness that, for seven days, these soldiers and myself had nothing to eat but a piece of hide, steeped in water that we might be enabled to chew it when softened; and yet, for eighteen hours, we remained on the field of battle, until, at the same instant, we were struck by grape. Now that we have passed our frontiers, and are returned to our country, we know that the Emperor cannot profit by our ill treatment. Look at this arm; undressed for seventeen days, and a burrow for worms! Look at our bodies, worn down, and wasting for food. The Emperor may want us again. We are ready to serve him, but he shall know our condition that we may have his redress."[43]

In numbers the army was inadequate. Russia had prepared only to support Prussia as an ally. By the collapse of that power, she suddenly found herself compelled to face the mighty armies of Napoleon, receiving from Prussia but one weak corps, the remnant of the great host which had been destroyed at Jena and Auerstädt. The Russian army was, in 1806, organised in 18 divisions, each consisting of—6 regiments of 3 battalions each; 10 squadrons heavy cavalry; 10 squadrons light cavalry; 2 batteries of guns of position; 3 light batteries; 1 horse battery. The batteries were of 14 pieces each for field, and 12 for horse artillery.[44] Thus the division had a nominal strength of 18 battalions, 20 squadrons, and 82 guns.

At the end of 1806, the whole army was distributed thus:

43. *Wilson*, pp. 53, 54.

44.	Heavy field batteries	8	12-pndrs
		4	½ pnd howitzers (licornes)
		2	light howitzers (licornes)
	Total	14	
	Light field batteries	8	6-pndrs
		4	¼ pnd howitzers (licornes)
		2	small howitzers (licornes)
	Total	14	
	Horse batteries	12	6-pndrs

	Battalions	Squadrons	Guns
I. Imperial Guard under the Grande Duke Constantine, at St. Petersburg, 1st Division	33	35	84
II. The army in Poland under Marshal Kamenskoi, viz.: (a) 2nd, 3rd, 4th and 6th Divisions under Ostermann Tolstoi, Sacken, Gallitzin and Sedmaratzki, forming the 1st army, Commanded by Bennigsen. (b) 5th, 7th, 8th and 14th Divisions, under Tutchkow, Dochtorow, Essen., and Anrrepp respectively, forming the 2nd army, commanded by Buxhowden	147	170	504
III. The army of Moldavia, under Michelson: Divisions 9, 10, 11, 12, 13; of which 9 and 10 were commanded by Wolkonski and Müller respectively. These two divisions returned from the Turkish frontier, when the Prussian power collapsed, and joined Bennigsen's left on the Narew, in the middle of January, 1807	90	100	306
IV. Intermediary corps under Count Apraxim in Russia, comprising 15th, 16th, 17th, 18th Divisions	54	30	144
Totals	324	335	1038

Besides these, were the corps in Finland and Georgia, which constituted an entirely separate army.[45]

---

45. Jomini, *Vie de Napoleon*, ii. 334, note, from which figures down to this point are taken.

The force at first opposed to Napoleon consisted of the two armies comprised under No. II. Their strength may be taken, according to Hoepfner, as follows:

(a) Bennigsen's	49,000	infantry
	11,000	regular cavalry
	4,000	Cossacks
	2,700	artillery
	900	pioneers
Total	68,000 and 276 guns	

Perhaps Hoepfner thinks, considering various authorities, 60,000 combatants is a full estimate.[46]

(b) Buxhowden's:	29,000	infantry
	7,000	cavalry
	1,200	artillery
Total	37,200 and 216 guns[47]	

Dumas estimates the strength somewhat lower at—Bennigsen 55,000, and Buxhowden 36,000.[48] The divisions of the latter general had been at Austerlitz, and had not replaced the losses which they had suffered there. An army of reserve was being organised in the interior of Russia.

Kamenskoi's army thus, in November, 1806, consisted approximately of 90,000 men.[49]

The Prussian army was but a small remnant of the mighty force which had been destroyed at Jena, gradually reinforced and its losses repaired by such recruits as could be raised in what remained to Prussia of her territory, or as could escape from the conquered provinces. Excluding the garrisons of Graudenz and Danzig, the Prussian corps in Poland seems to have amounted to not more than 6000 men in December, 1806, and at no time up to the end of July to have exceeded 25,000. It consisted largely of recruits and young troops, with only a nucleus of better-trained soldiers.

THE GENERALS

Of the great master of war who "fills a space in the world's history far greater than that occupied by all the men of action, all the thinkers, poets, or writers of every age . . . who is still regarded by

---

46. *Hoepfner*, iii. 26, 27.
47. *Ibid.*, iii. 29
48. *Dumas*, xvii. 99 and 101
49. This is the estimate given by Wilson (p. 84, note.)

myriads as the greatest of human beings,"[50] it would be presumption to speak in the few lines which space will allow to be devoted to some of the principal leaders in this war. His achievements have filled the world, during more than a century, with wonder and admiration. This history of one of them cannot pretend to give an account of Napoleon himself.

He was, in many ways, his own chief of the staff: He went into details which no ordinary commander-in-chief could find time for, especially one burdened with the cares of supervising the Government and the foreign relations of a great state. But there was a limit to the powers even of Napoleon, and he required a subordinate to amplify and issue the orders which he dictated in outline.

For his purpose, Marshal Berthier was an ideal chief of the staff. He was no general, and he could never have filled the place of a Von Moltke; but he knew Napoleon, his ways and his wishes, and could elaborate, to the liking of his master, the brief orders which were what he usually received. "In short words he (Napoleon) thus enumerated his measures. Berthier separated them from each other, drew up each order separately, and addressed them to the several addressees."[51] "Berthier's position was more that of a chief of the cabinet with high functions, than that of a chief of the general staff."[52] These two quotations, from a modern writer, express tersely the duties which Napoleon demanded, and which, for many years, Berthier executed, generally to his satisfaction. There were occasions when he failed, as will be seen later; and when Napoleon once[53] ventured to leave him temporarily in a position similar to that of the modern German chief of the staff, before his own arrival at the front, the result was very nearly being disaster. He was a superlative, confidential secretary—nothing more.

Joachim Murat, at this period Grand Duke of Berg, is perhaps the most picturesque figure among Napoleon's generals. He was nominally in command of the right wing of the army; but it is extremely improbable that his Imperial brother-in-law would ever have trusted him to act alone, once operations had fairly begun. He owed his position more to his connexion by marriage with Napoleon, and to the impossibility of getting him to serve loyally under any other command but that of the Emperor, than to his military merits. Brave to

---

50. Wolsley, *Decline and Fall of Napoleon*, p. 193
51. *Nation in Arms*, p. 73
52. *Ibid.*, p. 74.
53. At the commencement of the campaign of 1809.

a fault, vain and ambitious, with but limited intelligence, he was the beau ideal of the leader of a cavalry charge. Yet he was not, in any sense, a great cavalry general. His ideas of reconnaissance were vague, his information often defective and misleading. Even on the battlefield he sometimes handled his cavalry very indifferently. With his gaudy uniform and his theatrical displays at the head of his cavalry, with his habit of playing for the admiration of the enemy as well as of his own men, one cannot help regarding him as a poseur. Yet there was in him something chivalrous, hardly to be expected in a man of his humble origin. His last letter to his wife, before his miserable death in 1815,[54] shows that he was not devoid of feeling. As King of Naples, he was far from being a failure, and it may be doubted whether the Neapolitans would not have flourished more under his dynasty than under the Bourbons.

In command of the left wing was Marshal Bernadotte, Prince of Ponte Corvo, afterwards King of Sweden, a man of a very different stamp. Calm, selfish, calculating, and astute, of much more polished manners than most of Napoleon's marshals,[55] he was endowed with considerable powers of command. Him the Emperor could, as far as ability was concerned, trust in a semi-independent command. He had, or his master professed to think so, fallen short of his duty at Austerlitz, and, again, when he failed to support Davout at Auerstädt.[56] There was no love lost between him and the Emperor; Bernadotte had even been at times in opposition to Napoleon, notably in the case of the Imperial title. Did Napoleon employ him in the field because he feared him, and thought it dangerous to leave him behind in France? The question seems worth consideration.

54. *Biogr. Gen.*, art. "Murat."

55. De Fezensac (p. 132) describes his only meeting with Bernadotte, and extols the superiority of his manners and behaviour to that of the other marshals. Bernadotte even carried his consideration so far as to offer to keep De Fezensac for a night's rest, instead of sending him back to Ney at once. The offer was declined on the score of duty.

"His own people said that he (Bernadotte) would have been a hero in his own cause, but his disposition was thoroughly exclusive. He only opened his heart when everything depended on him alone; then it became full of ardour, generosity, and devotion for his own people, who found in him all the seductions and fascinations of a great soul. But to endure an equal or a superior; to help on the glory of another, whoever he might be; such an effort was always either impossible or intolerable to him" (*De Ségur*, p. 296).

56. Napoleon says that, after Jena, he had ordered Bernadotte's trial by court martial for his conduct on that day, but abandoned the idea on personal grounds (*Mémoires pour servir*, vii. 215, note on Bernadotte's Mémoires).

Marshal Davout,[57] commanding the 3rd Corps, had distinguished himself lately by his magnificent conduct of the battle of Auerstädt. It was he who had really ruined the Prussian army on the fatal 14th October, though it would not have been like Napoleon had he publicly allowed the full credit to his lieutenant. With the exception only of Masséna, he was probably the ablest of the marshals, both as a strategist and a tactician. He was a stern disciplinarian, but, apparently, popular with his men, and subordinates.[58] He was ever solicitous for their sustenance and shelter.

In the army generally, Marshal Ney occupied a position in some ways analogous to that which Murat held in the cavalry. The "bravest of the brave," he was the equal of Murat in personal courage, his superior in intelligence and comprehension of the requirements of war. His general good nature made him a favourite with his subordinates; his sudden outbursts of temper frightened them, and often involved him in quarrels with his equals or superiors.[59] As a soldier, he was at his best commanding the rearguard of a retreating army. Before Friedland, in the north of Portugal, in the retreat of 1812, Ney seemed to be a great soldier. None knew better how long it was possible to hold in safety a covering position, more precisely the moment when it was necessary to evacuate it and seek the next favourable locality in which, by a bold stand, to check the advancing enemy and afford time to the main body of his own army. In the front, or detached, he seemed to lose his head, would be carried away by ambitious projects, and some-

---

57. The name of this marshal is frequently spelt Davoust, sometimes Davoût. Both seem to be incorrect. The form Davout is used in Napoleon's correspondence, in Berthier's, by the marshal's nephew, the present Duc d'Auerstädt; finally, there is no misreading possible of his own very legible signature on numerous despatches and order, in the *Archives Historiques* in Paris

58. He was "a man of probity, of order, and of duty above all" (*De Ségur*, p. 296). After Eylau we find him complaining, in an order to Morand commanding the 1st Division, that many men had skulked out of the battle on the pretext of assisting the wounded to the rear (*Archives Historiques*, daily correspondence, 10th February, 1807). The remedy he recommends for this state of affairs is "*la savate avec du gras.*" This was a summary form of punishment inflicted by the men themselves on their defaulting comrades. The delinquent was tied up, and each man of his company, passing by, administered a sound blow or two on the bare flesh with a shoe. This system of barrack-room justice is, or recently was, in force in the French army in the case of petty thefts, etc.

59. "He knew not how to administer a calm reprimand. He either said nothing or else exceeded all bounds. Despite this violence of character, his heart was good, his spirit perfectly just, his judgment sound; very precious qualities in a soldier" (*De Fezensac*, p. 133)

times run great and unnecessary risk, almost in defiance of orders. There is something very pathetic and natural in the man which blots out the faults and compels admiration. Ney, "his third horse killed under him, alone near an abandoned battery, striking, in his rage, the bronze muzzle of an English gun,"[60]—Ney, baring his breast to the bullets of the soldiers he had so often led, in that last tragic scene near the garden of the Luxemburg, appeals to us, not unsuccessfully, to forget his weaknesses and his faults.

Napoleon boasted that he had no friends. His feelings towards Jean Lannes were perhaps nearer akin to friendship than he would admit. This marshal was one of the few old comrades to whom Napoleon, even as Emperor, allowed the familiarity implied by the use of the second person singular in speech. At his deathbed the stern Emperor relaxed, and gave vent to his grief. He had watched Lannes' progress as a commander, and had seen him steadily improving.[61] Impetuous, and ever ready to throw himself into the thickest of the fray, Lannes was yet not rash, and on more than one occasion in the Polish campaign he fought a good and patient battle against very superior numbers. He feared neither the enemy nor the Emperor; to the latter he would, at times, unbosom himself, even regarding Murat, in terms which would not have been tolerated from another.

Soult, a man more of the stamp of Bernadotte than of Ney, was, beyond doubt, a capable commander. He was unpopular with his subordinates.[62] Of his capacity as a general, Wellington said that he respected him, but that, "though his plans seemed always to be admirable, he never knew when to strike."[63]

Masséna, the "darling child of victory," of whom Wellington said that he was the best of the marshals, and "I always found him where I least desired that he should be"[64] played but a minor part in the campaign. Yet it might well have been one of infinite importance, calling for the exercise of all the patience and endurance which he displayed in the defence of Genoa, combined with the vigour and fire of the victor of Zurich.[65] He was, it can hardly be denied, the most brilliant of the marshals, and the best fitted for the command of an army.

---

60. Houssaye, *Waterloo*, p. 374.

61. *"Je l'avais pris pigmée, je l'ai perdu géant,"* said Napoleon (*Mém. de Ste. H.*, vol. i., pt. 2, p. 10).

62. *"Exécré par le corps entier des officiers"* (Houssaye, *Waterloo*, p. 58).

63. Brialmont, *Life of Wellington*, Gleig's translation, iv. 155.

64. *Ibid*, iv. 155.

65. Unlike Augereau, *"Masséna vaincu était toujours prêt à recommencer,"* said Napoleon (*Mém. de Ste. H.*, vol. i., pt. 1, p. 313).

Mortier calls for little remark. He was a general of average capacity, good enough for the command of a corps, hardly suited for independent command of an army.

The name of Bessières will always be associated with the command of Napoleon's Guard. He was not in the first rank amongst the marshals, and acting, as he generally did, under the personal command of Napoleon, he had no special opportunity for establishing a reputation for originality or independence.

Augereau was a curious mixture. His style of dress and his manner gave the impression of a braggart, which he was not. He was wanting, said Napoleon, in steadfastness and perseverance. Even a day of victory seemed to discourage him. His intelligence was not great, his education very little; yet he maintained order and discipline among his men, and was beloved by them.[66]

Lefebvre had served Napoleon a good turn on the 18th Brumaire, when he marched his grenadiers into the chamber of the Five Hundred, and cleared it at the most critical moment. His master repaid him with the marshal's baton, and the Dukedom of Danzig. The latter was probably better deserved by his chief engineer, Chasseloup. A hard-headed, courageous old soldier, Lefebvre was not a general of any capacity. To his artillery officers at Danzig, he said, *"Je n'entends rien de votre affaire: mais fichez moi un trou et j'y passerai."*[67] The words illustrate his character.

Amongst the commanders of French divisions were many men who attained, in later years, great distinction—Victor, Oudinot, Grouchy, and Suchet, all later made marshals, the last already greatly distinguished in the wars of the Republic in Italy; Morand, Friant, and Gudin, the excellent leaders of the three divisions of Davout's splendid 3rd Corps;[68] Vandamme, Rapp, Savary, Dupont, St. Hilaire, Lasalle, Milhaud, Carra St.-Cyr, Kellerman, Chasseloup, Latour Maubourg, were all names well known in the history of Napoleon's campaigns; but it is impossible, in the limits of this volume, to dwell on them.

The French generals were remarkable for their comparative youth. Napoleon himself was 37, Lannes and Soult were born in the same year as the Emperor, Davout was 37, Mortier 39, Murat 36, Bernadotte 43. The veterans were Augereau at 50, Berthier 54, and Lefebvre 52.

66. Napoleon's character of him (*Mém. de Ste. H.*, vol. i., pt. 1, p. 313).
67. *Biogr. Gen.*, art. "Marshal Lefebvre."
68. "Davout in a transport of joy replied, 'Sire, we are your Tenth Legion; the 3rd Corps will be to you, everywhere and always, what that legion was to Caesar" (De Ségur, *An A. D. C, of Napoleon*, p. 311). The boast had been justified at Auerstädt, and was to be so again at Eylau.

Of Marshal Kamenskoi, who commenced the campaign as commander-in-chief of the Russian armies, little need be said. A veteran lieutenant of Suwarow, he was now too old for war. His early measures in Poland were a mixture of impetuosity and hesitation. His violent character, which eventually led to his assassination by a peasant, rendered him unsuitable for supreme command.

Count Bennigsen, who succeeded him, was a Hanoverian. Born in 1745, he retired from his native army, and entered the Russian service in 1773. In that army he had a distinguished career in the cavalry.[69] He can hardly be described as a great general. If his plans of campaign were sometimes not wanting in originality and design, they failed in execution, or from Bennigsen's inability to modify them to suit changing circumstances. At times his conduct exhibited "a mixture of rash imprudence and of irresolution quite irreconcilable."[70] For the partial successes which he obtained in this campaign against the French, the valour and obstinacy of his troops, rather than his tactics, account.

Barclay de Tolly greatly distinguished himself in this campaign, in command of a division, especially at Eylau. His great claim to distinction, however, rests on his plan of campaign of 1812, when, as minister of war, he was responsible for the design, executed in part by himself, of drawing Napoleon to his destruction in the heart of Russia. Better had it been for Russia had that system been followed in 1807.

Prince Bagration, who was usually in command of Bennigsen's advance or rear guard, as the case might be, showed himself to be to the Russians what Ney was to the French. The excellence of his rear-guard actions will appear in the course of this history. He quarrelled, later, with Barclay, to whose scheme for the campaign of 1812 he was vehemently opposed.

The Ataman Platow, leader of the Cossacks, occupied a peculiar semi-paternal position amongst his wild troops. His personal influence with them was enormous, and his example would rally them against fearful odds. He had only to dismount and call upon his horsemen in order to stop the spread of disorder.

Of Prince Gallitzin, who led the Russian cavalry with ability, of Dochtorow, of the two Essens, of Anrepp, Müller, and Markow, it is unnecessary to make detailed mention.

One man, on the side of the allies, acquired a great reputation—

---

69. The personal appearance of the Russian commander is thus sketched by De Ségur: "A pale, withered personage of high stature and cold appearance, with a scar across his face" (*An A.D.C. of Napoleon*, p. 328). Available in a Leonaur edition.
70. Jomini, *Vie de Napoleon*, ii. 421.

Lestocq, the Prussian commander. His conduct was distinguished throughout by energy, firmness, and ability. It was more than once his fate to be exposed in a position where he could be cut from the Russians. On each occasion he extricated himself, from an almost hopeless situation, with the greatest ability. His march on Eylau was a masterpiece of patience and resolution, as well as of resistance to the temptation of a general action.

Marshal Kalkreuth, who acquired great glory by his defence of Danzig, had seen much of war, and was best known, before 1807, for his siege of Mayence in 1793. He was, however, at times wanting in resolution and perseverance. He more than once wanted to surrender, with a large body of troops, in the retreat after Jena, but was kept straight by Blücher and others.

CHAPTER 3

The Theatre of War

The theatre of the war to which most of the rest of this work will be devoted, lies between the rivers Bug and Vistula on one side, and the Niemen on the other. The south-eastern boundary of this area may be taken as a line joining Grodno to the point on the Bug where that river ceased to be the northern frontier of Gallicia. The north-western side abuts on the Baltic Sea. Within these boundaries lay a country for the most part flat, marshy, and thickly wooded—a country resembling, except in the last respect, the broads of Suffolk and Norfolk. There are no heights of any importance, and it is only in the north-western corner, from Graudenz on the Vistula to Marienburg, and for a few miles to the east, towards Hohenstein, that it is possible to describe the country as anything but an undulating plain. Here the underlying rock of the Polish plain crops out, and gives rise to hills which, in places, reach an elevation of 500 to 700 feet above the sea, amongst which are imbedded the lakes about Osterode, Pr. Holland, and Mohrungen. The bulk of the military operations of 1807 occurred in the flat country farther east. Across this tract, in a direction but slightly north of east, there extends from near the Vistula about Graudenz to the Niemen south of Kowno, a broad belt of lakes and marshes of all sizes and shapes. Individual lakes attain in places a length of 8 or 10 miles; chains of lakes with narrow strips of land between them extend to much greater distances. Some of the lakes are long and narrow, others of fantastic trace, with long, finger-like bays protruding into the country in all directions. The belt of lakes, roughly speaking, averages 25 miles in breadth, and includes hundreds of sheets of water and marsh, varying in size from the lakes above described to mere ponds, which could only be shown on a very large scale map.

The forests, which in ancient times clothed the whole of this country, had, in 1807, and even now have, only partially been cleared.

It was often, for a distance of many miles, impossible to find an area sufficiently clear of continuous forest to allow of the deployment of considerable forces. The great forest of Johannisburg extended, almost continuously, for 45 miles north of the upper Narew, with a breadth varying from 6 to 15 miles.

The principal waterways of this tract were the following: The Vistula, rising in the Carpathian Mountains, is, even at Warsaw, a large stream with a bed of several hundred yards in breadth. From Warsaw to a point some 20 miles below Thorn (a distance of nearly 130 miles as the crow flies) the river flows generally north-west between low banks, in a broad marshy bed, studded with innumerable islands. At this point it turns sharply to a direction slightly east of north, the right bank begins to acquire some height and, in the neighbourhood of Graudenz, rises to the dignity of a range of hills. Some 30 miles south of the Gulf of Danzig, the s.ream divides, the right branch flowing north-east and falling into the Frisches-Haff, the great lagoon which stretches from 20 miles east of Danzig to Koenigsberg. The left branch flowing north nearly to the sea, again subdivides, part of it falling into the western end of the Frisches-Haff, the rest running west to Danzig, where it turns north into the Gulf of Danzig. The river and the Frisches-Half thus separate from the main land the long, low, narrow strip of land known as the Frische-Nehrung, in which a breach, at Pillau towards its north eastern extremity, affords an outlet to the sea for the lagoon and the waters which flow into it.

The principal affluent on the right bank of the Vistula is the Bug, which, after forming the northern boundary of Gallicia, joins the Vistula 18 or 20 miles below Warsaw. At Sierock, the Bug receives on its right hank another considerable stream, the Narew, which, flowing from the western frontier of Russia, as it was in 1806, passes Lomza, Nowogrod, Ostrolenka, and Pultusk. Both rivers are military obstacles of importance, subject to heavy floods in wet weather, fordable only in seasons of drought.[1] A short way below Ostrolenka, the river Omulew reaches the Narew; which again, a few miles above Pultusk, receives the Orezyc. Both are small streams with a course of 40 or 50 miles from the north-west. Close to its junction with the Vistula, the Bug is joined by the Ukra, a stream of somewhat greater importance which rises near Soldau, about 60 miles north.

The only other stream of the slightest importance which reaches

---

1. The united stream below Sierock is sometimes spoken of as the Narew, sometimes as the Bug. The latter seems more correct, the Bug being the larger stream, and it is adopted in this work.

the right bank of the Vistula, in the theatre of war, is the Drewenz, flowing from the Osterode lakes to the Vistula, above Thorn.

The Pregel, in so far as it concerns the campaign, flows west, past Wehlau, into the Frisches-Haff at Koenigsberg.

Two other rivers which played a great part in 1807 require mention. The Passarge, originating in the lakes south-east of Osterode, flows nearly due north to the Frisches-Haff near Braunsberg. In its upper course it is of importance only where it spreads out into lakes or marshes. Even in its lower reaches it is not a very important stream, and, except when in flood, is fordable in many places.

The Alle, starting not far from the source of the Passarge, flows generally parallel to it at a distance of 8 or 9 miles, up to a point just north of Guttstadt; there it turns to the north-east, and, flowing in a tortuous course past Heilsberg, Bartenstein, and Schippenbeil, it joins the Pregel at Wehlau, 3o miles east of Koenigsberg. It is a more considerable stream than the Passarge, and, even as high up as Heilsberg, it is only fordable after a drought.

The tributaries of the rivers which have been described were in no case of importance, from a military point of view, in themselves; they became so only from their connexion with the marshes, which they fed or partially drained.

The general features of this country were plains of sand, or of mud in wet weather, intermixed with heaths, bogs, forests, lakes, and morasses.

Across this area there passed no metalled road; the best of the communications were mere banks of earth, not even revetted except where their passage across marshes rendered it impossible to maintain them without artificial support. By the droughts of summer or the frosts of winter, these so-called roads were hardened to a consistency which allowed of the passage of artillery with as much ease as is ever possible where unmetalled roads have to be used. When soaked with rain, or dissolved by thaws, they became almost impassable. Napoleon jokingly said that in Poland he had discovered a new element—mud. In wet weather the slush attained a depth to be measured in feet, not in inches. In December, 1806, the infantry sank to their knees, often deeper, in the soft roads; the horses to their hocks; the guns to their axles: sometimes even guns absolutely disappeared in the clayey mire. Double and quadruple teams could not drag them along as fast as the 1¼ miles an hour which the infantry with infinite labour could cover.[2]

---

2. The following references to the works of writers who took part in the campaign, will serve to show the terrible condition of the communications in open weather. De Fezensac's account of his journey to make (continued on next page)

The best of the roads were such as have been described, the worst were mere tracks leading from one village to another. The four principal reads between the Vistula and the Pregel were—

(1) From Danzig to Warsaw by the right bank of the Vistula;

(2) From Danzig to Koenigsberg by Dirschau, Elbing, and Braunsberg, not far south of the Frisches-Haff;

(3) From Warsaw to Koenigsberg by Sierock, Pultusk, Makow, Prasznitz, Willemburg, Bartenstein, Preussisch Eylau, and Kreuzberg;

(4) The road from Pultusk to Ostrolenka, Lomza, and thence towards St. Petersburg.

The more unfavourable portion of the theatre was the southern half, inhabited by Poles. It was devoid of large towns, sparsely populated, backward in every respect. Farther north, the names of the villages and towns indicate the German origin of the population. Large industrial villages were comparatively frequent and there was a general air of prosperity which was lacking in the country of the Poles. "Old Prussia offers, compared with Poland, the greatest triumph of civilisation over barbarism and of light over darkness. On one side numerous industrial wealthy towns, rich farms, and admirable cultivation; on the other, paltry hamlets, huts side by side with a palace: yet there is no difference in the soil. Customs, government, religion, these are what constitute nations."[3]

The climate of this tract is inhospitable. The icy blasts, which reach it from the frozen north, produce in winter a climate almost arctic in its severity. In summer the heat is great, for Europe, though of short

explanations to Napoleon on behalf of Ney. He started on the 15th January in wet weather; his conveyance broke down, and he had to go for miles at a footpace with wretched horses. Then came frost on the 17th. He had to cross the Bug in a boat on the 18th, as the bridge had been broken by the floating ice (pp. 134-135).

Bernadotte, writing of the operations towards Soldau in December, says, "The roads were frightful; the artillery could not follow, and one marched all day to cover three or four leagues" (7½ miles) (Report on 1st Corps, Arch. Hist.).

"The Geld on which we were about to fight was converted into a lake of mud, where soldiers and horses could scarcely march" (Lannes' report on Pultusk, Arch. Hist.). "The country over which the army passed (25th December) was clayey and marshy, the roads were frightful. Horsemen, infantry, and artillery could only get over them in the face of almost insurmountable difficulties. It took two hours to march a short league" (2½ miles) (Davout, p, 132).

"We fought and marched in mud; we should have died of cold and misery without movement" (Comeau, p. 288).

3. Jomini (Vie de Napoleon, ii. 354).

duration. Hot days are succeeded by damp cool nights, a condition of climate resulting in the prevalence of fevers. The dampness of the country, especially in the autumn and spring, its want of a well-defined watershed, and the consequent frequency of marshes and of sluggish streams, choked with the decaying debris of the forests, render it unhealthy and malarious. Of every 196 sick in the French hospitals in 1807, as many as 105 were cases of fever.[4]

In connexion with military operations it is not so much the terrain that is of importance in Poland as the climatic and seasonal conditions.[5] In summer the country is open, and practicable in all directions for all arms. The difficulty in operations arises from the often oppressive heat. In winter, when every lake, pond, marsh, and river is locked in the embrace of severe frost, these features, as obstacles, are obliterated. The only hindrances to progress are the forests, the snow, and the severity of the cold. In spring and autumn, rain swells the lakes and the rivers, and the roads are almost impracticable for the passage of wheeled traffic, owing to the sea of mud which covers them.[6]

---

4. Daru quoted by Dumas, at p. 487, vol. xix.

5. The winter of 1806-7 was exceptional. Comparatively mild autumn weather, alternating with frosts, lasted far later than usual. The following account of the weather, during the campaign, is abstracted from the writings of persons who went through it, chiefly from the correspondence of Napoleon.

"The weather, which had been magnificent during the month of October, and the first part of November, (then) became horrible. It rained and snowed incessantly. Provisions became very scarce; no more wine, hardly any beer, and what there was exceedingly bad, muddy water, no bread, and quarters for which we had to fight with the pigs and the cows" (Marbot, i. 240).

On the 18th November, 1806, no frost, sunshine every day, the roads too heavy to allow the Emperor to travel, except in country conveyances. Duroc's carriage overturned in the mud (Corr. 11,497).

Early in December, bright, dry, cold weather (Larrey, iii. 22).

15th December.—No frost, sunshine every day (Corr. 11,494).

17th December.—Thaw rendering roads very heavy (Corr. 11,497).

26th December.—Complete thaw for last two days (Rapp, p. 127, and others).

31st December.—Frost set in again (Larrey, iii. 61).

8th January.—Alternate snow and thaw (Corr, 11,584).

1st to 10th February.—Frost and snow (all authorities).

10th February.—Thaw set in (Larrey, iii. 61).

17th February.—Cold has ceased, and snow melted (Corr. 11,822).

18th February.—Rain and thaw. April weather (Corr. 11,823).

21st February.—Alternate frosts and thaw (Corr. 11,845).

26th February.—Loamy ground so slippery from thaw as to render cavalry and artillery useless (Wilson, p. 246). (continued on next page)

Much of what has been said regarding the character of the country beyond the Vistula applies equally to that between the Oder and the Vistula. Within the theatre of operations, when the French reached Warsaw, there were still four fortresses in the possession of Prussia.

1. Danzig, on the left bank of the Vistula near its mouth. The strength of this place will be fully dealt with when the siege is described.

2. Koenigsberg, at the mouth of the Pregel, the capital of old Prussia, a poorly fortified city but an immense depot of stores of all sorts.

3. Pillau, a fortified pentagon commanding the narrow outlet from the Frisches-Haff to the Baltic.

4. Graudenz, a fort situated to the north of the town of the same name, important as commanding a principal passage of the Lower Vistula. It held out against the French throughout the campaign. It was too small to be of great value, and too much isolated. The siege was not worth pressing with any great vigour, seeing that it was easy to mask the place with a comparatively small force.

28th February.—Frosts and thaw alternately (Corr, 11,907).

17th March.—Cold weather again. Two feet of snow in last three or four days (Corr. 12,064).

2nd April.—Weather flue, but still cold. Three or four degrees of frost (Corr. 12,263).

6th April—Freezing hard (Corr. 12,322).

17th April.—Raining (Corr. 12,394).

21st April—Frost. January weather (Corr. 12,437).

2nd May.—Fine. Leaves coming out. (Corr. 12,505).

16th May.—Weather like April in France (Corr, 12,593).

10th June.—Rain at night (Larrey, iii. 78).

14th June.—Hot days, cool damp nights (Larrey, p. 84).

6. "It has never yet," says Von der Goltz, "occurred to any one to write a strategy and tactics for the different seasons of the year; and yet their influence is certainly quite as great as that of terrain, which has often been treated so longwindedly" (Nation in Arms, p. 327). The remark applies with special force to Poland.

Napoleon at Eylau

JEROME NAPOLEON

JOACHIM MURAT AND HIS WIFE CAROLINE BONAPARTE
KING AND QUEEN OF NAPLES

Passage of the Vistula at Thorn

FREIHERR VON BENNINGSEN

PRINCE BAGRATION

THE ATAMAN PLATOFF

Eylau from the Landsberg Road

MARSHAL BESSIERES

MARSHAL MASSENA

MARSHAL LAFEBVRE

GENERAL VICTOR

MARSHAL MORTIER

Napoleon giving orders to Oudinot at Friedland

The raft at Tilsit

Napoleon at Tilsit with the Tsar and King and Queen of Prussia

The First Campaign—
Pultusk and Golymin

The Plan of Campaign and the Passages of the Vistula and Bug

"Je n'ai jamais eu un plan d'opérations," was a saying of Napoleon. He did not imply that he had no general scheme, no fixed goal towards which to direct his operations. What he did mean was, that he made no pretence to deciding beforehand precisely when and where he would meet the enemy, and how he would dispose of him when met. Whilst fixing his eye steadily on the end at which he had decided to aim and laying down the earliest movements, he recognised that, once the enemy was encountered, the further direction of operations must depend on changing circumstances, from day to day and from hour to hour.

When he first arrived in Berlin he could, until the fragments of the Prussian army had been destroyed, come to no more definite decision than that he must, sooner or later, encounter and defeat the Russians. On that point he was certain, and he did not hesitate to proclaim it publicly to his victorious army.[1]

As news of the surrender of Hohenlohe and Blücher, the capitulation of Magdeburg, the destruction of the other remains of the Prussian army west of the Oder, and of the slow advance of the Russian armies towards the Vistula came in, he began to see his way more and more clearly. From the first he had recognised the desirability of taking up his quarters, for the winter, east of the Vistula.[2] By doing so he would place himself in a position to open the campaign next spring against the Russians without having to delay his advance by the pre-

---

1. Corr. 11,093, dated 26th October, 1806.
2. "It was desirable for the success of ulterior operations not to allow the enemy to cross the Vistula; otherwise we should have been obliged to take cantonments in a bad position between the Vistula and the Oder, or else to recross the Oder and winter in Prussia. That would have uncovered the operations in Silesia, and have allowed the Prussians to recruit all the Poles who came (continued on next page)

liminary operation of forcing the passage of a great river, the Vistula. He would cover completely the operations for the subjugation of the Silesian fortresses, he would support and secure the moral and material assistance of the Poles, he would be able to cover the sieges of Danzig, Colberg, and Stralsund, from which places he had to fear a descent by sea upon his left flank and rear. Finally, he would wrest from Prussia almost all the territory from which she might hope to recruit her shattered army, leaving her nothing but the Baltic provinces of Old Prussia. His goal, for the present, was the establishment of cantonments on and beyond the Vistula, with his advanced corps pushed out far enough into Poland to leave him breathing space and to afford sufficient room to enable him, in the event of his being seriously attacked, to concentrate east of the Vistula, for the defence of its line, without risk of a disaster. Should he be able to attain that end, or even should he find himself compelled to winter between the Vistula and the Oder, or behind the latter river, he would still require a base secured by the possession of the fortresses of the Oder in its whole course. Should he winter beyond, or on the left bank of the Vistula, the Oder would form a secondary base on which to fall back, if necessary. Should he find progress beyond the Oder impossible, it would become his front line, with the Elbe in support.

In the end of October and the beginning of November he was uncertain as to the fate of the ruins of the Prussian army of Jena; Magdeburg still held out against Ney; Blücher might yet escape and threaten his communications west of the Elbe, or pass by sea to join the King beyond the Vistula. He had little information as to the situation and movements of the advancing Russians. He knew not whether he would have to meet them on a battlefield not far east of the Oder or whether they were still beyond the Russian frontier, farther to the east of the Vistula than he was to the west.

On the 5th November he writes fully to Davout, whom he had promptly sent eastwards from Berlin. He directs the marshal to advance on Driesen and Meseritz, beyond the Oder, and to scour the country in advance with 2500 dragoons under Beaumont. On no account was his infantry to pass Driesen and Meseritz without further orders. As far as the Emperor's information at present went, it was im-

---

under our standards" (Savary, iii, 20).
"If I let the Russians advance I lost the support and the resources of Poland; they might decide Austria, which only hesitated because they were so far off; they would carry with them the whole Prussian nation which would feel the necessity of doing everything it could to retrieve its disasters" (Jomini, *Vie de Napoleon*, ii. 334).

probable the Russians could reach Warsaw for another fortnight. On Davout's right, Jerome, with 24,000 men, was attempting the capture of Glogau; if he succeeded he would march on Custrin, which had pusillanimously capitulated, and was temporarily garrisoned by 2000 Baden troops. If Weimar (i.e. Blücher) surrendered to Soult, Bernadotte, and Murat, they, with Lannes from Stettin, would be available to support Davout's advance. When Magdeburg should fall before Ney, he also would be in hand.[3]

All was still uncertain as regards the extent of the advance. Two days later the clouds began to lift. Blücher had surrendered on the 7th; Magdeburg was on the point of capitulation, and actually fell next day. It seemed that Bennigsen, with the first Russian army, had not more than 50,000 men, and that it was very improbable they could all reach the Vistula before the 20th at the earliest.

Davout was, therefore, to reach Posen on the 9th, when Augereau would have arrived in support at Driesen. At Posen he was to construct enormous bakeries for the supply of the army which would concentrate on it. Nevertheless, Davout was to avoid engaging the Russians should they, perchance, have arrived on the Vistula. If they had not been brought to a halt by the result of the operations against the Prussians, the Emperor proposed, for the present, to halt at Posen, which he thought it beyond the limits of possibility for Bennigsen to attack before the 18th. Should the Russians be further delayed, the Emperor's plans might be changed.[4] At the same time, Chasseloup was directed to fortify Stettin against a surprise, as a support to the left of the base on the Oder,[5] and numerous orders for the collection of ammunition and supplies of all sorts at Posen were issued.[6] For the protection of his left rear against the sea, precautions were also taken. To Louis Buonaparte his brother had no intention of trusting the command in this direction. On the 5th November, the Emperor wrote to Mortier, in Hanover, that Louis' health would probably necessitate his return to Holland.[7] On the 11th, Mortier was appointed to the command on Louis' departure. The ill health of the latter was, perhaps, diplomatic only. The army under Mortier was ordered to seize Hamburg, and confiscate all the great stores of English merchandise there.[8]

3. Napoleon to Davout, dated Berlin, 5th November, 1806 (Corr. 11,176).
4. Corr. 11,196 and 11,199, both to Davout, darted Berlin, 7th November, 1806.
5. Corr. 11,178, dated 5th November, 1806.
6. Corr. 11,187 to 11,190, dated 5th November, 1806
7. Corr. 11,175, dated 5th November, 1806.
8. Corr. 11,269, dated 16th November, 1806.

It soon became abundantly clear that no trouble to the west of the Vistula was likely to arise from a Russian advance in winter. Davout had encountered practically no opposition as far as Posen, his cavalry was well out in front of him, meeting with no serious resistance.

The occupation of Warsaw, at any rate, was of vital importance as assuring the support of the Poles. This political consideration was of paramount importance, and turned the balance in favour of an advance on the Upper Vistula. From a purely military point of view the Emperor would possibly have preferred to operate in the angle of the river about Thorn, spreading his cantonments eastward, with his flanks resting on the Vistula above and below Thorn. To the Lower Vistula, as a base, there was the objection that his communications would be more open to a raid from Pomerania than they would be farther south. It is true they were more exposed to Austria if he advanced on the southern line; but then, if Austria entered the arena, the whole advance must have been abandoned until she had been annihilated.

The Emperor, on these considerations, decided to advance, at least as far as the line of the Vistula from Warsaw to Thorn. The conduct of the Russians, when he reached Warsaw, would show whether it was safe to push on beyond the great river.

The advance was to be in echelons with Davout and Murat on the right in front. As those marshals progressed beyond the re-entrant angle of the Vistula below Thorn, their communications would be exposed to enterprise from the river. To protect them on this side, the corps of Lannes, Augereau, Soult, Bessières, Ney, and Bernadotte would move in succession on Thorn, the three first-named then turning to their right up the lift bank of the river towards Warsaw.

In this way, any attempt by the enemy, across the river between Thorn and Warsaw, against the communications of one corps, would be taken in flank by the corps following. When Davout and Murat arrived in Warsaw, the corps of Lannes, Augereau, and Soult would be along the river below it, within call, whilst Bessières, Ney, and Bernadotte would be at, or approaching, Thorn. Thorn and Warsaw would be strongly held, when taken, as the extremities of the advanced base.

To cover the right flank of Murat and Davout, the corps of Jerome was available, until the proximity of the Austrian frontier, as it turned northwards to the Bug, should form a protection, so long as Austria was quiet. Murat, who was to command the right wing of the army, would be able, should the Russians show signs of standing to fight at, or in front of, Warsaw, to dispose of 80,000 men, a force far superior to any Bennigsen was likely to have.[9]

On the 24th November, the Emperor left Berlin, on the 25th, he was at Custrin. He was, at this time, carrying on negotiations with the King of Prussia for an armistice, the idea of which he had refused to entertain until he had gathered in all the fruits of his victories at Jena and Auerstädt. The terms which he now offered were such as Prussia could not possibly accept, unless she were prepared to cut herself loose from the Russian alliance and to throw herself on the mercy of the French. They were—

(1) The Prussian army to be withdrawn behind the Vistula;

(2) The French to occupy the right bank of the Vistula, from the Austrian frontier to the mouth of the Bug, as well as Thorn, Graudenz, Danzig, Colberg, Lenczyca, the Silesian fortresses of Glogau and Breslau, and all Silesia on the left bank of the Oder;

(3) The rest of East Prussia, and Prussian Poland to be unoccupied by either party;

(4) The King of Prussia to obtain the withdrawal of all Russian troops from his territories during the suspension of arms.

---

9. *Corr.* 11,302, to Murat, dated 24th November, 1806. In this letter the Emperor shows Murat the strength of his wing thus:

1st Cavalry Reserve (Murat)

Beaumont's and Klein's dragoons	4800
Becker's dragoons	1200
Nansouty's cavalry	2400
Milhaud's cavalry	800
Total	9200

	Infantry	Cavalry
3rd Corps (Davout)	22,000	1200
5th Corps (Lannes)	16,000	1200
7th (Augereau)	16,000	1200
Part of the 9th Corps (Jerome)	12,000	2000
Totals	66,000	5600

Grand totals—66,000 infantry, and 14,400 cavalry = 80,400 men

The Russians could not, Napoleon thought, have more than 30,000 or 40,000 men at Warsaw. The remaining French forces might be expected to be as follows: Ney at Posen on the 24th. Soult at Frankfort on the 25th. Sahuc's cavalry at Posen on the 29th. Lasalle's (at Posen) on the 20th. Grouchy's (at Posen) on the 29th. Bernadotte was still behind.

The last condition it was beyond the power of the King to comply with; the others would have the effect of leaving Napoleon master of the situation on the recommencement of hostilities, and he would naturally protract peace negotiations till the season was suitable for his advance. He would then be able, holding all the passages of the Vistula, to place his army in Poland long before the Russians could reach it, and Prussia would, meanwhile, have had little territory from which to recruit a fresh army. On the 27th November,[10] Napoleon informed Talleyrand that the King had, as he must have expected, refused to ratify the armistice. The period of negotiation had been utilised by Napoleon in vigorously pressing his advance.

On the 10th November, Davout was at Posen, where he had arrived the day before; Lannes was at Schneidmühl on his left, on the Stettin-Bromberg road; Augereau was at Custrin; Jerome, leaving 6000 Wurtemberg troops to besiege Glogau,[11] was moving towards Kalisch on Davout's right.

On the 18th, Davout had reached Sempolno, nearly half way from Posen to Warsaw, and Nansouty's cavalry was as far forward as Konin on the Wartha. Cavalry pushed out in all directions, especially towards Bromberg and Thorn, had forced the small bodies of Prussians in front of them to fall back towards the Vistula. Lannes was before Thorn, into which Lestocq, with the Prussians, had retired, after partially burning the pile bridge. Augereau was at Bromberg. Davout's left was, therefore, well protected. Lannes had, however, been unable to induce the surrender of either Graudenz or Thorn. Jerome with part of his corps was at Kalisch. Ney and Soult were in second line, Bernadotte still marching, from Lubeck, on Berlin.

On the 24th November, as Davout and Murat continued their advance on Warsaw, Lannes, who had remained till then in front of Thorn, commenced his movement up the Vistula, protecting their left. The small fort of Lenczyca, surrounded by marshes, about equidistant from Thorn and Warsaw, and about half as far from the river as it was from either place, was evacuated by the Prussians and occupied by Davout. It was at once set in order as a great advanced magazine, immense quantities of stores and ammunition being collected in it.

The first Russian cavalry were met and driven back by Murat at Blonie. On the evening of the 28th November, he entered Warsaw

---

10. Corr. 11,311, dated Meseritz, 27th November, 1806.

11. Glogau surrendered on the 2nd December, and Vandamme, with the Wurtemberg division, moved to the siege of Breslau, where he was joined by Jerome from Kalisch, with the Bavarian division. Breslau did not surrender till the 9th January.

as the Russians passed the Vistula to the suburb of Praga on the right bank, burning the bridge after crossing. Even now, Napoleon could hardly believe that Bennigsen would leave him, uncontested, the passage at Warsaw. He wrote to Murat, on the 1st December,[12] "If the enemy commits the folly of evacuating Praga, seize the *faubourg*, and construct a strong bridge head." On the 30th, Davout arrived with Morand's division and part of Gudin's, the rest of the infantry being between Blonie and Warsaw, the light cavalry spread along the left bank of the Vistula down to a point opposite the mouth of the Bug.

Lannes was now on the Bszura at Lowicz and Sochaczew. Augereau, from the mouth of that river to Wroclawik, above Thorn, touching, with his right, Lannes' left at Sochaczew. His light cavalry, on the left, waiting for the arrival of Ney, manoeuvred towards Bromberg.

On the 2nd December, the anniversary of the Imperial coronation and of Austerlitz, Napoleon issued to his troops one of the stirring proclamations with which he was wont to announce the opening of a new campaign. On the present occasion there was special need for a strong appeal to the enthusiasm and devotion of his soldiers who, in the past fifteen months, had served the Emperor so well. They had begun to feel the desire for a period of rest before renewing their exertions; they looked with repugnance on the idea of at once entering on a fresh campaign in the wilds of Poland, in the midst of mud and snow. They had already learnt something of the terrors of Polish weather in their march from Berlin, and there was much grumbling at the idea of going beyond the Vistula.[13] Here is the proclamation: "Soldiers! A year has to-day passed since you were, at this very hour, on the memorable field of Austerlitz. The Russians, fleeing in terror, or surrounded, were yielding their arms to their conquerors. Next day they sent overtures, deceitful overtures, of peace. Scarce had they, thanks to a perhaps culpable generosity, escaped from the disasters of the third coalition, when they entered upon a fourth. But their ally, on whose tactics they founded their chief hopes, is now no more. His strong places; his capital; his magazines; 280 of his standards; 700 of his guns; 5 of his great fortresses are all in our hands. The Oder, the Wartha, the deserts of Poland, the rigours of the season, have all failed to arrest for an instant your advance; you have braved all, surmounted all, everything has fled at your approach. Soldiers! we shall not lay aside

---

12. *Corr.* 11,332, dated Posen, 1st December, 1806.
13. "Our soldiers were less satisfied; they showed a lively repugnance to cross the Vistula. Misery, the winter, the bad weather, had inspired them with an extreme aversion for this country" (*Rapp*, 118).

our arms until a general peace has affirmed and assured the power of our allies, and restored to our commerce its liberty and its colonies. We have conquered on the Elbe and the Oder, at Pondicherry, and in our Indian colonies; at the Cape of Good Hope, and in the Spanish colonies. Who can give the Russians the hope of balancing destiny? Who can authorise them to thwart such great designs? Are not they still, as we are, the soldiers of Austerlitz?"

It is now time to examine the situation of the Russian armies and the small Prussian corps, with the outposts of which alone the French had so far come into collision.

On the 1st December began the Russian retreat from the Vistula before the French threatening a passage, not only at Warsaw, but also lower down at Wroclawik and Zakroczin. The 6th division (Sedmaratzki) fell back, from Praga, over the Narew to Sierock. The 4th division retired, between the 2nd and 4th December, from Pultusk to Ostrolenka with Bennigsen's headquarters. The 2nd division from Plonsk to Rozan, the 3rd from Prasznitz to a post midway between Makow and Ostrolenka. The advance guard of Barclay de Tolly retired from Plock to Novemiasto, behind the Sonna. Only a few hundred Cossacks remained on the Vistula.[14] The Prussians under Lestocq had been guarding the line of the Lower Vistula from Thorn, far too long a line for their weak force. Lestocq, nevertheless, protested against Bennigsen's orders for his retreat.[15] He was compelled to obey, especially as the retirement of Bennigsen would expose his left flank. On the 5th December, his headquarters were at Gollub, on the 6th at Strasburg. The detachments lower down fell back on Deutsch Eylau, Bischofswerder, and Löbau.[16]

On the 2nd December, Praga was occupied by a French regiment. On the 3rd, Milhaud's light cavalry passed the Vistula and proceeded towards the Bug. Between the 3rd and 8th, Davout's three divisions crossed the Vistula and occupied the small triangle between it, the Bug, and the Austrian frontier, which left the Bug a few miles above Sierock and met the Vistula a short way above Warsaw. Davout's headquarters were at Jablona, his outposts stretched along the left bank of the Bug from its mouth to the Austrian frontier. As long as Austria was neutral, this frontier now safeguarded Davout's right; Jerome's corps could devote itself to the Silesian sieges. Lannes' corps replaced Davout in Warsaw and Praga. Its headquarters were in Warsaw on the 5th December.

---

14. Hoepfner, iii. 69.
15. Hoepfner, iii. 67.
16. Ibid., iii. 70.

Immense energy was being displayed in repairing the bridge and in constructing redoubts, so as to make of Praga a powerful entrenched camp and bridge head.[17] This work was of the utmost importance as supporting the right of the new base on the Vistula, and as a cover to a retreat, should that be necessary.

Whilst Murat and Davout were completing the passage of the Vistula on the extreme right, Ney had arrived on the left of the line, in front of Thorn, now held only by a rearguard left by Lestocq. On the evening of the 6th December, a few French companies, commanded by Colonel Savary, passed the river in boats which had been collected under shelter of the islands. After a little sharp fighting, the Prussians, whose strength was small, were driven out of the town. More French troops passing over, a battalion and two squadrons followed the Prussian rear guard as far as Gollub. Having forced them to continue their retreat, the French returned to Thorn, and the repair of the bridge was at once taken in hand, though not, apparently, with so much energy as was desirable, for it was not completed till the 15th December.[18]

As Warsaw was required for a support to the right of the base on the Upper Vistula, so Thorn was required for the left. The old fortifications were ordered to be restored, in order to make of the place a bridge head covering the passage.[19]

To support Ney, Bessières, with the second cavalry reserve, passed at Thorn.

Bennigsen had ordered the retreat from the Vistula with a view to uniting with the 2nd Army under Buxhowden (who, in the beginning of December, had only just passed the Russian frontier,[20] and could

---

17. *Dumas*, xvii. 111, 112.

18. De Fezensac (p. 128) gives this date, mentioning that even on the 13th troops had still to cross in boats. The wooden bridge had been burnt, and its restoration was no easy matter.

19. Chasseloup was instructed to take in hand the fortification of the bridge head at Thorn; but first he was to attend to Praga, where an entrenched camp, large enough for 40,000 men, was required. He was also to submit a plan for fortifying one of the islands at the mouth of the Bug. Another *tête de pont* was required on the Bug, at the mouth of the Ukra (*Corr.* 11,463, dated 13th December, 1806).

20. The Russian western frontier in 1806 was very different from what it now is. Starting from the Baltic some 10 miles north of Memel, it ran south-east to the Niemen (or Memel) river, 25 miles east of Tilsit. Thence it ran east along the river for about 60 miles. From this point it ran nearly due south, following the Niemen nearly to its source, and thence in the same direction, to the Bug and the Austrian frontier. This, the nearest point on the frontier to Warsaw, and to the Vistula, was 90 miles east of that city.

not arrive on the Vistula before the 15th) before attempting to oppose seriously the French advance. Buxhowden, learning the retreat of the 1st Army, halted his own nearly thirty miles east of Ostrolenka, the headquarters of Bennigsen. The two commanders were vying with one another for the chief command. Both saw it was impossible for Marshal Kamenskoi, rapidly losing his reason, to retain his position long, and, it is to be feared, their jealousy may have influenced their actions. No sooner,[21] however, had Bennigsen retreated than he perceived his mistake in allowing the French, unchallenged, to pass the Vistula.[22] No doubt he could not have prevented their passage; but he might, at least, have, for the moment, delayed their acquisition of the two important *têtes de pont* of Praga and Thorn. He decided again to

---

21. Dumas (xiv., 425-429) gives a note, furnished to him by Bennigsen, on the latter's motives for not defending the line of the Vistula. After pointing out the inferiority of his numbers, he rightly remarks that he would have committed an unpardonable fault in attempting to defend the long line of the river above Thorn. If he attempted to defend Thorn and Warsaw, the French could cross between them, thus cutting him in two. The argument loses its force when we consider Bennigsen's subsequent orders to Lestocq to retake Thorn after its occupation by Ney.
22. A statement in the Arch. Hist. gives the positions of the French army on the 5th December.

Imperial Guard, Posen	Reserve of Grenadiers (Oudinot), Berlin	
Bernadotte	1st Corps	Marching on Posen, due there on 7th
Davout	3rd Corps	Warsaw and Blonic. Light Cavalry on left bank of Vistula from Warsaw to the Bszura
Soult	4th Corps	About Posen
Lannes	5th Corps	Sochaczew, Lowicz, and along the Vistula below the mouth of the Bszura
Ney	6th Corps	Opposite Thorn, and at Bromberg, etc
Augereau	7th Corps	In front of Blonie. Light Cavalry opposite Thorn, under orders to rejoin the corps
Reserve Cavalry	Lasalle marching on Warsaw	
	Milhaud on right bank of Vistula towards the lower Bug	
	Wattier concentrating on Kutno	
	Nansouty, Wiskitki, etc	
	D'Hautponlt, Ohermulki	
	Klein, Mosna, etc	
	Grouchy, near Posen	
	Beaumont near Willanow	
	Sahuc marching on Sempolno	
	Becker in front of Blonie	

Several of the cavalry positions are not marked on the maps.

advance. The recovery of Praga was hopeless; but he could hope to check Napoleon at the Bug, which had not yet been passed, and he might still possibly recover Thorn, where the French had shown less strength. Whilst he, with the main body of his army, again advanced to Pultusk, he sent a hurried order to Lestocq, to attempt the re-occupation of Thorn. It was too late. When Lestocq arrived before the place, which he had evacuated only two days before, he found Ney's force too strong for him. He was forced to retreat again to Strasburg, his rearguard being roughly handled by Ney, and to take up a position towards Lautenburg, on the left bank of the Drewenz.

Bennigsen's fresh forward movement was not more successful; for he was shortly informed of the further progress of the French, now to be narrated. Murat's orders were, when he had passed the Vistula at Warsaw, to endeavour also to pass the Bug.[23] This operation was undertaken by Davout, on the 10th December, with Gauthier's brigade of Morand's division. The points selected for the passage were Okunin, about two miles above Nowydwor, and Nowydwor itself, the principal passage to be at the former.

At 5.30 a.m. on the 10th, in the dark, Gauthier sent across the river at Okunin, by boat, ninety men, with orders to take post silently one hundred paces from the river on the farther side. They were not to fire, unless attacked. Effecting the passage undiscovered, they were quickly supported by more troops, and, at 7 a.m., a sharp fusillade was opened by the French at Gora, higher up the river, in order to induce the belief of a passage being intended there. There was no such intention, and the action was confined to fire across the river.

As the force opposite Okunin gathered strength, a reconnaissance was pushed forward towards Pomiechowo, a village on the right bank of the Ukra, about four thousand paces north of the point of passage. Simultaneously, another force had crossed opposite Nowydwor, landing in safety. The Russians in Modlin, near this landing-place, were forced to fall back on Pomiechowo, their retreat to which was threatened by the French troops from the Okunin crossing. They passed the Ukra, under fire from this force, by the Pomiechowo bridge.

Davout at once hurried on the construction of a bridge at Okunin, and of a *tête de pont* on the opposite bank. By evening he was firmly posted, with Morand's division, on the right bank, and had a defensible work, covering his bridge, well flanked, owing to the re-entrant angle of the river, by batteries on the left bank, above and below it.

---

23. Corr. 11,332, dated 1st December, 1806, to Murat.

On the 12th, Augereau's advance guard, passing the Vistula, without opposition, at Zakroczin, was able to protect the construction of a bridge head between Zakroczin and Utrata.

Bennigsen, hoping that by seizing Modlin on the 11th, when Augereau was still beyond the Vistula, he might force the French back across the Bug, possibly even over the Vistula, sent a regiment of jägers and one of hussars across the Ukra at Pomiechowo, at 7 a.m. This force drove the French 85th regiment from Pomiechowo, and occupied a position between that village and Koszewo. Davout, reinforcing the 85th with the 5th, again attacked. By 2 p.m., after a sharp combat, the Russians were compelled to re-cross the Ukra.

Informed of Augereau's crossing, and aware that Soult was approaching the Vistula on Augereau's left, Bennigsen, once more abandoning his forward movement, determined to defend the line of the Ukra.

Osterman Tolstoi's division (the 2nd) was at Nasielsk on the evening of the 11th. On the 13th, he was at Borkowo, on the Ukra, leaving Davout, unmolested, to strengthen his position opposite Okunin.

Soult marched from Posen on the 13th in echelons of divisions[24] to Wrocklavik, and was preparing to cross there, with such boats as he could collect, when he received orders[25] to march up the river, to cross as near as possible to the mouth of the Bszura, and march on Plonsk to join Augereau. Selecting as his point of passage the re-entrant angle near Dobrzyckow, he crossed unopposed there[26] with St. Hilaire's and Legrand's divisions, whilst Leval's passed at Plock, some distance lower.

Bernadotte's corps, arriving at Posen only on the 8th December, was not at Thorn till the 20th.

On the 13th December, Napoleon dictated, at Posen,[27] the following orders:

Bessières, with the 2nd cavalry reserve from Thorn, to advance to the right on Biezun, Rypin, and Soldau. Ney's light cavalry on Strasburg. Bessières would thus find himself midway between Thorn and Pultusk, in a position definitely to ascertain the Russian movements.

Soult, passing the Vistula on the 16th at Wrocklavik, to join Bessières at Lipno. When the junction was effected, Soult's light cavalry would move to the right on Plonsk, to facilitate the passage of Augereau at Zakrocrin, of Wattier at Wyszogorod, and of Davout at Nowydwor. Bessières' objects were: (a) to sweep the plain, and join

---

24. *Hoepfner*, iii. 81.
25. *Dumas*, xvii. 115.
26. *Ibid.*, xvii. 116.
27. *Corr.*, 11,458.

Soult; (b) to push the enemy over the Ukra: (c) to reconnoitre towards Pultusk and Willemburg; (d) to compel the Prussians to retreat.

Leval (Soult's corps), crossing at Thorn in support of Bessières, was to be at Lipno on the 7th. St. Hilaire, followed by Legrand (both of Soult's corps), to pass at Wrocklavik on the 16th. Thus, on the 18th, Soult would be, with his three divisions, across the Vistula, his right at Dobrzyckow, his left at Rypin. Ney, Bernadotte, and Lannes in second line. Ney to make for Strasburg, his place at Thorn being taken by Bernadotte and the Guard who would arrive there on the 18th. For the present no further movements could be definitely indicated, but, if the enemy did not mean to make a stand, infantry would be useless for his pursuit.

Scarcely had Napoleon passed these orders, when he received a despatch from Murat, dated midnight of the 10th December, describing the passage of the Bug, and asserting that the enemy had evacuated the left bank of the Narew. This changed his views, and induced him to believe the enemy was in full retreat. He at once issued fresh orders.[28] Murat was directed in pursuit with all his available cavalry (about 30,000 men), including that of Davout, Augereau, and Lannes, to link himself to Bessières towards Biezun, to endeavour to interrupt the road from Pultusk to Koenigsberg, and to harass the enemy's rear-guard to the utmost. With this great cavalry force, Murat would have such a superiority of that arm that he would be master of the situation, and could accept or refuse battle, as might seem best in the circumstances of the moment. Meanwhile, the infantry would secure as much rest as possible. Davout to occupy Sierock, and, possibly, send one division to Pultusk. Augereau to halt at Zakrocrin and Wyszogorod, drawing supplies from Plonsk and Blonie. Soult towards Plonsk. Lannes to concentrate at Warsaw. Napoleon had himself intended going to Thorn, but the reported retreat had changed his views, and he was bound for Warsaw. To Ney he wrote that his infantry would be useless for the pursuit, and he could protect his left with his light cavalry.[29]

It was time for the Emperor to be at the front. He left Posen on the 16th. The roads were so bad that he had to travel in a country conveyance, and Duroc, overturned in his carriage, broke his collar-bone.[30] Late at night on the 18th, the Emperor reached Warsaw, where, notwithstanding the hour, there was the wildest enthusiasm amongst the Poles. Next day, he was besieged with petitions and deputations seeking the reconstitution of the Polish kingdom. He replied to them as he

28. Corr., 11,465, dated 13th December, 1806.
29. Corr. 11,462, dated 13th December, 1806.
30. Corr. 11,497. 43rd bulletin.

had replied from Berlin. His one desire, as well as that of his soldiers, at this time, was to be allowed peaceably to occupy cantonments for the remainder of the cold season; but it was, at the same time, necessary to gain space and drive the Russians from his front.[31] He had discovered the inaccuracy of Murat's report as to the general retreat of the enemy, and had once more modified his orders, thus—

Ney to move on Gollub with advance guard at Rypin, light cavalry towards Strasburg and Culm.[32] Leval to occupy Thorn between the departure of Ney and the arrival of Bernadotte; then to join his own corps and support Ney at Gollub.[33] Bernadotte to arrive at Thorn, and await orders there, after relieving Leval on the evening of the 17th.[34] Soult to march between the Vistula and Biezun, so as to reach Plonsk on Ney's right.[35] Bessières, with his cavalry, to drive the enemy on Soldau, and to send parties along the Ukra and towards Plonsk, to meet the cavalry of Augereau. Murat to cover Ney's advance.[36] Further orders were sent to Bernadotte, on the 17th, to leave one division at Thorn, and, with the other two, to support Ney and Bessières, who would be subordinate to him as the senior marshal.[37] Augereau was ordered to be at Plonsk on the 22nd with Milhaud from the cavalry reserve.[38] Davout to pass all his corps, except one regiment, to the right bank of the Bug.[39] Murat also to send over Lasalle, Klein, Nansouty, and Beaumont.[40] Lannes to move from Warsaw to the left bank of the Bug towards Jablona and Zegrz, and the Guard to take his place at Warsaw,[41] which would be defended by Poles.42 All was now ready for the French advance.

As for the Russian positions, Marshal Kamenskoi had, at last,

31. "It is time to take up our winter quarters which can only be done after we have driven off the Russians" (*Corr.* 11,501, to Davout, dated, Warsaw, 9th December, 1806). To Clarke he wrote from Lowicz, on his way to Warsaw, that the armies were facing each other, the French on the left, the Russians on the right bank of the Narew, and that it was possible that in a week there would be a battle which would make an end of the affair" (*Corr.* 11,500).

"Not wishing to let the enemy shut us in on the Vistula, and feeling, on the contrary, the necessity to give ourselves a broader sphere in front of Warsaw and Thorn, I at once took the offensive" (Jomini, *Vie de Napoléon*, ii. 339).

32. Berthier to Ney, 15th December, 1806.

33. Berthier to Leval, 15th December.

34. Berthier to Bernadotte, 15th December.

35. Berthier to Soult, 15th December.

36. Berthier to Bessières, 15th December. The despatches in this and the for preceding notes are printed in full in *Dumas*, xvii., *"Pièces justificatives."*

37. Berthier to Bessières, 17th December.

38. Berthier to Augereau, 21st December. (continued on next page)

joined his armies on the 21st December at Pultusk. Old and worn out in body and mind as he was, he was yet all for a forward movement towards the Ukra in support of the troops there. Gallitzin, with an infantry regiment, 2 cavalry regiments and 18 guns, was sent from Pultusk to Glubowo, 6 miles north-east of Novemiasto, to support the 3rd division; Sedmaratzki, with the 6th division, was ordered to advance to Zbroski; Buxhowden's 5th and 7th divisions to march from Ostrolenka on Novemiasto, whilst his 8th and 14th divisions marched on Pultusk.[43]

Barclay de Tolly was, with 6 battalions, 1 hussar and 1 Cossack regiment, and 6 guns, on the Ukra about Kolozomb and Sochoczin. Dorochow, with 3 battalions, 1 cavalry, 1 Cossack regiment, and 6 guns, part of the 2nd and 4th divisions, at Borkowo. Osterman, with the rest of the 2nd division, stood from Borkowo on the Ukra to the Narew. Bagavout, with 3 battalions, one regiment of Cossacks, and one gun, was at Zegrz, supported in rear by another battalion and a regiment of Cossacks. Litow, with two infantry regiments, supported Barclay and Dorochow. Sacken, at Srenszk, stretched a hand to the Prussians, whose left was there and right at Lautenburg.[44]

39. Berthier to Davout, 22nd December.
40. Berthier to Murat, 22nd December.
41. Berthier to Lefebvre, 22nd December, and Berthier to Lannes, 23rd December.
42. Berthier to Gouvion, governor of Warsaw, 23rd December. This, and the despatches quoted in the preceding five notes, are quoted in *Dumas*, xvii., *"Pièces justicatives."*
43. *Hoepfner*, iii. 84.
44. *Ibid.*, iii. 82, 83.

CHAPTER 2

Passage of the Ukra and Operations of the 24th and 25th December

The Ukra falls into the Bug a short way above the French bridge at Okunin. At its mouth it branches right and left, forming a triangular island which is divided into two unequal portions by a channel. Davout had already crossed the right branch of the river, and occupied the island up to the channel. During the night of the 20th December, he seized the rest of the island, expelling the Russian detachment which occupied the part beyond the channel. There thus remained only one branch of the Ukra for him to pass.

On the morning of the 23rd, Napoleon proceeded to reconnoitre the position for the crossing which he proposed. Mounting by a ladder on to the roof of a cottage on the island, he soon decided on his plan, and dictated, on the spot, the necessary orders.[1]

From opposite Pomiechowo on the Ukra, to Czarnowo on the Bug, there runs a bank above flood-level of the rivers. Between this bank and the island occupied by Davout, the ground, like the island itself, is low, swampy, partially wooded, and liable to floods. From the left branch of the Ukra, across the broadest part of the low ground to the bank, is a distance of some 2500 yards. On and below the bank was posted Osterman Tolstoi's force of 9 battalions, 2 squadrons, 1 regiment of Cossacks, 14 field guns, 6 light guns.[2] Davout had Morand's division in the island, Friant's near Pomiechowo, Gudin's at the Okunin bridge. Napoleon had decided on a night attack, and his orders were consequently given in great detail, and with the utmost care.[3] They were executed with wonderful exactitude by Davout's corps, perhaps the best in the army.

---

1. For this account of the passage of the Ukra, compare *Hoepfner*, iii. 88-94; *Dumas*, xvii. 135-147; *Davout*, 115-127.

2. *Plotho*, p. 16.

3. For the orders in full, see *Dumas*, xvii. 136-138.

At 7 p.m. Morand's division was formed, with its advanced portion in three columns in the island, as far as possible from the enemy. Each of these leading columns had a strength of one battalion. A company of voltigeurs was detached from each column as escort to the guns which were, under cover of the voltigeurs' fire, able to take position and open a fire of grape across the left branch of the river, on the Russians in the low ground. The river was then passed by the voltigeurs in boats brought up from the Bug, and three bridges, one at either extremity, and one in the centre of the branch, were constructed, the work being protected by the troops which had passed in boats. As the bridges were completed, the rest of the leading columns crossed and advanced into the low ground. Behind them came a regiment (the 17th) of light infantry and 3 squadrons of cavalry. Behind these the rest of Morand's division.

Petit, with a detachment of Gudin's division, crossed the upper bridge and pushed up the left bank of the river. To support his frontal attack on the Russian right, 6 guns enfiladed it from Pomiechowo. To alarm the enemy with the idea of a passage at Pomiechowo, a quantity of damp straw had been lighted in the bed of the river in that direction, creating a dense smoke. Cavalry had also been sent up the right bank to raise apprehensions, as well as to link Davout's corps to Augereau's. A detachment of 50 men, under Perrin, crossed 100 paces above the island, and helped to protect Petit's left. Finally, 2 guns and 30 picked marksmen, moving up the right bank, slightly in advance of Perrin, flanked with their fire any attempt to attack his or Petit's front on the left bank.

No great difficulty was found in expelling the Russians from the low ground, and Morand advanced against the left of the main position in echelons by his right.

The 17th Regiment, in advance of Morand's main body, hurried forward, with more valour than wisdom, to the attack of Czarnowo. The fury of its onslaught, for the moment, staggered the defenders, and the French infantry burst triumphantly into the batteries in front of the village. Their triumph was short-lived, for the defenders, quickly rallying, drove their rash assailants back with the bayonet. Support was not at hand, and the advance was for the moment stayed. The main body, however, soon came up, and a fresh attack was organised. One battalion of the 30th turned Czarnowo by a ravine leading to the Bug, another advanced against the front of the village, and the third against the (French) left of it, through a pine wood. The rest of Morand's division, with cavalry behind the centre, followed in support. Still, the first attacks were met and repulsed by Osterman's infantry with a stubborn calmness which was proof against the élan of the enemy. Osterman, however, could not but perceive that, with fresh troops constantly feeding Morand's fighting line, it was impossible for him long to hold out with his inferior force. Fearing the loss, with that of Czarnowo, of his heavy artillery, he despatched it in the direction of Nasielsk. The fight for Czarnowo continued long with the greatest fury. In the end, the superior numbers of the French enabled them to gain a firm footing in the village and, forcing the enemy out, they were able to deploy on the plateau beyond.

On the opposite wing, Petit's attack had, in the meanwhile, been equally successful. At first he had only 400 men, besides Perrin's detachment on his left. Aided by a vigorous cannonade from the 2-gun battery at Pomiechowo, he was able to carry the Russian redoubts, from which the artillery was withdrawn towards Czarnowo, only just in time to save it from capture. The absence of pursuit soon showed the Russians how weak the French left was, and they launched a strong force of cavalry against Petit. His men, calmly holding their fire till the cavalry were close upon them, repulsed this and several other attacks by infantry upon the captured redoubts. Davout was able to reinforce Petit with more troops of the 3rd division, and every attack made upon him was open to the flanking artillery fire from Pomiechowo.

Osterman's troops had now, at 4 a.m., been for 12 hours under arms, for 9 under fire. The general, seriously alarmed by the loss of Czarnowo, determined on retreat. To cover it, he still continued his attacks on Petit, and kept up a vigorous fire in front. At this juncture, being reinforced by 3 battalions and 4 squadrons, he was able to draw off his troops, still in good order, towards Nasielsk.

It is probable that the loss on the French side exceeded that of the Russians, who had 1392[4] killed and wounded.

Napoleon's decision to attempt the passage by night was remarkable, and unusual with him. He was using for it the best troops in his army, and the accuracy with which they carried out his programme fully justified his confidence in them. Any deviation from his orders, any hesitation, on the part of the officers in leading, or of the men in following, might have led to disaster. On the other hand, the passage

4. Davout states his loss at 807, but this is probably below the mark, and appears to exclude Petit and part of the cavalry. The loss in officers was specially heavy, as was to be expected in a night attack where bold leading was essential to success (*Davout*, p. 127). Plotho (p. 24) says Osterman Tolstoi reported his loss as only 500. Hoepfner (iii. 93) gives 1392, including three generals wounded.

by daylight would have been attended with immense risk and difficulty. The bridges would have had to be constructed under the fire of the Russian guns commanding all the low ground, the advance across which could not fail to be attended with much greater loss than was incurred at night.

Friant's division, which had bivouacked between Pomiechowo and Koszewo, marched at 4 a.m. on the 4th, and following the same route as Morand's, was on the battlefield by daybreak. It at once took over the pursuit from the victorious troops, now exhausted by a long night of continuous fighting. Passing through Psucin, Friant arrived near Nasielsk soon after midday. Rapp, with Marulaz's cavalry, and Lemarroy, with a regiment of dragoons, were already engaged with the Russians, whom they had driven out of the village, and who had now taken up a position on the rising ground beyond, their cavalry resisting the French in the meadows on the left and in front. Dorochow from Borkowo had by this time joined Osterman.

Friant, himself attacking in front, sent his voltigeurs to threaten the Russian retreat by their left. So successful was the flank attack that three guns were taken and the Russians driven back to the wood. Friant had not been able yet to bring up his guns over the muddy roads. The Russians still held to the woods, and it was not till night had fallen that they were compelled, by constant attacks of superior forces, to continue their retreat to Strzegoczin, abandoning some of their guns in the mud. Davout's 1st and 2nd divisions bivouacked, during the night of the 24th-25th December, in and beyond Nasielsk. The 3rd, which had marched up from the Okunin bridge, was behind.

On the 25th, all the divisions marched in the direction of Novemiasto; but, finding a strong Russian column in position at Kaleczin, where the Novemiasto-Golymin and Nasielsk-Ciechanow roads cross, Davout changed his direction to that of Strzegoczin, whence he dislodged the enemy without difficulty. The corps bivouacked that night in and behind Strzegoczin. Lannes' corps, following from Okunin, was on Davout's right rear on the 24th, and at Zbroski on the night of the 25th.

Whilst Davout's corps had been effecting the passage of the Ukra at its mouth, the next corps on the left, Augereau's, had moved from Plonsk[5] early on the 24th, reinforced by Wattier's and Milhaud's cavalry. Its march was directed against Barclay de Tolly, holding the upper passages of the river at Kolozomb and Sochoczin. Both bridges

---

5. It had arrived there from Zakroczin on the 23rd (*Hoepfner*, iii. 96).

had been burnt, and there was an earthwork beyond that of Kolo-zomb defended by artillery, and by three battalions and two squad-rons. At Sochoczin, three battalions, and three squadrons held the left bank. The two forces were linked by three battalions in a wood between them.

Against Sochoczin marched Heudelet's division, with Milhaud's cav-alry attached; against Kolozomb Desjardin's division, and Wattier's cavalry.

Whilst the 16th Light Infantry lined the right bank on either side of the Kolozomb bridge, Savary,[6] with the grenadiers of the 14th, forced his way across by utilising some planks which the Russians had not burnt,[7] and which served to span the gaps in the partially destroyed bridge. The French were met at Kolozomb by the Rus-sian infantry and hussars, but, being quickly reinforced, compelled the enemy to retreat towards Novemiasto, leaving in their hands six guns in the earthworks. Lapisse, meanwhile, had been sent some 3000 yards down the river to surprise, at Pruski, the enemy, who had no guns there. The Russian position at Kolozomb was a very strong one, with the river in front and a wood behind, and they had twelve guns. Lapisse passed successfully, but an attempt to pass 1000 yards above Kolozomb failed.[8] Heudelet had been less successful. There was no ford in front of him. Attempting to restore the bridge, under cover of his infantry and artillery replying to the Russian fire, his first attack was beaten off with heavy loss. In a fit of temper, for which he is se-verely blamed by Marbot,[9] he again sent forward his men, who were once more repulsed. Any serious attack at Sochoczin was unnecessary, seeing that a crossing at Kolozomb, farther east, must infallibly result in the retreat of the Russians at Sochoczin. It was only necessary to hold them at the latter place by a demonstration preventing them from assisting their comrades at Kolozomb. Accordingly, as soon as Desjardins was across at Kolozomb, two of Heudelet's brigades were summoned thither by Augereau. The passage at Sochoczin was soon after left open by the retreat of its defenders. Milhaud, pursuing the retreating Russians, captured the baggage of their 2nd division. The French loss at these crossings is given by Augereau at 66 killed and 452 wounded, about equally distributed between the two divisions. Savary was killed at Kolozomb.

Augereau now reassembled his corps. His light cavalry, (Durosnel)

---

6. Brother of the future Duc de Rovigo.
7. *Marbot*, i. 245.
8. Augereau (*Archives Historiques*).
9. *Marbot*, i. 246.

moved up the Sonna towards Ciechanow, to expedite the Russian retreat, and the main body pursued the Russians towards Novemiasto till stopped, short of that place, by darkness.[10] On the 25th, Augereau occupied Novemiasto and his advanced guard got as far as Bond-kowo, his 1st division to Gatkowo, and his 2nd to Gostymin.[11] On Augereau's left was Soult's corps. It reached Gora, west of Plonsk, on the 4th, and marching in the direction of Sochoczin and Ciechanow, was at the former on the night of the 5th, with light cavalry at Oirzen. The Guard was with the Emperor that night at Lopaczin. Murat, with all of the 1st cavalry reserve which had not been detached, was, on the night of the 25th, at Sochoczin. He had, on the 24th, attacked Sacken at Lopaczin. With his retreat already threatened by the forward move-ment of the French against Barclay on his right, and Osterman on his left, Sacken gave way before Murat, who, in the pursuit, forced the Russian 1st Division to make the best of its way towards Pultusk. Part of it, under Pahlen, was driven towards Ciechanow.

To bring up the story to the night of this dismal Christmas Day, it remains to describe what was happening towards Thorn, between the Prussians on the one hand, and Bessières, Ney, and Bernadotte on the other.

On the 28th December, Lestocq had retreated from Strasburg to Lautenburg, leaving Bulow to defend the defile at Gurzno.[12] On the 9th, Grouchy, with Bessières' advance guard,[13] seized Biezun. The point was of great importance to Lestocq; through it he communi-cated directly with the Russian right at Sochoczin, from which it was distant less than two marches. On the 21st, Lestocq sent a detachment through Soldau and Kuczbork to attempt the recapture of Biezun.

---

10. *Archives Historiques.*

11. Augereau (*Archives Historiques*) says he only reached Novemiasto on the 25th, which is less than Hoepfner (iii. 68) gives him credit for.

12. Prussian official account quoted by Wilson (p. 253).

13. Bessières 2nd cavalry reserve was about 6000 strong (Berthier to Bessières, 17 December, *Dumas*, xvii. 456. It's constitution was—

Light Cavalry division	Tilly
2nd Dragoon division	Grouchy
4th Dragoon division	Sahuc
2nd Cuirassier division	d'Hautpoult

(Soult's report, *Archives Historiques*). It was constituted on the 16th December 1806, and again broken up on the 12th January, 1807, when the constituent troops were thus distributed—Tilly's and Sahuc's divisions were made over to Bernadotte; Grouchy's to Ney; D'Hautpoult's was sent to Thorn and the neighbourhood. ("*Journax de Marche*," *Archives Historiques*)

It was at Kuczbork on the 22nd, and consisted of two infantry regiments, a regiment of dragoons, two of hussars, and a battery of horse artillery. On the 23rd, it appeared before Biezun, where Grouchy had now been joined by Bessières, with infantry and artillery. The attempt was a complete failure. The Prussians, charged by Grouchy, were driven back two miles beyond Kuczbork, with the loss of 500 prisoners and 5 guns, besides killed and wounded.[14] On the 24th, the detachment continued its retreat to Soldau. Ney, whilst this detachment was in front of Biezun, marching from Strasburg, came upon Bulow's rearguard at Gurzno. On the 24th he drove it before him to Kuczbork, where it joined the Biezun detachment in its retreat to Soldau. From Kuczbork, Ney sent Marchand's division to operate against the Prussians at Mlawa and Soldau.[15] With his other division he remained in support behind Marchand's left.

Lestocq's corps, in the hope of ascertaining the intentions of the enemy and of maintaining communications with the Russian right, was scattered over a front of some 10 or 11 miles, from near Lautenburg, on the right, to Neidenburg and Mlawa, on the left. The whole strength of the Prussian corps was not above 6000 men.

At Soldau, there appear to have been no more than one battalion and 8 or 10 guns.[16] Marchand had, according to his own statement, only two regiments of infantry, supported later by the rest of his division from Mlawa. Ney was at Gurzno with his 2nd division.

---

14. *Hoepfner*, iii, 138-140, where a full account of the action is given.

15. This is not quite Dumas's version, but see the next note for evidence in support of this account.

16. Dumas (xvii. 189), basing his statement, apparently, on Marchand's report, says there were 6000 Prussians entrenched at Soldau. Hoepfner denies this, and gives full details of the distribution of the corps (iii. 145, etc.). His account is the more probable on the face of it. Against 6000 men in a strong position covered by a stream, a canal, and a lake on its left, Marchand could hardly have succeeded so easily as he did in capturing the town. Had he done so, Lestocq would scarcely have led back to the storm of the captured position a force which had yielded so easily when it had the advantage of the defensive. It is curiously difficult to fix with certainty the date of the action at Soldau. Hoepfner gives the 25th; Dumas also. De Fezensac (131) says it was on the same day as Pultusk, the 26th. Jomini does not specify the date clearly. Bernadotte (Archives Historiques) gives the 5th. The "*Journaux de Marche*," of Ney's corps (in the *Archives Historiques*), unlike those of Davout, Soult, Augereau, and Bernadotte, are very brief, mere diaries, giving the positions occupied by the corps on each day. There are two versions of the manuscript; the one which is rather fuller as regards details of positions, makes no mention whatever of days of battle. The other merely states, in a column of remarks, that there was an action on a particular date at a place gamed. Against the 25th December (continued on next page)

Notwithstanding the strength of the position, the weak Prussian force was unable to make a serious resistance. Marchand was master of Soldau soon after 2 p.m. Having ascertained the direction of Ney's advance, Lestocq had concentrated his troops and returned to recapture Saldau. The attack on it was made from the Neidenburg road, about 5 p.m. Despite the valour with which the Prussian troops fought, they were unable to get beyond the outer edge of the village, whence, after desperate hand-to-hand fighting, they were driven back. Lestocq, whose left had meanwhile been driven in from Mlawa, retreated during the night on Neidenburg, whither he was slowly followed by Ney.[17]

The same night, Bernadotte was marching to support and replace Ney at Mlawa and Soldau. Bessières, with headquarters at Bobarzin, occupied the country about Mlawa, Raciaz, etc.[18]

Thus the Prussians, on the night of the 25th-26th December, were completely severed from the Russian right, and retreating, away from it, towards Koenigsberg. Ney, Bernadotte, and Bessières were interposed between the allies; Soult was also marching to turn the Russian right; the rest of the French army, opposed to their front, was towards Golymin and Pultusk.

The Russian position at the same time was as follows: Kamenskoi had ordered a general retirement on Ostrolenka, artillery being freely abandoned to avoid hampering the movement. Bennigsen, with the divisions of Osterman Tolstoi, Sedmaratzki, and part of those of Gallitzin and Sacken, was at Pultusk; Gallitzin, with the rest of his own division, was retiring on Golymin; the rest of Sacken's was moving on the same place from Ciechanow, but, owing to its having been driven by Murat northwards, was farther from Golymin than Gallitzin was. Of Buxhowden's army, Dochtorow's division was east of Gallitzin, on the road through Golymin to Makow; Essen's and Anrepp's were at Popowo, on the Bug, preparing to retire direct to Rozan and Ostrolenka up the peninsula between the Bug and the Narew.

---

it has the entry "combat de Mlawa," against the 26th, "combat de Soldau." The matter, however, seems to be set at rest by a letter from Marchand to Ney (Daily Correspondence, 26th December, in *Archives Historiques*), in which he says, "Yesterday (i.e. 25th) I occupied Mlawa and Soldau. At Mlawa I had no serious difficulty, but it was different at Soldau, as I had only two regiments with which to attack 6000 men." This seems to show that Ney was not in person at Soldau. The "*Journaux de Marche*" show his headquarters as Gurzno on the 24th, 25th, and 26th December.

17. Ney did not move his headquarters beyond Soldau till the 29th, when they were at Neidenburg ("*Journaux de Marche*," 6th Corps, *Archives Historiques*).

18. "*Journaux de Marche*," *Archives Historiques*.

Bennigsen resolved, disobeying Kamenskoi's orders, to stand and fight at Pultusk. The marshal was himself with Bennigsen, but broken in body and mind, he left the army early next morning for Grodno where his eccentric conduct showed that he was no longer fit for command.[19] At this point the gallant but worn-out old lieutenant of Suwarrow disappears, except for a brief moment, from the scene.

19. "On his return to Grodno he went, without his shirt, into the streets, and then, sending for a surgeon, pointed out all his wounds, groaned as he passed his hand over them, and insisted on a certificate of his incapacity to serve" (*Wilson*, 83, note). Truly a pitiful ending to the career of a gallant old soldier.

CHAPTER 3

The Battles of Pultusk and Golymin
26th December, 1806

PULTUSK[1]

The town of Pultusk lies on the right bank of the river Narew, the general course of which here is nearly due north and south.[2] The greater part of the town is in the low ground, and is intersected by a small branch of the stream. It spreads, however, also on to the bank, which is somewhat steep and rises to a small elevation to the west. The river is passed by the road from Strzegoczin and Golymin below the infall of the small branch. That road runs to the north-west over the height already mentioned, then falls into a slight depression, again rises and mounts the height to the south-east of the village of Mosin, and, passing through the centre of a large wood, continues its course close to the south side of Mosin. The height on which stands the large wood is a plateau of some extent which, narrowing into a fairly wide ridge,[3] continues to the south-east nearly to the river bank, where it is bounded, towards the town, by a considerable ravine falling into the low ground about one thousand paces from the Golymin road. The plateau and ridge form a natural screen, hiding from the forest on their west and south, the town and all the lower portions of the Golymin road. In front of a person coming from Pultusk there appears, from the ridge of this screen, a shallow depression, bounded on

---

1. This account of the battle of Pultusk is based on a comparison of those given by (a) *Dumas*, vol. xvii., pp. 164-171; (b) Sir R. Wilson; (c) *Hoepfner*, vol. iii., pp. 109-119; (d) *Davout*, pp. 131-137; (e) Lannes' report, *Arch. Hist.*
2. The river at the bridge appears to have a breadth of about 100 yards. At the date of the battle it was running very high, owing to the thaw, and was covered with blocks of floating ice.
3. The wood measured about 1800 paces at right angles to the Golymin road, and about 1200 at its greatest width along the road.

its farther side by the forest, to which the ground again slightly rises, and covered in places, especially opposite the Mosin heights, by outlying thickets and woods.

The position chosen by Bennigsen for his main line of battle practically coincided with the line of the Golymin road, from Pultusk to the point where it enters the wood on the Mosin heights.

On this line, the left resting on the town and the right on the Mosin wood, he drew up his main body in three lines. In first line he placed 21 battalions of the 2nd and 3rd divisions. Behind these, at about 300 paces' interval, stood, in second line, 18 battalions, and behind them again, in third line, towards the left, were 5 battalions of the 5th and 6th divisions. The artillery of the main body was disposed in advantageous positions along the front of the first line.

On the right, Barclay de Tolly was thrown forward into the south-western half of the great wood. With three jäger regiments he held the edge of the wood, whilst two battalions of another regiment stood in reserve in the wood on the Golymin road, thus forming a continuation through it of the first main line. The third battalion supported a battery placed outside the wood, astride of the road, commanding the approach from Golymin. In the space between the wood and Mosin was a regiment of Polish cavalry. There were more guns, masked by a hedge, facing the Nasielsk road.

The Russian general had a similar advanced position on his left wing, designed to cover the Narew bridge. Here Bagavout stood, beyond the deep ravine, with 10 battalions, 2 squadrons of dragoons, 600 Cossacks, and one battery. His cavalry was pushed forward along the Warsaw road. These troops were all drawn from the 6th division. The advanced posts of Barclay and Bagavout[4] thus occupied the two extremities of the screening ridge, which has already been described. To link them to one another, there were posted along their ridge 28 squadrons of regular cavalry.

Owing to the conformation of the ground, and the position of the advanced wings with their connecting line of cavalry, the main lines, on the Golymin road, were concealed from the view of an enemy debouching from the forest by the Warsaw and Nasielsk roads. But, at the same time, the fire of the greater portion of the Russian artillery was masked by the cavalry line.

In the valley, beyond the cavalry and extending into the outlying

---

4. Bagavout began the battle with 5000 men before he was reinforced (Bennigsen's despatch, *Wilson*, p. 235). He was between the river bank and the extremity of the ridge, extending on to the slope heading up to it.

woods in front of the forest, was a long line of Cossacks, supported, in front of Barclay's position, by 10 squadrons of hussars. Lastly, one battalion of Anrepp's division (14th) stood to guard the bridge on the left bank of the Narew. Anrepp himself was on the march, under Kamenskoi's orders, from Popowo, near the Bug, to Rozan and Ostrolenka.

Such was the position in which Bennigsen prepared to receive the French attack, which might fall upon him either from the direction of Warsaw and Nasielsk or from that of Golymin. He had taken special precautions to cover the bridge, not only by his strong detachment under Bagavout, but also by keeping his reserve behind his left flank, ready to support that commander. From the outskirts of Pultusk to Barclays battery on the Golymin road was a distance of about 4500 paces. The Russians had two lines of retreat, one by the right bank of the Narew, through Makow to Ostrolenka, the other over the bridge by the road on the left bank *via* Rozan. The latter was decidedly longer, as it passed round the outside of the great bend of the river. Therefore, Bennigsen's right flank, covering the shorter line by the chord, was specially sensitive to attack.[5]

Lannes, with his two divisions, commanded by Suchet and Gazan, marched from Zbroski at 7 a.m. on the 26th December. The distance to Pultusk is but five miles; to the point where he must meet Bennigsen's foremost troops scarcely four. Yet even this march, short in actual length was a tedious and difficult one. The weather had recently been an alternation of frost and thaw. During the last two days a decided thaw had set in. It had penetrated deep into the ground, aided in its action by constant showers of rain, of sleet, and of snow, which melted as it reached the surface of the earth. The ground had become more and more sodden, and the unmetalled roads had degenerated into lines of mud which, ground and churned by the passage of men and horses, acquired a depth that rendered all movement, not only irksome, but difficult in the extreme. For the artillery, it was still more difficult to forge a way through these terrible roads, even with the aid of double, treble, and quadruple teams. For the infantry, a rate of progression exceeding 1¼ miles an hour was not generally practicable.[6] The men were generally halfway up to their knees in sticky mud, often much farther.

---

5. *Hoepfner*, iii., 111. Behind his left wing lay both the road to Makow by the right bank, and that over the bridge. The former, however, shortly turned to the northwest, so that it was liable to be severed, farther on, behind the right wing.

6. "The country was clayey and cut up by marshes; the roads were frightful. The cavalry, infantry, and artillery, were lost in the depths of mud. None could get out of them save by untold labour" (*Rapp*, p. 127). "It took two hours to cover a short league" (*Davout*, p, 132). One league = 4 kilometres = 2½ miles.

Davout officially records that several men, including an officer whom he names, spent the night after the battle on the field, simply because they were unable to move backwards or forwards in the mud.[7] Rapp makes a similar statement.[8] Lannes himself wrote: "The rain and the hail overwhelmed our soldiers"; and, again "The field, on which we were about to do battle, had been converted into a sea of mud, through which soldiers and horses could with difficulty march."[9]

By incredible exertions, the whole corps had been got forward on the 5th from Czarnowo, with its artillery complete, till the first division reached Zbroski, and Gazan's, in second line, was a mile behind. The corps had marched 15 miles. The troops bivouacked in misery during a night of storms of snow, hail, and rain.

Where Lannes had started his corps on its march towards the enemy, of whose presence in force at Pultusk he was aware, he himself rode forward, with an escort of two squadrons, to reconnoitre the position. As he emerged from the forest on the Nasielsk-Pultusk road, he saw before him, on the ridge covering Pultusk, Bennigsen's cavalry, and the front of his advanced wings, the whole covered by the line of Cossacks in the intervening depression. He had already had to clear some of the Cossacks out of the thickets on his side. The town of Pultusk, and Bennigsen's main lines, were hidden from him by the rising ground. It was not till considerably later that he realised the magnitude of the force with which he had to do battle. Could he have known the odds in numbers against which he had to contend, perhaps even Lannes' brave spirit would have quailed; for he knew of no succour likely to reach him from his left,[10] and he did know that there was nothing behind him.

Presently, Claparède, coming up with the 17th Light Infantry as advance guard, drove in the Cossack outposts, and enabled Lannes to see better what was in front of him. His position was difficult and dangerous, but he had the Emperor's clear orders for the capture of the Pultusk bridge, and he was not the man to hesitate, whatever the

---

7. *Davout*, p. 136.

8. *Rapp*, p. 127.

9. Lannes' report on the battle to Berthier, dated 27th December, in daily correspondence (*Arch. Hist.*). The report is written by Victor, then Lannes' chief of the staff.

10. Lannes had no information of the approach of Davout's 3rd division. Indeed, Davout had no orders to send it to Lannes' support. He merely directed it to keep from that marshal's left flank a Russian column retreating, apparently, on Pultusk from Strzegoczin (*Davout*, p. 132). Berthier's despatch to Lannes (dated 26th December), which reached him about 10 a.m., says: "Marshal Davout is about to advance on Strzegoczin and Golymin." The orders of the same date to Davout merely direct him on the last-named places, and in no way indicate that he was to assist Lannes.

difficulties. It was now about 10 a.m., and he had just received the Emperor's order.[11]

As his troops slowly came up, he marshalled them, under cover of the woods, in two lines, covering, as far as he could, the whole length of the Russian position. In first line he ranged the whole of Suchet's division, less the 40th regiment. In second line was Gazan's division, plus the 40th from Suchet's. On the right of his first line, he placed Claparède with the 17th Light Infantry, and Treilhard's Light Cavalry, in support, opposed to Bagavout's detachment. The centre, under Wedell, consisted of the 64th regiment and one battalion of the 88th. On the left were the other battalion of the 88th, the 34th, and Becker's dragoons, the whole led by Suchet in person. The left wing was covered, more completely than the centre and the right, by detached woods, and its strength was thus concealed from Barclay de Tolly, to whom it was opposed. The few guns which had, so far, arrived were disposed in front of the centre and the left. Gazan, with the second line, followed the first at about three hundred paces. The battalions were mostly deployed and their front covered by a swarm of skirmishers. The second line comprised only two regiments of Gazan's and the 40th. In reserve there were the two battalions of the 21st regiment (Gazan's division).

The strength of Lannes' corps may be taken at about 20,000 men, whilst Bennigsen had between 40,000 and 45,000.[12]

---

11. These are the orders referred to in the last note. They inform Lannes that the enemy's centre is pierced, that one or two regiments may have remained at Sierock, if so, they will certainly be captured. The marshal is to advance on Pultusk, to pass the Narew there, and at once to construct a bridge head. Clearly the Emperor had no thought of any serious resistance to his advance at Pultusk (cf. despatch quoted in full, *Dumas*, vol. xvii., pp. 485-487). The estimate seems at least 3000 too high. The same authority (iii, 10) gives Bennigsen's strength, allowing for sick, detachments, etc., as 40,600 men, viz. 66 battalions, 55 squadrons, 7 field batteries, and 2½ horse batteries (128 guns). Sir R. Wilson (p. 273) gives 45,000. Lanes' strength was 24 battalions and 27 squadrons. If, as Hoepfner reckons, he had 20,000 men, the battalions may be reckoned at 750, and the squadrons at 80 men. Assuming Davout's battalions to have had an equal average strength, d'Aultanne's force could not have exceeded 7000, and the whole French force engaged would not amount to over 27,000. Napoleon (*Corr.* 11,305), sending orders to Murat, mentions the strength of Lannes' corps as 16,000 infantry and 1200 cavalry. Becker's dragoons he puts at 1200, which would give Lannes 18,400 in the morning. To this must be added, in the afternoon, one-third of Davout's infantry, which Napoleon states in all to be 22,000. Lannes' total in the afternoon would then be only 25,300.

12. Hoepfner gives Lannes 20,000 men in the morning, and 30,000 at the end of the battle, though it is difficult to suppose he is right in estimating Gudin's division of Davout's corps at 10,000.

The attack commenced about 11 a.m. on the right, with the advance of Claparède's men against Bagavout. The French moved forward with enthusiasm to the attack. They felt that behind them lay the dripping woods and the sodden ground on which they had spent the preceding night, and through which they had been toiling since seven o'clock. In front of them was Pultusk, where, if they reached it, they might hope to spend a less wretched night. The enemy defending it they had already beaten at Austerlitz; they had not yet learnt what was his capacity for stolid, dogged resistance. Lastly, they were fighting under the eyes of a marshal whom they adored, and who was always ready to lead them in person where the battle raged most hotly.

Bagavout's cavalry and Cossacks, no match for the French infantry, were driven in without difficulty. The next opponents of the French were the 4th Jägers, whom Bagavout sent forward. Cheering, and regardless of the heavy artillery fire with which they were smitten by the Russian guns,[13] the French infantry drove the jägers backwards and leftwards, until they reached seven squadrons, under Koschin, on the left of the cavalry line joining Bagavout to Barclay. Seeing the attack on Bagavout, Bennigsen had despatched to his aid four battalions, under Osterman, from the reserve and first line.[14]

Simultaneously with Claparéde, Wedell, with the French centre, had moved forwards, and now changed direction to his right, intending to fall on Bagavout's right flank, whilst Claparède attacked him in front. In doing so he, necessarily, exposed his own left flank to Koschin's cavalry and the defeated jägers who had fallen back on it. Koschin, quick to see his chance, charged at once through a blinding snowstorm which concealed his approach until his men were actually in the midst of Wedell's leading battalions, sabring them right and left.[15] But the storm, which had aided him so far, now, in turn, prevented Koschin's seeing the advance, against his own right flank, of Wedell's half of the 88th. That battalion was just in time to save those in front of it, attacked by Koschin in flank and by two battalions of jägers and Bagavout's cavalry in front. In the confused, hand-to-hand struggle which ensued, each side claims to have annihilated the enemy. In the end, the Russians had to retire, and the fight came to a standstill, Bagavout falling back on his old position, and Koschin towards the rear of the left wing.

---

13. Bagavout's battery (14 guns) was on his left, close to the river bank.
14. Two from the extreme left of the 1st line, and two from the reserve in 3rd line (*Wilson*, p. 272).
15. This combat occurred in the angle, on the French side, between the Nasielsk and Warsaw roads, about 250 yards from either.

Treilhard's cavalry now advanced. A Russian hussar regiment in front of it waited till it approached, and then, wheeling leftwards, exposed the French cavalry, on the ridge, to the fire of a battery in the main line, which had previously been masked. From it the French suffered severely.

It is now time to return to the movements which had been going on simultaneously on the French left. Lannes, having started his attack on the right, hurried off to look after Suchet's column advancing to the storm of the Mosin heights. The 34th Regiment led the way with a swarm of skirmishers and *chasseurs à cheval* in front, accompanied by the intrepid Lannes, as well as by Suchet.

Fired by the example and encouragement of their leaders, the 34th, bursting into the front of the wood, carried all before them. Barclays men were driven in confusion back through the first half of the wood on to the reserve,[16] on the Golymin road. The Russian battery in the wood was momentarily captured, but the reserve turned the scale; the battery was recovered, and the 34th driven into the midst of the wood through which they had just triumphantly fought their way. They were saved from disaster by the arrival of the 2nd battalion of the 88th, which, it will be remembered, was attached to this wing. In the outer half of the wood, on the French side of the road, a furious personal conflict raged with varying success. Whilst the French first line had thus, on the whole, gained ground against the detachments of Bagavout and Barclay, the end line had followed steadily, and it now occupied the ridge which had, at the beginning of the battle, been held by the Russian regular cavalry joining the wings. The cavalry had retired behind the main lines, and Gazan's men were thus exposed to the full stress of the artillery fire from the, now unmasked, batteries in front of Bennigsen's main position.[17]

The battle had raged for several hours. The French had made but little progress. The right had failed to dislodge Bagavout completely from his original position, their centre had not got beyond the ridge occupied in the morning by the Russian cavalry. There replying, as best it might with a very inferior force of artillery, to Bennigsen's guns in the main line, it was suffering severely from their fire. On the left, Lannes and Suchet were, with difficulty, maintaining themselves, in the nearer half of the great wood, against Barclays superior force. There seemed every prospect of Lannes' whole corps being compelled to a disastrous retreat.

---

16. Two battalions, *vide supra*, p. 91.
17. Of the total of over 120 guns, Barclay had 28, and Bagavout 14. There were another 14 in Osterman's reserve. Thus, Gazan was exposed to the fire of nearly 70 guns.

But now a change came over the scene. The short day, which would close by 4 p.m., had scarce two hours to run, a premature darkness was threatened, owing to the stormy, cloudy weather. At this juncture, Bennigsen was warned, by the Cossacks on his right, of the approach, by the Golymin road, of a strong hostile column. Davout's 3rd division, commanded temporarily by his chief of the staff d'Aultanne, had started at 6 a.m. from Kowalavice, about two miles short of Strzegoczin, in pursuit of a Russian column which appeared to be falling back on Pultusk, and which it was ordered to fend off from the left flank of Lannes' corps.

Finding in front of him a considerable body of cavalry escorting guns and stores, d'Aultanne followed it without seriously engaging himself. The enemy, in his retreat, was forced, by the state of the roads, to abandon 14 guns and a large number of wagons. Satisfied with his progress, the French commander was about to bivouac for the night, when he heard, on his right, a heavy cannonade, showing him that Lannes was hotly engaged. The large number of guns indicated that the enemy must be superior in this arm at least; for d'Aultanne could infer that Lannes had had the same difficulty as himself in moving up artillery. With a just appreciation of the situation, he resolved to move at once to Lannes' assistance. By the route which he had followed he had had to march about double the distance Lannes had, and he had, moreover, been delayed by fighting, and collecting the abandoned guns and waggons.[18] It must, therefore, have been somewhere towards 2 p.m. when he arrived in view of the Russian right on the Mosin heights. With a double team he had succeeded in dragging up one gun; with that he satisfied himself that Mosin was only occupied by Cossacks. He had no time to concert measures with Lannes, to whom he sent notice of his advance, in echelon from his right, in the direction of the Golymin to Pultusk road. He had 9 battalions.[19] His right echelon, in front, skirted the woods opposite Barclays right; the left echelon rested on the little brook which flows past Mosin to the Narew. He was first attacked by the Polish cavalry regiment from between Barclays position and Mosin; that was easily beaten off.

Meanwhile, Bennigsen, alarmed for his right, had wheeled back the whole right of his main lines so as to face the Mosin wood. He thus greatly lessened the volume of artillery fire which Lannes' centre had to bear.

---

18. For this account of d'Aultanne's march, see *Davout*, pp. 132–134.
19. His whole cavalry force consisted of 70 chasseurs, and 100 of Rapp's dragoons. His artillery was not up except the one gun just mentioned (*Davout*, pp. 132 and 134).

When d'Aultanne's right echelon arrived opposite the angle of the Mosin wood, he changed direction to the left, forming for attack, in columns of half battalions at 50 paces' interval, and at once advanced in the midst of a heavy snowstorm. The new direction which he had assumed brought him obliquely on the right of Barclays position, his right directed on the extreme left of Lannes' left wing, still fighting in the wood.

As the attack advanced, Barclay fell back towards the now refused right wing of the main line. From this, there hurried to his assistance two infantry regiments and 20 squadrons. At the same time, Bennigsen directed the fire of a powerful battery, from the Golymin road, against the French in the outer half of the wood. Thus strengthened, Barclay once more advanced into the wood beyond the road. At last, the French 34th, which had so long and so gallantly maintained itself in the wood, was forced back out of it. The result of its retreat was to create a great gap between it and the right of d'Aultanne's force, whose flank was thus exposed. Into the opening so made poured the 20 squadrons of Russian cavalry. Both Lannes and d'Aultanne, separated by this mass of cavalry, were in imminent danger when the situation was saved by the firm conduct of the 85th Regiment of d'Aultanne's division. Disorder was already spreading in his ranks, as well as in those of Lannes. It was increased by the darkness which had now settled down. The Russian cavalry was received with a steady fire from the 85th, formed in squares and facing the right flank of the intruding enemy. That cavalry was compelled to fall back, though it several times charged d'Aultanne's lines. Order had, however, been restored by the exertions of Piré and Gauthier, and the charges failed. The last of them was made about 8 p.m. in the midst of another violent snowstorm.

Shortly before this, d'Aultanne had received a message from Lannes, begging him to stand firm, as the marshal was about to renew his attack. After waiting for an hour, and seeing no signs of the promised attack, d'Aultanne decided to retire to the woods along whose edge his right had advanced.

The further doings of the French centre and right have still to be related. When Bennigsen turned most of his guns to the support of Barclay,[20] Gazan, in the centre, was able to direct his artillery against the right flank of Bagavout's detachment, and to support a fresh attack on him by Claparède and Wedell. Bagavout was overpowered, and driven back across the ravine in front of which he stood. His guns were captured, but he was promptly reinforced by five fresh battalions.

20. About 2 p.m.

To support him, Osterman established a strong battery behind his right. Bagavout once more urged forward his troops across the ravine. After a long and desperate fight, the French, unable to maintain their forward position, were borne back across the ravine in confusion. A bayonet charge, by a regiment under Somow, had completed their overthrow.[21] They were unable to retain the guns which they had taken, and which now again fell into Bagavout's hands.

Exhausted by many hours' fighting, following on a severe march, Lannes' corps was not fit to continue the battle, in which they had for four hours fought against double their numbers. Even with d'Aultanne's division they had scarcely equalled three-fourths of the Russian strength.

Weary and sullen, they fell back in good order, unpursued, to the positions which they had occupied before the action commenced. Beyond that they did not retreat. Bennigsen's story, that his Cossacks, next morning, found no French within eight miles of the field, may be dismissed as a fable. Possibly the story may have been carried by Cossacks scouting in the direction of d'Aultanne, who, thinking Lannes could now take care of himself, since Bennigsen had retreated, marched off, before dawn on the 27th, to rejoin his own corps, leaving the ground unoccupied in the direction of the Golymin road.

During the night, Bennigsen decided on retreat. The greater part of his army, passing to the left bank of the Narew, marched by the circuitous road on that side to Rozan on the 27th, and on to Ostrolenka on the 28th.[22] The night of the 26th-27th had been one of calm, succeeding the tempest of the day. Lannes was in no state to pursue on the 27th. His losses had been very heavy in the savage hand-to-hand fighting throughout the 26th. His and d'Aultanne's losses are greatly understated by the French. On the whole, it is probable that they were not less than 7000 in killed, wounded, and prisoners. The Russians, too, had lost heavily; 5000 is, perhaps, not too high a figure at which to estimate their casualties.[23]

---

21. Lanes (*Arch. Hist.*) states that a fresh attempt (apparently the one here described) was made against his right about 3 p.m., but was arrested by Gazan.

22. Writing on the 28th December to Murat, Napoleon says that part of the troops from Pultusk had retired by the right bank. Murat is ordered to ascertain whether they had gone direct to Rozan or by Makow. If the enemy were standing at Makow, they were not to be attacked until an overwhelming force was collected (*Corr.* 11,512).

23. Wilson puts the French loss at 10,000 killed and wounded, the Russians at 3000 killed without mentioning wounded (*Wilson*, p. 273). Elsewhere (p. 81), he puts the Russian loss at less than 5000 men, and the (continued on next page)

Both sides lay claim to the victory in this well-contested battle. It is difficult to award the palm to either. What ground Lannes gained he lost again, and he had been so severely handled that he could not molest Bennigsen's retreat. Bennigsen, on the other hand, though he had repulsed the attack of a very inferior force, had not been able, or had not dared, to pursue it. He was, rightly, nervous lest the advance of Napoleon's centre on Makow should cut his line across the bend of the river to Rozan and Ostrolenka. He could not feel sure that Lannes' attack would not be renewed next day by a stronger force. Then, if he lost the Pultusk bridge, almost inevitable a ruin would stare him in the face. So badly did he think of his position, that he preferred reaching Rozan by a 22 mile march on the left bank of the river to risking the direct march of only 15 or 16 by the right.

Having decided, contrary to Kamenskoi's orders,[24] to stand and fight at Pultusk, Bennigsen might well have used his position to better advantage, and, at least, have inflicted a decisive defeat on Lannes. Had he fallen vigorously on the French corps at the beginning of the battle, and advanced with his right, he would probably have rolled it up and driven it into the river before d'Aultanne could come up. He could still have kept a strong reserve behind his right wing to ward off any attack from the Golymin direction. But his disposition of his troops was not calculated to favour any such bold action. Instead of meeting the French advance with over 100 guns posted on the ridge, he masked the greater part of his artillery by the curtain of cavalry which he drew between the advanced wings under Barclay and Baga-vout. Consequently, the French, whilst encountering strenuous resistance from these two commanders on either wing, had nothing, at first, opposed to their centre but cavalry and Cossacks. It was only when these retired that the Russian batteries behind could open on the en-

---

French at 8000 at least. Hoepfner (iii. 118) says that, though the Russian official accounts state the French loss at 10,000, other Russian authorities say 7000 killed and wounded, and 700 prisoners. The French admit only 600 or 700 killed, and 1500 wounded. This is the figure given by Dumas (vol, xvii., p. 174), and by Lannes (*Arch. Hist.*). The marshal puts the Russian loss at 2000 killed, 3000 wounded, 1800 prisoners. Dumas says more than 2000 dead Russians were found on the field, and 1500 wounded, incapable of being moved. The French, as the attackers, might be expected to lose more heavily than the defenders. They were exposed to a terrible artillery fire, telling heavily on the close formations. On the other hand, in the personal conflict which constituted so large a part of the battle, losses would probably not differ greatly. Plotho (p. 36) calculates the Russian loss at only 3000 or 4000 killed and wounded.

24. *Wilson*, p. 80

emy's centre. What their effect would have been had they, with a considerable force of infantry, been where the cavalry were, can be judged from the way in which they arrested Gazan's advance, until their fire was diverted by d'Aultanne's appearance. But for the weakness of the Russian centre in front, Wedell's move to the right, to support Claparède against Bagavout, would have been impossible.

Bennigsen could well have placed 10,000 infantry and 50 or 60 guns where his cavalry were, still keeping a strong reserve of infantry. The cavalry, standing behind his right wing, could have issued on the French left flank and rear as soon as the first attack had failed, as it must inevitably have done. Then, with 25,000 infantry against him in front, as well as a powerful artillery, with 38[25] squadrons and a strong force of Cossacks attacking his left and rear, and, finally, with practically no reserve at his command, it is difficult to see how Lannes could have escaped total destruction. The battle would have been over in two or three hours, well before d'Aultanne could arrive, and that officer would, naturally, not have risked an attack without the support of Lannes.

Bennigsen reported that he had been attacked by 60,000 French under Napoleon in person. If he was, in good faith, under this delusion it will account for his want of vigour. But surely his intelligence should have been better!

He reported to the Tsar that "the succours, so much desired by General Buxhowden, did not arrive in time, although it was scarcely distant from me two miles,[26] in the neighbourhood of Makow, and that it had halted halfway to afford me all the advantages of my victory."[27]

Buxhowden is unjustly blamed here; for he had Kamenskoi's orders to retreat on Ostrolenka, and he was doing so with Dochtorow's and Tutchkow's divisions by Makow, and with Essen's and Anrepp's from Popowo. Kamenskoi was with Bennigsen the night before the battle, and Buxhowden had no fresh orders from him. It is true that Dochtorow did recall part of his division to support Gallitzin at Golymin, but the cases were not altogether parallel. He was merely supporting a rearguard retreating by the same road as himself.

---

25. 28 from the ridge, and 10 from in front of Barclay (*vide supra*, p, 91).
26. German miles of 4½ English. Distance, therefore, was about 9 miles, English.
27. Bennigsen's despatch, quoted by *Wilson*, p. 336. The translation is not very clear, nor well punctuated, but the meaning can be gathered. The proper translation would appear to be "the succour so much desired by me from General Buxhowden, although distant from me scarcely 2 miles, in the neighbourhood of Makow, did not arrive in time to afford me all the advantages of my victory; it had halted halfway."

Lannes seems to have made the best of an extremely unpleasant position. He was put in it owing to the Emperor's false intelligence as to the enemy's lines of retreat. His orders to Lannes, already quoted,[28] indicate clearly his belief that there was no considerable force at Pultusk. They do not even provide for Lannes' action in the event of his finding himself outnumbered. Napoleon, in fact, believed that the enemy was marching on Makow, and all his efforts were directed against the right of the Russian army and its rear, now that it was separated by Ney, Bernadette, Bessières, and Soult from the Prussians. Lannes received his orders only as he reached the field of battle. They were so positive that he could hardly have justified failure to follow them to the letter. Moreover, he had already commenced the action before he was fully aware of the immense superiority of Bennigsen's numbers.

He was hampered in his attack by the necessity for keeping a strong second line to fall back on. If there was one thing he was certain of it was that there was no strong supporting force between him and Czarnowo. At 2 p.m. his position was more than ever hazardous, and he must have felt that a strong offensive return against his left flank could not but involve him in disaster. That it would eventually have come, but for the unexpected arrival of d'Aultanne, can hardly be doubted. The promptitude of the latter commander in marching to the sound of the guns is highly commendable.

GOLYMIN

Whilst Lannes was fighting, at Pultusk, his uphill battle against very superior numbers, another action was in progress in front of Golymin, 12 miles to the northwest.[29]

At that village, Gallitzin had collected parts of his own division. The portion of Sacken's which had been driven northwards by Murat was also on its road to Golymin. The rest of these divisions had retreated on Pultusk and formed part of the army under the personal command of Bennigsen on the 26th December. When Gallitzin reached Golymin, about 8 a.m., his troops were too exhausted by their difficult march to continue it farther towards Makow. He had, moreover, to wait for Sacken's men. The same morning, under

---

28. *Vide supra*, p. 94.
29. The chief authorities consulted for this battle are: (a) *Hoepfner*, iii. 122, etc.; (b) *Dumas*, vol. xvii., p. 180, etc.; (c) *Davout*, pp. 137-140; (d) *Marbot*, i. 246, 247; (e) *Rapp*, p. 128. etc.; (f) Augereau's report in the *Archives Historiques*.

orders from the Emperor,[30] Augereau marched off Desjardins' division, at 7.30 a.m., from Kaleczin.[31] The other division (Heudelet's) was ordered to start at 9 a.m. They were to march *viâ* Sonsk, whilst Durosnel, with the light cavalry, was to cut the road between Ciechanow and Golymin, collecting on it baggage abandoned by the enemy. Murat, with part of the reserve cavalry, followed, marching by Garnowo.[32] Gallitzin had, overnight, informed Dochtorow, who was marching in advance of him on Makow, of his own march to Golymin, and had warned him that the French were advancing to the attack from all directions. This message Dochtorow received simultaneously with Kamenskoi's orders for his retreat on Makow. Nevertheless, leaving his division to continue its retreat meanwhile, he himself, with a musketeer regiment and one of dragoons, remained at Golymin to receive Gallitzin.[33]

Scarcely had the latter collected and organised his wearied troops at Golymin when the rear-guard, of 2 squadrons, was attacked by Murat's advance guard. Gallitzin sent 3 squadrons of cuirassiers to endeavour to arrest the French advance, and so to give him some time to rest his men, before again proceeding towards Makow. The rear-guard, thus strengthened, succeeded in repulsing Lasalle, who led Murat's advance, to the woods from which he had issued.

Presently there appeared, at Ruskowo, the head of Augereau's column. Seeing that, in the exhausted condition of his troops, retreat without fighting was no longer possible, Gallitzin proceeded to make the best arrangements he could to meet the French.

The position of Golymin, though almost absolutely flat, was one of great strength for a defensive action against an enemy advancing from the west. The ground is slightly elevated to the north and north-west of the village, but the rise is very gentle. Except on the north, it is almost entirely surrounded by woods interspersed with marshes, which,

---

30. Orders from Berthier to Augereau, dated Lopaczin, 26th December. (Printed in *Dumas*, xvii. 487, 488.) In the same order he was warned that, should he hear heavy firing on his right, it would mean that Davout was seriously engaged and must be assisted by Augereau moving towards Strzegoczin.
31. He went round by Sonsk on the Sonna. By this route the distance to Ruskowo is about 10 miles.
32. This is the direct route. From Kaleczin to Garnowo, about 6 miles. He had to start from Sochoczin, and was somewhat delayed until the Emperor was satisfied that the force in front of Davout at Strzegoczin was retreating on Golymin. See three despatches from Berthier to Murat, dated Lopaczin, 26th December, printed by *Dumas*, xvii., pp. 488-491.
33. *Hoepfner*, iii. 123.

owing to the weather prevailing on the 26th December, were in their most impracticable condition. The outer edge of these woods abutted, at a distance averaging 3500 paces from Golymin, on the open marshy plain over which the French line of approach passed. The side most open to attack was the rising ground, towards Wadkowo and Wola-Golyminska; but even here there was a large wood, between Wadkowo and Golymin.

Into the woods and ground about Kaleczin[34] Gallitzin sent Tcherbatow with a regiment of infantry, and 4 light guns. With the rest of his troops, he posted himself in front of Golymin. His first line comprised 6 battalions of infantry, and what remained of two cavalry regiments, from which he had already made detachments. In reserve he held a regiment of cuirassiers, 2 squadrons of hussars, and the troops of the 7th (Dochtorow's) division.

On arrival at Ruskowo,[35] Augereau sent Heudelet, when he arrived some time after Desjardins, to the left to attack by Wadkowo, which he occupied without difficulty. Desjardins moved forward, from Ruskowo, towards Golymin. At this moment, Murat arrived with Milhaud's and Klein's[36] cavalry divisions and was joined by Marulaz with Davout's light cavalry, moving by the Strzegoczin road. They advanced, in two lines, against the Russian cavalry, which gave way before them, retiring into the woods, where the French horsemen were unable to follow.

Meanwhile, Augereau's two divisions, which had been unable to bring up their artillery, moved forward, Desjardins from Ruskowo, Heudelet from Wadkowo.[37] Heudelet had but poor success. The resistance of the Russian cavalry and infantry was so strenuous that,

---

34. A hamlet 400 or 500 paces west of Golymin, not to be confounded with the place of the same name from which Augereau started.

35. Looking to the state of the roads, and the distance they had to march, this could hardly have been before 2 or 2.30 p.m., the time which Marbot (pp. 246, 247) gives. He was himself with Augereau's cavalry. It was already getting dark, owing to the shortness of the day and the gloom of the sky.

36. Including Lasalles' advance guard and Marulaz, there must have been between 6000 and 7000 cavalry at Garnowo.

37. Desjardins' division was the first on the field. On its left, on arrival at Ruskowo, it found many hostile troops. Augereau therefore sent orders to hurry up Heudelet, and left one of Desjardins' brigades in Ruskowo, to protect the rear of the other moving on Golymin, till Heudelet's arrival on the left. Heudelet, advancing between Wadkowo and Golymin, was attacked in flank by cavalry, but had time to form squares and repulse it. He was so constantly attacked by the cavalry that he had to keep his troops permanently in squares. (Augereau, *Arch. Hist.*)

wanting the support of guns, he could advance but a short way. Desjardins' division, which, unlike Heudelet's, had been completely successful at the passage of the Ukra, attacking with more impetuosity, at first drove back Tcherbatow's infantry regiment. Reinforced by a battalion sent him by Gallitzin from the reserve, Tcherbatow placed himself, sword in hand, at the head of his men, and again led them forward to the attack. Desjardins lost the ground which he had gained, but rallied, and once more advance against the foe. His men, when within 50 paces of the Russians, were brought to a standstill by grape fire.[38]

After this, the fight in front of Augereau degenerated into a combat of skirmishers, which lasted, with varying success, well into the evening. On the whole, the French left (Heudelet) slowly progressed towards turning the Russian right. So far, Gallitzin's small force had held its own with success. There was yet another strong French column with which he had to deal on his left.

Davout had started, with his 1st and 2nd divisions (Morand's and Friant's), from Klukowo and Strzegoczin at daybreak.[39] Marulaz, with the cavalry, was in advance, and, as already described, had joined Murat in driving the Russian cavalry back from Garnowo on the woods towards Golymin. On his way, he had captured 20 guns, 80 ammunition wagons and 200 others, abandoned by the retreating Russians in the mud. He and Murat were now awaiting the arrival of the infantry for the attack of the wood. The Russian infantry were preparing for its defence. Gallitzin, warned of the approach of Morand, had sent 3 fresh battalions into the woods and marshes on Tcherbatow's left, and 2 squadrons on to the Pultusk road. At 3 p.m. the Russian right had been reinforced by 2 cavalry regiments of the 7th and 8th divisions, arriving from Ciechanow. This force had succeeded in getting past Durosnel, by whose cavalry it was attacked on the road. Davout's 1st division (Morand) had to march 7 miles from Strzegoczin to Garnowo, and the 2nd (Friant) 8½ from Klukowo.

On arrival, Morand formed his 1st brigade in battalion columns for the attack of the wood. The 2nd brigade (d'Honnières) was behind him. It was 3.30 before the 1st brigade was ready. Darkness had fallen, though the scene was illuminated by the burning village

---

38. Desjardins' 2nd brigade, in its advance, was overwhelmed by grape when within 50 paces of the enemy. It was forced to retire 200 yards, and to form squares in front of Kaleczin (Augereau, *Arch. Hist.*).
39. *Davout*, p, 131.

of Garnowo, which had been fired by the Cossacks as they left it. This light facilitated the direction of the fire of the Russian guns.[40] As the brigade charged into the wood, with its voltigeurs in front, the Russian infantry, to free their limbs for the struggle, threw off their knapsacks. Their resistance was obstinate, but the vigour of the French attack overcame all opposition. Fighting hand to hand with their favourite weapon, the bayonet, the infantry of Gallitzin was slowly driven back through and out of the wood, leaving it strewn with their dead and wounded, and with 4000 knapsacks, which, in the agony of the struggle, the soldiers had no opportunity to recover. As in Augereau's case, Davout could attack only with infantry, for his guns had fallen behind. Perceiving that the enemy was attempting to retreat to the right by the Makow road, Davout despatched d'Honnières' brigade, in that direction, to attempt to turn the wood and to advance on Golymin by the Pultusk road. The 51st Regiment moved into the wood in front of Osiek, on the near side of the Pultusk road, whilst Rapp with his dragoons charged, on the road, the Russian cavalry. Himself at the head of his men, Rapp, ever in the forefront of the battle, bore back the Russian horsemen in confusion towards Golymin. But, in doing so, he fell into a trap. The marshes on either side were filled with Russian infantry, standing up to their waists in the bog, safe from any attack by cavalry.[41] From their fire, Rapp's men suffered heavily. The general himself was wounded, and his dragoons were compelled to fall back into line with their own infantry. To avoid what appeared to be probable useless loss, Morand did not attempt to advance beyond the border of the woods towards Golymin. There he took post, with Rapp's dragoons in reserve, for the night. Friant's division had not come into action at all.

Gallitzin and Dochtorow had now begun their retreat on Makow. Their troops, instead of obtaining some rest at Golymin, had had a full day of fighting. Perhaps, even that was less exhausting than plodding along the miry roads: at least, it was less disheartening. Dochtorow was the first to move off, as the storm of combat lulled. It was not till 9 p.m. that Gallitzin was able to move the last of his troops from the battlefield. He first withdrew his guns,

---

40. *Marbot*, i. 248. He also mentions that the uniform of Murat's white cuirassiers made them a prominent object for the direction of the Russian fire. Many of the villages, says Marbot, were on fire. Probably Ruskowo and Wadkowo were so. Augereau (*Arch. Hist.*) mentions, as burning, the village between Kuskowo and Golymin, i.e. Kaleczin.
41. *Rapp*, p. 128.

which marched slowest and with most difficulty. Next followed his cavalry. Behind them was the main body of the infantry. Last of all came the outposts, covering the rear of the infantry. When the battle gradually died away, the Russians in Golymin were almost surrounded; the Makow road was the only one open to them. It was midnight before the head of Dochtorow's detachment joined Tutchkow, and the remainder of his own division, at Makow, 10 miles from Golymin.

As regards the proportion between the numbers engaged on either side, the case of Pultusk was reversed at Golymin. Gallitzin's own force was 15 battalions and 20 squadrons,[42] a regiment (3 battalions) of infantry from Dochtorow and a regiment of cavalry. At 3 p.m. he was joined by two cavalry regiments retiring from Ciechanow, as well as some of Sacken's infantry.[43] It would seem probable, therefore, that he at no time had available more than 16,000 or 18,000 men.

The French had Augereau's two divisions, two of Davout's (one of which was only in reserve), and part of the cavalry reserve; alto-

---

42. *Wilson*, p. 82. That authority asserts that Gallitzin was reinforced by part of Dochtorow's and Tutchkow's divisions towards evening. It does not appear probable that any of Tutchkow's troops took part in the battle. Dumas (xvii. 176, 177) says Gallitzin had parts of his own and Sacker's divisions and the whole of Dochtorow's—in all, 28 battalions, 45 squadrons. On this question the authority of Hoepfner seems preferable, as to only part of Dochtorow's being present. Napoleon (*Corr.* 11,305, dated 24th November, 1806), writing to Murat, recapitulates the strength of that portion of his wing of the army which was afterwards present at Golymin. Setting off losses (Davout and Augereau had both suffered considerably in the recent actions) against recruitments in December, it is probable the strength was slightly below what is given by the Emperor, *viz.*:

1. Cavalry Reserve	Dragoons–Beaumont (with Rapp)	4,800
	Klein (with Murat)	800
	Milhaud's light cavalry	
2. Corps Cavalry	Davout's	1,200
	Augereau's	800
	Total	7,600
3. Infantry	Davout (2/3 only)	14,600
	Augereau	16,000
	Total	30,600
Total cavalry and infantry		38,200

43. Augereau had sent Durosnel's light cavalry towards Pamirs to cut off the enemy's baggage. Coming on Sacken in force, retreating on Golymin, he turned in that direction, pressing the retreat. Reaching the field about nightfall, he endeavoured to effect a diversion by attacking the Russian right (Augereau's report, *Arch. Hist.*)

gether about 37,000 or 38,000 men. The Russian losses are put at
795,[44] but were probably somewhat higher. Davout states the loss of
the 1st division at 222,[45] and Dumas says the French total losses were
about the same as those of the Russians.[46]

The action was a much smaller affair, in every way, than that at
Pultusk; the duration and vigour of the combat were less. Gallitzin
was at a great disadvantage as regards numbers. To make up for this, he
had two batteries of artillery (28 guns), while the French had failed
to bring to the front any of theirs. The Russian position was an extremely strong one naturally, especially when the enemy were unable
to bring artillery to bear on the woods and on the Russian lines.
Again, Gallitzin had an advantage in being attacked piecemeal by the
different columns as they arrived in succession. Augereau's effort had
practically collapsed before Davout arrived on the scene at all. Murat,
too, was unable to do anything beyond driving the hostile cavalry
before him back into the woods occupied by infantry. The action
was a disjointed one on the French side. Davout's assertion[47] that "an
hour after nightfall the corps of Marshal Augereau was engaged with
the enemy, nearly a league to the left of the 3rd Corps; the darkness,
and the uncertainty as to the point of this attack, rendered impossible any concerted action," shows this clearly. Davout, advancing in
front of Garnowo, was exhibited to the view of the defending force
by the light behind him of the burning village, whilst his opponents
were hidden from him by the darkness and the woods. When all is
said, these advantages were but a poor compensation to Gallitzin for
his numerical inferiority; it cannot be denied that his resistance, with
exhausted troops, is deserving of the highest praise. So brave was his
defence that Murat wrote to the Emperor, "We thought the enemy
had 50,000 men."[48] It appears doubtful if Augereau's corps occupied
Golymin before the early morning of the 27th, when no unwounded
Russians remained there.[49] The exact time of its entry is not of great
importance, as it is certain that it was, in the end, unopposed.

---

44. *Hoepfner*, iii. 126.

45. *Davout*, 140.

46. *Dumas*, xvii. 126. It is difficult to believe that the losses on either side were not
somewhat higher than 800. Plotho makes the Russian loss 553 killed and wounded,
and 203 prisoners.

47. *Davout*, p. 139.

48. *Hoepfner*, iii. 126.

49. Dumas (xvii, 185), who says it was the 27th. Marbot (i. 247), who was with Augereau, says they got into Golymin on the night of the 26th, and found it littered with
dead and dying. Augereau's own account (*Arch. Hist.*) is not clear on the subject.

Napoleon, if we may accept the testimony of Jomini speaking in his name, was more disappointed with the indecisive result of the action of Golymin than with that of the battle of Pultusk.[50] His failure to get beyond Golymin on the 26th, still more Soult's failure to pass Ciechanow,[51] destroyed the hope of cutting the Russian line of retreat with his left, and driving them against the Narew.

---

50. *Vie de Napoleon*, ii. 342.
51. His light cavalry reached Ciechanow on the 26th, just after the enemy had left it. That night the 1st and 2nd divisions were in front of Ciechanow, the 3rd at Paluki, some 5 miles farther on (Soult's report, *Arch. Hist.*).

CHAPTER 4

The First Winter Quarters and Events Outside Poland

WINTER QUARTERS

On the 7th December the French army occupied a line extending from Neidenburg, on the left, down the valley of the Orezyc, to Pultusk on the right. There was already a bridge head at Okunin, on the Lower Bug; others were at once commenced, on the Bug at Sierock, and on the Narew at Pultusk. The 5th and 7th Russian divisions reached a point about eight miles north-west of Rozan. Bennigsen was at Rozan, where he was joined by the divisions of Anrepp and Essen from Popowo.

On the 28th, Napoleon stopped the advance of his troops.

Bennigsen, finding he was not pursued with any energy, first took position in the angle between the Omulew and the Narew, opposite Ostrolenka. Buxhowden's army was on his right, between Ostrolenka and Myszienec.[1]

Marshal Kamenskoi reappeared for a few hours at Ostrolenka, but, as it was ascertained that the orders he gave did not emanate from the Tsar, it was decided to disregard them. He again returned to Grodno, finally disappearing from the scene.

Of the two Russian generals, Buxhowden was the senior. Bennigsen, however, was not inclined to serve under him, and looked for the chief command, which he considered his stand at Pultusk would ensure to him. Consequently, he, with his own army and the 8th and 14th divisions of Buxhowden's, which had been prevented from crossing by the destruction of the Ostrolenka bridge, marched up the left

---

1. Jomini (*Vie de Napoleon*, ii. 343) says the retreat on Ostrolenka was disapproved by Bennigsen, who, losing sight of the ensemble of the campaign, fancied that, in checking Lannes at Pultusk, he had gained a great victory over Napoleon.

bank of the Narew to Nowogrod, reaching it without mishap on the 1st January. Buxhowden was 9 miles to the north-east of Nowogrod, at Plock. The two portions of the army were connected by a temporary bridge, the frequent destruction of which, by floating ice, furnished Bennigsen with a convenient excuse for not joining Buxhowden, and for thus maintaining a semi-independent command. He could not, however, disobey his senior's summons to a council at which the future plan of operations was discussed. What it was, and how it was carried out, may be left for description until the French settlement in winter quarters has been detailed.

Napoleon, now out of touch with the Russians, flattered himself that he would be allowed, without further molestation, to take up his quarters, for the rest of the cold season, in the broad stretch of country between the Vistula and the Omulew.[2] His army was discontented at the hardships it had to undergo in terrible weather, and he himself required time to complete the organisation of his magazines, hospitals, and transport.[3]

From Pultusk, and from Warsaw, he issued numerous orders, detailing the position of each corps in the cantonments which he proposed to occupy.[4] They were finally summarised in a note by Berthier, dated 7th January, on the general disposition of cantonments, of which the following is an abstract.

1. Cavalry without Infantry

Latour-Maubourg, with the 5th and 7th Hussars, in the country between Plock and Wyszogrod; cantonments not to extend far, and this brigade to refit and rest.

Milhaud, with the two regiments of his brigade which had suffered most, to rest on the right bank of the Vistula between Plock, Dobrzyn, and Borkowo.

Klein–Dobrzyn to Bobrownik, guarding the small stream running from Gollub to the Vistula.

---

2. "I think all is finished for this year. The army is about to take up its winter quarters" (*Corr.* 11,523, to Josephine). The Emperor returned to Warsaw on the 2nd January (*Corr.* 11,549, 48th bulletin).

3. There was great disorder, at this time, in the commissariat at Warsaw, which the Emperor had to remedy. His orders, placing under each marshal the control of supplies in his own district, did not, at first, work satisfactorily. The marshals, considering themselves supreme, hampered and interfered with the collection of supplies by the civil commissaries. Napoleon had to issue severe orders to check this (*Savory*, iii., 27).

4. These orders will be found printed in full in *Dumas*, xviii., pp. 288-309. It is not very clear in Dumas whether the note was by Berthier, but the original in Paris dispels any doubt (*Arch. Hist.*).

Nansouty, with his heavy cavalry division, on the Pilica about Rawa, on the road from Warsaw to Breslau.

D'Hautpoult's cuirassiers, with their artillery, about Thorn—the regiments in Gollub, Rypin, and Sierps.

Espagne's cuirassiers to move forward from Posen to Petrikau, behind Nansouty.

Guard cavalry, excepting four squadrons at Warsaw, with artillery, ambulances, etc., between Warsaw and Biela, along the left bank of the Vistula and the Pilica.

All the small depots of cavalry, with the artillery park of the army, to collect at Lenczyca.

Each command to concentrate at its headquarters, and await orders, should the enemy take the offensive.

2. Infantry Corps with Cavalry attached

Bernadotte with Sahuc's dragoons; headquarters at Osterode, occupying the districts of Elbing and Marienwerder.[5]

Ney, having his supplies, depots, park, and workshops at Thorn, to occupy Soldau, Mlawa, Chorzel and their neighbourhood, with outposts at Willemburg. His corps would link that of Bernadotte to Soult, with whom he would settle the limits of cantonments.

Soult, using Plock in the same way as Ney used Thorn, to occupy Prasznitz, Makow, Sochoczin, Noviemasto, and the Plock district, having in front of him, beyond the Orezyc, Lasalle's light cavalry and Milhaud's brigade, with the exception of the two regiments ordered to rest on the Vistula.

Augereau, using Wyszogrod as his base, to occupy the surrounding district up to the right bank of the Ukra, not carrying his left beyond the stream passing Bodzanow. Should he find himself cramped here, he was at liberty to extend to the rear, on the Bszura, west of the Vistula, as far as Lowicz.

Davout's limits were, in rear, the left bank of the Ukra, from its mouth to the little river Ziclini. Thence to near Golymin, and on to near Pultusk. He was also to occupy the whole country between the Narew and the Bug, up to Ostrolenka.

Lannes to hold Sierock and the neighbourhood. His light cavalry in the villages on the right bank of the Bug from Sierock to Brok. Gazan's division, of the same corps, was to hold the triangle between

---

5. The Polish corps, then numbering 7000 under Dombrowski, was made over to Bernadotte for the blockade of Graudenz (*Corr.* 11,535 and 11,536, dated 2nd January). That fortress was effectually blockaded on the 18th January, after a small fight, in which the garrison was driven in. (Bernadotte's report on 1st Corps, *Arch. Hist.*).

the Bug, the Vistula, and the Austrian frontier. Suchet's division in Praga and the suburbs of Warsaw. There also was Gudin's division of Davout's Corps and the infantry of the Guard.

Orders issued for the collection of supplies, and the establishment of hospitals at the bases fixed for the various commands, at Marienwerder for Bernadotte, at Thorn for Ney, at Plock for Soult, at Wyszogrod and Lowicz for Augereau, at Pultusk for Davout, and at Warsaw for Lannes.

It will be noted that, with the exception of Pultusk, all these centres were on or behind the Vistula. The Emperor's desires were clearly stated to be, "not to have any encumbrance on the right bank of the Vistula, so that there might be no obstacle to the evacuation of that country should His Majesty see fit to order it."[6]

At the places named, was ordered the collection of every sort of supplies, and the preparation of workshops for the repair of harness, clothes, and artillery. Baking was to be carried on to a much greater extent than was required for the daily consumption of the army, a large supply of biscuit being thus accumulated.

In case the enemy should take the offensive, the points of concentration for the corps were—Ney at Mlawa, Soult at Golymin, Davout at Pultusk, Lannes at Sierock, Augereau at Plonsk. It will be observed that nothing is said of a point of concentration for Bernadotte, which would seem to point to Napoleon's not believing he could be attacked without warning from the corps on his right. Any marshal attacked in force was at once to concentrate, and warn the others.

With his troops thus quartered, Napoleon's right and centre were covering an area of country which it was well within their power to defend against any force they were likely to encounter. The corps, from Ney on the left to Lannes on the right, covered roughly the segment of a circle, the centre of which was at Wyszogrod, and the arc extended from Neidenburg and Willemburg, down the right bank of the Omulew and across the country from near Ostrolenka, to Brok, on the Austrian frontier. Bernadotte's corps alone was unduly extended towards Elbing and the Frisches-Haff. The whole of the arc was covered by light cavalry, and any one of the corps behind it could be promptly reinforced from flank and rear. Napoleon seems to have thought it extremely improbable that the enemy would assume the

---

6. Ney, Bernadotte, and Soult, alone, owing to their distance from the river, were allowed to have small intermediate hospitals and depots of supplies. The words quoted in the text are a good instance of the caution displayed by Napoleon, and his prevision of all possible eventualities.

offensive, still more improbable that, if he did so, he would attack Bernadotte. He would appear to have under-estimated the Russian generals' enterprise of design.

He urged on the fortification of important points of support to his line. At Sierock a double *tête de pont*, on the Bug and the Narew, was to be constructed; another on the Narew, at Pultusk; a third at Modlin. The passage of the Vistula at Warsaw was to be covered by a strongly fortified camp at Praga, supported by works on the left bank. Finally, Thorn was to be fortified as a bridge head.[7] Even should he be forced to abandon temporarily the right bank of the Vistula, Napoleon looked to being able to hold the left, as well as bridge heads on the right bank at all important points from Warsaw to Thorn. Thus, when he recommenced operations in the spring, he would not have to force the passage of a great river.

The object of Bernadotte's extension towards the Baltic was to cover the siege of Danzig, which place, as a standing menace, whilst in the enemy's hands, to his communications, the Emperor desired to capture before the time came for a fresh advance. For this siege, and for the blockade of Colberg and Graudenz, the 10th Corps was now constituted, and placed under the orders of Lefebvre.[8]

Napoleon himself took up his quarters at Warsaw on the 2nd January, 1807. Great as were the attractions of the Polish capital and its delightful society,[9] it is certain that Napoleon, had he been left undisturbed there, would have taken good care that it should not

---

7. *Corr.* 11,585.

8. The command was first given to Victor, but he was captured by a Prussian party from Colberg. Though he was, shortly afterwards, exchanged against Blücher, this misfortune cost him his chance of the Dukedom of Danzig, and, for a time, his marshal's baton. A letter (*Arch. Hist.*, daily correspondence), from him to the Emperor, describes his capture, as he was changing horses, by disguised Prussian soldiers, and peasants. He is very indignant at what he considers this unfair capture, and begs the Emperor to remonstrate with the King of Prussia. Napoleon hardly appears to have taken the same view, as he made no difficulty about exchanging Victor for Blücher. The constitution of the 10th Corps at this time was—

(1) Dombrowski's Polish division, about 7000.

(2) A brigade of French infantry, about 4000.

(3) Two regiments French chasseurs.

(4) Baden troops (for blockade of Colberg), about 6000.

(5) Legion of the North, about 4000.

(6) A French cavalry brigade.

About 25,000 in all. To these would be added the Hessian troops so soon as Zayonchek with his Poles could relieve them of the duty of blockading Graudenz (*Corr.* 11,680). (continued on next page)

have become a Capua, either for himself or his army. There was no rest for him. He was employed night and day in making innumerable arrangements, and conducting business of every sort, from the provision of supplies for his army to the supervision of affairs at home and abroad.

Here he may be left for the short period of cessation of serious hostilities, whilst the course of events elsewhere than at the principal seat of war is briefly sketched.

SILESIA

Though Napoleon's chief efforts against Russia were made on the Vistula, it must not be forgotten that he was, at the same time, carrying on operations, military or diplomatic, in furtherance of his projects over the whole of Europe, from France to Turkey, from Swedish Pomerania to Southern Italy, and even to Persia. It is with the operations on the Vistula alone that this history can deal in detail, but a brief outline of events elsewhere is essential.

Silesia, when the advance to the Vistula commenced, was still unsubdued. Though not held by any important Prussian force in the open field, its fortresses[10] were strongly garrisoned, and would afford rallying-places for Prussian levies, to say nothing of being a strong support for Austria, should she make up her mind to intervene. Obviously, these places could not be left on the right rear of the French army.

The first siege undertaken was that of Glogau, which surrendered, after some bombardment, on the 2nd December, to Vandamme and the Wurtemberg troops. The two Bavarian divisions had, at this time, moved with Jerome to Kalisch. Until Napoleon was in possession of Warsaw, he required these divisions to protect his right flank as it moved eastwards. At Warsaw, he was able to rest it on the Austrian frontier in safety, so long as that power remained neutral. Jerome was, therefore, at liberty, in the beginning of December, to return to the assistance of Vandamme and the Wurtemberg division, who had at once, on the surrender of Glogau, proceeded to partially invest Breslau. On the 10th, Jerome reached Breslau. On the 15th, the bombardment

9. (on previous page) It was at this time that Napoleon first made the acquaintance of the beautiful Countess Walewska. Of her devotion to him, which continued even t the days of St. Helena, there can be no shadow of a doubt. Of the reality of his love for here there is, perhaps, not quite the same certainty. In any case, it is clear that he did not allow it to interfere with his energetic attention to his army and his schemes.
10. They were Glogau, Breslau, Schweidnitz, Glatz, Neisse, Brieg, and Kosel

was continued, the governor having refused to surrender. Deroi's division and Mazanelli's cavalry brigade, which had been left at Kalisch, were now summoned, as it appeared that the Prince of Anhalt Pless had raised the peasantry in support of detachments from the other garrisons. Vandamme, left alone owing to the departure of Jerome in response to the Emperor's summons, attempted an assault of Breslau on the night of the 22nd-23rd, but it was delayed by various accidents, and was beaten off. The Prince of Anhalt was approaching. On the 24th, his badly organized levies were routed by Minucci's division, and their 6 guns captured.

The batteries in front of Breslau had now been strengthened by some of the artillery taken at Glogau, the ditches were frozen over, and the governor negotiated for a surrender. The negotiations were broken off on his hearing that the Prince of Anhalt was again advancing to his relief with rallied and increasing forces. The Prince, evading the troops sent to meet him, arrived near Breslau, whence he was repulsed, and in his retreat was badly cut up by the detachments which he had escaped in his advance.

The governor of Breslau, now losing all hope of succour from without, and fearing that the thick ice on the ditches would expose the place to an assault, surrendered on the 7th January. The corps of Jerome now had at its disposal the captured artillery for the sieges of the remaining fortresses. Napoleon, considering the subjugation of Silesia practically complete, appointed his brother Jerome governor of the province, and left Vandamme to carry out the sieges.[11]

POMERANIA

Protection for his left flank was equally essential to the Emperor. To Mortier, with the 8th Corps,[12] was confided the task of occupying and defending the conquered country between the mouths of the Elbe and the Oder, including the territory to the east of Stettin as far as Colberg. He had to watch Swedish Pomerania, and to threaten Stralsund and the Island of Rugen, which might be used as bases for descent by the English and Swedes.

On the 12th December, he occupied a central position on the right back of the Peene, his right at Uckermunde, left at Demmin, and

---

11. About this time Napoleon estimates his army in Silesia at over 30,000 men (*Corr.* 11,575)
12. It comprised Granjean's and Dupas' divisions; 3 cavalry regiments, 2 companies of foot artillery, and 2 of Dutch light artillery.

headquarters at Anklam. The Swedish troops on the opposite bank fell back on Stralsund. Between the 16th December and the 4th January, Mortier was reinforced by four infantry regiments.[13] To put a check on the frequent expeditions from Colberg, he occupied Usedom, Schweinmunde, and Wollin, at the mouths of the Peene and the Oder. On the 6th January, a detachment, attacked by Prussians from Colberg, at Wollin, successfully drove them off. Mortier, refusing to be drawn into petty fights, occupied a line behind the Peene, from Uckermunde to Treptow. Nothing more occurred here before the end of January.

TURKEY AND PERSIA

At the Ottoman Court, Napoleon was must ably represented by his Corsican compatriot, General Sebastiani. The Ambassador's clever combinations of threats and promises were aided by the injudicious invasion, towards the end of November, of Moldavia and Wallachia by Michelson with 50,000 or 60,000 men.[14] The demands of England and her threats of bombarding Constantinople were also of assistance to him.

The action of Russia, in this imposing upon herself the task of observing Turkey with a considerable force, at a time when she wanted every available man to oppose the French in Poland, was most unwise. Sebastiani was able, by the end of December, 1806, to persuade the Sultan to declare was against his Northern neighbour. The Tsar, compelled by the pressure in Poland to withdraw two out of the five divisions with Michelson in Moldavia and Wallachia, sought to procure a diversion by England towards Constantinople. On the 29th January, the Sultan, egged on by Sebastiani, declared war against England also.[15]

In February a British fleet passed the Dardanelles, and appeared before Constantinople. All was at once confusion there. Sebastiani, in imminent danger of his life, kept his head, urged on the defence of

---

13. 22nd and 58th of the line, and 12th and 15th light infantry.

14. Michelson at first had 90 battalions, 100 squadrons, and 306 guns. Of these, 36 battalions and 40 squadrons were withdrawn to Poland in December 1806 (Jomini, *Vie de Napoleon*, ii. 344 (note) and 346). According to the same author (ii. 336) Michelson at first had 80,000 men. This seems too high and estimate. Plotho (pp. 69-70) calculates the Russian forces as 500 per battalion, 80 per squadron, and 200 per battery of 14 guns. These figures would give Michelson's original army at 58,200, and the numbers remaining later as about 35,000. Napoleon himself, in the end of January, estimated them at 30,000 (see *ante*, p. 13, note 1).

15. Napoleon, in seeking the co-operation of Turkey, appears to have had an eye to using her against Austria also. "Austria is muzzled; if she moves, notwithstanding my army of Italy, I will bring the Turks to the gates of Vienna, and my Poniatowski will not be for them a Sobieski" (*Comeau*, p. 285).

the capital, and amused the British Admiral, Duckworth, with negotiations, until the latter found the defences so strong that there was no course left by a retreat again through the Dardanelles—no easy matter, under the heavy fire of the now completed batteries on either shore.

On the Danube, nothing of importance occurred during the campaign in Poland; but Napoleon, by assisting the Turks with the loan of French officers, and by threats of the advance of Marmont's corps[16] from Dalmatia, succeeded in keeping paralyzed a considerable force under Michelson, which could have been employed to much greater advantage in Poland.

With Persia, too, he carried on negotiations in the spring, which sufficed to alarm Russia in the East, and detain there troops which might otherwise have given assistance in the main theatre of war. With the affairs of Turkey and Persia it will not be necessary, now that their general bearing on the war has been indicated, to deal further.

---

16. The 2nd.

PART 3

The Campaign of Eylau

CHAPTER 1

The Movements Up to the Battle of Eylau

At the council of war, held by Buxhowden, at Nowogrod, on the 2nd January, a plan of operations had been decided on.

The 14th division, and the two divisions under Essen I., now approaching from Moldavia, were to be left between the Bug and the Narew to watch and occupy the French right wing. The remaining 7 divisions would assemble by the 5th January, between Biala and the right bank of the Narew, for an advance, behind the Johannisburg forest, into East Prussia against the French left wing.

But it did not at all suit Bennigsen's views to undertake these operations under the chief command of his senior, and rival, Buxhowden. Seizing, therefore, on the breaking, by floating ice, of the bridge at Nowogrod as a cover for his action, he marched, on the 6th, up the left bank of the Narew, by Lomza, to Tykoczin, with the 2nd, 3rd, 4th, 6th, 8th, and 14th divisions, arriving there on the 8th. Thence, crossing the Narew, he marched for Goniondz, where he received the Tsar's orders conferring on him the Order of St. George, in recognition of his action at Pultusk, and, what he prized still more, the chief command of the army, from which Buxhowden was recalled. On the 12th January, he crossed the Bobra, now covered with thick ice by the frost, which had commenced on the 31st December.[1] On the 14th, he was at Biala, where Buxhowden surrendered the command to him and left the army.

At Goniondz was left Sedmaratzki's division (6th),[2] to cover the movement of the main army, and to keep up its communications with Essen I. and the two Moldavian divisions.

---

1. This date is taken from *Larrey*, iii. 22.
2. Instead of the 14th, which had originally been ordered to stay behind, and was now carried forward.

Lestocq, meanwhile, had fallen back, after the action of Soldau, towards Gilgenburg, on the night of the 6th December. On the march he changed direction towards Neidenburg, with the result that there was considerable confusion, and it was not for several days that the Prussians were collected at the latter place. On the 7th January, Lestocq, after retreating from Neidenburg to Oertelsburg and Sensburg, reached Rastenburg.[3] On the 10th, he marched to Angerburg, north of the Lotzen lake. On the 11th he moved westward again to Drengfurth, failing in an attempt to recapture Schippenbeil from Ney, who had taken it the previous day. On the 16th, he was at Barthen.[4] On that date, Bennigsen had reached Arys, between the lakes of Spirding and Lotzen. He had marched from Biala, on the 15th, in four columns, the movement of which was completely concealed from Soult's cavalry, on the Omulew, by the intervening forest of Johannisburg.

Napoleon's marshals had faithfully carried out his wishes, with the sole exception of Ney. The keynote to the Emperor's dispositions was the avoidance of all forward movements calculated to rouse the enemy to activity. He desired to leave the Russian bear to hibernate quietly, if he would do so, whilst he himself was busy making every preparation to awake him in the spring. Hibernation was, as has been seen, not the Russian scheme, but Ney did not know that. He had received a general indication of the Emperor's plans on the 4th January, but his cantonments were not, in that order, precisely specified.[5]

The orders of the 4th January were surely clear enough in their spirit to indicate to Ney the undesirability of an offensive advance; yet, early in January, he began to move towards Koenigsberg. His motives, according to De Fezensac,[6] were the search for a country better supplied with provisions, and an advance against Koenigsberg itself. On the 2nd January, his light cavalry was marching on Guttstadt by Passenheim and Oertelsburg. On the 8th-11th, his headquarters were at Wartenburg; from the 12th to the 20th, they were at Allenstein, and he had his troops dispersed all over the country at Bischofsburg, Bischofstein, Seeburg, Wartenburg, Guttstadt, Queetz, Gottkendorf,

3. For this account of Lestocq's movements, see Prussian official account in *Wilson*, pp. 253-254.
4. Not Bartenstein.
5. On the 4th January, Berthier had written to Ney: "The Emperor, not wishing to make any offensive movements with his armies during the winter, desires you to take such cantonments as will protect Marshal Soult's left and Marshal Bernadotte's right." The distinct specification of Soldau, etc., was on the 7th.
6. *Souvenirs Militaires*, p. 134.

Neidenburg, Bartenstein, Oertelsburg, Mensguth. He had even, as far forward as Schippenbeil, a battalion of grenadiers supporting his light cavalry still farther out.[7]

On the 9th, he proposed a strong reconnaissance to see if the enemy were still in Koenigsberg, but abandoned the idea in consequence of fresh news. On the 10th he took and occupied Schippenbeil, which Lestocq failed to recapture on the 11th. On the 14th, he estimated that he had in front of him Lestocq with 9000 men, and Ruchel, garrisoning Koenigsberg, with 4000. At the same time, he wrote that he had no positive news of Bernadotte and Soult, though he had incidentally heard of Sahuc's and d'Hautpoult's cavalry divisions passing Neidenburg. He adds that he is occupying a well-supplied country, and his men are living in abundance.[8] On the 15th, Bernadotte wrote warning Ney that he was exceeding his orders in advancing.[9] On the 16th January, Ney writes to Berthier[10] that he is negotiating with Lestocq and Ruchel for a delimitation of the hostile fronts, and an armistice requiring four days' notice for termination.

It is hardly surprising that the Emperor, when he at last heard of Ney's proceedings, was furious. He believed that Ney had long ago received the definite orders prescribing his cantonments. It was only on the 8th that the Emperor received information, and his despatches, for days after, show traces of his anger.[11] He was still ignorant, on

---

7. "*Journaux de Marche*," 6th Corps, *Arch. Hist.*
8. Ney to Berthier, 14th January, *Arch. Hist.*
9. Copy enclosed in a despatch from Bernadotte to Berthier, on 15th January, *Arch. Hist.*
10. *Arch. Hist.*, daily correspondence, 16th January.
11. On the 18th, Berthier writes to Ney: "I have submitted to the Emperor your letter, and one from Marshal Bernadotte informing him of the movements you have made without his orders. He desires me to convey to you his displeasure. . . . His intentions are not to go to Koenigsberg; had he so proposed he would have issued orders. The Emperor, in his general projects, requires neither advice nor plans of campaign; no one else knows his designs, and it is our duty to obey. His Majesty is all the more surprised at the movements you have made, inasmuch as he had already explained to you the circumstances under which you were not to act without orders. . . . The Emperor knew the Prussians were retreating; that was no reason for you to spread your corps over 20 leagues. He orders you to take up the prescribed cantonments: do so gradually, for this is the first retrograde step the Emperor makes. The adjutant-commandant Jomini will explain to you how much the Emperor is annoyed at the movements you have made without orders." Again he wrote, next day: "The Emperor has been extremely astonished to see by a despatch received from Marshal Soult, as well as from your own, that, not only have you disobeyed his Majesty's orders relative to your winter (continued on next page)

the 26th, of Bennigsen's march, with the bulk of his army, against the French left, though he saw that something was going on in that direction.[12] Despatches travelled slowly in the difficult country, and the wintry weather which now prevailed. A severe frost had set in about the 17th, after some broken weather.[13] The Emperor's information was, therefore, several days behind time. Nevertheless, he had, from the 23rd, had suspicions, and he, at least, expected heavy reprisals for the irritation of Ney's march on Koenigsberg. From the 25th, commences a series of orders calculated to meet any eventualities on the left. Only two days earlier, Lefebvre had been ordered to proceed with the new 10th Corps towards Danzig. He was now directed to hold fast at Thorn.[14] Espagne was to march on Thorn;[15] Augereau to pass the Vistula with his troops from the left bank, and concentrate at Plonsk;[16] Oudinot to leave Kalisch, and reach Lowicz by the 31st.[17]

---

quarters, but that you have even counselled Marshal Soult to do the same. I reiterate the order to return to the positions indicated to you for winter quarters; the Emperor is unchangeable in his plans, and, but for political considerations, would have made mention in the orders of the day of the non-execution of his orders by your corps." On the 19th, Berthier, writing to Soult, says: "His Majesty hopes that this is the last occasion on which Marshal Ney, by his flighty dispositions, will expose himself to the danger of compromising the fate of the army by such grave faults." De Fezensac (p. 136) had been sent to carry a despatch from Ney, and he returned with Jomini and the reply. From Jomini he heard that the Emperor was specially enraged by the armistice which Ney was negotiating with the Prussians, and had remarked that other generals had been tried by court martial for less grave offences. Yet Ney's conduct was not quite so bad as the Emperor pictured it. In the *Archives Historiques* there is a despatch from Ney to Berthier, dated 18th January, in which the writer says: "I received yesterday (17th) the duplicate copy of the dispositions ordered on the 7th for the definite quarters of all the corps, and have given orders for my troops to return in succession to the neighbourhood of Chorzel, Soldau, and Mlawa." How Berthier's despatch took 10 days to reach Ney is not explained. Still, with Berthier's letter of the 4th before him (*supra*, p. 129, note), Ney clearly did not act in the spirit of his instructions. Even now, he protested against the country he was ordered to occupy as being void of supplies, and a "veritably cemetery" (*Arch. Hist.*, daily correspondence).

12. On the 26th, Berthier wrote to Soult: "The ill-considered point made by Marshal Ney appears to have determined the enemy to make a movement to his right."

13. See De Fezensac's account of his journey with Ney's despatch (*Souvenirs Militaires*, p. 136).

14. Berthier to Lefebvre, dated 25th January (printed in *Dumas*, xviii. 3381.

15. Berthier to Espagne, 25th January (*Dumas*, xviii. 341).

16. Berthier to Augereau, 25th January (*Dumas*, xviii. 339).

17. Berthier to Oudinot, 25th January (*Dumas*, xviii, 341).

Bernadotte was told[18] that, owing to Ney's aggression, the enemy was moving to the right. He was to hold the line of the Passarge, and was even to go so far as to propose to the enemy to fix that river as a boundary, intimating to him that the Emperor had no intention of moving on Koenigsberg, and had recalled Ney. Should he attempt to force Elbing, the Emperor was prepared to break up his winter quarters, in order to prevent a passage of the Vistula by the enemy. Elbing was not to be seriously defended. If it was attacked determinedly, Bernadotte was to fall back so as to cover Thorn, raising the blockade of Graudenz if he felt it necessary, and drawing the troops before it partly to Thorn, and partly across the Vistula.

On the 26th,[19] again, Ney was told that Soult would now occupy Willemburg and Chorzel, with his point of concentration moved forward from Golymin to Prasznitz, whilst Ney's own rallying-point was changed from Mlawa to Neidenburg. These orders, it was remarked, were issued on the assumption that the enemy proposed wintering in front of Ney; a remark which clearly shows that the Emperor had not yet grasped the full meaning and extent of the Russian movement.

On the 27th, he was convinced that Bennigsen aimed at nothing less than cutting off the extended French left, and, by a movement on the Lower Vistula, endeavouring to force the whole army to repass the river.

Such, indeed, was Bennigsen's scheme—a well-conceived one, which had a good chance of success if well executed against a general of ordinary capacity. The objections to it were: first, the difficulties of execution in such country and such weather; and, secondly, the natural boldness of Napoleon, who could ill afford, after the checks at Pultusk and Golymin, to expose his prestige to another blow by yielding to the initiative of the enemy, and contenting himself with the line of the Vistula, even with its well-protected points of issue at Warsaw, Modlin, and Thorn. His great disinclination for a fresh campaign in this season is clearly shown by his despatch, of the 26th January, to Bernadotte,[20] which, at the same time, indicated that he was prepared, in the last resort, to undertake it.

Now that he saw it was inevitable, he prepared to make his blow a crushing one. His scheme was to pivot on his left at Thorn, and, wheeling forward his right and centre, to drive Bennigsen into the angle between the Lower Vistula and the Frisches-Haff, or against the latter.[21]

---

18. Berthier to Bernadotte, 26th January (*Dumas*, xviii. 341).

19. Berthier to Ney and Soult, both dated 26th January (*Dumas*, xviii. 343, 344).

20. *Vide supra*, p. 134, note (1). (continued on next page)

The movements which he had been ordering during the last few days were all calculated to facilitate such a plan.

Murat was to assemble d'Hautpoult's, Klein's, and Latour-Maubourg's brigades at Raciaz, whilst the Emperor himself proceeded with his headquarters to Prasznitz and Willemburg.[22] Soult, raising his cantonments, to concentrate on Willemburg.[23] Ney to cover Soult's left, and, with Augereau now marching on Mlawa, to unite him to Bernadotte.[24] Lefebvre was ordered to assemble his corps at Thorn for

21. What Napoleon's intentions were is clearly indicated in Berthier's despatch of the 28th January to Bernadotte. "The intention of the Emperor is to pierce the enemy's centre, and to drive to his right and left such of the enemy's troops as may not have retired in time; but, holding fast to his system, which is to cover Thorn, that should be the object of your movements. You would then rejoin the left of the army, regaining, even by the rear if necessary, your communications with Marshal Ney . . . the more deeply the enemy is involved the better" (printed in *Dumas*, xviii. 366). We may well believe that the Emperor's secret hopes went further than this. If Bennigsen, unaware of his impending fate, should push on south-westwards in pursuit of Bernadotte, it might well happen that he would become so deeply involved as to find himself in front of Thorn with the Lower Vistula barring his way westwards, watched as it was by part of Lefebvre's corps spread down the left bank. In his front he would find Lefebvre entrenched in Thorn. Wheeling to their left, and driving Bennigsen on to the river, would be the corps of Bernadotte, Ney, Soult, Augereau, Murat, and the Guard. In that case destruction, or at the best a precarious retreat on Danzig, would stare him in the face. A letter from the Emperor to Lefebvre (*Corr.* 11,711, dated 28th January), warns him that the enemy, finding his left turned by Napoleon's wheel, might march on Thorn, or across the Vistula. Lanfrey (*Hist. de Napoleon*, iv. 45-46) thinks Napoleon only hoped to cut off 15,000 or 20,000 Russians. It is true that, in his proclamation of the 30th January (*Corr.* 11,739), he talks of driving the enemy across the Niemen, and that in writing to Clarke at Berlin (*Corr.*, dated 27th January, 1807) he warns him to be on the look-out for 15,000 or 20,000 of the enemy, who might be driven across the Vistula. That, however, by no means implies that this was the limit of the Emperor's hopes, or that he did not expect to cut off a great many more east of the Vistula, before they could reach it. See also the concluding words of note 24 below.

22. Berthier to Murat (2 despatches), dated 27th January (*Dumas*, xviii. 348, 349).

23. Berthier to Soult, 27th January (*Dumas*, xviii. 352).

24. Berthier to Ney, 27th January (*Dumas*, xviii. 352). Whether Bernadotte should be able to maintain himself at Osterode, or whether he should be compelled to retreat on Thorn, Ney and Augereau were to maintain the line between his right and Soult's left. If, however, there should appear to be danger of Bernadotte's being anticipated at Thorn by the enemy, Ney was to cover that place. "The Emperor does not wish to re-occupy his winter quarters before he has destroyed the enemy."

25. Berthier to Lefebvre, 27th January (*Dumas*, xviii. 350). Lefebvre was to collect (*a*) his French brigade; (*b*) 12 guns now on their way from Warsaw; (*c*) Espagne's cavalry; (*d*) if the siege of Graudenz had been raised, (continued on next page)

the protection of that all-important fortress.[25] Davout to keep his advanced posts in position, and, under cover of them, to concentrate towards Pultusk.[26] Bernadotte's first object was to hold on at Osterode, and cover Thorn, till Lefebvre had assembled there, raising, if necessary, the siege of Graudenz.[27] Bessières, with the Guard, to pass the Narew on the 28th, and march on Pultusk on the 29th, leaving 15 guns for Oudinot at Warsaw.[28]

Lannes' corps, and Becker's dragoons, were left to cover the right of the army towards Ostrolenka, and in the peninsula between the Narew and the Bug.[29] As Lannes took up his position, Davout would move forward by Ostrolenka and Makow to Myszienec, where he would leave all his corps, except Gudin's division, by the 31st. Becker's dragoons would quietly replace the light cavalry, which, in turn, would, equally unobserved, replace Soult's at Myszienec. Gudin's division, for the present, not to go beyond Pultusk.[30]

By these movements, the Emperor expected to have his army, by the 31st, in the following positions:—

Lefebvre at Thorn, and down the left bank of the Vistula. Bernadotte on his right. Augereau and Ney uniting Bernadotte with Soult and Murat in the direction of Willemburg, with cavalry pushed towards Oertelsberg. Davout at Myszienec. Lannes' corps and Becker's dragoons towards Ostrolenka. The Guard and Gudin in second line, in the angle between Davout and Lannes.

Everything being thus in readiness for the French advance pivoting on Thorn, it is necessary to return to the movements of the Russians and Prussians during the latter half of January, which had induced the Emperor, much against his will, to resume active operations.

Lestocq, driven by Ney from Schippenbeil on the 10th January, failed in an attempt to retake it, and took post about Friedland. It was in this direction that a proposed armistice between the opposing forces had so aroused the anger of Napoleon against Ney.

Bennigsen, meanwhile, in furtherance of a promise to the King of

---

the Hessian division; he was to keep his Poles on the left bank, watching it as far down as possible. His objects were defined to be (*a*) the defence of Thorn, and the restoration of the bridge, damaged by floating ice: (*b*) the watching of the left bank of the Lower Vistula as far as possible; (*c*) the protection of Bromberg; (*d*) the formation of a reserve to the left of the army, and, possibly, an advance on Danzig.

26. Berthier to Davout, 7th January (*Dumas*, xviii. 353).

27. Berthier to Bernadotte, 27th January (*Dumas*, xviii. 354).

28. Berthier to Bessières, 27th January (*Dumas*, xviii. 355).

29. Berthier to Lannes, 28th January (*Dumas*, xviii. 359).

30. Berthier to Davout, 28th January (*Dumas*, xviii. 361).

Prussia that he would defend Koenigsberg,[31] had reached Arys on the 16th, and Rhein on the 18th, without his movement being discovered by Ney, or by Soult, across whose front he had marched behind the Johannisburg forest and the Spirding lake.

Ney, on the 19th, ignorant of the storm which was gathering on his right flank, and not yet having received Napoleon's peremptory orders to withdraw, still had his cavalry at Schippenbeil. There it was encountered by Gallitzin, on the 9th, with 40 squadrons, the Russian advance guard, exploring the roads from Rhein towards Koenigsberg on the right, and Bischofstein on the left.[32] On this date Lestocq, standing fast, effected his union with the Russian right. Bennigsen marched with three advance guards under Markow, Barclay, and Bagavout. On the 10th his headquarters were at Roessel, midway between Rastenburg and Bischofstein, his cavalry driving in Ney's with loss, and even surprising the cantonments of parts of the corps which had still not begun their march. Lestocq closed in towards the Güber, and, on the 21st, he and the Russians were abreast on the line from Schippenbeil to Bischofstein. At the latter place Colbert, with Ney's light cavalry, retreating from Schippenbeil and Bartenstein, was attacked by the advance guard, and driven back with heavy loss on to Seeburg. Bennigsen's advance guard penetrated, on the 21st, as far as Heilsberg. On the 22nd and 23rd, the Russian main body halted, whilst the advance guard moved on towards the Passarge. On the latter date, Ney had succeeded in making good his retreat, though not without loss, to Neidenburg, whence he extended his corps towards Soult on his right, and Bernadotte on his left.

Lestocq, on the 22nd, marched from Schippenbeil towards Bartenstein, pushing outposts towards Landsberg. On the 3rd, he marched on Landsberg, so as to keep clear of the Russian columns,

---

31. *Wilson*, p. 242.

32. Hoepfner (iii., 172) gives, on the authority of the original reports, the allied strength thus:

7 Russian divisions under Bennigsen	66,000
Sedmaratzki's 6th division at Goniondz	8,000
Corps of Essen I. at Bransk	18,000
Lewstocq's Prussians about Friedland	13,000
Total	105,000

Deducting (*ibid.*, p. 177, note) about 3000 men connecting Benningsen with Sedmaratzki, he puts the force advancing from Rhein against Ney at 76,000 Russians and Prussians.

and sent his advanced troops towards Mehlsack and Wonnditt. That morning Rouquette, on the Heiligenbeil-Braunsberg road, reported having been driven back by Bernadotte's advance guard, which, for the moment, induced Lestocq to suppose the marshal was marching on Koenigsberg. However, when he reached Mehlsack on the 24th, he found that Bernadotte had abandoned Braunsberg, and fallen back on Preussisch Holland. On the 24th, the Russian headquarters were at Heilsberg. Markow's advance guard surprised and, after a sharp fight in Liebstadt, captured about 300 French cavalry and infantry.

Bernadotte had scarcely reached the Frisches-Haff with his left wing when he received news from his chief of the staff, Maison, at Osterode, of the Russian offensive movement, and Ney's retreat.[33]

Maison, without waiting for orders from his chief, with admirable promptitude warned Pacthod, who was at Mohrungen, with one infantry regiment, and directed the concentration of Rivaud's division at Osterode, of Drouet's at Saalfeld, and the retirement of the dragoon brigade from Hohenstein[34] Bernadotte, on the left, ordered the assembly of Dupont's division, Laplanche's dragoons, and the light cavalry at Pr. Holland, and directed Rivaud to hold Osterode, blocking the defiles leading to it, whilst Drouet should advance, on the 25th, from Saalfeld to Mohrungen, in order to support Pacthod's regiment there, and to give security to the march of Dupont from Pr. Holland to Osterode.

On the 25th, Bennigsen's headquarters reached Arensdorf, his left column, passing the Alle at Guttstadt, reached the Passarge at Deppen, the advance guard going forward to Alt-Reichau on the road to Mohrungen. The right column marched through Arensdorf to Liebstadt.

Lestocq, who had turned towards Mehlsack when he thought Bernadotte was moving on Koenigsberg, had to make a very long march to reach, with his headquarters, Schlodien, on the 25th. His

---

33. Maison received the news from Ney (operations of 1st Corps, *Arch. Hist.*). Ney has been accused of not sending warning of the Russian advance to Bernadotte. This passage clears him.

34. Bernadotte's orders had prescribed the following cantonments for his corps:
Dupont's Division: Pr. Holland, Elbing, Frauenberg, Braunsberg.
Rivaud's Division: Osterode, Mohrungen, Deutsch Eylau.
Drouet's Division: Saalfeld, Christburg, Riesmuhl with detachments at Marienburg and Marienwerder.
Light Cavalry: To occupy the whole length of the Passarge.
4th Division of Dragoons: One brigade at Hohenstein, communicating with Ney; the other in reserve between Pr. Holland and Elbing (Bernadotte's report, *Arch. Hist.*)

outposts were towards Mulhausen, Pr. Holland, and Mohrungen—4 battalions still behind the Passarge. In this position he was joined by Rouquette, now released, by Bernadotte's retreat, from guarding the road to Koenigsberg near the Frisches-Haff.

ACTION OF MOHRUNGEN, 25TH JANUARY

It was at Mohrungen, on the 25th, that there occurred the first serious action between the advancing Russians and the retreating French. Markow, with the advance guard of the right wing, had learnt from the prisoners taken at Liebstadt, that Bernadotte was on the march for Mohrungen. Pushing on, he arrived near Mohrungen about noon on the 25th.[35] There he found Bernadotte with 9 battalions and 11 squadrons made up partly from Pacthod's regiment, partly from Dupont's division arriving from Pr. Holland, and partly from Drouet's from Saalfeld.[36] Seeing the Russian advance, Bernadotte sent to hurry up Dupont to his assistance, and prepared, with what troops he had, to attack Markow. That general took up a position on the heights in front of Georgenthal, north of Mohrungen. In first line he placed two regiments of infantry, in second line one regiment. Two battalions of another regiment, with the third in reserve, advanced towards the defile of Pfarrersfeldchen. In front of them, towards Mohrungen, was a regiment of hussars. To the right front of Georgenthal were 2 battalions of jägers, and in the village itself 3 more battalions—altogether 17 battalions and one regiment of hussars, besides cossacks.[37]

Scarcely had these dispositions been made when, about 1 p.m., Bernadotte's cavalry attacked the hussars. The latter, at first victorious, were forced by the French artillery to retire, and take post to the left of Georgenthal. The French cavalry, in turn, were brought to a standstill by the Russian guns.

Bernadotte now sent urgent orders to Dupont to make for the Russian right flank, marching from Hagenau by Koenigsdorf and Wi-

---

35. Bernadotte (*Arch. Hist.*) thinks that Ney had abandoned Alleistein with too much precipitation, thus leaving Bernadotte exposed on his right flank. After the series of rebukes and peremptory orders he had received, it seems scarcely fair to blame Ney for following to the letter his orders from headquarters.

36. Bernadotte reached the field, just as Markow appeared, with one battalion 9th Infantry, the 27th and 94th Regiments, and Laplanche's dragoon brigade (Bernadotte, *Arch. Hist.*). The same authority puts the enemy's strength at 20,000, which was considerably too high.

37. Bernadotte says that when he arrived, the plain in front of Pfarrersfeldchen was "inundated" by Cossacks (*Arch. Hist.*).

ese, whilst he himself attacked in front. He carried Pfarrersfeldchen with a rush, and advanced against the main Russian position.[38] Darkness was already falling on the field, when the two jäger battalions began to fall back before his attack. They were supported by their reserve, but Dupont's flank attack, from Wiese on Georgenthal, new began to make itself felt. Notwithstanding the brave resistance of 6 battalions detached against Dupont, Markow felt himself outmatched, and compelled to retreat. At this moment Anrepp arrived on the field, announcing that he was hurrying up the cavalry of the Russian right wing. He was mortally wounded as he moved to the front. Following up the retreating Russians, the French lost heavily. Dupont had now succeeded in defeating the two regiments opposed to him, and was nearing Georgenthal. In this moment of victory, Bernadotte heard firing behind him at Mohrungen, but was unable to judge of the strength of the force which had, apparently, taken him in rear. Abandoning, therefore, the pursuit, he marched his men back on Mohrungen.[39]

The cause of the noise was an inroad of Russian cavalry upon the baggage in Mohrungen. Gallitzin, with the cavalry of the left wing, had reached Alt-Reichau, and sent forward 3 squadrons, under Dolgoruki, supported by 6 more under Pahlen, to reconnoitre through the defile between the Narien and Mahrung lakes.[40] This force, reaching the western side of the lakes at nightfall, moved on Mohrungen, which they found almost denuded of troops, but full of baggage, and supply columns. The place was promptly attacked, its defenders captured, and the baggage plundered. Beyond it, the cavalry met Bernadotte, retracing his steps with his troops, and was compelled to retreat, carrying with them some 360 French prisoners, 200 released Russian and Prussian prisoners, and a quantity of plunder.[41] They lost, however, part of

---

38. For the attack of Pfarrersfeldchen, Bernadotte employed the battalion of the 9th, and one of the 27th. He pushed forward 4 guns on to a height commanding the village. The 9th were at first beaten off from Pfarrersfeldchen, whilst the 27th made steady progress against the wood on the right. The attack was then reinforced by the 2nd battalion, 27th, and by the 8th light infantry, with the 94th in reserve, and dragoons in support. The 1st battalion of the 27th, at the wood, lost, but again recovered, its eagle.

39. Bernadotte (*Arch. Hist.*) points out the danger of his position, liable, as he was, if defeated, to be cut from Rivaud's division at Osterode.

40. According to Danilewski, the sound of the battle at Mohrungen did not, owing to the stormy weather, reach Gallitzin, so that Dolgoruki's arrival was, in a sense, accidental (see *Hoepfner*, iii. 185).

41. According to Wilson (p. 35, note) they found in Bernadotte's personal baggage 12,500 ducats which he had levied for himself in (continued on next page)

their force, which had been surrounded when it rashly advanced too far towards Pfarrersfeldchen.

The action in front of Mohrungen might have involved Bernadotte in a serious disaster, had Markow promptly sent for assistance, from Gallitzin on his left, and from Anrepp on his right. The Prussians were, perhaps, too far off to be able to render much assistance; yet they had, at Hagenau, to some extent hindered Dupont's junction with Bernadotte. Bernadotte should have taken measures to guard the defile between the lakes on his right rear.[42] Probably he felt that he had not sufficient troops available to be able to spare any for this purpose.[43] Had he been able to do so, his right flank and rear, to a distance of some miles, would have been admirably protected. Till Dupont's arrival, he was in a considerable inferiority in numbers, and by that time the mischief was done. The loss in this action was heavy, probably about 2000 on either side.[44]

Lestocq on this day (25th) reached Hagenau as day closed, after an engagement with part of Dupont's division on its retreat from Pr. Holland.[45] Proposing to free Elbing from the enemy, the Prussians started on the 26th for Pr. Holland, but were ordered by Bennigsen to advance on Liebstadt. When they had got halfway there, a fresh order directed them on Hagenau again, to be prepared to support an attack on Mohrungen next morning. After some twenty miles of

Elbing, as well as a quantity of plate bearing the arms of minor German states, from which it had been taken. Bernadotte's servant, when asked to point out his master's property, denied that these articles were part of it. They were, however, found in the marshal's own quarters, and in such quantity that he could hardly have been ignorant of their presence. If this story is correct, the future King of Sweden cuts but a sorry figure in the episode. His own account (*Arch. Hist.*) of the movements of his corps omits all mention of the irruption of Russian cavalry into Mohrungen.

42. The military importance of the lakes in this direction is well brought out in the critical remarks of Count von Waldersee (representing Marshal von Moltke) on the 66th problem set by Von Moltke in 1882 (*Moltke's Tactical Problems*, text, p. 164). In the problem the western army is supposed to be endeavouring to join an army corps to the north, and has to guard its flank against an army east of the lakes.

43. De Fezensac (p. 140) says Bernadotte had only 9000 against 16,000, but it is not quite clear whether he refers to the earlier portion of the action, or to the later period when Dupont had arrived. At the latter period the French probably had a superiority of numbers.

44. This is the number admitted by Wilson as the Russian loss. Bernadotte gives his own losses as 700 or 800, whilst patting that of the enemy at 1600 (report in *Arch. Hist.*).

45. Lestocq, unlike Gallitzin, had heard the cannon at Mohrungen (*Hoepfner*, iii. 186), from which it may be inferred that a strong east wind was blowing.

marching and counter-marching, they were much where they had been in the morning.

Bernadotte, on the 26th, fell back on Liebemühl, avoiding the direct road to Osterode, which was rendered dangerous by its proximity to Gallitzin's force at Alt-Reichau.[46]

Bennigsen occupied Mohrungen with part of his main army on the 26th, the rest coming up on the morning of the 27th. His right advance guard moved on Liebemühl, the left on Allenstein, the former place having been evacuated by Bernadotte who had continued his march on Löbau, where he was joined by d'Hautpoult's cuirassiers on the 29th, from the neighbourhood of Gollub. He thus commanded 17,000 infantry, and 5000 or 6000 cavalry, on the 30th. On the 28th, Bennigsen found himself at Mohrungen with his troops wearied by 10 days of marching. He decided to rest and replenish his stores.

Lestocq he again sent off farther to the right. On the 29th, that general reached Rosenberg, with outposts towards Freystadt, Bischofswerder, and Deutsch Eylau. Rouquette's detachment had marched on Marienwerder. The Prussian advance had resulted in the raising of the blockade of Graudenz by the Hessians. Bennigsen's right advance guard extended to Saalfeld, his left to Guttstadt. On the 30th, he sent Bagration to Deutsch Eylau to strengthen his link with the Prussians, whilst he proposed to march himself towards Allenstein. On the 31st, Lestocq was at Freystadt, with outposts at Lessen, Schönau, and Schwarzenau, and 100 cavalry between him and Graudenz, which was being rapidly provisioned. Bagration, with the right advance guard of the Russian army, was at Deutsch Eylau with detachments on the Drewenz. The left advance guard, and the 2nd division, were in and behind Allenstein, with a detachment, under Barclay, at Osterode. The 5th, 7th, and 8th divisions under Tutchkow were at Samrodt, between Mohrungen and Pr. Holland; the 13th and 14th divisions, commanded by Sacken, with headquarters at Gotteswalde, were on the march south of Osterode; reserve, 4th division under Somow, at Guttstadt; Bennigsen himself was in Mohrungen; cavalry of the left wing was as far forward as Hohenstein and Passenheim.

---

46. Bernadotte's report says that the enemy's movement on his left flank, threatening to cut him from Thorn, compelled his retreat. His corps was completely assembled only on the 28th, at Roecken on the road to Löbau. On the 30th and 31st, he was drawn up there for battle. On the latter day at noon, he marched for Strasburg, his rear guard being roughly handled by the enemy at Brattian. He did not leave Strasburg to advance again till the 4th February (*Arch. Hist.*).

On the same date, the French positions were:—Lefebvre on the extreme left, at and about Thorn, and down the left bank of the Vistula; Bernadotte at Strasburg; Ney at Gilgenburg; Augereau at Neidenburg and Janow; Guard (Bessières) at Chorzel; Davout, with two divisions, at Myszienec, and Gudin's at Prasznitz; cavalry reserve (Murat) and Soult, about Oertelsburg and Willemburg; Savary, with the corps of Lannes (who was ill at Warsaw), at Brok on the Bug.

Bennigsen was under the impression that he had succeeded in his enterprise, almost without a blow, and that Napoleon was about to recross the Vistula between Thorn and Warsaw. On the 1st February, the scales fell from his eyes, and he saw, not only the full disposition of the French army, but also the whole of Napoleon's great scheme for his destruction.

Whatever might have been the effect of Bennigsen's move in inducing a general of ordinary capacity to abandon the country beyond the Vistula, Napoleon was the last person to follow such a course. Bennigsen had not yet appreciated his boldness, and he was, therefore, surprised when the Emperor himself conveyed to him, unintentionally, a full statement of his scheme. Bennigsen's flank march against the French left is a good example of the futility of a good design if not supported by equally good execution. His first fault was his waste of time, and force, in marching up the Narew, and not joining Buxhowden directly. His second was the direction of his march from Rhein towards the head of Ney's column, instead of towards its rear. Had he turned boldly to the south-west, he must, almost infallibly, have separated Ney from Soult, and destroyed the greater part of the former's corps. He would also have anticipated Bernadotte at Mohrungen and Osterode, and separated Dupont's and Drouet's divisions from Rivaud's, forcing them, probably, to cross the Vistula.

With Ney's corps, and two-thirds of that of Bernadotte, cut off, Napoleon's position beyond the Upper Vistula would have been one of extreme peril. It is difficult to see how he could have maintained himself on the right bank.

Bennigsen lost two days by halting on the 22nd and 23rd—the fatigue of his troops probably rendered this inevitable. His halt at Mohrungen was, nevertheless, fortunate for him, for it was then too late to cut off Ney or Bernadotte, and a further advance would have plunged him more deeply into the trap which Napoleon had now prepared for him.

Napoleon, too, had underestimated his adversary's capacity for designing a bold move.[47] It was not till the 27th January that he was

---

47. That is if the design was Bennigsen's at all. There is some reason for believing it was not his, but Buxhowden's.

convinced that the movement against his left was anything more than a reply to Ney's aggression. As a matter of fact, Ney had no part in influencing the Russian scheme, for it was decided on before the marshal began to move northwards.

The Emperor, convinced at last that he must, unwilling though he was, enter on a fresh campaign, lost no time in pressing it to what he hoped might be a final decision.

On the 30th January, Berthier sent orders to Bernadotte to concentrate wherever he might be, but to be careful to cover Thorn, until he was certain Lefebvre was there. Once there, the latter would be able to hold it, if necessary, for a week, which was more than would be required of him.[48] The place was of infinite importance, as the hinge on which the whole French movement was to turn.[49]

Napoleon had left Warsaw on the night of the 29th January. On the evening of the 30th, he was at Prasznitz, on the 31st, at Willemburg. The marshals had been warned that the advance would commence on the 1st February.

From Willemburg a despatch was sent to Bernadotte by Berthier. It ordered the 1st Corps to join the left of the army under the immediate command of the Emperor. The march was to be concealed from the enemy by being made at night; a light cavalry regiment was to be left behind to keep up the bivouac fires all night, and then, in the morning, to retire slowly on Thorn, turning back any French convoys it might meet, and warning Lefebvre that he was now dependent on his own resources. If possible, Bernadotte was to reach Gilgenburg, though, if he found serious difficulty, he might continue to cover Thorn. The despatch gave details of the positions of the other corps, and contained the significant words, "It is unnecessary for me to tell you that the Emperor, desiring to cut off the enemy, would prefer your joining his left; but he must trust, in this, to your zeal and your knowledge of the actual circumstances in which you are."[50]

---

48. Berthier to Bernadotte, dated Prasznitz, 30th January, *Dumas*, xviii. 374.

49. In *Corr.* 11,711, dated 28th January, Napoleon warns Lefebvre that the enemy, finding himself turned by the French advance from the right, may march on Thorn.

50. Berthier to Bernadotte, dated Willemburg, 31st January, *Dumas*, xviii. 380. A second despatch was sent off at 7 p. m., in which Berthier states that the Emperor does not understand Bernadotte's meaning when he says that the enemy is manoeuvring against the left by Mlawa. He only knows of one Mlawa, but that is not on Bernadotte's left. The despatch continues: "I have sent you orders an hour ago; you will be guided by what has passed on the 31st; if the enemy is, as you suppose, in retreat on Osterode, you will pursue him prudently; nevertheless, His Majesty hopes he will not have been in time to escape altogether." (continued on next page)

Here was Napoleon's whole plan of campaign, stated with the lucidity which characterised his despatches. This all-important paper was given by Berthier to the first officer who came to hand. A young officer, fresh from one of the military schools, was on his way to join his regiment in Bernadotte's corps. He might as well be utilised to carry the despatch. Naturally, he knew nothing of the country he had to cross, nothing of the enemy's positions, and he probably was only able to get a very sorry mount.[51] This unfortunate young man fell in with a party of Cossacks sent forward by Bagration towards Strasburg. He was captured before he could destroy the papers, and the inestimable prize reached Bennigsen, after being read by Bagration, on the 1st of February. Only one copy having been sent, Bernadotte received no orders, and, therefore, stayed where he was.

Then follows a long complaint of the delay in carrying despatches. The officer with Bernadotte's despatch had been 15 hours on the road. This second despatch is not given by Dumas. The fate of these two despatches is narrated in one from Bernadotte (*Arch. Hist.*), dated 3rd February. In it he explains that what he meant about Mlawa was that, whilst 8000 or 10,000 of the enemy were manoeuvring on his left, another column was reported to be moving towards Mlawa on his right, and the Emperor's left. He goes on to explain that he only received the second despatch, dated 31st January, 7 p.m., on the 2nd February. The one of an hour earlier never reached him, and he is ignorant of what the orders were. He had ascertained from the villagers that it was captured by Cossacks at Lautenberg from a young officer of the *Ecole Militaire*, who was carrying it. The captain who carried the second despatch had heard the same story. The next despatch from Berthier to Bernadotte is dated 3rd February, 4 a.m., and says it appears possible Bennigsen will fight at Liebstadt, in which case the Emperor desires Bernadotte to join his left, *via* Osterode, for the battle. The next is dated 5th February, 8.30 p.m. It says that Ney has cut off the Prussians. The Emperor believes Bernadotte to be at Osterode, but has no news of him. He hopes Bernadotte is approaching the enemy by Liebstadt, or by Guttstadt, from Osterode. On the 6th, at 3 a.m., Berthier again writes that Ney had taken 3000 prisoners from Lestocq. Bernadotte is urged to try and come up with this disorganised corps, as Ney is wanted to join the Emperor's left (*Arch. Hist.*, daily correspondence). Evidently, Bernadotte's despatch of the 3rd February, announcing the capture of Berthier's of the 31st January, had not reached headquarters yet, and the Emperor was still ignorant of the marshal's position. The first despatch of the 31st January was sent *en clair*. Jomini (*Vie de Napoleon*, ii. 359) makes the Emperor say that it would have been wiser to use a cipher, and that he afterwards adopted this practice.
51. It appears to have been the custom in the Grand Army to assume that every officer carrying despatches was properly mounted, and knew the country, whereas the contrary was more often the case. "An officer always had an excellent horse, he knew the country, he was never taken prisoner, he never met with an accident, he arrived quickly at his destination; and this was so little doubted that a second officer was by no means always sent. All this I knew," says De Fezensac (p. 116), speaking of his mission with orders to Ney on the 8th February.

For Bennigsen, obviously, an early retreat was the only possible course. He "had fallen headlong into the trap; his attention was fixed on Bernadotte, whom he was pursuing. He was rushing blindly on his destruction,"[52] when his eyes were suddenly opened by the captured despatch, whilst there was still time to avoid the noose.[53] Yet he was unwilling to seek safety in rapid retreat; moreover, he had, if possible, to gain some time for Lestocq and Bagration to join him. The former knew nothing of the French movement. The latter had read the despatch to Bernadotte before forwarding it, and acted on the information. On the 1st February, the advance of the French right wing commenced by the movement of Murat with the light cavalry, and of Soult's corps on Passenheim, from which Dolgoruki was driven back on Allenstein. Soult's light cavalry was sent to Mensguth to safeguard the right.

Ney reached Hohenstein the same day. Davout, from Myszienec, sent Marulaz with his light cavalry, 2 infantry regiments, and 2 guns, to reconnoitre towards Johannisburg. Gudin's division was at Chorzel. Lefebvre was ordered to pursue the Prussians, as they retired between Marienwerder and Osterode, and to reinvest Graudenz.[54]

On this day, Bennigsen ordered his army to concentrate on Jonkowo. The reserve, from Guttstadt, and Sacken, from Seeburg, were called up. Barclay was to wait at Allenstein for Dolgoruki, retiring from Passenheim. Bagration had, of his own accord,[55] started for Liebemühl and Allenstein, leaving his Cossacks to attack Bernadotte's outposts, and induce him to believe in an advance against himself. On the 2nd February, Murat and Soult occupied Allenstein, which was evacuated by Barclay's advance guard. It retired to Gottkendorf, whilst Bennigsen assembled the greater part of his army behind the heights of Jonkowo. There he took post, his right resting on a marshy wooded valley, his left on the Alle at Mondtken, his front covered by a small brook—now, of course, frozen over.

Ney nearly reached Allenstein, Augereau was half a day's march from it, Davout was moving on Oertelsburg, after leaving a strong

---

52. Jomini, *Vie de Napoléon*, ii. 355.
53. "This intelligence, which ought not to have been unexpected, created some surprise" (*Wilson*, p. 89).
54. Hoepfner (iii. 198) observes that Napoleon seems to have overlooked the fact that they could have retreated in safety on Danzig. The garrison of Graudenz had been closely blockaded and driven into the fortress on the 18th January (Bernadotte, *Arch. Hist.*). They were very short of supplies, and on the point of surrender, when relieved, and their magazines replenished by Lestocq (*Wilson*, 144).
55. In consequence of his perusal of the captured despatch to Bernadotte.

rear-guard[56] at Myszienec to keep up the communication with Savary. The Guard reached Passenheim. On the 3rd February, Ney and Augereau, arriving at Allenstein, drove the Russian outposts on their main body. Napoleon, hearing of the Russian position at Jonkowo[57] ordered the Guard to Allenstein, and himself reached Gottkendorf about mid-day.[58]

Under cover of Ney's horse artillery, he threatened Bennigsen's front with Ney's and Augereau's corps and St. Hilaire's division of Soult's. Soult himself, with his two other divisions, went down the right bank of the Alle to seek a crossing at Bergfried, which would bring him out on the left rear of the Russian army. Davout, who had been attacked as he was on his way from Oertelsburg to Wartenburg, received orders to turn towards Spiegelberg and join Soult's right. Guyot's light cavalry, of Soult's corps, was directed on Guttstadt; Gudin's division, on the march from Prasznitz, was ordered to Oertelsburg by Mensguth.

Action of Bergfried, 3rd February

For the protection of the bridge over the Alle at Bergfried, Bennigsen had posted the 14th division (Kamenskoi) and 3 Prussian batteries. Four battalions undertook the defence of the defile, whilst the rest remained in reserve. One battalion held the village of Bergfried, on the right bank.[59] The Prussian guns, on the heights of the left bank, commanded the approaches to the bridge and flanked the village, but the left bank above and below Bergfried, and the heights behind, do not appear to have been occupied by Russian infantry, so that the defence was confined to the defile itself.

It was 3 p.m.[60] when the head of Leval's division appeared before Bergfried. Two batteries were brought into action against the Prussian guns, a third enfiladed the defile from the heights to the left of Berg-

---

56. The rear-guard consisted of the 11th Regiment, the 2nd battalion 85th, and the 2nd Regiment of chasseurs à cheval (*Davout*, 159-160).

57. This place is called Jonkendorf on the modern map. The name has been retained here in the form used in all accounts of the campaign.

58. Up to the 3rd February, Napoleon was very doubtful as to the enemy's intentions. On that day he writes to Murat: "Everything leads to the belief that the enemy will try to re-unite at Guttstadt; it is impossible to believe he will allow his left flank to be turned;" but he goes on to express his anxiety lest the enemy, instead of retiring, should march by Mohrungen, Liebstadt, or Osterode on Allenstein (*Corr.* 11,792).

59. Soult (*Arch. Hist.*) says the Bergfried position was defended by 8000 men, who were later reinforced by a second division of equal strength. This seems excessive.

60. Sunset about 4.40 on this date.

fried. The 24th Light Infantry was directed to the attack of the village and bridge, whilst Vivier, with the 4th of the Line and a battalion of the 28th, attempted to cross the Alle below Bergfried.[61]

The frontal attack on Bergfried was repulsed by the artillery and infantry fire of the defenders. A second, enveloping attack was more successful, but a heavy fire of case prevented the French from promptly following up the Russian infantry, as it crossed the bridge in retreat.

Pressing the attack with great vigour, Leval's infantry broke over the bridge, forcing the guns to retire. Presently rallying, the Russian infantry charged again with the bayonet. Carrying the enemy before them, they retook the hotly contested bridge, in a desperate hand-to-hand fight on it and the causeway. One Russian company, in the heat of the moment following across the bridge, was almost destroyed, and forced to retire.

Vivier, during this period, had not made much progress, though some French accounts pretend that he succeeded in taking the heights on the left bank, thus leaving the passage open to Leval, and inflicting heavy loss on the enemy. The Russians, on the other hand, say a fresh attack on the bridge was repulsed. Soult himself says that, though he drove the enemy across the bridge, and Vivier's flank attack compelled him to retire, yet the division of Leval bivouacked that night on the heights above Bergfried, on the right bank, keeping only outposts on the left bank. Legrand was at Spiegelberg and Braunswalde, one brigade at each place. St. Hilaire, who in the morning had had a successful brush with the enemy, was at Kaltflies.

Soult's account vouches for the finding of 800 dead Russians on the field, and puts his own loss at 300. The losses were probably more equal.[62]

Bergfried was certainly not the decided success that Napoleon represented it to be. Even accepting the account most favourable to the French, they had done no more than get across the river, and could not risk occupying the farther bank in force at night. The attack, commencing only an hour and a half before sunset, was too late to enable Soult to take part, on that day, in the fight at Jonkowo. As, however, he had reached a position threatening Bennigsen's left rear, the position at Jonkowo was no longer tenable.

In front of Bennigsen, Napoleon confined his operations to a de-

---

61. Dumas (xvii. 346) says Vivier was to ford (*passer á gué*) the river. Wilson (p. 89) says: "The Alle was long frozen, but impassable on account of the snow that rested on its bed." What Vivier had to ford was not water, but soft, deep snow.
62. Soult, *Arch. Hist.*

laying action, awaiting the expected turning movement of Soult and Davout. Nothing beyond a desultory exchange of artillery fire occurred in this part of the field.

The Emperor still hoped that Bennigsen would remain to fight next day, in which case, with Davout and Soult descending on his rear, he must almost certainly have been destroyed.

At daybreak on the 4th, the Emperor moved forward, Murat in front of the centre, Ney on the right of Jonkowo, Augereau on the left, Soult, from Bergfried, towards Mondtken. It soon appeared that Bennigsen, aware not only of Soult's presence at Bergfried, but also of the capture of Guttstadt by Guyot on the previous evening, had retreated during the night, leaving only a strong rear-guard to waste Napoleon's time by inducing him to deploy for battle. The course which he followed, in retreating northwards, was Bennigsen's only chance of assuring his communications with Koenigsberg, which were seriously compromised by the loss of Bergfried, and by Davout's advance on Guttstadt.

The Russians marched in three columns, under Sacken, Gallitzin, and Tutchkow, on Wolfsdorf and Arensdorf.

The rear-guard followed, also in three columns, under the general command of Bagration; Bagavout on the right, Markow in the centre, Barclay de Tolly on the left. They were followed and harassed all day by Ney, Murat, and Soult.

A sharp cavalry fight occurred between Ney and Bagavout at Waltersmühl. Bagavout, reinforced by Bagration, and touching Markow's column, kept up a running fight till nightfall put an end to it. Murat pushed on to Deppen, whence he drove the enemy after a cavalry combat. Soult, closely following the Russian left column, and frequently attacking it, reached at nightfall, Heiligenthal, Ankendorf, and Alt Garschen. Davout, with Friant's division and his light cavalry (Marulaz's), reached Rosengarten in rear of Soult; Morand's division at Wartenburg, Gudin's, towards Oertelsberg.[63] Augereau bivouacked at Pupkaim, behind Murat.

Bennigsen, still anxious for the junction of Lestocq, who, with the longer distance he had to traverse, had only reached Liebstadt[64] on

---

63. *Davout*, p. 152.

64. Lestocq reached Deutsch Eylau from Freystadt on the morning of the 3rd February. Later in the day he was at Osterode, where he received a despatch from Bennigsen, urging his junction with the Russian right. On the 4th, he was marching through the defile between the Marien and Mahrung lakes, with outposts towards the passages at Deppen and Waltersdorf.

the evening of the 4th, once more took up a position, as if for battle on the morrow, at Wolfsdorf, on the road from Liebstadt to Guttstadt. The news of the French occupation of Guttstadt, and his consequent anxiety for his communications, decided him once more to make a night march, leaving Lestocq to his fate. Early on the morning of the 5th he marched through Arensdorf on Frauendorf, halting 1½ miles short of it, at Burgerswalde.

Napoleon, convinced that Bennigsen was making for Landsberg, continued to manoeuvre by his right with the corps of Soult and Davout, whilst Ney and Murat delayed the Russian rear-guard. The two wings were connected by the Guard and Augereau's corps, under the Emperor's immediate command. Davout was ordered to march direct on Guttstadt; Soult to pursue between Guttstadt and Liebstadt, towards Arensdorf, but in touch with Davout's left; Murat to reconnoitre towards Liebstadt and Wolfsdorf, attacking the enemy with his main body should he find him in position. Ney would push the enemy towards Wolfsdorf and Arensdorf.

Ney had scarcely started, when it was reported that there was a strong hostile force on his left, south of Liebstadt, seeking to cross the Passarge. The Emperor at once ordered him, with his two divisions and Lasalle's light cavalry, to the left bank of the Passarge, towards Liebstadt. At 11 a.m. he was attacked by Lestocq's advanced troops,[65] and driven back into the Waltersdorf defile. A wood, in which was the French advance guard, was stormed and taken. Ney, arriving with his whole force in three columns, attacked the wood, and drove the Prussians from it with heavy loss. Continuing the pursuit till dusk, he forced the enemy[66] to retreat between the lakes of Mohrungen.

Ney had only defeated an advance guard which was trying to cross towards Bennigsen's supposed position. Lestocq, with the main body, succeeded in reaching Wusen, on the right bank of the Passarge. Ney arrived at Liebstadt, thus cutting off the advance guard which he had driven on Mohrungen.[67]

---

65. 5 or 6 battalions, 3 cavalry regiments, and a horse artillery battery.
66. Dumas (xvii. 355) says 2000 prisoners and 16 guns were taken, besides killed and wounded. Hoepfner (iii. 211) shows that this is an exaggeration. Only 8 guns were engaged on the Prussian side. On the 6th February, at 3 a.m., Berthier wrote to Bernadotte that Ney had taken 3000 prisoners from Lestocq, on the road between Schlitt and Liebstadt, and had pursued him towards Mohrungen. Bernadotte was urged to fall upon, and complete the ruin of this beaten corps, this allowing Ney to join the Emperor's left (Berthier's correspondence, *Arch. Hist.*) Jomini (*Vie de Napoleon*, ii. 357) says Lestocq lost 16 guns and many prisoners.
67. Napoleon was by no means certain what troops (continued on next page)

Whilst these events were occurring on the French left, Bennigesn, detaching a force[68] to hold Heilsberg and protect his left flank, continued his retreat on Landsberg, his rear-guard constantly stopping to fight. He took position for the night at Frauendorf, his rear-guard strongly posted at the entrance to the woods 1½ miles short of it.

Soult, reaching Freymarkt, through Wolfsdorf and Arensdorf, had an advance guard of 2 battalions, and his light cavalry, a mile or two farther on. Murat, after aiding in Ney's fight, also reached Freymarkt.

Davout sent Marulaz, with a handful of cavalry, to Heilsberg, which he occupied without opposition, but was presently driven out and back on Reichenberg. Morand's division and Gudin's reached Guttstadt; Friant's with Davout himself, arrived at Benern and Freymarkt, where it joined Soult. On its march, news reached it of Bennigsen's detachment moving to Heilsberg.

Continuing his retreat during the night of the 5th-6th February, Bennigsen reached Landsberg.

On the morning of the 6th, Napoleon detached Davout with Morand's division against Heilsberg; Friant's following on Launau. Just as Davout had succeeded in ejecting the enemy from Heilsberg, Friant appeared from Launau and took up the pursuit, with Marulaz, towards Eylau, inflicting some injury on the enemy on the road. Gudin only reached Heilsberg after it was captured. On Davout's left, Durosnel's light cavalry brigade maintained his communication with the corps moving on Landsberg. The latter marched in a single column, Murat in advance, followed by Soult and Augereau, through Frauendorf.

ACTION OF HOF, 6TH FEBRUARY

Bennigsen, himself going on to Landsberg, had left his rear-guard between Glandau and Hof. Barclay de Tolly there commanded 4 infantry regiments, 3 of cavalry, 2 of Cossacks, and a horse artillery battery. In his front he stationed 1 battalion of jägers, with 2 squadrons of hussars, and 2 guns. About 3 p.m. the head of the French column appeared, led by Murat. The Russian advanced force, now reinforced by 2 more squadrons, was quickly driven in. Barclay, finding that he would have to sacrifice himself for the benefit of the army, drew up his little force in front of Hof, behind a marshy stream. Immediately

had opposed Ney. This was perhaps due to the fact that Lestocq had Russians with him as well as Prussians. The Emperor (*Corr.* 11,781) writes to Talleyrand that his only fear is that it is nothing by the Prussians whom Ney had intercepted.

68. 3000 men (*Wilson*, p. 93). Davout (p. 154) puts the force at 4 Russian regiments, several thousand cavalry, and 20 guns.

behind the bridge, he placed a hussar regiment, supported in rear by 2 regiments of infantry, and another of hussars. On the wooded heights to his right, he posted a jäger regiment with some hussars; on his left, another jäger regiment, also in a wood.

The French skirmishers, advancing about 3 p.m.,[69] against the Russian left, were driven back when their opponents had been strengthened by one of the jäger regiments from the centre. Murat next, leading the dragoons he had with him and followed by d'Hautpoult's cuirassiers, hurried across the bridge. Their formation constricted by the narrow defile, the dragoons were overwhelmed, before they could reform beyond it, by the onslaught of the Russian hussars and Cossacks, and were carried back in confusion across the bridge. The reserve Russian regiment, following over the bridge without orders, was in turn overthrown beyond it, and pushed back across it by the French. The flight of this regiment broke the other also, and both were hotly pursued until their horse artillery brought the French cavalry to a halt, and compelled them to retire.[70] Again reinforced, Murat once more advanced, but was checked by an infantry regiment in squares. This afforded time for the rally of the Russian hussars who yet again drove off the dragoons. At last, the cuirassiers, led by d'Hautpoult, came to their rescue, and by sheer weight bore down the Russian dragoons, driving them in wild confusion on the infantry squares, killing, wounding, and capturing many of the Russian horsemen. Two standards and 4 guns also fell into the hands of the victors.[71]

Barclay hastened through Hof to take a fresh position on the other side. On his right the jäger battalion on the wooded height had been surrounded, and was compelled to force its way with the bayonet to another wood in rear.

---

69. *Wilson*, p. 95. The Russians placed 8 picked battalions with their right on Hof, and their left on a wood, their front covered by a deep ravine and 8 guns. The Emperor ordered the cavalry to attack without waiting for Soult (*Marbot*, i. 254).

70. Soult says the first cavalry attacks were repulsed, but d'Hautpoult's cuirassiers bore down everything before them, and broke a Russian square. Ledru's brigade reached the Hof plateau at the same time as the cuirassiers (*Arch. Hist.*). Marbot (i. 254) says the Emperor thought it better to attack with the cavalry without waiting for Soult. The light cavalry was first repulsed, then the dragoons; finally d'Hautpoult's cuirassiers crashed through all opposition. Speaking of Murat's handling of the cavalry at Hof, Jomini (*Vie de Napoléon*, ii. 356) remarks that he insisted on passing his brigades, in succession, through the defile of a marshy brook, thereby exposing them to defeat in detail.

71. The Russian regiment thus defeated was the Petersburg dragoons. In its flight it broke two of the supporting battalions, riding over them, and exposing them to terrible loss at the hands of the pursuing French cavalry (*Wilson*, pp. 95, 96).

In Hof, Barclay found 5 fresh battalions, which Bennigsen had sent with Dolgoruki to his assistance. Leaving him there, Barclay went to his left wing, where the French, strongly attacking the wood, were endeavouring to cut off from Landsberg the battalion stationed in it. At the same time Dolgoruki was attacked in the centre. Reinforced by Gallitzin[72] with two cuirassier regiments, he succeeded in holding his ground till nightfall, when the whole rear-guard fell back over the little brook which crosses the road between Hof and Landsberg. On either side of this, the contending armies faced one another, during the night, in close contact.

The Russian loss in this engagement was 5 guns, 2 standards, and more than 2000 men.[73] That of the French was rather higher.

On this day, Ney was still opposed to Lestocq, who marched on Engelswalde, near the Mehlasck-Zinten road, with his rear-guard at Körpen and Bornitt, towards the Passarge. He was not molested on the 6th by New, who, from Liebstadt, reached Wormditt, where he received an order from Napoleon to march on Landsberg, and form the left of the army in the battle which the obstinate resistance at Hof had led the Emperor to believe would be fought next day at Landsberg. Davout was, at first, ordered to march on Landsberg on the 7th for the expected battle, but was later diverted towards Eylau.[74] Napoleon still believed that Bernadotte was following, and would account for, the Prussians. As a matter of fact, Bernadotte, owning to the capture of the despatch of the 31st January, had only received orders on the 3rd February, and was still two marches behind, at Mohrungen.[75]

But Bennigsen had no intention of fighting at Landsberg. During the night he marched for Pr. Eylau. The rear-guard, under Bagration, did not leave Landsberg till 8 a.m., when, after an hour's fighting, it

72. The Prince Gallitzin, whose death in this action is mentioned by Wilson, was not the commander of the Russian cavalry, but a younger man of the same name who had just joined the army.

73. Soult (*Arch. Hist.*) gives the Russian loss at 8000, of whom 3000 were killed, and 1500 prisoners. It seems that this must be an exaggeration. His own losses he gives as—

Legrand's division	1750
Light cavalry	210
Totals	1960

but this takes no account of the losses among the dragoons and cuirassiers. He also gives the guns taken as 11. The Russian losses in the text are those given by Hoepfner (iii. 216).

74. *Davout*, pp. 156, 157.

75. *Bernadotte, Arch. Hist.* His marches in his fresh advance were: 4th February, Strasburg to Löbau; 5th, at Löbau; 6th, Löbau to Osterode; 7th, Osterode to Mohrungen; 7th Mohrungen to Reichertswalde.

was driven out by Murat and Soult. Bennigsen, marching, during the latter part of the night, in a single column on the Landsberg–Eylau road, was compelled to clear it by sending his heavy artillery round to the left to rejoin him at Eylau.

Napoleon promptly followed with Murat, Soult, and Augereau, countermanding the orders to Davout and Ney to join his right and left flanks at Landsberg. Ney was ordered to march from Landsberg on Kreuzburg.[76]

---

76. He was at Liebstadt on the 5th, on the 6th at Wormditt, behind the Drewenz (the small stream near Wormditt), with a detachment at Pr. Holland; on the 7th he bivouacked outside Landsberg, on the Kreuzberg road (Ney, *Arch. Hist.*, "*journaux de marche*").

CHAPTER 2

The Battle of Eylau

ACTION OF THE 7TH FEBRUARY

The road from Landsberg to Koenigsberg passes, for the first 9 miles, through alternate plain and forest, finally emerging, in a clearing, about a mile and a half before it reaches the large village of Preussisch Eylau. In front of this forest there stretches, to the north, east, and south, an undulating plain, the greatest elevation on which amounts to no more than a hillock. In the foreground, on the left of the road, is the lake of Tenknitten, extending half a mile north-west to the village of the same name; to the right is the Waschkeiten lake. The space of 1000 yards between the two lakes is occupied by slightly elevated ground, with a fairly marked height across the road.

Half a mile before the road reaches Eylau, it begins to descend a slope to the valley, in which the village is situated. Viewed from this point, the depression bears a strong resemblance to some of the open valleys of Norfolk and Suffolk.[1] The height of the near edge is inconsiderable; that of the farther side, beyond Pr. Eylau, still less. The substantial village lies chiefly in front, stretching some little way right and left of the road. Towards the right of it, the church and cemetery stand on a well-marked mound. The houses, as well as the church, were, in 1807, solidly constructed, and afforded good cover to a force defending them. Through the valley, from Rothenen a mile south-east of Eylau, past Althof two miles north-west of it, flows a little stream, the Pasmar. Under the near slope of the valley is a long marshy lake. There are several other ponds in the valley, and on the eastern plateau.

On Eylau converge the roads from Landsberg, Kreuzberg, Koenigsberg, Friedland, Bartenstein, and Heilsberg. Beyond the village the ground

---

1. Jomini describes the valley as "an undulating plain bounded on three sides by more accentuated country and hills, among which are several lakes" (*Vie de Napoleon*, ii. 360).

soon begins to rise again, and attains the crest of the opposite plateau at a distance of 1000 paces from the outskirts of Eylau. This side of the valley resembles the other in contour. Its crest is rather low on the Landsberg-Koenigsberg road, somewhat higher farther east by the village of Serpallen, where the highest point in the neighbourhood, the Kreegeberg, overlooks the whole scene. On the arc of a circle, drawn with the Eylau church as its centre and a radius of 2500 yards, will be found the village of Schloditten, on the Koenigsberg road; the hamlet of Anklappen on that to Domnau and Friedland; and Serpallen in the valley, a little to the left of the road to Bartenstein. Behind Schloditten is Schmoditten;[2] behind Anklappen lie Kutschitten and Lampasch; to the north of Serpallen is Klein Sausgarten: all places of importance in the great battle.

The horizon beyond Schmoditten is bounded by forest; there are extensive birch woods in the centre of the triangle, the angles of which are represented by Anklappen, Kutschitten, and Klein Sausgarten,—more woods beyond Serpallen, and between Rothenen and the western edge of the valley; behind the spectator is the forest through which has passed the road from Landsberg. In summer, all this scene is a sheet of ripening wheat and rye, interspersed with green meadows, and picked out by the darker colours of the woods, and by the blue of the lakes and ponds—a scene to which the horrors of war seem wholly foreign.[3] Very different was the view on this 7th of February: cold and desolate, much more appropriate as a setting to the bloody scenes which were to be enacted there in the next few hours. The whole surface of the country was wrapped in a white pall of deep snow, against the, as yet, unstained purity of which the black woods, the villages, and the troops[4] stood out in sharp relief. The undulations and the elevations, never very strongly marked, were even less discernible than when colour and shade were there to lend assistance to the eye.[5]

---

2. As will be seen, Dumas appears to have confused these two very similar names.

3. "In our pursuit of the Russians (in June) we passed by Eylau. Three months before, we had left the fields covered with snow and corpses; now, they presented a lovely carpet of green, studded with flowers" (*Marbot*, i. 276)

4. Larrey (p. 84) remarks that Baron Gros' picture of Napoleon at Eylau very correctly shows how the dead and wounded on the field showed out in sharp contrast to the background of snow (frontispiece).

5. See illustration of Eylau in this volume photographed from the Landsberg road in March, 1901, when the battlefield, as in February, 1807, was covered with snow. The picture of Napoleon at Eylau by Baron Gros conveys the same idea. It may be remarked that this large painting appears to represent the moment just before the attack on Eylau on the 7th. Bagration's troops are passing in retreat through the intervals of Barclay de Tolly's division, drawn up to cover the retreat, with guns posted on the small elevation in front of the church.

The lakes and streams were obliterated by the thick covering of snow which lay on their frozen surface. So firmly were they locked in the grasp of frost, and so completely concealed by the snow, that troops of all arms, horses, wagons, guns, passed over their frozen surface, without the men being aware that water lay beneath their feet. There was no repetition of the shelling of the ice at Austerlitz, which played such ghastly havoc with the Russians there.[6] The gunners knew not there was ice; had they known it, it is by no means certain that they could have broken it through the three feet or more of snow protecting it from all but a plunging fire which could not be brought, in that flat country, to bear on it.[7]

Such was the scene which met the eyes of Bennigsen's troops as they wearily left the forest, after their 9 miles night march from Landsberg, on the forenoon of 7th February.

Passing across the western plain and the valley, Bennigsen carried the main body of his army to the eastern slope, and there ranged it, ready for the great battle which he had determined to fight. To cover his operations,[8] he left a strong rear-guard on the Ziegelhof plateau, as that to the west was styled. This force was commanded by Bagration, who posted it thus.[9]

On the rising ground crossing the road, a short way after it passes the hamlet of Grünhofchen, was the horse artillery, commanding the mouth of the defile between the woods. Immediately behind the guns were, on the right, standing on the frozen surface of the Tenknitten lake, one grenadier regiment; in the centre, and on the left, two musketeer regiments. In second line was another grenadier regiment. In front of the guns, covering the whole of this line, and passing back, leftwards, to and along the north-western shore of the Waschkeiten lake, a jäger regiment was extended in line of skirmishers. Behind the Tenknitten lake, north of the road, was another musketeer regiment, with some artillery in front of it, on the slope down to the lake. Behind this advanced force,

---

6. Since this passage was originally written, Mr. J. H. Rose has shown that the Austerlitz incident has at least been greatly exaggerated.

7. As will be seen shortly, the 18th Regiment of Soult's corps came under artillery fire (chiefly grape, it is true), when on the ice, without its being broken.

8. This was one motive assuredly. Bennigsen also assigns, correctly no doubt, as his motive the protection of the line of march of his heavy artillery. Owing to his having to march from Landsberg on a single road, he was forced, in order to avoid blocking his column, to send his heavy guns by a more circuitous route to the north. (See Russian official account, printed by *Wilson*, p. 238).

9. Bennigsen began his retreat from Landsberg at dusk on the 6th, and was in position at Eylau by noon on the 7th (*Wilson*, p. 96).

not far from where the descent to the Eylau valley commences, were ranged the troops of the 8th division, their left resting on the Heilsberg road, their right on that of Landsberg. In front of the left were 14 guns, on the edge of the Waschkeiten lake. In the space between that lake and the long lake at the foot of the slope, 25 squadrons stood in three lines. On the right, beyond the Landsberg road, were 10 more squadrons. Farther to the right front, behind the village of Tenknitten, were posted the Petersburg dragoons, who had suffered such a disastrous defeat on the previous day. Barclay de Tolly was charged with the defence of Eylau itself. Part of his artillery held the church height on his left, covered by infantry in front and on the left. The rest of his infantry and artillery were in Eylau, and at the saw-mill on its right rear.

It was 2 p.m. when Murat's cavalry, followed by the head of Soult's corps, began to arrive at the edge of the woods about Grünhofchen. After the experience of the previous day at Hof, the cavalry did not hurry alone to the attack of the position. Soult sent forward on the left the 18th Infantry, on the right the 4th, against the ridge across the road.[10] Schinner's and Vivier's brigades, as they came up, moved to the right, through the wood to Grünberg farm, to turn the Russian left. Augereau, arriving later, was ordered to turn the enemy's right by Tenknitten. At first, however, the 18th and 46th were unsupported in their attack on the centre. The 18th, somewhat in advance of the 46th, crossed the end of the frozen Tenknitten lake under a heavy artillery fire. Changing direction to the right, against the Russian position, and already shaken, they were charged with the bayonet. To complete their discomfiture, the Petersburg dragoons, burning to avenge their overthrow at Hof, crossed the lake and fell impetuously on the left of the 18th, which had not time to form squares.[11] It suffered severely, and was thrown into complete disorder. Fortunately for this regiment, Klein's dragoons came on the scene, and, charging the Russians, relieved the pressure on it, though not till the disaster had occurred. Just after this catastrophe, the 46th reached the Russian front. It was attacked several times, but succeeded in maintaining order in its retirement.

---

10. This action is described in Soult's report, *Arch. Hist.*

11. According to Hoepfner (iii. 223) both battalions of the 18th were overthrown by this charge. Dumas (xviii. 7) says only one battalion was broken. This is also Napoleon's version (*Corr.* 11,796). Soult's report (Arch. Hist.) is not precise on the point. He admits the 18th lost one of its eagles, but says he believes it was buried in the snow when the regiment broke; it might be found at the bottom of the lake near the road, as it would have sunk when the ice melted. This remark shows that the 18th were actually on the frozen lake when attacked, and that artillery fire did not break the ice.

Soult, placing his guns on the rising ground about Scheweken and Grünhofchen, opened fire on the Russians. Schinner and Vivier had, by this time, got forward in the wood on the right, which had delayed their progress. Augereau, too, was moving on Tenknitten. When, therefore, the attack on the Russian centre on the road was renewed by the rest of the divisions of Leval and Legrand, supported by St. Hilaire's, the Russians, feeling the danger on both flanks, were already retiring on Bagration's main body near the edge of the valley.

Vivier and Schinner moved on both sides of the Waschkeiten lake. The former overpowered the cavalry between the lake and the valley, thus outflanking Bagration and compelling him to retire on Eylau. There his men passed through the intervals of Barclays troops, drawn out at and in front of the village.

Napoleon was now master of the whole plateau—from the forest to the edge of the valley. His loss had been so heavy that, three weeks later, when the Russians again returned to Eylau, they found a hillock, on the scene of Soult's first attempt, literally cased with dead bodies.[12] The opposing armies were ranged on opposite sides of the valley, into which, like a great bastion in front of the Russian line, protruded the position of Barclay de Tolly.

It was not within the scope of Napoleon's intentions to storm Eylau that night. He would have preferred to halt on the easily defensible position of the western plateau, until the arrival of Davout on his right, and of Ney on his left, should enable him to attack Bennigsen with his whole army. Bernadotte, he hoped, had relieved Ney of the pursuit of Lestocq. Into the assault of Eylau on the evening of the 7th he was forced by circumstances beyond his control. Part of the deserve cavalry followed the retreating Russians into and beyond the village, so did some of Soult's corps. The action there became so severe that it soon reached a stage at which it was impossible to break it off.[13]

---

12. *Wilson*, p. 96.

13. The statement in the text differs from most of the previous accounts, and requires proof. Wilson, Alison, Thiers, Jomini, and Hoepfner, all assume that Napoleon designed the attack on Eylau on the 7th. Dumas goes further, saying, "Napoleon, gaining the necessity of its (Eylau's) occupation, . . . ordered Soult to drive the enemy from it." The first piece of evidence in favour of the view adopted in the text is the statement of Marbot (i. 255), which, taken alone, would perhaps not outweigh the authorities quoted. Marbot, who was attached to Augereau's staff, positively states that he heard the Emperor remark to Augereau on the western plateau, "They wanted me to carry Eylau this evening, but I do not like night fighting; moreover, I do not wish to push my centre too far forward before Davout has come up with the right, and Ney with the left. I shall wait, (continued on next page)

As Bagration and Markow retreated through Eylau, they were covered by Barclay's men and guns in the gardens and houses of the village. Here Markow and Bagavout separated, the latter going towards Serpallen, the former turning to the left towards Schloditten.

Legrand's and part of Leval's division, both of Soult's corps, arrived in front of Eylau by the Landsberg road, and one regiment pushed through, but was promptly charged and driven back.[14] The rest en-

therefore, till to-morrow, on this high ground, which can be defended by artillery, and which offers an excellent position for our infantry. When Ney and Davout are in line, we can march simultaneously on the enemy." In this Augereau expressed his concurrence. Meanwhile, the Emperor's personal baggage having come up, was, owing to a misunderstanding carried forward into Eylau. The Russians began plundering it, Soult's men endeavoured to rescue it, and the enemy, believing a serious attack to be intended, brought up reinforcement,. The battle thus developed beyond the point at which it was possible to break it off. Napoleon's remark is, on the face of it, eminently reasonable, and such as might have been expected from him. Augereau's report makes no allusion to it; but, it must be remembered, he was on the sick-list when the report was written, and, in any case, he would not necessarily record a remark made to him personally, not concerning his own corps. The next item of evidence is the *Relation d'un Témoin Oculaire*. This pamphlet is attributed by Sir R. Wilson to Napoleon himself. It was published in Paris in 1807, and obviously must have been approved by the Emperor, if not inspired by him. On p. 9 the following remarks occur: "The dispositions for turning the enemy's rear-guard were no longer necessary once the rear-guard had rejoined the main army. The Emperor gave orders to remain in order of battle on the plateau of Eylau. But Vivier's brigade, which had been ordered to turn the left of the rear-guard, advanced to the Eylau cemetery, and there found itself engaged." The last item of evidence is Soult's account of the operations of his corps (*Arch. Hist.*). He says the Russians were followed into Eylau by part of the Reserve cavalry and by the 24th infantry of his own corps, which pushed into and beyond the village, but was driven back again. An impulse had been imparted to the troops, in consequence of which they got engaged in Eylau to such a degree that it was impossible to withdraw them without great risk. Besides, in the misery in which the troops were, Eylau, with its shelter and its supplies, was an irresistible attraction to them. Whatever the danger of the attack, it was impossible to withdraw the infantry. The whole tone of the report (dated Elbing, 15th November, 1807) is that of an apology for a movement which Soult felt to be undesirable, and knew was against the Emperor's wishes. The cumulative evidence of these statements of eye-witnesses, notwithstanding discrepancies in detail, appears to lead irresistibly to the conclusion that the storming of the village was forced upon the Emperor and Soult against their better judgment. Once taken, Eylau could not be abandoned. Besides, by this time, the Emperor appears to have been led to believe that Bennigsen was again retreating (Jomini, *Vie de Napoleon*, ii. 358).

14. It is a little difficult to say for certain what happened in the left part of Eylau. Soult (*Arch. Hist.*) says the 24th Regiment passed right through it, but, being attacked on the farther side, was driven back into the (continued on next page)

countered a strenuous resistance from Barclays infantry, from 2 guns at the junction of the Kreuzberg and Landsberg roads, and from the artillery in front of the church.

Whilst they were vainly endeavouring to get forward into the streets, Vivier's brigade was reforming in several columns on the ice-covered lake below the western heights. The bank on its eastern side sheltered them from the artillery at the cemetery. As these fresh troops, supported by St. Hilaire's division, advanced to the storm of the cemetery and church, the combat in the streets became more and more embittered and sanguinary. At 5 p.m. the church and cemetery were carried by storm, Barclay being severely wounded in the gallant defence which he made there. Vivier had previously succeeded in getting into the cemetery, but had been forced out by a counterattack. He now established himself in the church and cemetery, where his brigade spent the night surrounded by the dead and dying victims of the fearful struggle.[15] Bagration was preparing to evacuate the rest of the village, when Somow, with the 4th division, was sent forward from the main position beyond, to retake Eylau at any cost. Led by Bagration on foot, the division advanced to the attack in 3 columns. They had much to endure from the French infantry fire, and from the guns which swept the streets with grape. By 6 o'clock, nevertheless, they had succeeded in recapturing the village. Then came a sudden change. At 6.30, Bennigsen withdrew the 4th division again to the eastern heights, covering its retirement with the Archangel regiment of infantry in line of skirmishers, and with two battalions advanced, on its right, to the saw-mill. Barclay drew off to the left of Bagavout at Serpallen; and Eylau, once more evacuated, was quietly reoccupied by the French by 7 p.m.[16]

The firing on both sides died fitfully away as the Russians reached their station on the uneven edge of the valley. No attempt to follow them was made, but, presently, Napoleon moved Legrand's division just beyond Eylau, into the space between the Koenigsberg and the Friedland roads. Schinner's brigade was in the houses near the church; Ferey's held the left of the village.

outskirts. This seems to lend some colour to the assertion of Wilson (p. 96), that the village was at first evacuated under a misapprehension of orders, and then re-occupied.

15. Soult's report, *Arch. Hist.*

16. Dumas fixes the final occupation of Eylau so late as 10 p.m. (xviii. 8). Wilson says that at the commencement of the French advance on Eylau the village was evacuated by the Russians, owing to some misapprehension of orders (*Wilson*, p. 96). (*Vide supra*, p. 167, note.)

From the church height towards Rothenen, St Hilaire's division bivouacked in the open. Beyond him, on the extreme right, Milhaud's cavalry occupied the ground in front of Rothenen and Zehsen. Grouchy's and Klein's dragoons were behind Eylau, left and right respectively of the Landsberg road. On Ferey's left, were the cavalry brigades of Colbert, Guyot, Bruyère, and d'Hautpoult. Still farther to the left, was Durosnel's cavalry of Augereau's corps.

In 2nd line Augereau's corps bivouacked in and in front of Storchnest and Tenknitten. The Guard infantry was on the heights occupied in the afternoon by Bagration's main body; the cavalry of the Guard on the right of the Landsberg road, in line with its infantry.[17]

Bennigsen's army was thus disposed for the night. His first line extended along the heights from Schloditten to Serpallen, passing across the Friedland road at a distance of only 1000 paces from Eylau.[18] The ground, it must be remarked, was not an even glacis-like slope, such as was that in front of St. Privat in 1870. It was a series of hillocks and slight transverse depressions, like that of the Suffolk valley, with which comparison has been made. The descent on the French side was similar. On the extreme right, commencing from Schloditten, Markow commanded 12 cavalry regiments, with 6 more somewhat in advance of his line. Beyond his right were some Cossacks, seeking communication with Lestocq. From his left, the line was continued by 11 infantry regiments, each with two battalions deployed in front;[19] and the 3rd, a little distance in rear, in column. In front of Serpallen was Bagavout, with 2 infantry and 2 hussar regiments. There, too, was what remained of Barclays force. In 2nd line were 10 regiments of infantry in column at battalion intervals.

In these two lines were the 2nd, 3rd, 5th, 7th and 8th divisions. The 4th had halted, in its retirement, across the Koenigsberg and Friedland

---

17. This is the position assigned to the Guard by the "*témoin oculaire*," whom there is no reason to doubt in this case. Hoepfner (iii. 228) places the Guard cavalry behind Ferey, and next to Klein. He also says there were 18 line regiments of infantry with the Guard on the western heights.

18. Wilson (p. 98) describes the Russian position as about two miles long and one deep, bounded by fir woods, except in rear of the right and in continuation of the left. Pr. Eylau had no species of work to protect it, and was in a hollow about 300 yards in front of the Russian right centre on the hill which rose above the village so as to overtop the houses.

19. Jomini (*Art of War*, p. 295) remarks that this was also the order used by Napoleon at the Tagliamento. It is, he says, "suitable for the offensive-defensive, because the first line pours a powerful fire upon the enemy, which must throw him into more or less confusion, and the troops formed in column may debouch through the intervals and fall with advantage upon him while in disorder."

roads, in front of the main line. The 3rd line consisted of 5 regiments of infantry of the 14th division, and formed the reserve in front of Anklappen, under Kamenskoi.[20] The rest of the cavalry was behind the centre and left wing, partly deployed, partly in column.

The right was commanded by Tutchkow, the centre by Sacken, the left by Tolstoi, the reserve by Dochtorow, the cavalry by Gallitzin.[21] Sixty horse artillery guns were at Anklappen.[22] The rest of the artillery (400 guns and howitzers) was ranged in front of the 1st line, but behind the advanced position of the 4th division. There was a great battery of 70 heavy guns opposite Eylau, another of 60 on the right, and a third of 40 between the centre battery and Kl. Sausgarten. These three great masses of guns were in addition to the more widely distributed batteries along the line.

In these positions, the two armies prepared to pass the night following the terrible combat of the evening, and preceding the far more awful struggle of the morrow. It requires a strong effort of the imagination to picture the horrors of that night. The valley and the heights on either side, deeply buried in snow, were lit by the bivouac fires of 120,000 men. The flames flickered in the icy north wind which swept along the positions, carrying with it the smoke from the damp wood, and the constantly falling snow. Not even the pale light of all these hundreds of fires could impart warmth to this arctic scene. The men crowded round the fires for warmth, hardly for rest; for what rest was possible in such circumstances? Between the opposing lines of fires stood the outposts of the armies, and the sentries, who, on their cheerless posts, must have thought with envy even of their companions behind them. So close were the main lines that—

The fix'd sentinels almost receive,
The secret whispers of each other's watch;
Fire answers fire; and through their paly flames
Each battle sees the others umber'd face.[23]

---

20. Quite a different person, of course, from the commander-in-chief of the beginning of the campaign.

21. Bennigsen had 7 divisions, viz. the 2nd, 3rd, 4th, 5th, 7th, 8th and 14th. Sedmaratzki, with the 6th, was left at Goniondz, and the two divisions which had come from Moldavia were between the Narew and the Bug. The 1st was the Guard, not yet at the front.

22. The idea of maintaining a separate artillery reserve has, in modern times, been abandoned. Regarding this reserve at Eylau, Jomini remarks (*Art of War*, p. 289) that it had a powerful influence in enabling Bennigsen to recover himself when his line had been broken through between the centre and the left.

23. Shakespeare, *K. Hen. V.*, act iv., chorus.

The French had some shelter in the houses and in the blood-stained church of Eylau. Milhaud's men were protected by Rothenen, Augereau's by Tenknitten and Storchnest. A large proportion, however, had no means of guarding themselves from the bitter blast and the frequent snowstorms. If the sufferings of the French were great, far greater were those of their enemy. Schloditten and Serpallen could only shelter a few on the extremities; Anklappen was a mere hamlet, in which Bennigsen and his staff could scarce find accommodation. During the night, the cold increased in intensity; the thermometer, which stood at 14° Fahrenheit. on the evening of the 7th, had by morning fallen to 2° above zero.[24] The sufferings of the wounded were terribly aggravated by the cold. In Eylau, a hospital had been extemporised in the largest building. In the morning, when the village was no longer suitable, temporary hospitals were established in barns on the Landsberg road; but the straw, and even the thatch, had been taken from them for the cavalry horses, so that they were exposed on all sides, and the sufferers had to be laid on the remaining debris of straw, sprinkled as they were with snow. So intense was the frost, that the very instruments fell from the hands of the attendants as they waited on the operating surgeons.[25]

Food was lacking to both sides. In the villages nothing was left but potatoes and water. Augereau and his staff with difficulty obtained a loaf or two of bread.[26] The provision trains had not been able to follow closely the long French column, marching from Landsberg on a Single road. The Russians suffered still more severely from hunger and cold. For days previously "the soldiers had to prowl and dig for the buried food of the peasantry; so that, between search of provision and duty, they had scarce time to lie down, and when they did, they had no other bed than the snow, no shelter but the heavens, and no covering but their rags."[27]

If the French commissariat, on which Napoleon had lavished so much care, was unable to provide his army promptly with the necessaries of life, how much worse must have been the case of the Russians, whose commissariat arrangements were almost non-existent! How terrible must have been the sufferings of their wounded, for whose relief on the battlefield there was, at present, no provision!

---

24. *Larrey*, iii. p. 37. The temperatures given by him in terms of Reaumur's scale have been reduced to those of Fahrenheit's for the text.
25. *Larrey*, iii. 38.
26. *Marbot*, i. 256.
27. *Wilson*, 94.

The man on whose boundless and unscrupulous ambition all these miseries were due, Napoleon, having completed the arrangement of his army, retired to a house in Eylau, whence the most staring evidences of the mortal combat had been hastily removed. There, sitting on a chair, he slept for some hours in the midst of all the carnage, the dying and the dead.[28] All around, his men were pillaging the village, and ransacking it for food.[29] If his hopes were buoyed by visions of another Austerlitz or Jena on the morrow, he still had ever before him the possibility of another Pultawa. He alludes more than once, in his correspondence from Poland, to the fate of Charles XII. He had met with unexpected resistance at Pultusk, at Golymin, at Bergfried, and at Hof. Might not the coming battle result in defeat?

Bennigsen, too, was doubtless full of apprehension. Whatever he might have written of his previous battles, he knew well that he had not yet won a real victory. Were he decisively defeated, his army, driven upon Koenigsberg, might be ruined and compelled to surrender in the *cul de sac* between that fortress, the sea, and the Curisches-Haff. On the other hand, he knew that Austria was only waiting for a distinct, not necessarily decisive, defeat of the French to throw in her lot with the allies. Now, if ever he was to have it, was his chance to win eternal renown by a victory over the hitherto unconquerable Emperor. To

---

28. This is the generally accepted version (see *Alison*, vii. 347, and *Thiers*, vii. 415.) The plan of the battle in the account of the "eye-witness" shows, as Napoleon's sleeping place, on the night's of the 7th, 8th, and 9th, the plateau where his Guard were. If it is true that Napoleon himself was the author of this work, there is an obvious reason for his not admitting that he slept in Eylau on the 7th, and more than a mile to the rear on the 8th. The admission would imply that the results of the battle of the 8th had been such as to render Eylau unsafe. On the other hand, when the Guard were present, the Emperor usually slept in their midst, though on the eve of Jena the 40th of the line was the regiment honoured. On this occasion, he would have had to sleep in the open to be with the Guard. Once more, in favour of his seeping in Eylau, is Jomini's (*Vie de Napoleon*, ii. 358) assertion that Murat reported the enemy to be in retreat. It is not certain at what hour the news, if given, was ascertained to be incorrect. If he believed in the retreat, the head of his army was the best place for Napoleon. De Fezensac (p. 145) was at Eylau on the night of the 7th-8th, and mentions Berthier's being in the village. Presumably, Napoleon also was there, especially as de Fezensac, who left the village at 8 a.m. on the 8th, mentions the Emperor mounting his horse about that time, as if he himself had seen it. The matter is finally disposed of by Soult's report of the operations of the 4th Corps (*Arch. Hist.*). He says that the Emperor fixed his headquarters in Eylau, where he and Murat had the honour of joining him.

29. "The total pillage of a town, taken as Eylau had been, can scarcely be avoided" (Jomini, *Vie de Napoleon*, ii. 358).

Bennigsen defeat meant the possible loss of an army; to Napoleon it meant, not only the loss of his army, but, possibly, the destruction of the military despotism which he had built up with such infinite care and skill. So mighty were the issues which hung upon the result of the approaching struggle.

The strength of the forces[30] arrayed against one another, at and near Eylau, has been the subject of most contradictory statements. On full consideration of the various accounts and authorities, it will not probably be far wide of the mark to take the forces on the field at daybreak

---

30. To commence with general accounts, the following numbers are given by the authors named:

	French	Russians/Prussians
Alison (vii. pp. 345, note, and 344)	80,000	75,000 (including 10,000 Prussians)
Thiers (vii. pp. 414, 415)	63,000	90,000
Dumas (xviii. 9 and 12)	68,000	80,000
Wilson (pp, 98, 99)	90,000	60,000 (Russians only)
Plotho (pp. 69, 70)	90,000	65,000-70,000 (Russians + Prussians)
Rustow (i. 316)	69,000	64,000

Bennigsen, in his official account (*Wilson*, p. 238), says: "I marched out of Landsberg the 25th January (i.e. 6th February, new style), my army only consisting of 70,000 men, different detachments of it having been separated." He plainly does not include, in the 70,000, either Lestocq's corps or the detachment sent to Heilsberg. The latter consisted of 3000 men (*ibid.*, pp. 93, 94), but may have been reduced to 2000 by the fighting at and near Heilsberg. Lestocq reached the field with about 7000 men, including those he left in Althof to oppose Ney (he had 5584 against Davout alone (see *ibid.*, p. 106, and *Hoepfner*, iii. 235). Thus there would appear to have reached the field between 2 p.m. on the 7th and the evening of the 8th, about 72,000 Russians and 7000 Prussians, say 78,000 in all, after allowing for losses on the march from Landsberg. It is far from clear on what grounds Wilson reduces the Russians to 60,000 in face of the despatch which he publishes. Bennigsen puts Napoleon's forces at 90,000. In an article "More Light on St. Helena," by Sir Herbert Maxwell, in the Cornhill Magazine, for January, 1901, the following passage occurs: "In answer to a question put to him (i.e. to Napoleon, by Sir George Cockburn) relative to the greatest number of men he ever commanded, he said he had 180,000 at the battle of Eylau, and 1000 pieces of cannon. The allies had nearly the same number" (p. 31). There must clearly have been some misunderstanding here. It is beyond the possibility of doubt that Napoleon had not 100,000 men at Eylau, much less 180,000. The most hostile chronicler does not rate his number over 90,000, and all are agreed that his guns were inferior in number to the 460 of Bennigsen. The numbers given in the article are about what Napoleon commanded at Wagram, which was also the battle in which he had the largest army. Is it not possible that he misunderstood Sir G. Cockburn's question, or that the latter may have confused the name Löbau, used in connexion with Wagram, with Eylau? The "*témoin oculaire*" (p. 11) says 80,000 Russians were drawn up in a space sufficient only for 30,000. From the statements of the strength of corps in February in (continued on next page)

on the 8th February at 67,000 Russians and 49,000 French. Napoleon was expecting the arrival of Davout, with 15,100, on his right, and of Ney, with 14, 500, on his left. To join Bennigsen's right, Lestocq, facing Ney at Hussehnen, with 9000 Prussians and Russians, was under orders to march, as quickly as possible, *via* Althof, to Schloditten.

---

the Archives Historiques, it is not possible to arrive directly at a conclusion as to the French strength. The statements are, for the most part, noted as being correct up to a much later date than February 7th, generally the end of March or beginning of April. By that date, the losses of Eylau had been repaired and the corps raised to a greater strength by troops from France and Italy. The only course left is to work, as Alison did, on the January statements. The strength of the corps which took part in the battle are thus shown in the statements for January, the latest available before the date of the battle (statements, *Arch. Hist.*).

Imperial Guard (excluding Oudinot)	9,199	of all arms on 20th January
3rd Corps (Davout)	19,757	of all arms on 15th January
4th Corps (Soult)	19,643	of all arms on 1st January
5th Corps (Ney)	16,039	of all arms on 1st January
7th Corps (Augereau)	14,966	of all arms on 15th January
Reserve cavalry (excluding the 4th dragoon division, with Bernadotte, and the 5th with Savary)	17,706	of all arms on 1st February
Total	97,310	

For Davout's corps, we have his own statement of the strength at Eylau, after deducting losses and the detachment at Myszienec, viz. 15,500. Soult lost at Bergfried at least 700, at Hof he admits 1960. He must have lost quite 3000 altogether in the advance to Eylau. Ney can hardly have lost less than 1500 at Waltersdorf and the other actions. Augereau's loss may not have been above 500, as he had little fighting in the advance. The Reserve cavalry fought every day of the march on Eylau, and its loss can hardly be taken at under 2500. It suffered severely at Hof. The guard lost little, say 200. Deducting these losses, and taking Davout's corps at the figure he gives, the French strength is reduced to the following round figures:

Guard	9,000
Davout	15,100
Soult	16,750
Ney	14,500
Augereau	14,500
Murat	15,200
Total	85,050

But some allowance must he made for stragglers and detachments. On the whole, it is improbable that Napoleon had much over 82,000 or 83,000 men. Of these, 29,600 (Ney and Davout) were not on the field at daybreak on the 8th. In calculating the French strength at that hour, the losses of the 7th must be deducted. These were probably quite 4000, therefore they had not more (continued on next page)

Bennigsen was astir at 5 a.m. He directed Dochtorow to withdraw the 4th division from the position, towards Eylau, which it had occupied during the night; also the 7th division from its place in the line. With these two divisions, and the reserve at Anklappen (14th division), he formed two deep columns, each with a front of one battalion, and placed them on a height behind his centre, on either side of the Friedland road. The Archangel regiment moved back from the sawmill to the right wing, whilst Markow filled the gap left in the line of battle by the withdrawal to the reserve of the 7th division.

Napoleon also, now convinced that Bennigsen had no intention of continuing his retreat behind the Pregel, made changes in the position of his corps. The Guard infantry, and artillery moved forward from its bivouac to a position behind the church. Augereau's corps took post, in columns of brigades, with its left about 1000 paces behind the church. At 8 a.m. it again moved forward to the line of the church, on which its left rested. Desjardins' division (9 battalions) was in 1st, Heudelet's (8 battalions) in 2nd line. To make room for Augereau, St. Hilaire, with 8 battalions, moved to his right, and formed line in front of Milhaud's cavalry (18 squadrons); Legrand and Schinner were in front of and in Eylau; Vivier and Ferey extended the line from the left of Eylau to the windmill heights in front of the saw-mill.

Behind Augereau, were d'Hautpoult's 12 squadrons of cuirassiers, to the right of the Guard infantry. Behind him were 12 squadrons of the Guard cavalry, and, on their right, 12 squadrons of Grouchy's dragoons. Klein took Milhaud's place in rear of St. Hilaire, and Milhaud moved to the right. The light Cavalry took post on the left, from the windmill height towards Althof. It comprised the division of Lasalle and the brigades of Bruyère, Guyot, Colbert, and Durosnel.

One regiment of Guard infantry, the 18th of the line, and 2 guns remained, in reserve, at the bivouac between Tenknitten and Was-

---

than about 48,000 or 49,000 men. From Bennigsen's force of 78,000, must be deducted 7000 Prussians, and (say) 4000 for losses on the 7th. This leaves him 67,000 at the same hour. Hoepfner (iii. 227) allows him only 58,000, but there seems no sufficient reason to disbelieve Bennigsen's own statement that 70,000 marched from Landsberg, besides the detachment at Heilsberg. The total allied forces Hoepfner (iii. 235) puts at 63,500, the French at 80,000 (iii. 229). The fairest conclusion seems to be that Napoleon had a superiority of about 4000 or 5000 in numbers, which was counteracted by the superiority of 110 guns on the other side. The strength of the two armies was, therefore, approximately equal. Up to 11 or 12 on the 8th, Napoleon was decidedly the weaker; he was not the stronger until quite the end of the battle, when Ney had arrived.

chheiten. The artillery was ranged along the whole front, from opposite Serpallen to the saw-mill. The Emperor took his stand near the church. Day broke gloomy and wild. No "sun of Austerlitz," drawing off the morning mists and exhilarating the men, rose in front of the French army. Low, heavy clouds, swept across the grey sky by a gusty and freezing wind, from time to time discharged their snowy contents with violence in the faces of the shivering soldiers. At such times, so dark became the atmosphere that the Russians could not even distinguish Eylau.[31] The snow prevented the commanders from seeing their troops, the howling north wind rendered it impossible for the soldiers to hear the word of command. At times, it was not possible to see ten yards off. The action at such moments had the character of a night attack.[32]

In the midst of this turmoil of the elements, before Napoleon had completed his last arrangements, Bennigsen, about 8 a.m., commenced the battle with a tremendous artillery fire directed on Eylau. The French, in and behind the village, were, to some extent, sheltered by the houses and by the mounds which closed up to it.[33] The Russians, on the other hand, standing out, when the atmosphere was clear, in sharp relief against the white snow on the bare slope, without any cover whatever, were exposed from head to foot to the fire of the French guns.[34]

The Russian fire, at first somewhat wild,[35] increased in intensity, as did that of the French. The preponderance in numbers of the Russian guns made up for the inferiority of the marksmanship.

Despite the awful fire, the French left pushed forward, whilst the centre and right gained the slight elevations in front of the Bartenstein road. The light cavalry, on the left, got as far forward as the fulling-mill on the stream, 500 yards below the saw-mill. Legrand, advancing to the storm of Tutchkow's position, was met in front by two infantry regiments of the Russian right wing, and charged in left flank by 2 dragoon regiments. He was driven back towards Eylau with considerable loss. Napoleon, thinking the Russians meditated the recapture of the windmill height, and an advance against Eylau from that direction, sought to disengage his left by an advance from his right.[36] With this

31. *Hoepfner*, iii. 237.
32. *Davout*, pp. 169-171.
33. *Wilson*, p. 101; Marbot, i. 257.
34. *Wilson*, p. 98.
35. *Wilson*, p. 101.
36. *Hoepfner*, iii. 240.

object in view, he directed St. Hilaire to move forward, bearing off somewhat to his right, whilst Augereau acted in like manner.[37] By this movement St. Hilaire would come into touch with Davout, who was now gradually coming up, and the army, pivoting on Eylau and wheeling to the left, would drive in the Russian left wing. It was soon after 10 a.m.,[38] when this advance began. At that moment a terrible snowstorm burst upon the field. The snow, driven full in the faces of Augereau's infantry, blinded them, and caused them to lose all sense of direction. Instead of bearing to their right, as ordered, Desjardins' division, followed by Heudelet's, took a direction to the left, towards the Friedland road. They thus passed partially in front of the batteries at Eylau, which, in the darkness, fired on their own troops.[39] The corps thus diverged rapidly from St. Hilaire's, which had kept the prescribed line. Presently it found itself, unexpectedly, close in front of the Russian line, at the point where the right wing joined the centre. Augereau had the leading brigade of each division deployed, the second behind it in squares. One battalion, which had gone more to the right, was alone in the midst of the Russian position. The corps artillery was at the church.

Desjardins and Heudelet were met by an overwhelming fire of grape from the great central battery, which was alone sufficient to disorder them and cause immense losses.[40] Seeing their advance, Bennigsen had moved forward part of his two great reserve columns. This

---

37. The "*témoin oculaire*" defines the Emperor's intention as being that Augereau should join St. Hilaire's left, so that the two might form a line oblique to that of the enemy, uniting Davout to Eylau.

38. St. Hilaire, quoted by Soult in his report (*Arch. Hist.*), says it was 10 a.m. when he received the order for his advance. St. Hilaire's division was practically taken from Soult's command on this day, and kept under the Emperor's direct orders. Soult, therefore, incorporates St. Hilaire's report in his own, which deals with the action of the other two divisions (Legrand's and Leval's). A report (*Arch. Hist.*) by Parmentier, who became chief of the staff of the 7th Corps after Eylau, gives 8 o'clock as the time when Augereau moved to the line of the church, and 8.30 as the hour at which the advance commenced. St. Hilaire's account seems the more probable.

39. *Marbot*, i. 257.

40. "Desjardins' division was half destroyed by grape and by the sabre; Heudelet's fared no better" (Jomini, *Vie de Napoleon*, ii. 360). In the Archives Historiques there is a report from Compans, who succeeded temporarily to Augereau's command, showing how frightful must have been the losses of the division. In the first place, he gives a list of about 30 officers killed and wounded; but this only includes regimental officers of and above the rank of *chef de bataillon* and the general's staff. It goes on: "Each division showed in the evening only about 700 men present." They had gone into action 7000 strong each! Of course, many (continued on next page)

body, after firing a volley in the faces of the shaken French, charged with the bayonet. Simultaneously, a brigade of the 4th division and the Russian cavalry came upon the unhappy French corps. No troops could withstand such an onslaught in front and on both flanks, especially when the Russian cavalry were in their midst before they were perceived through the snow. Almost every regiment was broken; the whole mass fled in the wildest confusion, followed, bayoneted, sabred by the victorious Russians. As the snow cleared, Augereau—of whom Napoleon said that he wearied even with a day of victory,—wounded, ill,[41] disheartened, saw the remnants of his corps pouring back into Eylau in broken detachments. One regiment, the ill-fated 14th,[42] was still on the slope, formed in a rough square on a small mound, surrounded on all sides by infantry, cavalry, and Cossacks, fired into by musketry and artillery, stabbed by the long lances of the Cossacks, sabred, suffering every conceivable woe, yet gallantly fighting to the death. The marshal had not a battalion in condition to attempt its rescue. He sent, in succession, the officers of his staff to urge the 14th to retreat if possible. Two of them disappeared in the hosts of the enemy, and were heard of no more. At last, Marbot succeeded in reaching the doomed regiment. Retreat was impossible. The eagle was carried off by Marbot, though he nearly lost his life in doing so. Firm to the last, the isolated regiment fought, unsupported, refusing to surrender.[43] Not one officer and scarcely a soldier escaped.

Napoleon, from the church, watched the course of this awful disaster to Augereau on his left, whilst he saw St. Hilaire, on his right, not

---

stragglers must have turned up later, but the remark shows the utter demoralization of the corps. Augereau's official report (*Arch. Hist.*) admits a loss of 929 killed and 4271 wounded—total 5200. This takes no account of prisoners, and even so it is, perhaps, below the mark. Jomini says Augereau's corps found that they were at a great disadvantage against cavalry, as their muskets had been so damped by the snow as often to fail to go off (*Art of War*, p. 305).

41. On the morning of the 8th February Augereau sent a note to Napoleon, saying he was too ill to command in the field any longer, and proposed, with the Emperor's permission, to retire that day. Napoleon, in reply, requested him to keep the command for one day longer. Meanwhile, the battle had begun, and Augereau sent another note, to say that he would be with his corps even if he had to go on to the field in a sledge—a mode of conveyance which he actually did employ till he reached his corps. He retired from the field about 4 p.m. (*Arch. Hist.*, daily correspondence).

42. It had led Augereau's advance (*Marbot*, i. 257). It was the regiment which had stormed the bridge at Kolozomb on the 24th December, having its colonel, Savary, killed there. The snowstorm cleared off after half an hour (*Témoin Oculaire*, p. 13.).

43. *Marbot*, i. 263, etc.

destroyed, it is true, but checked, his left attacked by cavalry in the gap between it and Augereau's corps, unable to make any progress.

The triumphant Russians, following on the heels of Augereau's ruined corps, were breaking into Eylau. Even they, with the snowstorm at their backs, had partly lost their way. One *"colonne perdue,"* as Napoleon described it,[44] which he estimates at 4000 to 6000 men, had wandered into the western street of Eylau, and had approached close to the position of the Emperor. Behind him, the Guard was moving forward to his rescue. Beyond the Russian column, Bruyère's cavalry, by direction of Murat, was preparing to charge it in rear. The Russians were actually amongst the French hospitals in the barns in rear of Eylau. The terrified wounded who could walk were endeavouring to escape. Even the others, trying vainly to follow them, were only induced, by Larrey and his assistants expressing loudly their intention of remaining where they were, to desist from the vain attempt.[45] The Emperor was in the most imminent danger of death or capture. A stray bullet, a little more hurry by the Russian column, might have changed the whole history of Europe. Napoleon alone, in the midst of all this confusion, standing on the mound with only his staff and a single squadron, his personal guard, maintained his calm and his presence of mind.

Before the Guard infantry[46] could reach the spot, the Russians would be upon him. The Guard refused to fire; they considered it was their duty to charge with the bayonet without firing;[47] they were blind to the consequences of delay. Every instant gained was of vital importance to their Emperor. He employed the only means he had to gain a few moments. The squadron of his personal guard was ordered to charge. Rushing upon almost certain death, with loud shouts of *"Vive l'Empereur,"* this little band of heroes fell furiously on the head of the Russian column. It was the attack of the pigmy upon the giant, but it gained the necessary time. Before this squadron was exterminated, the Guard had reached with the bayonet the front, Bruyère with the sabre the rear of the Russians. Their destruction was inevitable, and was as complete as had been that of Augereau's larger force. The latter's corps had been wiped out. Marbot goes so far as to say that it had but 3000 men left out of 15,000.[48]

---

44. *Commentaires de Napoleon.*

45. *Larrey*, iii. 40.

46. A battalion under Dorsenne was in front, and made the attack (*Dumas*, xviii. 20; *Témoin Oculaire*, p, 13).

47. *Témoin Oculaire*, p. 13, and *Dumas*, xviii. 20.

48. *Marbot*, i. 257. Hoepfner (iii.244), with more exactitude, states Augereau's loss at 929 killed and 4271 wounded—total 5200. This is Augereau's own figure (*Arch. Hist.*).

The situation of the French centre—Davout not yet having come up in force on the right, Ney being still far behind on the left, Soult's corps repulsed, Augereau's destroyed—was most critical. Napoleon recognised that only heroic measures could save him from destruction. Bennigsen failed to see that now, before Davout could bring substantial help, he still had time for the attack with superior forces of the French left, rolling it up on the centre. As soon as the Emperor saw the formation of the gap between St. Hilaire and Augereau, due to the latter's false direction, he ordered Murat to place himself at the head of the cavalry reserve,[49] and, followed by Bessières with the Guard cavalry, to make a supreme effort against the Russian centre with this treat body of 70 or 80 squadrons.[50] In such circumstances Murat showed to his greatest advantage. Splendidly mounted, in gorgeous uniform, surrounded by a staff only second to himself in brilliancy, his countenance inflamed with the lust of battle, he was the beau-ideal of the cavalry leader. Grouchy's dragoons, moving out over the ground beyond the Bartenstein road, crashed into the right flank of the Russian cavalry which had repulsed St. Hilaire, scattering it in all directions. Grouchy himself had his horse killed, but was remounted by an *aide-de-camp*. Rallying after the charge, he again led his 2nd brigade to support his 1st[51] Milhaud, at the same time, faced Bagavout's detachment, at and behind Serpallen which it had to evacuate. Having defeated the cavalry on the flank of St. Hilaire, Grouchy's dragoons, led by Murat in person, wheeled to their left against the cavalry of the Russian centre, which was now brought forward to meet them. On his right, Murat was joined by d'Hautpoult's cuirassier division, and this great line of cavalry, followed by others, poured in successive waves up the slope.

The Russian cavalry, going down before the shock, were driven back

---

49. "A commander may sometimes feel obliged to push his cavalry forward alone, but generally the best time for charging a line of infantry is when it is already engaged with opposing infantry. The battles of Marengo, Eylau, Borodino, and several others prove this" (Jomini, *Art of War*, p. 305).

50. Murat's report (Arch. Hist.) shows as engaged on this day, in this part of the field—2nd division cuirassiers, 1st, 2nd, 3rd dragoon divisions
These may be taken, roughly, at—

2nd cuirassier division	1900
1st dragoon	2000
2nd	2200
3rd	3100
Guard cavalry	1500
Total	10,700

51. Grouchy's report, *Arch. Hist.*

upon their infantry. Murat's portion of the line was met by fresh cavalry, and again compelled to retire: d'Hautpoult's heavier horses and men broke through everything. As the Russian horsemen scattered to the right and left of him, they were charged in flank by fresh lines of cuirassiers, and cut to pieces. D'Hautpoult, reckless of grape, of infantry fire, and the bayonet, fired by the praise he had received from the Emperor for his action at Hof, burst through the line of guns, sabring the gunners, or forcing them to seek shelter under their pieces. On rode the cuirassiers through the first line of infantry where one battalion, striving to resist by force this line of steel-clad warriors, was ridden over by them. Through the second line they forced their way. It was only when they had reached the reserves, standing with their backs to the Anklappen woods, that the charge had expended its force, after passing over 2500 yards.[52]

Bessières, following with the Guard cavalry, the chasseurs in 1st line, and joined by Grouchy, who had been checked by the Russian 2nd line when d'Hautpoult passed through it, fell upon the Russians, as they began to reform behind the cuirassiers, again carrying death into their ranks. Joined by the 5th cuirassier regiment and the mounted grenadiers, this second wave of cavalry again broke through the two Russian lines before it lost its force. The men and horses, exhausted and breathless from their long gallop and the tremendous exertions of the fight, were surrounded by the Russian cavalry, infantry, and Cossacks reassembling after their defeat. Twice broken, the Russian lines had, with indomitable courage, twice re-formed behind the intruding cavalry.[53] The French had to cut their way back as they had come. Exhausted cuirassiers of d'Hautpoult's division, which had gone the farthest, went down before the lances of the Cossacks, who could not have resisted them for a moment when fresh. Some broke back direct in the line by which they had come, others, passing behind the Russian lines, rejoined the French left; very many met their death in the midst of the Russian army. The brave d'Hautpoult himself received his death wound.[54]

---

52. Grouchy's report, *Arch. Hist.*

53. Jomini remarks that the retirement was as difficult as the advance, for the Russian troops re-formed, facing to their rear, behind the French cavalry (*Vie de Napoleon,* ii. 361).

54. "A regiment of French cuirassiers had, during the storm, gained an interval in the Russian line between their centre and left wing; but the Cossacks and some hussars, immediately as they were perceived, bore down upon them. The cuirassiers, apparently like men stupefied by the magazine of their own enterprise, and unprepared for success, rushed with a considerable detour through the rear of the camp, and then turned towards the right of the Russian right wing, but their bodies successively tracked the course, and only 18 escaped alive" (*Wilson*, p. 193).

This tremendous charge, costly though it had been, had yet served its purpose in checking the ardour of the Russian centre, thus enabling Napoleon to hold his own, whilst he anxiously awaited Davout's turning movement on the right.[55] He had, besides the cavalry, his artillery, Soult's corps, seriously reduced in numbers, the remnant of Augereau's, and the Guard.[56] The last-named had not been seriously engaged, and was unshaken. Augereau's troops assembled to the right of Eylau, the cavalry reserve more towards Kl. Sausgarten with Klein in 1st, Grouchy in 2nd, and d'Hautpoult in 3rd line. The Guard infantry was midway between Eylau and Serpallen; the Guard cavalry on the right of the infantry, behind the reserve cavalry. The left wing remained as before. It was now about 11 a.m. Till noon, Napoleon held on determinedly to Eylau and the line of the Bartenstein road. After that hour, Bennigsen had his hands full elsewhere, and the battle became little more than an artillery duel in the direction of Eylau. The tide of victory on which Bennigsen had so far floated was about to ebb.

Davout, at 2 p.m. on the 7th, had received orders from Berthier[57] to take position, in column, on the road from Bartenstein, so as to have the head of his column at a distance of about 3 miles from Eylau. His divisions, accordingly bivouacked in these positions: Friant's between Perschen and Beisleiden, about 4 miles from Eylau; Morand at Zohlen, a short way in rear; Gudin, near Bartenstein, 10 miles from Eylau. Marulaz, with the light cavalry of the corps, joined Friant and Davout, from the neighbourhood of Eylau, after Soult had taken up his position.[58]

---

55. The cavalry charge was, on a far larger scale, almost as desperate a remedy as the charge of Bredow's brigade at Mars la Tour, on the 16th August, 1870. The loss in Murat's charge cannot be precisely ascertained, but Grouchy gives his alone at nearly 250 killed and wounded. There were engaged in this charge on the French side one division of cuirassiers, three of dragoons, and the Guard cavalry. The cuirassiers lost more heavily than the others. Probably the total losses of the reserve cavalry were somewhere between 1000 and 1500. Even after the charge, they suffered heavily from the Russian artillery, under whose fire they stood all day.

56. "At 11 a.m. Soult's corps had suffered much; Augereau's, so to speak, no longer existed. All was lost but for the firm face I maintained for three hours, at the cemetery, with the Guard, the cavalry, and the artillery, which I myself directed" (Jomini, *Vie de Napoleon*, p. 366).

57. Davout, p. 158.

58. Davout (p. 160) state; the strength of his divisions thus:

1st division (Morand) about	6000
2nd division (Friant), less 111th regiment left at Myszienec	4000
3rd division (Gudin), less 2nd battalion of the 85th at Ortlesburg	4500
1st and 12th chasseurs, the 2nd being left at Myszienec	600
Total	15,100

All these divisions were ordered to march for the battlefield two hours before daybreak. Friant, with Marulaz in advance, took the direction of Serpallen. Morand followed. Gudin started at 3 a.m., on account of the greater distance he had to march. It was not yet day when the cavalry encountered and drove in the Cossacks. Soon after sunrise, Friant drew up his division in order of battle on the heights short of Serpallen, which village Bagavout had evacuated as he approached, and which was now occupied by some companies of the (French) 48th regiment.[59] Marulaz was on the right, Morand in 2nd line, behind Friant. There appears to have been same delay here, waiting for the approach of Gudin, for Davout's attack did not become serious till towards noon.[60]

Davout, whilst waiting, caused a reconnaissance to be made, searching for the right of St. Hilaire's division, with which he required to connect his own left. Between eleven and twelve, a body of cavalry appeared on Friant's right; against it was sent Marulaz, supported by the 33rd regiment, and followed, in the direction of Klein Sausgarten, by the rest of Friant's division.

Bagavout had been reinforced by the 14th division (Kamenskoi) from the reserve. The cavalry were repulsed by Marulaz and the 33rd, but were immediately supported by infantry. Friant, attacked by the Russian infantry and by the rallied cavalry, was engaged in a long and severe combat. Finally, the enemy retired in good order before him, covering their retreat by a heavy artillery fire from the heights behind Serpallen.

Morand, meanwhile, sending his 1st brigade to the left to link him to St. Hilaire, who was again moving to the attack of the heights in front of him, took the 2nd brigade through, and by the left of Serpallen. He was met by a heavy artillery fire from the heights, 400 yards in front of him. To this, but an inadequate reply could be made by his light artillery. The 17th regiment was on his right in echelon of reserve. The 51st and 61st[61] were kept by Davout ready to support either Morand or Friant, as circumstances might require, until the arrival of Gudin's main body as reserve enabled him to send the 51st to support Friant, the 61st to follow Morand, and strengthen the union of his left with St. Hilaire.

Friant, still suffering severely from the guns in the direction of the

59. Bennigsen, in his official account (*Wilson*, p. 238, etc.), says Bagavout repulsed an attack on Serpallen about daybreak. There is no mention of this either in Hoepfner or Davout. Wilson himself (p. 102) says the attack was repulsed "some time after" the defeat of Augereau, and that, when the village was fired, the snow and smoke drove in the faces of the Russians. If so, the wind must have gone completely round at that time.

60. Jomini (*Art of War*, p. 198) puts the hour as late as 1 p.m.

61. Both of Gudin's division.

Kreegeberg, received orders to take Klein Sausgarten with one battalion of the 33rd. Lochet, with this battalion, broke his way into the village. He was not at once supported, and, after half an hour, attacked by infantry and cavalry, which, passing from the left wing of the Russian line beyond Kl. Sausgarten, reached his right flank, he was forced to withdraw. Outside the village, he and Marulaz maintained a stationary and sanguinary fight amongst the stockaded enclosures in which sheep were wont to be folded at night, to protect them from wolves. The Russian cavalry were thus driven off by the 33rd, the 48th, and the 51st. The enemy's infantry reinforced continued to gain ground as they vigorously assaulted the 33rd, the 48th and Marulaz's cavalry. Locket was killed here. At last, with the assistance of its artillery, Friant's division succeeded in again advancing into Kl. Sausgarten, where he firmly established himself.

Whilst the fight thus progressed on Davout's right, Morand and St. Hilaire, in front, and to the left of Serpallen, had to sustain very heavy fighting. So great was the loss in the 13th light infantry, that it had to be replaced in the fighting line by a battalion of the 17th from the reserve. The 61st, at this period, took post on Morand's right. To the left of it the 17th and 30th continued the line till it joined the right battalion (10th light infantry) of St. Hilaire. At first, the advance of St. Hilaire prospered. Firing as they moved, his men compelled the Russians to yield before them, abandoning 30 guns, which fell into Morand's hands. Suddenly, in the midst of their success, the 10th light infantry, forming the link between the two divisions, was charged by 20 squadrons under Korff. This cavalry, which had been concealed, partly by the inequalities of the ground, partly by a snowstorm, coming upon the left of the French regiment, drove it in confusion away from its own division, back to the right on the division of Morand. Disorder spreading into this division also, it was pushed back on Serpallen. The arrival of Klein's dragoons, from behind St. Hilaire, saved the situation, and drove off the Russian cavalry which had done so much harm.

During this combat, Davout had found it necessary to again strengthen Friant, on his right, with the 12th regiment from Gudin's division. On this side, also, the Russians had executed several fierce assaults, accompanied by heavy loss to both parties, but in the end unsuccessful.

Osterman had now retreated, from in front of Morand and St. Hilaire, to a position behind the Kreegeberg—a movement which, by exposing the right flank of Kamenskoi and Bagavout in front of Klein Sausgarten, compelled them also to retire and join Osterman's left.

Nothing could stop the advance of Friant. As he moved towards Anklappen, Morand and St. Hilaire were able to reoccupy the small hills beyond Serpallen, from which they had been driven, as just described, by Korff's cavalry, supported by infantry. From them Morand was not again ousted. With three regiments on them, he served as a pivot for the wheel of Davout's right, from Kl. Sausgarten towards Kutschitten and Anklappen. St. Hilaire, who had assisted in the recapture of these heights, was now, by the Emperor's order, again drawn to Morand's left, which he connected with the reserve cavalry (Klein in 1st, Grouchy in 2nd, d'Hautpoult in 3rd line). Beyond the reserve cavalry, were the remains of Augereau's corps, on the right of Eylau. The Guard infantry behind these, stood halfway between Eylau and Serpallen; on its right, behind the reserve cavalry, was the cavalry of the Guard. The whole left wing was posted as in the morning. Bennigsen, who had, since Davout's attack began, been constantly moving troops from his right and centre to the aid of his left wing, now ordered the latter to retire behind Anklappen, whilst the right and centre held fast with their diminished forces. Davout, placing a battery of 30 guns on the Kreegeberg to support his movement, pushed forward his infantry even into the farmstead of Anklappen. From the latter the 48th regiment was again forced to retire by superior numbers. Whilst this first attack on Anklappen was proceeding, Davout had detached the 30th towards his right. Milhaud's dragoons were now at his disposal. Then, with part of the 51st, and 4 companies of the 108th, he sent against the Russians of Bagavout and Kamenskoi in the birch wood to the right of Anklappen, whence they drove the enemy. The French right was still protected, against the attacks of the Cossacks, and cavalry, by Marulaz's squadrons.

The Russians, driven from these woods, retreated, constantly pursued, on Kutschitten. At the same time, the attack on Anklappen was renewed by Gauthier, with both battalions of the 25th, whilst the little wood, on the left of the farm, was invaded by a battalion of the 85th. Both attacks were successful, though they met with vigorous resistance. The troops pursuing the defenders of the larger wood towards Kutschitten, were equally happy in taking that village. The hour was about 5 p.m., the Russian left wind was in full retreat. With the loss of Kutschitten the direct road to Russia had been intercepted. The troops began to break up; the whole plain between Kutschitten and Schmoditten was covered with men, mostly wounded, bending their steps towards Koenigsberg.

The French left wing and centre, terribly crippled by the morning's events, still occupied their original positions. The Russians, in this part of the field, could only spare enough troops to retain their own line. Neither side had strength left for a renewal here of the morning's struggle, the artillery alone continued the slaughter. From a point about 1000 paces south of Eylau, Napoleon's right wing and the Russian left, turned at right angles across the plateau on the Russian side. The French front extended from this point to Kutschitten, with a kind of bastion projecting northwards from its centre, where Davout's most advanced troops held Anklappen. The battle seemed to be lost for Bennigsen.

Another startling change was about to come over the fortunes of the field. Before describing it we must leave, for a time, the armies in the positions described, and turn back to trace the movements of the two actors, Ney and Lestocq, whose appearance on the scene caused the change.

About 7 p.m., on the 7th February, part of Lestocq's corps, followed and harassed by Ney,[62] had reached Hussehnen, about 7 miles from Eylau to the north-west. His rear-guard, with infinite difficulty in cutting a road through the forest for its artillery, only came up at 6 a.m. on the 8th.

At 3.30 a.m. Lestocq received from Bennigsen an order directing him to march, with his corps, on Pr. Eylau, and to take post on the right wing of the Russian position. He ordered the baggage column to assemble, at 5 a.m., at Bomben, and to march, north of the fighting column, to the river Frisching, en route for Koenigsberg. Colonel Maltzahn, with the remnant of the advanced brigade which had suffered so heavily at Waltersdorf, was also ordered in the same direction, to cover the Koenigsberg road. One battalion, and one squadron were sent, by Dollstadt and Muhlhausen, on to the Eylau-Koenigsberg road. Esebeck, with his dragoons, the Russian Kaluga regiment of infantry, and half of a horse artillery battery, was to support the detachment at Wittenberg. All the heavy batteries were ordered to march at once, by Althof, to strengthen the Russian artillery on the battlefield. The troops which had not yet arrived were to take a short rest at Hussehnen, and then follow Lestocq. At 8 a.m. that general started, with 35 squadrons, 10 battalions, and 1½ batteries of horse artillery, to march on Eylau by the direct route, viâ Wackern, Schlautienen, Domiau, Görken, and Roditten. As the head of the column emerged from the forest at Schlautienen, Ney was seen approaching their right flank from Bornehnen. To stop his advance, Lestocq sent one battalion,

---

62. Ney reached Landsberg and bivouacked there on the evening of the 7th. Thence he despatched de Fezensac on a mission to Napoleon at Eylau. The 6th corps appears to have left Landsberg in the small hours of the 8th (*de Fezensac*, p. 245).

whilst he pushed another, with half a horse artillery battery, on to the heights running east from Schlautienen. At the same time, the direct road to Althof was abandoned, in favour of a more circuitous one by Pompicken and Graventien.

As Ney drove in the flanking force of two battalions, he advanced his guns towards the Schlautienen heights and Wackern. He had received orders at 7 a.m, to march on Kreutzburg, and to drive the Prussians from the Koenigsberg road towards Bernadotte, who was supposed to be marching direct on that place.

As the tail of the Prussian column was leaving Wackern, the head of another French force was seen approaching from the south-west. A company of infantry was sent into the wood in front of Wackern, to delay, as much as possible, this fresh column. So vigorous was the attack of this company that the troops behind it were enabled to get clear of the village. As the French, following up with infantry and artillery, drove in this weak rear-guard, they occupied Wackern. One Prussian company had to force its way out with the bayonet. As Ney's men passed right and left of Wackern, 5 Prussian squadrons and a half battery were forced aside, on to the Kreuzburg road, notwithstanding the fire of their guns. The brave stand at Wackern had given time to the Prussians left to rest after their night march to overtake the rest of the corps at Pompicken. They had set out from Bomben as soon as they heard the guns at Schlautienen.

At Pompicken another stand was made. Ney was, once more, delayed while Lestocq pushed steadily on with his main body, by Graventien, to Althof, constantly fending off Ney's advance against his right flank and rear, whilst avoiding a general[63] action. It was only at 2 p.m. that Ney received Napoleon's orders, directing him to take post on the left of the army, and attack the Russian right. The orders had been despatched at 8 a.m., but the officer carrying them was delayed by various circumstances,[64] and only reached Ney at the hour named.

---

63. Lestocq himself says he had the greatest difficulty in avoiding being drawn into a general action (see his report, *Wilson*, p. 257).

64. The officer was de Fezensac, who has left a full account of his journey (p. 145). He knew Ney was marching on Kreuzburg, as ordered, so he attempted first to join him direct, *viâ* Pompicken, in the position he expected the marshal to have reached. Finding the difficulties too great, seeing that he did not know the country, he returned to Landsberg, and thence followed Ney, whom he reached at 2 p.m. He adds that Thiers asserts that Napoleon sent orders on the night of the 7th to Ney and Davout to march on Eylau. In so far as concerns Ney, he vouches for the incorrectness of this statement, and for the fact that Ney received no such orders till 2 p.m. on the 8th. As regards Davout, it is admitted that he had his orders on the 7th.

The marshal would, it might be supposed, naturally march to the sound of the 700 or 800 guns which had been thundering, about Eylau, since 8 a.m. Incredible as it may seem, no sound of that tremendous conflict reached his ears. The wind was unfavourable, and it is agreed by all authorities that the sound did not travel against it through the snow-laden atmosphere.[65] Even from the heights between Drangsitten and Graventien, though Lestocq could clearly see the flash and the smoke of the guns, he could hear no sound.[66]

It was 1 p.m. when the Prussians approached Althof. A battalion was left to hold the village and bridge of Drangsitten,[67] covering the march of the corps to the Russian right wing at Schloditten. Scarcely had Lestocq formed his troops at Althof when an urgent message reached him from Bennigsen, requiring him to march to the aid of the now retreating Russian left wing. All the troops he now had available for this purpose were 9½ battalions, 29 squadrons, and 2 horse artillery batteries—5584 combatants.[68] With this small force, he set out, through Schmoditten, for Kutschitten.

The scene of rapidly increasing disorder, augmented by the ever-growing fire of Davout's batteries, and the triumphant advance of his right against the Russian left, has already been described. Arriving at Schloditten in three columns, the Prussians began to meet Russian officers (who openly spoke of a lost battle on the left), and disorganised bodies of troops, leaving the battlefield. These Lestocq stopped, and gathered up to return with him to Kutschitten. His artillery, coming into action ahead of the corps beyond Schloditten, beheld the heights, between Anklappen and Kutschitten, swarming with the enemy's skirmishers, every man standing out sharp and clear against the background of snow. Heavier bodies occupied Kutschitten and its neighbourhood; behind that village stood Marulaz's light cavalry. The Prussian general judged that, could he but tear Kutschitten from his grasp, the outflanking enemy would himself, in turn, be outflanked. For the assault, the Russian Wyburg regiment took post a short way to the left of Schöning's regiment; farther to the left were the Ruchel and Towarzycs regiments, with 200 Cossacks who

65. Jomini, *Vie de Napoleon*, ii. 364.
66. *Hoepfner*, iii. 235.
67. The stream was, of course, frozen, but its bed was filled with deep, soft snow (Lestocq's report, *Wilson*, p. 259, note).
68. Dumas (xviii. 32) estimates that 9000 Prussians left Hussehuen, and 2000 were left at Althof; thus Lestocq arrived on the field with 7000. But he makes no mention of, or allowance for, the detachments towards Koenigsberg. The figures accepted in the text are those of Hoepfner, based, apparently, on official documents.

had rallied to the Prussian corps. As reserve, behind these columns, followed, deployed, the grenadier battalion Fabecky. Behind again, the Prussian cavalry in column.

With loud cheers, the centre column moved direct on the village, the other two passing to the right and left of it. The right column was faced by French infantry, which it drove back into the great birch wood. The centre column, rushing through a storm of grape, chased the French defenders of Kutschitten into and through the village. These, endeavouring to stand behind the village, found themselves taken in rear by the Prussian left column, which, after driving on Marulaz's cavalry, had wheeled to its right and come down upon the back of the village. Of the 51st regiment and the four companies of the 108th in Kutschitten, hardly a man escaped. Quarter was not much asked, or given, in the deadly struggle. Three of the guns which Davout had taken were recaptured.

Kutschitten successfully stormed, Lestocq again drew out his troops, on the heights beyond, for the attack of the birch wood, wheeling them to the right of their original line of advance. His arrival, and the firm countenance of his men, had already effected wonders in restoring the Russian line behind Anklappen. On the right he posted the infantry regiment Schöning, then the grenadier battalion Fabecky, and the regiments Ruchel and Wyburg. His cavalry were in 2nd line. The Towarzycs regiment protected his left, the Cossacks held in check the French cavalry towards Kl. Sausgarten.

Their spirits raised by a glimpse of the setting sun, supported by their artillery on the heights to the right and left, the line marched on the birch wood. The frontal attack drove in the skirmishers, and carried back Friant's columns 50 yards into the wood, whilst the regiment Ruchel went against their right flank.

Stubborn was the French resistance; for half an hour the issue hung in the balance. At last, charging and charging again with the bayonet, the Prussians carried the wood, and drove Friant into the open between it and Kl. Sausgarten. Davout, so recently riding on the crest of the wave of victory, now felt success slipping from his grasp. He had lost Kutschitten and the birch wood; and, at the same time, Bagavout and Kamenskoi, rallying beyond Anklappen, supported by the artillery of the left wing, had once more stormed the hamlet. The French, driven from the burning farm, fell back in disorder towards Kl. Sausgarten. Davout realised fully his danger. Collecting his guns on the heights between Kl. Sausgarten and the birch wood, he rode amongst the disheartened troops. "Here," he cried, "the brave will find a glorious death; it is the cowards alone who will go to visit the deserts of Siberia." Not in vain was his appeal made. The fire of his artillery, beating upon the Prussians as they showed themselves on the edge of the wood, exhausted by 12 to 14 hours of continuous marching and fighting, at last checked them, and they slowly retired into the wood. For some time, the artillery combat continued in the darkness which had overshadowed the gloomy scene. Gradually it died away, neither side being fit for more fighting. It was 10 p.m. as the last shots were fired on this side of the field, now once more illuminated by bivouac fires. Davout's corps stretched from in front of Kutschitten on its right,[69] past the Kreegeberg, in the direction of Eylau, touching St. Hilaire's right.

It still remains to narrate the movements of Ney, following to the battlefield Lestocq, whom he had failed to drive away from it. At the bridge of Drangsitten, Ney encountered the rearguard left by Lestocq. Falling back on Althof before him, this rearguard once more stood there. Attacked in front and on both flanks, it formed square and slowly retired on the main body of its corps, which it reached, near Kutschitten birch wood, about 9 p.m.

It was 8 p.m. when Ney formed for the attack of Schloditten, with Belair's brigade and one brigade of Lasalle's light cavalry, which had stood all day on Napoleon's left. The village, filled with Russian wounded and vehemently defended by their troops, was only carried after a severe action. The rest of Ney's corps was drawn out between Althof and Schloditten.

The latter village, being on the road to Koenigsberg, Bennigsen could not afford to leave it in Ney's hands. To retake it he sent the Taurisch grenadier regiment, whilst a Prussian battery continued to fire on it from the heights towards Kutschitten.

Belair's troops stood, covered by the walls and houses of Schloditten, patiently reserving their fire till the Russians were almost on them. Then they opened fire with such deadly effect, at close range, that the attackers quailed before the storm and fell back.[70] But it was

---

69. This differs from the French accounts. Davout (pp. 168, 169) affirms that all the Russian attacks on Anklappen were beaten back with loss, and that his left held the hamlet for the night. Dumas (xviii. 34) tells the same story. That of Hoepfner (iii. 251) and of Lestocq himself (quoted, at p. 259, by Wilson) has been preferred as the more probable. It seems clear that Davout's left, had it retrained at Anklappen, would have been in a position far more exposed than would ever have been suffered by so able a tactician as that marshal.

70. Hoepfner (iii. 253) and Bennigsen (quoted by Wilson, p 241) assert that the attack was successful, Ney being driven out at the point of the bayonet. Dumas (xviii. 36), and other French authorities, say (continued on next page)

no part of Ney's intention to hold Schloditten against the enemy, if he continued in force there. Presently he withdrew his brigade from the village, which was entered, about 2 a.m., by the Russians, without opposition.

Gradually, with dying gasps of artillery fire, the battle had subsided

---

the assault was repulsed. Dumas falls into confusion between the similar names, Schloditten and Schmoditten, for it is the latter which he represents as the objective of the Russians, though Ney never occupied it. Jomini (*Vie de Napoleon*, iii. 364) says Ney was attacked by Sacken's division, which had suffered less than the others, and that, though he maintained himself near Schmoditten (sic), the attack imposed upon him, and he took position at some distance from the Koenigsberg road. The historical summary in the Annual Register for 1807, denies the Russian success against Schloditten. De Fezensac alleges that Belair repulsed the assault on Schmoditten (*sic*), and Ney and his staff spent the night there, in the house of a peasant who had been killed. He adds the picturesque detail that they all supped off one wretched goose, the only food procurable, which Ney generously shared with his staff (p. 148). The plan of the positions at the end of the battle in the account of the "*témoin oculaire*" shows Ney as holding Schloditten and the ground behind it; Lasalle's light cavalry between Schloditten and Schmoditten. Careful search in the Archives Historiques has resulted in the version of this much-disputed episode given in the text. From Althof, Ney wrote a pencil note to Berthier (*Arch. Hist.*, daily correspondence) saying he had pushed Lestocq on Schmoditten, and had occupied Schloditten with the 1st brigade of Marchand's division (Leger Belair's), but he did not intend to hold the village after 2 a.m. if the enemy remained in force in his front. At this time Marchand's 2nd brigade was in front of Althof, Gardanne's 2nd brigade was behind it—his first had been left behind to watch the Prussians who had marched from Pompicken on Koenigsberg. This latter brigade rejoined Ney just as he closed his despatch. Lasalle's light cavalry and a brigade of dragoons were behind Althof. This despatch, signed by Ney, appears to have been written about 8.30 or 9 p.m., just after the capture of Schloditten. An unsigned paper, probably sent by Ney at a later hour, distinctly affirms the repulse of the Russians at Schloditten at 10 p.m. In the correspondence of the 9th February, there is a hasty note from Soult to Berthier, dated 3 a.m., in which he says that, though the enemy had occupied Schloditten, he appeared to be diminishing in strength on Soult's front. He encloses, for Berthier's information, the despatch from which he derived the news about Schloditten. It is a pencil note from Dutaillis, Ney's chief of the staff. It confirms the repulse of the Russian attempt on Schloditten at 10 p.m., adding that Ney had, later, evacuated the village, in accordance with his previously expressed intention. The Russians had re-occupied it only at 2 a.m. These scraps of paper, written by the actors in the midst of the slaughter, for the information and guidance of brother generals, not with a view to publication, bear on the face of them the stamp of truth. To doubt that they are a genuine expression of what the writer believed is impossible. He might be mistaken in some matters, but it is incredible that he should be so in regard to such a patent fact as the success or failure of the attempt to recapture Schloditten. The despatches are hidden away in masses of correspondence which probably have not been searched for years.

along the whole line. The positions of the French centre and left remained as they had been before Lestocq's arrival, except that the line had been prolonged by Ney, between Althof and Schloditten.

The right, too, retained its position as far as the crest of the eastern heights. Thence, instead of extending straight to Kutschitten, with the centre advanced to Anklappen, the extreme right passed, in front of the Kreegeberg, to Klein Sausgarten, and the rising ground in front of the village. Close in front of it were Lestocq's Prussians and Russians.

The whole valley, its slopes and the plateaux on either side, were a scene of the most appalling carnage and suffering, the outcome of this fearful struggle of two days.[71]

Scattered all over the surface lay dead and wounded men and horses, staining with their life-blood the trampled snow. In places where the battle had been fiercest, the bodies lay closer: where the French 14th regiment had fought to the last, on the slope in front of Eylau, their position was marked by a square of corpses. Outside the square lay the bodies of men and horses, slain in their attempts to break the desperate regiment. The same scene was repeated, in reverse, below the Eylau church, where the Russian column had so nearly saved Europe from years of the Emperor's tyranny, but had itself been exterminated. In and behind Kutschitten, lay the remains of its 800 French defenders, of Davout's corps. In rear of the French position, the eminence near Tenknitten still wore its ghastly cuirass of human bodies.

To add to these horrors, the ghouls of the battlefield, the followers, and even the transport soldiers, roamed amongst the dead and dying, stripping and robbing them of everything, down to their very boots. The wolves from the neighbouring forests only awaited the satisfaction of these human wild beasts to enjoy their share of the ghastly feast. It was, to quote the title of a picture in the Salon of 1901, "*l'heure des fauves*." Marbot, left for dead, coming to his senses when his boot was being pulled off his foot by a transport soldier, seems to consider the latter's conduct quite natural, and even remarks, almost with surprise, that his plunderer was ready to return his clothes, when he found who he was, and that he was not yet dead.[72] The starving Russians were still, like the French, in search of what food might be found in the villages, on the dead, anywhere. Osterman could collect only 2170 men out of his whole division.[73] The rest were dead, wounded, or marauding.

---

71. The day after the battle, Ney, riding over the field, viewing all this slaughter, remarked to his staff, "*Quel massacre! et sans resultat*" (*de Fezensac*, p. 149).

72. *Marbot*, i. 267.

73. *Hoepfner*, iii. 255.

The French troops were almost more broken in spirit than their enemies, who, at any rate, had the consolation of having scored a success at the end of the battle. There were no enthusiastic cries of "*Vive l'Empereur*," as there had been in the morning. All was despondency, gloom, and misery. At 11 p.m. a strange council of war was held on the Russian left wing. Bennigsen had summoned his generals, and there, in the midst of the carnage and the snow, the situation was discussed by these men on horseback. The commander-in-chief expounded to the surrounding circle his views and intentions. He had, he said, no bread[74] to feed his troops, no ammunition to replenish their empty pouches and caissons. He had no course open but retirement on Koenigsberg, where he would find stores and ammunition in abundance.

The generals besought him to hold on. Knowing and Tolstoi offered at once to renew the attack, and complete the victory, which they believed was theirs. Lestocq, summoned to the council whilst he was actually preparing again to move against Davout, added his entreaties. Bennigsen was firm; he knew he had lost at least 20,000 men, and he did mot know that the French loss was even greater. He insisted on retreat, and then, exhausted by 36 hours on horseback, he sought a short period of repose, in a house resounding with the shrieks of the wounded and dying who filled it.

About midnight the Russians, about 2 a.m. the Prussians, began reluctantly to abandon the field which they had so gloriously held.[75] Lestocq, with his corps, took the road towards Domnau and Friedland. The rest of the army moved towards Muhlhausen, on that to Koenigsberg. Schloditten, evacuated by Ney, was held as a protection to the right flank.

As day broke on the 9th, Napoleon, from his bivouac on the scene of the first encounter of the 7th, scanning with anxious eyes the field of the battle, to renew which his army was so little prepared, saw that, this time, the reported retreat of Bennigsen was indeed true. On the northern horizon were to be seen groups of Cossacks covering the retreat of the army, which had already disappeared in the forest beyond.[76]

---

74. "The Prussians had provisions; but the Russians had no other sustenance than the frozen snow. Their wants had induced numbers, during the battle, to search for food in the adjoining villages, and the plain was covered by foraging parties passing and repassing" (*Wilson*, p. 109, nine).

75. It was about 3 a.m. when Soult first noticed the diminution of the enemy in his front. See his hurried despatch forwarding that of Dutaillis, quoted above, p. 200, note.

76. Wilson (p. 109) says that Osterman, owing to some mistake in his order to retreat, did not move from his ground till 9 a.m. on the 9th, and then passed unmolested across the French front. This story is incompatible with the French account, and is not mentioned by Hoepfner. On the whole it seems improbable.

Murat was at once launched after the enemy, but his cavalry, broken and exhausted by their exertions of the previous day, were in no condition to carry on a pursuit after the heart of their leader.[77] It may be said that they followed, rather than pursued. On the night of the 9th Bennigsen halted at Wittenberg, beyond the Frisching; on the 10th, he continued his march to Koenigsberg, there taking post in front of the Friedland gate, his left resting on the Pregel, his right covered by the detachments made from the Prussian corps at Hussehnen, and driven from it at Pompicken. Lestocq's corps, marching off in far better order than the Russians, reached Domnau on the 9th, and was forced beyond it by Marulaz's pursuit.[78] On the 10th, it reached Allenburg.

The losses of both sides in this sanguinary battle will, perhaps, never be known with exactness. The best estimate that seems possible, on a consideration of the various accounts, would put the loss of the Russians and Prussians at about 25,000, that of the French from 3000 to 5000 higher, in killed and wounded. Prisoners, on either side, were comparatively few.[79] The hand-to-hand fighting was too fierce to allow of quarter being freely asked or given.

---

77. The "*témoin oculaire*" (p. 21) says the French would have marched on Koenigsberg on the 9th, but for a change of weather, which rendered the roads impracticable once more. There was a thaw after the battle, but it did not commence till the middle of the day on the 10th. Larrey, who appears to have kept a regular diary, says (iii. 61) that a fall of icy rain on the morning of the 10th was the prelude to the thaw which set in during the day.

78. Lestocq says he left his van at Domnau and established his headquarters at Friedland on the 9th (*Wilson*, p. 261).

79. Napoleon's bulletins are, as usual, clearly false as to losses. They give them at 1900 killed and 5700 wounded on the French side: at 7000 killed and 12,000 to 15,000 wounded on that of the enemy. The latter is a curious underestimate, for Napoleon. Plotho (p. 74) gives the Russian loss as 25,000 killed and wounded. Altogether in the campaign he thinks they lost 10,000 killed and 15,000 wounded, and the total loss of both sides, between the 20th of January and the 9th of February, he puts at the appalling total of 60,000 killed and wounded. The French losses at Eylau are very difficult, the Russian almost impossible to estimate. The largest loss that Napoleon ever admitted was 18,000 (*Mémoires pour servir*, viii. 67). Davout admits that his corps lost 5007. Augereau gives his loss as 5200, exclusive of prisoners; it was probably higher. Marbot (i. 279) goes so far as to say it was 12,000 out of 15,000. There is no complete statement, in the *Archives Historiques*, of the loss of the cavalry reserve. Grouchy, in his report (*Arch. Hist.*), says his division lost about 250 killed and wounded. The cuirassiers lost much more heavily. It will not probably be too high an estimate to take the loss of the cavalry, including the on the left and the Guard cavalry, at 2500. The Guard infantry was scarcely engaged, but can scarcely have lost less than 1000. It, as well as the cavalry, had to stand all day under the fire of the Russian artillery. Soult admits 8250 killed and (continued on next page)

When the French army issued, in the afternoon of the 7th, from the woods towards Landsberg on to the Ziegelhof plateau, it seemed uncertain, says Soult,[80] whether the whole Russian army, or merely a rear-guard, was in front of it.

The conduct of the action against the Russian rear-guard was, at first, somewhat disjointed on the side of the French. Soult's centre moved so much faster than his right wing that the frontal attack, on the Russian extreme rear-guard, commenced and failed before the flanking movement was ready. It would seem that the assault should have been delayed until it could have been supported by Augereau on the left, and Schinner and Vivier on the right, as it eventually was.

It has been shown that the storming of Eylau, on the evening of the 7th, was probably far from what Napoleon desired. The remark which Marbot alleges he heard fall from the Emperor's lips admirably sums up the case. Napoleon knew that Davout could hardly be in a position to afford help, on the right, before the following day was well advanced. Ney's last orders had directed him on Kreuzburg, and his orders to march to the battlefield were not even despatched till 8 a.m. on the 8th. This failure to call Ney direct from Landsberg, on the night of the 7th, is an omission, on the part of the Emperor, which it is very difficult to explain. Ney was bivouacking that night close to Landsberg,[81] ready to start early next morning for Kreuzburg, as he actually did. Had he received orders by midnight of the 7th-8th, instead of at 2 p.m. on the 8th, he would have been before Schloditten many hours sooner than he was, and, marching on the shorter line, would have anticipated Lestocq there.[82]

Whatever the cause of this neglect may have been, it was clear that, if Napoleon occupied Eylau on the night of the 7th-8th, and if Bennigsen held firm on the eastern heights, the French centre would be in a very exposed situation.

Nor could the Emperor hope to face Bennigsen with equal forces.

---

wounded (report in *Arch. Hist.*). He probably lost 10,000. Ney must have lost quite 1500. These figures, taking Augereau at 8000, give a total of 28,000. Bennigsen's despatch (*Wilson*, 238-42) gives the loss on his side at 12,000 killed and 7900 wounded. It is unlikely that the wounded were less than the dead. Assuming they only equalled them, the total would be 24,000.

80. Soult's report (*Arch. Hist.*).

81. Ney, *Arch. Hist.*

82. Napoleon afterwards said that, unless Lestocq had been pressed, he might have fallen on the French left and rear (*Mémoires pour servir*, etc., viii. 66). This scarcely seems to cover the case.

He was nearly 30,000 men short of his full strength, so long as Davout and Ney were absent. Bennigsen was only 7000 below the strength he developed on the arrival of Lestocq.

With his superior numbers, on the morning of the 8th, Bennigsen, had he been a commander of the capacity of his adversary or even of that of Davout, might have rolled Napoleon's left upon his centre, and the whole in confusion on Davout, long before Ney could put in an appearance. The Emperor had not infantry to properly fill the position of his left wing, which consisted almost entirely of Lasalle's light cavalry and that of the corps of Soult and Augereau with part of the cavalry reserve.[83]

For four hours Napoleon's centre at Eylau was in the most imminent danger. It was only at noon, when Davout's flank attack became serious, that the intensity of the pressure, on the centre and left, was relieved. When Davout moved forward on Kutschitten and Anklappen, a vigorous attack from Eylau would probably have decided the battle in Napoleon's favour, but the French troops there were too shattered and exhausted, by the events of the morning, to attempt it.

The danger to the left wing did not escape the observation of contemporary critics. Marbot wonders at Bennigsen's failure to overwhelm Eylau before Ney and Davout arrived. Even Soult[84] says that, so late as the arrival of the Prussians, Bennigsen should have attacked the French left. Napoleon's own anxiety for it is shown by his stupendous efforts, with St. Hilaire's division, with Augereau's corps, and with the cavalry reserve, to distract attention from it.

At St. Helena he exhibits his sensitiveness to the imputation that he had attacked at Eylau piecemeal. He tries to prove that, if he had two corps detached, they were opposed by equal Russian detachments. He distorts the facts.[85] The Prussians, it is true, opposed Ney, but they were much inferior to him in strength. Davout, Napoleon says, was opposed by a force equal to his own, which he drove on to the field in front of him, and which (and not troops from Bennigsen's right) opposed him at Serpallen and Kutschitten. This is a misstatement. Davout found only 3000 men at Heilsberg, and they had all

---

83. Soult's report (*Arch. Hist.*) says there was nothing but cavalry to the left of Eylau. The village was a somewhat straggling one, and it was a little difficult to say precisely where it ended.

84. *Marbot*, i. 256. Soult's report, *Arch. Hist.*

85. *Mémoires pour servir*, etc., vol. viii. p. 67. Shortly after the battle, Napoleon wrote that the Russian army in column appeared to intend outflanking the French left when Davout appeared on the field (*Corr.* 11,796).

joined Bennigsen on the night of the 7th. His first fighting on the 8th was with Bennigsen's left wing, posted overnight. The only possible defence for an advance of the centre into the valley, the only ground on which Napoleon could accept it with equanimity, appears to lie in the false information which Jomini[86] alleges he received from Murat, that Bennigsen was retreating once more, as he had already done from Jonkowo, from Wolfsdorf, and from Landsberg. The report was not prima facie improbable; if true, it would have been well for Napoleon to be in Eylau. The fact that he left Augereau and the Guard on the western plateau during the night, seems to indicate that the Emperor believed it, for a time at any rate.

Another criticism, to which Napoleon, at St. Helena, showed his sensitiveness, concerned the formation of Augereau's corps in its disastrous advance at 10 a.m. He asserts that the corps was deployed under his own eyes, and that it could not have debouched in column in face of the heavy fire.[87] The wings, he says, were supported by columns. On this point Augereau's report[88] may be accepted. He states that the 1st brigade of each division was deployed, the end formed in squares in support of it. They were first overwhelmed by a terrible artillery fire, then charged by infantry, and finally by cavalry. In the constantly recurring darkness of the snowstorms, the only way to maintain concert of action was by very close contact of units, a rule which Davout observed in his attack.[89] Had this plan been adopted by Augereau and St. Hilaire, the disastrous deviation to his left of the former would, perhaps, not have occurred.

The great cavalry charge was a desperate remedy for a desperate situation. As the space between Augereau and St. Hilaire opened out, it became necessary to fill it somehow. Both outflanked, Augereau and St. Hilaire were being driven in opposite directions. All that Napoleon had left was his cavalry and the Guard. The latter was his last reserve, and he was always reluctant to use these picked troops till the last moment; therefore, the cavalry had to be sacrificed. Besides, they, with their superior mobility, played a part in clearing St. Hilaire's and Augereau's flanks which could hardly have been done in time by infantry.

---

86. "Murat announced to me that the enemy was retreating, which supposition was rendered plausible by the loss of Eylau" (Jomini, *Vie de Napoleon*, ii. 358).

87. *Mémoires pour servir*, etc., viii. 68.

88. *Arch. Hist.*

89. "The order had been given to close up, and not even to leave the regulation interval between one battalion and another at times when the snow, falling thickly, prevented the discernment of objects at a distance of ten paces" (*Davout*, pp. 169, 170).

The moral effect of this cavalry incursion into his very centre was, probably, great on Bennigsen, and damped his ardour for the general advance, which Napoleon had such reason to dread. The foolish pride of the Guard battalion, which insisted on charging with the bayonet, nearly cost the Emperor his life or his liberty.

By noon, the French centre and left were comparatively safe, owing to the vigorous action of Davout, whose splendid corps once more covered itself with glory, and was within a hair's-breadth of completing the ruin of the Russians. Lestocq was only just in time to stop the growing disorder. Still, even with the ground he regained, the Russian position, with its left wing *en potence*, and with Ney holding Schloditten on the other flank, on the road to Koenigsberg, was one of great peril.

Could either side have renewed this sanguinary struggle on the 9th, is a question impossible to answer. Still, Napoleon had two corps, Ney's and the Guard, comparatively uninjured, whilst Bennigsen had none. The Russian ammunition had nearly run out.[90] On the French side, Davout, at any rate, had got up his ammunition columns and replenished his supply.[91] Probably the reserve ammunition had also arrived by the Landsberg road.

Bennigsen's retreat was, doubtless, his wisest course. He had inflicted enormous loss on the French and had rendered it impossible for them to pursue with any vigour; better still, the blow to Napoleon's prestige in Europe had been very heavy.

The Russian general appears to have made no attempt to fortify his selected field of battle. There were no barricades or *abattis* in Eylau, none in Serpallen, nothing to check the progress of troops in the woods. In the prevailing frost, the ground was, of course, unworkable; but is it not possible that something might have been done with the snow? Might it not have been utilised, at least, to afford some concealment to the Russians on the bare face of the heights? As it was, they were silhouetted clearly against th e snow, and, when the sky was clear, offered a splendid target to the French artillery. Anything in the form of trenches in the snow would have seriously incommoded Murat's cavalry. The fact appears to be that it was not the way of the Russians to use the spade, even on a defensive field of battle, at this period, and they were probably not supplied with tools. Had the will to entrench been present, they might, no doubt, have worked the soft snow without proper tools.

Strategically, the plans of Bennigsen and Napoleon had alike mis-

90. *Wilson*, p. 107.
91. *Davout*, p. 171.

carried. The Russian commander aimed at cutting off Bernadotte; he stumbled upon Ney in a position where he, as well as Bernadotte, might have been destroyed, had the opportunity been properly utilised.[92] As it was, Ney's foolish advance towards Koenigsberg probably saved Bernadotte by the delay which it caused to the Russian march; his escape was indeed a narrow one.

As he and Ney fell back, Bennigsen became infected with the delusion that the most important part of his scheme had succeeded, that the Emperor was in full retreat across the Upper Vistula, his retirement being covered by the two marshals.

Napoleon's scheme was ruined, it is hardly too much to say, entirely by the capture of the despatch of the 31st January. It gave Bennigsen warning of what was coming quite twenty-four, if not forty-eight, hours before he could have gathered it otherwise. The importance of even twenty-four hours gained or lost at such a moment, was incalculable. It certainly saved Lestocq, who was the nearest to Thorn and the Vistula. Even if Bernadotte had got a second copy of the despatch, there would hade been a great alteration in the subsequent course of events. Wanting instructions, he was left hopelessly behind. At Eylau, Napoleon was deprived of the services of his corps which, if it had pursued Lestocq closely, would probably, with the aid of Ney, have disposed completely of him.

Even with his adversary's scheme laid bare before his eyes, Bennigsen risked much in marching on Jonkowo, instead of on Liebstadt.[93] Till he was well past the latitude of Guttstadt, he was in the most imminent peril of being cut from Koenigsberg, and driven on the Frisches-Haff. In favour of his delay, it must be said that he was apparently influenced by a loyal desire to give Lestocq time to rejoin him on his right. Even at Eylau, Davout's attack very nearly drove the Russians off the Koenigsberg road. Napoleon's expressed hopes of piercing the hostile centre, driving one half on the Niemen, and the

---

92. "Unfortunately, General Bennigsen was not acquainted with the full security in which General Ney confided, or, by directing the march on Wartemburg, instead of Bischofstein, the whole of the marshal's corps would, probably, have been obliged to capitulate" (*Wilson*, p. 84). "Instead of falling on the rear of his (Ney's) corps, disseminated in columns of regiments over 25 leagues, it (the Russian army) made a long detour to gain its head, and drive it back on its line of retreat; this fault allowed it to concentrate in an excellent position at Gilgenburg" (Jomini, *Vie de Napoleon*, ii. 353).

93. Bennigsen "saw the impossibility of continuing at Jonkowo, and regretted his movement from Mohrungen, since he now had to retire in presence of an enemy, and General Lestocq's corps was exposed to imminent hazard'; (*Wilson*, p. 91).

other on the Vistula and Frisches-Haff, failed completely; yet it was one of his boldest and best-conceived schemes.[94] It has not attracted such general attention as the march on Ulm or on Jena, because it failed, whilst they succeeded. In conception it equalled them; in execution it failed, chiefly, if not wholly, through the contretemps in connexion with Bernadotte. One result of the campaign was to cause the Emperor to transfer his advanced base to the middle and lower Vistula, and his main line of communications from the Posen-Warsaw road to that of Thorn.[95]

---

94. "In these campaigns I saw more, I understood more, I learnt more of war than I had in my preceding Campaigns, and even than I did in those which I saw afterwards. Napoleon owed there nothing to chance. Everything was arranged and foreseen. He did not seek to conquer only, or to invade; he sought to surpass a great warrior who had operated before him in those countries." "I have studied Napoleon on other theatres, but it is in this campaign that he seemed to me greatest, the man born a general, calculating calmly what was possible, difficult, or impossible. The last he left to the enemy; from the others he derived his own advantage and glory" (*Comeau*, pp. 228, 290).

95. Writing to Daru on the 12th February, he says that the line of communication will now pass through Thorn, not Warsaw (*Corr.* 11,804).

CHAPTER 3

Events on the Narew in January and February

No mention has, so far, been made of the movements on the extreme French right, where Savary was left in command of the 5th corps, to guard the approaches to Warsaw by the Narew and Bug, and to cover the right rear of the movement northwards. The corps at his disposal consisted of Suchet's and Gazan's divisions, with Becker's dragoon division; in all, about 18,000 men. Opposed to him, between the Narew and the Bug, were the two divisions from the army of Moldavia, under Essen I. There was also Sedmaratzki's 6th division at Goniondz, which might have to be reckoned with.

Savary's instructions[1] were, if he found Essen only in small force about Nur, to attack him. If, on the contrary, the Russian general had been reinforced, Savary would only hold Brok and Ostrolenka with cavalry. In any case his object was to cover the right bank of the Narew, from the mouth of the Omulew to Sierock, and to guard the latter place strongly, as well as the course of the Bug between it and the Austrian frontier. He was to bridge the Bug near Sierock, and to press on the completion of the *tête de pont* at Pultusk. If forced to retire on Pultusk with the bulk of his force, he would require a regiment to guard the Bug from Sierock to the Austrian frontier. The cavalry in Ostrolenka would require a small infantry force to support it.

Essen, meanwhile, had, on the 27th January, advanced from Bransk to Wyoki Mazowiecki, whence he reinforced Sedmaratzki with 3 infantry regiments from the 9th division.

On the 3rd February, the French were driven out of Ostrow. About this time, Savary received orders to abandon Brok and retire upon Ostrolenka, so as to strengthen his communication with the Emper-

---

1. Berthier to Savary, dated Praszmitz, 31st January, 1807; printed, Dumas, xviii. 377.

or's army. Dayout, it will be remembered, had left a detachment at Myszienec. Oudinot also was on the march from Lowicz to Prasznitz, to assist in filling the gap with his grenadier division.

When Savary took command of his corps, he found himself in the unpleasant position of being junior to his divisional generals. It is not very clear why Suchet, a tried lieutenant, should have been superseded by him. He found the troops suffering severe privations, marauding in large numbers in search of food. Therefore, in order to facilitate supplies, he marched to Ostrolenka by Pultusk, which, as he himself admits, exposed Becker, between the rivers, to great risk.[2]

After Eylau, Essen was ordered by Bennigsen to drive back Savary, who, at the same time, had made up his mind to assume the offensive. The French advanced cavalry captured a copy of Bennigsen's despatch. Savary also received information that Essen had sent 4000 or 5000 men across the now frozen Narew, at Tykoczyn, to turn his left.

He decided to hold Ostrolenka on the defensive, whilst he assumed the offensive on the right bank of the river. This was on the 15th February. In the low hills outside Ostrolenka he left 3 brigades, flanking them with batteries on the opposite bank. On the morning of the 16th, he moved out against the Russian force coming down the right bank. Gazan, meeting the enemy on the march, drove them back on a narrow road between two woods, before they had a chance of deploying. They were pursued for some 5 miles.

In the meanwhile, a brisk artillery fire, at Ostrolenka, warned Savary that his troops on the left bank were engaged. The Russians moving forward in three columns had been firmly met by Reille, commanding the three brigades in Ostrolenka, amongst which were part of Oudinot's grenadiers. Though he was driven into the town, the flanking artillery fire from across the river had already checked the Russians. Savary now passed the river with the rest of Oudinot's grenadiers and Suchet's division, the latter called in from the Omulew. Issuing from the town, Savary drew up his troops in two lines. On the left, leaning on the river, the grenadiers, and the cavalry; in the centre, Suchet; on the right, Campana's brigade (Gazan's division). In this formation he moved against the Russian position on the sand hills. Thence he dislodged them with a loss of about 1000 men and; guns.[3]

2. Savary remarks that, luckily for him, the Emperor's attention was too much taken up with the events in his own front to allow him to give much consideration to details on the Narew. But for this, he says, more forcibly than elegantly, "*j'aurais eu la tête lavée de main de maître pour m'y être mépris*" (Savary, iii. 46).

3. Hoepfner (iii. 280) says only 2 guns.

The Russian advance on the right bank had not been in as great force as Essen had intended. Sedmaratzki's division had been summoned to join Bennigsen, and there remained only the 3 regiments, under Wolkonski, which Essen had sent to reinforce him. After their repulse by Gazan, they also were ordered to join Bennigsen. After the failure of his attempt on Ostrolenka, Essen fell back again, on the 17th, to Wyoki Mazowiecki. Savary, under orders from the Emperor, holding Ostrolenka with a detachment and repairing the bridge there, confined himself generally to the occupation of winter quarters along the right banks of the Omulew and Narew down to Sierock. Oudinot, who had temporarily turned aside to assist Savary, resumed his march to Willemburg.

Savary's action at Ostrolenka, though not anything very remarkable as a victory, had been useful in disclosing the fact that the Russians were in no great strength on this side, and that Napoleon had little to fear from any attempt to strike his communications with Warsaw. When he had Masséna in command of the 5th corps, on the marshal's arrival from Italy, there was little need for anxiety, especially looking to the great entrenched camps which had been created at Sierock, Warsaw, and Modlin.

PART 4

Winter Quarters and Danzig

The Return to Winter Quarters and the Recruitment of the Armies

THE RETURN TO WINTER QUARTERS

Whether the terrible struggle at Eylau were a victory for the French or not, the very fact of its incompleteness was sufficient to inflict a severe blow on the reputation for invincibility of Napoleon, which had already been somewhat shaken by the indecisive results of Pultusk and Golymin, and the promptitude with which Bennigsen had resumed the offensive.[1]

It was absolutely necessary for the Emperor to convey to Europe, especially to Austria, the impression that he had conquered. The Poles, too, might be inclined to think that their hero was not invincible if he retreated too soon after the battle.

Anxious, therefore, though he was to give his troops their well-earned rest in cantonments, the Emperor was constrained by political considerations to remain some days on or near the battlefield, thereby showing that, if his army was too much shattered for him to dare a fresh advance on Koenigsberg, the Russians were equally not in condition to retrace their footsteps westwards. Even had the French corps been fit for a renewal of the campaign, its difficulties would have been vastly increased by the break-up of the frost on the 10th February. One more reason for delay was the necessity for clearing the country, by sending to the hospitals in rear the many thousands of wounded

---

1. Many French writers even do not attempt to represent Eylau as a victory. "The battle was long, very bloody, and, despite the paeans of victory and the bulletins, it is one of those which I have always held lost" (*Comeau*, p. 284). Savary (iii. 64) says that it could be considered a victory only if the retention of the battlefield, and the retreat of the enemy, can be considered alone to constitute victory. Ney's exclamation, "*Quel massacre! et sans résultat!*" (*de Fezensac*, p. 149) shows what that marshal thought of it.

French and Russians who were lying in every village near the scenes of the series of actions culminating at Eylau. Little or no attempt to bury the dead was made: they were left to the beasts and birds of prey. As Platow grimly remarked, when an armistice was proposed for this purpose after an action in March, the weather was so cold that there was no fear of pestilence from this source.[2] Besides, so long as the ground was unthawed, burial was almost a physical impossibility.

Napoleon at once issued orders for the removal of the wounded, no easy matter where carriages were scarce and could only be dragged through the snow and mud by double and treble teams.[3] Their sufferings, jolted, and shivering in the bitter cold, on open carts or sledges, must have been aggravated to a frightful degree. It was no short distance that they had to traverse, for the Emperor had resolved, at any rate, to abandon his forward position, where the difficulty of supplying his army was already felt.[4] He was uncertain even, whether he would be able to maintain himself beyond the Vistula at all. Therefore, he ordered the establishment of his hospitals at Posen, Thorn, Bromberg, and Gnesen, on or behind the great river.[5] So anxious was he that he sent Bertrand to open negotiations with the Prussian king, offering terms far more favourable than any suggested since Jena, and than those he subsequently granted, when he was in a position to dictate conditions.[6] To the credit of the king and his advisers, the offer was rejected.

---

2. *Wilson*, p. 125. Platow's words, according to this authority, were that "the weather, being cold, there was no danger of any inconvenience from their want of interment, and that he should give himself no thought about their obsequies, but he warned off, in future, all such frivolous messengers, unless they wished to increase the number of the unburied." Perhaps Sir R. Wilson would have better consulted the reputation of his hero by omitting this anecdote, which smacks strongly of the barbarian.

3. Marbot, one of the wounded himself, describing his journey, says: "So long as we were in that horrible Poland it required 12, sometimes 16 horses, to draw the carriage at a walk through the bogs and quagmires" (*Marbot*, i. 271). "The wounded, obliged to be moved in sledges in the open air to a distance of 50 leagues" (Napoleon to his brother Joseph, dated 1st March, 1807; see *Confidential Correspondence with Joseph*, No. 278, p. 231). "We had to add to our spring carriages, sledges and bad carts, the movement of which became more or less difficult with the thaws and frosts which alternated" (*Larrey*, iii. 48).

4. *Corr.* 11,805, dated 12th February, 1807.

5. *Corr.* 11,804, to Daru, dated 12th February, 1807.

6. *Corr.* 11,810, dated 12th February, giving instructions to Bertrand. That officer was to offer the restitution of the Prussian territories practically intact. He was to point out that, even if the position of Prussia were restored through Russia, the king would be, so to speak, a vassal of the Czar, which would suit neither Prussia nor France. Napoleon would prefer to make the (continued on next page)

On the 11th February, Bernadotte at last reached Eylau, and was sent on the road to Kreuzberg.[7] Murat was ordered to watch beyond the Frisching, supported by Ney on the Eylau-Koenigsberg road. Devout took up cantonments at Domnau, with cavalry towards Friedland. Soult was in the villages on the battlefield, the Guard at Eylau, and the remnant of Augereau's corps on the Bartenstein road.

Bennigsen called in the Prussians from Allenburg, but left some 2600 cavalry there and at Friedland. The latter place Davout seized on the 13th. The events of the next two or three days are of no interest or importance; there were a few small combats of cavalry, but neither side was in a condition to undertake any serious operation. Napoleon was, in fact, preparing everything for retreat to the position behind the Passarge, which he hoped to be able to gain unperceived, and to hold during the rest of the cold season.

On the 16th, the wounded having for the most part been removed, the Emperor considered he had stayed long enough near the scene of the great battle to show, at least, that he had not been defeated. The orders for retreat were issued, therefore, on that date to the following effect:[8]

On the 16th reserve parks, baggage, sick, and everything that would delay the march, to gain a start of 8 or 10 miles in the line to be followed by the respective corps. The march to commence on the 17th, all outposts remaining as they were, so as to deprive the enemy of any knowledge of the movement going on behind them.

Ney, commanding the rear-guard, with his own corps, with the cavalry divisions of Lasalle and Klein and the brigade of Guyot, would reach Eylau on the 17th, Landsberg on the 18th, and Freymarkt on the 19th. Campans, with the remains of Augereau's corps, was to start on the 16th for Heilsberg, with two battalions sent on as far as possible towards Guttstadt, to which place he would follow with the rest on the 17th.

Davout to reach Bartenstein on the 17th, Heilsberg on the 18th,

restoration himself, but he absolutely declined the idea of a conference at which England should be represented. Such a course would involve endless delay, and might spread over the next two years. Prussia was necessary to Europe, as well as to France, as a barrier against Russia. The throne of Berlin must be filled shortly, whether by a member of the house of Brandenburg, or by some one else. The person to whom it fell must, however, clearly understand that it was the gift of Napoleon alone.

7. Bernadotte's headquarters on the 11th, 12th, 13th were at Görken; on the 14th, 15th, 16th about Kreuzburg ("*Journaux militaires*," 1st corps, *Arch. Hist.*).

8. *Dumas*, xviii. 54-60, and the detailed orders printed at pp. 432-439 of the same volume.

Guttstadt on the 19th. The battalion of the 85th, which he had left at Oertelsberg, would rejoin him at Heilsberg.

Bernadotte was to reach Schlautienen on the 17th, Seefeld on the 18th, Wormditt on the 19th. The country on his left, towards Zinten and Mehlsack, to be watched by light cavalry; from Seefeld more light cavalry to be sent to Orschen.[9] Ney was to be kept fully informed of what was happening in Bernadotte's direction. Soult to reach Landsberg the 17th, Frauendorf 18th, and Liebstadt 19th.

Bessière's marches, with the Guard, were to Landsberg on the 17th, to Freymarkt on the 18th, and to Liebstadt on the 19th.

By these movements the army would, on the 19th, be on the line Wormditt—Liebstadt—Guttstadt, with Ney somewhat in advance at Freymarkt. It will be observed that Augereau's and Soult's corps, which had been so shattered at Eylau, were kept well away from any pursuit the Russians might attempt, if they discovered the movement before it was complete. The brunt of the pursuit would fall on the unshaken corps of Ney and Bernadotte. Napoleon clearly thought it unlikely that Bennigsen would interfere with his right. He hoped, and the event justified him, that the retreat would, owing to the maintenance of the outposts to the last moment, remain undiscovered till it was complete. It was only on the 19th that Bennigsen realised that his enemy was gone. Platow, on that date, entering Eylau, found there 1500 Russians and a few hundred French, whose wounds were so bad as to render their removal impossible. On the 20th, the main body began to advance. The Prussians occupied Domnau and Bartenstein. Here they were joined by Sedmaratski, who had now arrived and marched on their left to Seeburg. That evening, Lestocq received orders to send part of his force to act as the right of the allied army, holding the French left in check.

On the 21st, the Russian advance guard reached Landsberg, where more of the most severely wounded were found. There was some fighting between the Cossacks and the retiring French outposts in the village. The main body was at Eylau with its second line behind Kreuzberg; the reserve still behind the Frisching.

The Prussians were now partly on the right, partly on the left of the advance, while Bennigsen moved in a single column. Plotz, on the extreme right with part of the Prussians, crossed the Lower Passarge

---

9. On Bernadotte's pointing out the difficulty of moving his artillery by this route, he was allowed to move by the Mehlsack road, provided, always, he took good care to cover that to Landsberg (Berthier to Bernadotte, 16th February; printed, *Dumas*, xviii. 437).

at Braunsberg. Encounters with the last rear-guards of the French frequently occurred.

Napoleon, before he retreated, had announced[10] to his army, by proclamation, his intention of taking up his quarters nearer the Vistula. He boasted loudly the success of his operations against Bennigsen. The latter, at Landsberg, on the 25th February, in turn, appealed to his army with an equally exaggerated account of his alleged successes.[11]

Bennigsen hoped that Napoleon was still in retreat across the Vistula, but was not strong enough to dare to push him hard; the Emperor had no intention of reprising the river if he could help it, but he was far from certain that Bennigsen might not compel him to do so. He at once proceeded to issue orders for the assumption of winter quarters as he desired to hold them. His main line of communications was now changed. The route by Warsaw ceased to be his principal line,

---

10. Pr. Eylau, February 16th. Soldiers, —We had begun to enjoy a little repose in our winter quarters when the enemy attacked the first corps, and showed themselves on the Lower Vistula. We broke up, and marched against him. We have pursued him, sword in hand, 80 miles. He has fled to his strongholds, and retired beyond the Pregel. In the battles of Bergfried, Deppen, Hof, and Eylau, we have taken from him 65 pieces of cannon, and 16 standards, besides his loss of more than 40,000 men in killed, wounded, and taken prisoners. The heroes who, on our side, remain in the bed of honour, have died a glorious death. It is the death of a true soldier. Their relatives will always have a just claim to our care and benevolence. Having thus defeated all the enterprises of the enemy, we shall return to the Vistula, and resume our winter quarters. Those who may dare to disturb these quarters shall have reason to repent; for, whether beyond the Vistula or on the other side of the Danube, whether in the middle of the winter, or in the beginning of autumn, we still shall be found French soldiers and soldiers of the Grand Army. (Proclamation, quoted, *Wilson*, p. 200).

11. Soldiers, —As I was informed by my outposts that the enemy flattered himself he would cut us from our frontiers, I caused the army to take a different position, so as to mar their plans. The French, deceived by this movement, fell into the snare which I had spread for them. The roads by which they followed us are strewn with their corpses. They were drawn on to the field of Eylau, where your incomparable valour surpassed my hopes; and you have shown them all that Russian heroism can do. In that battle more than 30,000 French met their death. They have been forced to retire from every point, leaving us their wounded, their standards, and their baggage. I vainly endeavoured to draw them under the walls of Koenigsberg—there to complete their destruction. Only eleven regiments dared to advance. They have been destroyed, or taken prisoners. Warriors! you have now rested after your exertions; let us pursue these disturbers—let us crown our great deeds, and, after having, by fresh victories, given peace to the world, we will re-enter our beloved country. Our monarch awaits us to recompense your incomparable valour. In the arms of our wives and children, we shall console ourselves for all the misfortunes which have afflicted our dear country. (Bennigsen's Proclamation, quoted, *Dumas*, xviii. 66, 67).

being replaced by that of Thorn. The chief depot on that line would be Posen, whence canals afforded excellent communications, in open weather, with Magdeburg in rear, and Bromberg in front.[12]

The Warsaw line was by no means given up. It was necessary on all grounds, military as well as political, to retain the Polish capital. Savary's success at Ostrolenka had cleared the country, and allowed of the establishment of direct communication between Warsaw and the main army on the Lower Vistula, instead of forcing convoys to hug the bank of the river.[13] To strengthen the force at Ostrolenka, Jerome was ordered[14] to send to it a Bavarian division of about 10,000 men, as well as about 5000 or 6000 Polish levies. Napoleon had also added to it a tower of strength in the person of Masséna, whom he had summoned from Italy to take the command of his right. Masséna's relations with King Joseph at Naples had not been too cordial, and he welcomed the summons to more active duties in the field. He was, however, disappointed to find himself relegated to a secondary part of the theatre of war. He remarked to the Emperor, "Then, sire, it is a simple corps of observation that I am to command, on the rear of the Grand Army?"[15] The complaint was scarcely fair, for it was by no means impossible that the command might become of supreme importance, should the Russians once more attempt an advance on Warsaw. Moreover, as Napoleon explained to Masséna, he could hardly supersede men who had borne the brunt of the campaign in favour of the last comer, even if he were Marshal Masséna. Masséna's objects were (a) to cover Warsaw; (b) to hold in check the enemy's left; (c) to protect the country against incursions of Cossacks, and to maintain the communications of the army.[16]

---

12. *Corr.* 11,804, dated 12th February, to Daru.

13. On the 19th February, the Emperor sent orders for the construction of a good road from Warsaw to Osterode, behind the Ukra, passing through Zakroczin, Plonsk, Raciaz, Soldau, and Gilgenburg (*Corr.* 11,831). Osterode was to be the principal depot beyond the Vistula, and the construction there of great bread and biscuit bakeries was directed (*Corr.* 11,830, dated February 19th).

14. *Corr.* 11,811, dated 13th February, and orders of 24th February to Masséna (*Dumas*, xviii, 467).

15. *Masséna*, v. 316.

16. See full instructions to Masséna, dated Osterode, 25th February; printed. *Dumas*, xviii. 467, etc. He was, if possible, to maintain the line of the Omulew, with an advance guard in Ostrolenka, and the main body in Pultusk, Makow, and Prasznitz. If forced to do so, he could fall back successively on the lines of the Orezyc and the Ukra. In the last resort, he would have to defend the great entrenched camp at Praga and Warsaw. In the event of the Emperor's deciding to resume the offensive, he would send Masséna special orders. If the (continued on next page)

204

On the opposite flank, the capture of Danzig was urgently necessary, and orders were issued to Lefebvre, so early as the 18th February,[17] to proceed to its investment. The siege would be carried on, even if a retreat to the left bank of the Vistula were forced; in that case it could not be so effectually covered. Lefebvre would have the Poles, already assembled on the left bank, Menard's division of French troops, which ought to have arrived, and the Saxons, about to march from Posen.

To cover this great siege, and the blockades of Graudenz and Colberg, the following orders for cantonments were issued, on the 10th February.[18]

Osterode was fixed as the rallying-point for all the corps of the centre and left, in the event of the enemy main advancing. Augereau's corps ceased to exist, the small portion of it which had escaped at Eylau being distributed to others.

To Bernadotte was assigned the Lower Passarge, from its mouth to Spanden. He was to occupy Braunsberg and Saalfeld, with his troops cantoned in columns between the two; headquarters at Pr. Holland. Infantry and cavalry posts along the Passarge, watching all the passages so as to prevent a crossing by the enemy's light cavalry.

Soult would take up the line on Bernadotte's right, holding Wormditt, Liebstadt, Mohrungen, and Liebemuhl, having only advanced guards across the Passarge, and guarding its course from Spanden to Deppen. His troops, generally, would be in column from Wormditt to Liebemuhl.

Ney was to occupy Guttstadt and Allenstein, keeping cavalry and infantry posts between the Alle at Guttstadt and the Passarge at Elditten, watching the passages of the former river from Guttstadt to Allenstein. His park, ambulances, etc., somewhere between Allenstein and Osterode.

Davout was to occupy cantonments from Hohenstein to Gilgenburg, watching the country towards Passenheim and Willemburg with detachments.

These four corps were thus spread out like a fan, radiating from the centre at Osterode to the arc through Braunsberg, Wormditt, Gutts-

Russian main body acted offensively against the Emperor, Masséna would take the offensive, with a view to detaining Essen on the Narew, or to follow him if he slipped away. Were Masséna's corps attacked in great force, he would require to let go Pultusk, but should hold the bridge at Sierock as long as possible. By so doing, he would be in a position to follow the force which had driven him back, should it turn northwards against the Emperor.

17. *Corr.* 11,826, dated Landsberg, 18th February, to Lefebvre.
18. Orders printed in full, *Dumas*, xviii. 448, etc.

tadt, Allenstein, and Gilgenburg. The Guard, and Oudinot's grenadiers, were ordered to Osterode, Löbau, Rosenthal, Neumark, etc., forming a general reserve.

The headquarters of the cavalry reserve were also at Osterode. Sahuc's dragoons were made over to Bernadotte, another dragoon division to Ney, Millhaud's to Davout. Klein was to occupy cantonments at Elbing, and on the road to Pr. Holland. There also Durosnel was to refit his light cavalry. That under Lasalle was to go to Neidenburg and the neighbourhood. The three cuirassier divisions, which had suffered heavily before and at Eylau, were sent to the rear, about Riesenburg, Freystadt, Bischofswerder, Strasburg, etc.

The movements, commencing on the 21st, were to be completed by the 23rd, except in the case of Bernadotte. Each corps was to have a small hospital on the right bank of the Vistula, besides a larger one on the left. At Osterode, food was to be stored sufficient for the army for 10 days; two points between Osterode and Thorn were also to be selected, and kept stored with 5 days' supplies at each. At Thorn, 20 days' more supplies were to be collected and kept up, thus making 40 days' altogether in reserve.[19]

NAPOLEON'S MEASURES FOR INCREASING HIS FORCE

This seems to be the most convenient moment at which to interrupt the narrative of events for the purpose of sketching briefly the measures which, during the next four months after Eylau, the Emperor took for the purpose of reinforcing his army to a strength which should place beyond all doubt the result of the campaign in the spring or summer. He felt, too, that his prestige had suffered so severely that he must so strengthen himself in Germany as to render it almost impassable for Austria to dare the risk of interference, and, at the same time, to guard against an English descent, in support of the Swedes, on his left rear.

Such a descent he had always thought possible, though he estimated 25,000 men as the utmost number the expedition was likely to muster.[20] In the earlier stages of the war the possibility of its landing on the coasts of France was greater than it was now that the Emperor had transferred the seat of war to, and beyond the Vistula.

19. Berthier to Daru, 20th February, 1807, *Dumas*, xviii.; 453.
20. *Corr.* 12,135, dated 23rd March, 1807, to his brother Louis. Also *Corr.* 12,075, dated 18th February, in which he tells Clarke that it is even possible Berlin might be temporarily occupied by a raid from the sea. The estimate of numbers was certainly a liberally high one.

Under these circumstances, the Emperor felt that he could venture on a further denudation of the French and Dutch ports, and of the reserve at Paris, the void being filled by conscripts of 1807 and 1808; for he contemplated another draft on the military reserves of the future.[21]

Each of the 5 battalions in Paris, and the 6 at Brest, was reduced to 600 men, all above that number being drawn for the nucleus of fresh provisional regiments. The depots of the 65th and 72nd, in Holland, were required to provide 160 men each for the same purpose.[22] Zayonchek's Polish corps, which was destined to fill the gap between Masséna and the main army, was ordered to be recruited up to 25,000 men.

Napoleon's design was to create an army of observation in Germany, to be placed under the orders of Brune. Raising it to 60,000 or 70,000 men, and having available on its wings the corps of Mortier in Pomerania, and of Jerome in Silesia, he would have at his disposal at least 100,000 men in rear of his army on the Vistula. This great force could be moved forward on the Vistula, back upon the Elbe, north to the coast, or south against Austria, as circumstances might require.

The conscripts of 1808 were demanded by a message to the Senate, dated 20th March, 1807, about one and a half years before they were due.[23] Their distribution was laid down precisely, the principle of sending them where they were not likely to see active service being carefully observed.[24] From Italy were drawn, for the army of observation, the French division of Boudet and Molitor;[25] and other troops. Spain was called on to supply 15,000 men for the army of observation. The Prince of the Peace had been organising Spanish troops, nominally to be able to assist Napoleon if required, really to be prepared for action in the event of his defeat. The Spaniard's hand was forced by the Emperor's demand, and he meekly sent the troops.

---

21. *Corr.* 12,080, dated 19th March, Lacuée, in which Napoleon says he proposes demanding the conscription of 1808. Reckoning it at 80,000, he would send 36,000 to 5 legions of reserve, and 24,000 to complete the 3rd battalions at home. Thus the boys of under 20 would be kept back from the scene of active operations, for which he thought them unfit. Writing to Kellerman on the 4th June, he says that the conscripts of 1808 are too young for work at the front (*Corr.* 12,722).

22. *Corr.* 12,901, dated 28th February, to Dejean.

23. *Corr.* 12,100.

24. The distribution was thus—60,000 for the Active Army (20,000 for the 5 legions. 15,000 to Italy. 25,000 for the rear of the Grand Army.) 20,000 for the Reserve (10,000 to the legions. 5,000 to Italy. 5,000 to the Grand Army. (*Corr.* 12,228, dated 30th March.)

25. *Corr.* 12,232, dated 30th March.

In the latter half of April, the ports were once more drawn on for four divisions, to be replaced by the reserve legions and by conscripts. These four divisions would march parallel to the coast, following the English movements, and ready at any moment to meet a descent from the sea on their left.[26] To embarrass England, Admiral Decrés was ordered to make preparations in Brest, as if for a descent on Ireland. The Emperor believed an English expedition to be starting at the end of April.[27] Very complete instructions were sent to Brune for his action in every possible case.[28]

More cavalry was drawn from the army of Italy in May;[29] and, as the season for the resumption of hostilities approached, urgent orders were sent to Clarke[30] to hurry forward the provisional regiments; to Jerome, to forward all recovered invalids, especially cavalry, from Silesia;[31] to the Fusiliers of the Guard (2 regiments), to hasten their march through Germany, using carts as far as Bromberg.[32]

---

26. *Corr.* 12,435, dated 2rd April, 1807, to Lacuée. The Emperor again says he does not believe England able to embark more than 25,000 men. If the expedition, which he believed to be starting shortly, should appear to be making for the Baltic, the four divisions would march off thus, following its movement, and being replaced as they started by the legionaries and conscripts:

1st division from Boulogne	7,680 men
2nd division from St. Lo	6,540 men
3rd division from Pontivy	7,000 men
4th division from Camp Napoleon	4,480 men

27. *Corr.* 12,486, dated 29th April, to Decrés.
28. *Corr.* 12,494, to Brune, dated 29th April. His corps observation, irrespective of Mortier's and Jerome's corps, would for the present consist of 20,000 French troops (Boudet's and Molitor's division, from Italy), 14,000 Dutch and 14,000 Spaniards: the new draft from Spain could not arrive before June (*Corr.* 12,465). The left of this corps should be between the Elbe and the Weser, the centre between Lubeck and Demmin, the right between Demmin and the Oder, Molitor and Boudet at Magdeburg, the Spaniards in Hanover. If the English landed in Holland, Brune would move on that country. If they made for Hamburg, Brune would also go there. If Danzig was their objective, he would move to his right. Should they go still further east, he would lean on Stettin, leaving but a small force to resist a possible diversion towards Hanover. *Corr.* 12,495, dated 29th April, instructed Mortier to besiege Colberg and cover the coast from the Oder to the Vistula. If a landing were attempted at the mouth of the Oder, the marshal would lean to his left and support Brune; if at Colberg, all his forces (about 18,000) must unite to cover the siege, Brune supporting him. If Danzig or Koenigsberg were the landing-place, Mortier would march on the former, Brune moving up behind him.
29. *Corr.* 12,543, dated 6th May, to Eugene, and *Corr.* 12,567, dated 10th May.
30. *Corr.* 12,542, dated 6th May. (continued on next page)

Immense efforts were made to increase the supply of horses. Napoleon expected to have 80,000, of which 56,000 would be with the Grand Army.[33]

To the increase of his artillery he gave special attention, even going so far as to cast guns of a different calibre to utilise the ammunition captured from the Prussians.[34] By these and similar measures[35] the Emperor would have, in the middle or end of May, in addition to the garrison at home and the army on the Vistula, the strength of which will be dealt with later, roughly speaking, the following forces directly or indirectly covering him against possible aggression of the English and Swedes in the north, of Austria in the south of Germany, and of England in the south of Italy—

(a) Brune's army of reserve with the corps of Mortier and Jerome: 100,000[36]

(b) The army of Northern Italy, with Marmont's corps in Dalmatia, both threatening Austria's southern frontier: 72,000[37]

(c) Army of Naples: 52,000[38]

Altogether Napoleon cannot have had less than 600,000 men in different parts of France and Europe—a gigantic army at that period.

The issue of all the numerous orders necessary for these preparations was alone a heavy piece of work; but it was only a portion of

31. *Corr.* 12,545, dated 6th May.

32. *Corr.* 12,038, dated 15th March, to Dejean.

33. *Corr.* 12,038, dated 15th March.

34. Jomini, *Art of War*, p. 318.

35. A new provisional regiment was formed from the 3rd battalions of the 59th and 69th (*Corr.* 12,485, dated 29th April). There were 16 provisional regiments from which to recruit the army on the Vistula (*Corr.* 12,472, dated 25th April). Also 7 new provisional garrison regiments (*Corr.* 12,433, dated 21st April). On the 21st April, Napoleon notes, in a letter to Lacuée, that, out of 160,000 fresh troops expected by him, 113,000 had already arrived (*Corr.* 12,431, dated 21st April).

36. This does not appear to include the French troops marching up parallel to the coast from Boulogne, etc., but they would about compensate for the movement of Mortier across the Vistula at the re-opening of the campaign. On the 30th May, the Emperor, writing to Brune (*Corr.* 12,704), says that marshal will have, by July, 60,000 infantry, 6000 cavalry, and 7000 or 8000 men in the provisional battalions at Hameln, etc. This army, left in his rear, was not meant merely to check England. Should Austria move, it would have to go to Silesia and Gallicia, in which case it would be reinforced by 20,000 Poles, and 20,000 men in Silesia, and would have 100 guns. Its composition is summarised as: (*a*) Dutch troops; (*b*) Spaniards from Etruria; (*c*) Spaniards arriving in June from Spain; (*d*) Molitor's and Boudet's divisions; (*e*) Loison from before Colberg.

37. *Corr.* 12,543, dated 6th May, to Eugene.

38. Letter to Joseph, dated 1st March, 1807, No. 278, at p. 231, vol. i., *Corr.* with Joseph.

what the Emperor got through, in his seclusion from the distractions of the gay world, at Osterode or Finkenstein.[39] He had to deal with troubles at home, panic and a fall in the funds,[40] with matters of diplomacy all over Europe and in Persia, with a thousand great questions yet he found time to watch every detail concerning his army, its communications, and its supplies. Nothing seemed to escape him. It was he who called attention to the omission from a return of two regiments which had been overlooked at Luxembourg;[41] it was he who, by comparing hospital with regimental returns, discovered how many of his men were marauding all over the country. All this time he was being urged, by Murat and the other generals at Osterode, to retire to the left bank of the Vistula.[42] Napoleon's correspondence during March and April, teems with complaints of insufficient information from his generals, with orders for the establishment of bakeries, for forwarding supplies of all sorts, for the establishment of hospitals and the removal of the wounded, with demands for more boots and with instructions for reconnaissances and surveys. There is hardly any point on which he insists more strongly than the provision of ample supplies of boots. The principal central depot for boots and uniforms, as well as other stores, would now be Posen; thence, they could go by canal to Bromberg, and so to the army beyond the Vistula.[43] As the hospitals at the front became crowded with the sick and wounded, the less serious cases were transferred to Breslau and Glogau, where fine barracks gave good accommodation.[44] In this way the congestion of the main hospitals was relieved. To facilitate communications, bridges at Thorn, Marienburg, and Marienwerder were built, or completed.

Events on the Main Front in
February, March and April

In seeking to take up the winter quarters prescribed by Napoleon, on the 20th February, the corps of Davout, Ney, Soult, the Guard, and the cavalry reserve, had nothing but a rearward movement to make. With Bernadotte the case was different, for he had to spread his corps down the Passarge to Braunsberg.

---

39. "If the Emperor, instead of sitting in a hole, like Osterode, had gone to a large place, he would have taken three months to do all he actually did in one" (*Savary*, iii. 65).
40. *Savary*, p. 65.
41. *Corr.* 12,485.
42. *Savary*, 65.
43. *Corr.* 12,804, dated 12th July, to Daru.
44. *Corr.* 12, 102, dated 20th March, to Jerome.

On the 25th February, the Emperor received information that the Prussians were marching on Elbing with about 4000 men, and also on Guttstadt. His first care was to guard with Soult's corps, the bridge on the Passarge at Alken.[45] He seriously apprehended a general advance of the enemy, and he expressed his intention, in that event, of fighting a great battle on the Osterode plateau, where he calculated he could collect 95,000 men in thirty-six hours,[46] whilst he reckoned the enemy's whole strength at 55,000.[47]

On the 25th, the Prussians had passed, in part, the Passarge at Braunsberg, and had pushed cavalry and infantry into and beyond Stangendorf and Zagern. Lestocq was moving on the Passarge through Wormditt, which the French had evacuated, towards Alken and Spanden.

His right was ordered to move cautiously, on the 26th, towards Muhlhausen. On that day, however, Bernadotte sent Dupont's division, with three light cavalry regiments under Lahoussaye, and a dragoon brigade from Muhlhausen, to force the Prussians back across the Passarge at Braunsberg. Before these troops they retired.[48] Dupont, sending the 9th infantry and the 5th chasseurs to his right on Petelkau, himself moved direct on Braunsberg with 3 infantry and 2 cavalry regiments. He found the Prussians drawn up behind Stangendorf, with their left resting on Zagern. That village being carried by the French right column, the Prussians took up another position, behind a ravine, between it and Braunsberg.

Dupont, meantime, had carried the position behind Stangendorf. Once more the Prussians formed on the heights in front of Braunsberg. Hence, again overpowered, they were driven across the river beyond the town.

On the 27th, Dupont retired to the left bank, burning the Braunsberg bridge, and established himself at Braunsberg, Frauenburg, and Tolkemit. The Prussians lost at least 800 men in these actions.

---

45. *Corr.* 11,877, dated 25th February, to Soult.
46. *Corr.* 11,882, dated 26th February, and 11,889 of the same date, both to Soult.
47. Hoepfner (iii. 293) gives the allied strength as—

Russians	39,545
Prussians	11,300
Total	50,845

which the expected arrival of Sedmaratzki would raise to about 61,000 regular troops, and 6,300 Cossacks.
48. They retired to Heiligenbeil and Mehlsack, with outposts at Wormditt. "The loamy ground was so slippery from the thaw that cavalry and artillery were useless" (*Wilson*, p. 246).

On the 1st March the Prussians and Russians took up the following positions:

Russians:
Advanced guard (Platow) at and about Arensdorf, supported
  by the mass of the cavalry under Gallitzin, at Benern.

1st line	5th division (Tutchkow), Mehlsack
	8th division (Essen III.), Frauendorf
	3rd division (Sacken), Raunau
	2nd division (Osterman Tolstoi), Reichenburg,
	beyond the Alle
2nd line	7th division (Dochtorow), Plauten
	14th division (Kamenskoi), Stabunken
	4th division (Somow), Heilsberg
HQ	Heilsberg

Prussians:

1st advanced brigade	Grunau and towards Braunsberg
2nd advanced brigade	Schalmen, Anken, etc
3rd advanced brigade	Langwalde and along the Passarge
Supports	in Plaswich, Lindenau, Damerau, etc
Main body	in the neighbourhood of
	Hohenfurst and along the
	Mehlsack-Braunsberg road
Reserve	about Lilienthal, etc
HQ	Peterswalde

Ney, during these days, on the 26th February, sending one brigade forward again from Guttstadt into the Schmolainen forest, had badly cut up an advanced Russian regiment. Reinforced, the Russians turned the tables on him, forcing him to evacuate Guttstadt in the following night. The town was of importance to the French, as a support for the advanced portion of their line, and Napoleon was annoyed at Ney's retirement from it as there were only, the Emperor believed, 4000 or 5000 of the enemy in front of him.[49]

For its recapture measures were now taken. Ney had fallen back to a position with Deppen on his left, and the Emperor was inclined to think the enemy contemplated an advance against the right of the Grand Army. In that case, he would reply by a movement from Braunsberg, which would soon alarm Bennigsen for his communications with Koenigsberg, and put a check on the movement of the op-

---

49. *Corr.* 11,895, dated 27th February, to Soult.

posite wing. Bernadotte was therefore to support Dupont by a division at Muhlhausen.[50] To fill the gap between Davout and Masséna, Zayonchek's Poles were ordered to the neighbourhood of Neidenburg.[51]

Davout was now at Mohrungen, not within reach of Ney; but Soult could support Ney at Deppen, being, in turn, supported by Davout,[52] behind whom, again, would be the Guard and Oudinot.

On the 3rd March, whilst Bernadotte and Soult made demonstrations on the Passarge, Ney moved, with about 18,000 men, an Queetz, which he occupied without much difficulty. On the 4th he continued his movement through Guttstadt on Schmolainen.

There, finding Sacken had concentrated at Launau, he stopped, and, on the 5th, retired again to Guttstadt, whilst Bernadotte and Soult, Ney's object having been effected, recrossed the Passarge.

The Emperor was still apprehensive of a movement against his right, but was most anxious to hold on to his cantonments, and ordered them to be fortified as far as possible. "*Il faut remuer de la terre et couper du bois,*" he wrote to Soult, on the 5th March.[53] He now broke up and distributed to other corps the shattered remnant of the corps of Augereau, who had himself been allowed to return to France to get cured of his wounds.[54] Napoleon had now discovered that there were many stragglers from the army, including, he heard, even officers. For the arrest of these, and their return to the army, he issued stringent orders to Rapp, now governor of Thorn, and to Clarke.[55] Another point on which orders were issued was the strict blockade of the garrison of Graudenz by the Hesse Darmstadt troops.[56] They were placed under Victor, who was exchanged against Blucher early in March.[57]

Bennigsen appears really to have intended a further advance against

50. *Corr.* 11,905, dated 28th February, to Bernadotte.

51. *Corr,* 11,909, dated 1st March. This force should amount to 10,000 or 12,000 (*Corr.* 11,925, dated 4th March). It was afterwards ordered to be raised to 25,000. Its mission was to guarantee the flank from Neidenburg to Allenstein, to keep touch also with Masséna, and to protect the road on the right bank of the Vistula from Warsaw to Mlawa, Soldau, and Osterode (*Corr.* 11,957 and 11,958, dated 6th March).

52. *Corr.* 11,915, dated 2nd March, to Soult.

53. *Corr.* 11,939 and Corr. 11,962, dated 6th March, to Lefebvre.

54. The corps was distributed thus: 16th Light Infantry, 63rd, and 24th of line, to Bernadotte. 7th Light Infantry to Davout. 14th (almost destroyed) and 105th to Soult. 44th to Lefebvre (*Corr.* 11,951, dated 6th March, to Daru).

55. *Corr.* 11,951 and 11,955, both dated 6th March.

56. *Corr.* 11,904, dated 28th February.

57. The exchange is mentioned as having been effected in *Corr.* 11,976, dated 8th March.

Ney, and Napoleon considered it desirable to alarm him in the direction of Willemburg, where he thought it possible that there might be part of Essen's troops, whom it was Masséna's duty to retain on the Narew.[58] He accordingly sent Murat with about 6000 cavalry, part of Oudinot's grenadiers, and some of Zayonchek's Poles against it. The movement was supported by Davout from Allenstein and Hohenstein. Murat, finding only cavalry at Willemburg, occupied it on the 10th.[59] He was ordered[60] to advance as far as Wartemburg, and then, after waiting a day to pick up stragglers, to fall back again to Osterode.[61]

After this period, comparative peace reigned in front of the enemy's army. There were trifling outpost skirmishes here and there which are not worth detailing, but the Russian army had settled into winter quarters. On the 20th March its positions were:[62]

Bagration	with advanced guard, altogether about 11,000 men, besides artillery and Cossacks, at Launau	
Markow	with the cavalry of the right wing, about Reimerswalde and Heilsberg	
Right bank of Alle	Gallitzin's cavalry of the left wing	about Kerwienen, Kiewitten, etc
	2nd division (Osterman)	Lauterhagen, Roggenhausen, Krekollen
	14th division (Kamenskoi)	Gallingen, Kraftshagen, etc
Reserve	4th division (Somow)	Tolks, Albrechtsdorf, Borken, etc., on the left bank of the Alle
	7th division (Dochtorow)	about Tormitten, on the right bank
	Tolstoi	about Wargitten and towards Seeburg
	Platow with Cossacks	at Oertelsburg and Passenheim
Headquarters	Bartenstein	Point of assembly: Schippenbeil

---

58. *Corr.* 11,978, dated 9th March.
59. *Corr.* 12,000.
60. *Corr.* 12,008, dated 12th March.
61. Gazan's division from Masséna's corps was sent to Willemburg. The objects of this were explained by the Emperor to Masséna as: (continued on next page)

214

Bennigsen had, by the middle of March, received reinforcements of about 10,000 men, partly fresh regiments, partly stragglers and recovered invalids.

The Prussians were about at Heiligenthal, Zinten, and Plauten, with advance guards towards the lower Passarge.

Napoleon held to his old line, vigorously pressing the siege of Danzig and the strengthening, by fortification, of his main front.

Lefebvre was ordered to occupy the Nogat island, between the branches of the Vistula, and to drive the enemy as far up the Nehrung as possible, blocking his return by fortifications.[63]

Masséna was required to send Garan towards Willemburg, which was the key of the Omulew, and where he would strengthen the link with the centre.[64]

Even on the 22nd March, the Emperor did not feel sure that he could maintain himself on the right bank of the Vistula.[65] He was still intent on the idea of a great battle, about Saalfeld or Osterode, should the enemy advance, and he ordered positions for the purpose to be carefully surveyed.[66]

In these positions the main armies may be left whilst we describe, as fully as space will allow, the great siege which it was Napoleon's object to cover, Bennigsen's to raise. The operations in Silesia and Pomerania will also be very briefly indicated to their conclusion.

---

(1) that the division might be available on the third day at Osterode, should the enemy move in that direction; (2) to maintain communication between Masséna and the Emperor, and to hold Willemburg, which was the key of the Omulew (*Corr.* 12,016, dated 13th March).

62. *Hoepfner*, iii. 325, etc.

63. *Corr.* 11,962, dated 6th March.

64. *Corr.* 12,016, dated 13th March, to Masséna (see note, p. 239).

65. On that date he wrote to Daru that the country in which he was could not long feed his army. When the bridges and bridge heads at Marienburg, Marienwerder, and Sierock were quite complete, it would be necessary to consider whether he would not be constrained to lead his army to the left bank, in which case his chief positions would be Dirschau, Mewe, Schwetz, Bromberg, Thorn, and Wrocawik. Then the Marienwerder bridge would be of special importance (*Corr.* 12,120, dated 22nd March).

66. *Corr.* 12,321, dated 6th April. A most interesting document, showing how fully the Emperor appreciated the advantages, to the defensive, of the lakes and marshes, as a protection against turning movements.

CHAPTER 2

The Siege of Danzig

Space will allow of but a brief account of this great siege, which would require a volume to itself if it were to be fully described.[1] Scarcely was the battlefield of Eylau cleared when, on the 18th February,[2] Napoleon commenced his arrangements for the siege, which had been interrupted by Bennigsen's advance, necessitating the recall of Lefebvre to guard Thorn. Troops were already on the move in that direction.

The 10th corps, under Lefebvre, had to deal with the sieges of Danzig, Colberg, and Graudenz. It consisted of two Polish divisions under Dombrowski, the Baden contingent, a Saxon corps, two Italian divisions, and various French troops—altogether about 27,000 men and 3000 horses. About 10,000 men were French, the rest auxiliaries. The numbers available for the principal siege (Danzig) varied according to the requirements of the others, with which it is not proposed to deal. Graudenz was blockaded; but it was after all but a small fortress, and no great vigour seems to have been exhibited in the siege. It sufficed to effectually mask the place. On the 18th February, Menard and Dombrowski, near Mewe, drove back part of the Danzig garrison which had moved out in that direction.

A more serious affair occurred on the 23rd, when the same two generals attacked the Prussians in Dirschau. A body of 1500 was cut off in the town, where they made a brave resistance. Overwhelmed by numbers, they were almost entirely destroyed by the Poles, who, exasperated by race hatred and by the long resistance offered, gave but little quarter.

---

1. This account is based on that of Dumas (xviii. pp. 123-198), of Kirgener, Director of Attacks (*Précis du siège de Dantzich*, Paris, 1807), and of Hoepfner (iii., pp. 335-529).
2. Corr. 11,826, to Lefebvre, directing him to invest Danzig, and remarking that Menard's French division should now be at hand, that the Saxons were at Posen, and the Poles long ago ready.

With this effort, the endeavours of the garrison of Danzig to keep the enemy at a distance ceased, and they settled down in and about the city for the siege. Lefebvre, not considering himself strong enough to commence the siege, did not move beyond Dirschau till the 9th March.

At that period the civil population of Danzig numbered about 45,000. The city had somewhat declined in importance of late years, yet was still a very important port and market. Its fortifications had, in 1806, been much neglected, and were in very bad repair. It was only when the Prussian power collapsed, in the autumn of that year, that a siege began to seem probable. Then every effort was made to repair and strengthen the fortress. Much assistance in this respect was derived from the great stores of wood in the place. Palisades and earthwork formed a great feature in the new defences.

The fortress itself was situated in the low ground on the south bank of the left branch of the Vistula, which here flows from east to west before it finally turns north, just below Danzig, to the sea. Through the town runs the little river Mottlau, by damming which it was practicable to inundate the country for some distance from the fortifications of the east and south sides. In these directions the place could be rendered, in those days, practically impregnable. On the north side, it was protected from close approach by the river, from which it was only separated by 300 yards of marshy land intersected by channels. The enceinte consisted of bastioned fronts. On the west side the land rose above the enceinte to a height which commanded the town. On this height was constructed, with earth and palisades, another front, protecting the western enceinte, which, without it, would have been easily subdued. This outer line of works extended from the inundated south side to the Vistula.

The dominating parts, separated from one another by a valley, were those on the southern height of the Bischofsberg and the northern the Hagelsberg.[3] In front of the line, where it joined the Vistula, projected the large redoubt of Kalk, lying in the low ground with a smaller work

---

3. "As compared with the Hagelsberg, the front of the Bischofsberg was broader and the trace better. The Hagelsberg ditches, on the other hand, were deeper. The two works and their continuations formed a continuous connected line; once the last palisade at any point was passed, the besieger would command the whole line. The weakest point was between the Hagelsberg and the river, but an attack on that was flanked by the Kalk redoubt. There the ground was level and open. In front both of the Hagelsberg and the Bischofsberg it was broken, hilly, and difficult for works of approach. In conclusion, if the Bischofsberg and the Hagelsberg fronts had both abutted on a plain, the former would have been the stronger. The nature of the ground in front reversed their value. The (continued on next page)

beyond it. Even the Bischofsberg and the Hagelsberg fronts were not on the highest parts of the rising ground, and were, to some extent, commanded by the ground in front of them. This was obviated by the great height of the works themselves.[4]

Beyond the river, on the north, was the western extremity of the low island known as the Frische-Nehrung, stretching away east as far as Pillau, near Koenigsberg. The extreme western corner of the Frische-Nehrung, at the point where the Vistula changes its course from west to north, was separated from the rest by the navigable canal of Laake, connecting Danzig with the lower reach of the river. The triangular island of Holm, so formed, was of great importance in the siege. So long as the canal remained open, Danzig was directly connected with the sea. The mouth of the Vistula was guarded on its right bank by the fort of Weichselmunde. Opposite to this fort was a large entrenched camp, at Naufahrwasser, having the greater part of its front protected by the Sasper lake, and the channel joining it to the Vistula. It was further guarded by a double line of works.

Between Weichselmunde and Danzig, on the Nehrung, there was a large wood. The island of Holm and the Laake canal were defended by several redoubts and other works, which spread down the banks of the Vistula, connecting Danzig with Weichselmunde.

The artillery of the fortress consisted of 303 guns, 20 howitzers, and 26 mortars. In addition, there were 28 guns, 1 howitzer, and 3 mortars at Weichselmunde, and 51 guns, 2 howitzers, and 3 mortars at Neufahrwasser.

The two forts of the Bischofsberg and the Hagelsberg, on which the French approaches were afterwards directed, had 40 pieces each.

The garrison numbered nearly 16,000 men, including about 1600 cavalry. About 11,000 were in the fortress, the rest at Weichselmunde,

---

besieged, perceiving this, continued to occupy the orchards and suburbs before the Bischofsberg, until the besieger was irretrievably committed, by the progress of his works, to the attack of the Hagelsberg" (Kirgener, concluding observations, pp. 38-47).
4. The commanding engineers of the attack and defence were respectively Chasseloup de Laubat, and Bousmard, both famous in the annals of fortification, and each the inventor of a new system. The two systems were alike in their use of ravelins advanced beyond the glacis; but neither of the fronts attacked at Danzig was traced in this manner. These two famous engineers directed the operations of attack and defence, and, as is natural, the contest between two such representative men is full of interest. Lefebvre knew nothing whatever of military engineering, and was ordered to act entirely on Chasseloup's opinion in technical matters. Chasseloup, who had other work on hand, was ably represented in the details of the siege by Kirgener, who was constantly on the spot.

Neufahrwasser, on the Holm island, and on the Nehrung.[5] The besiegers are given by Hoepfner as 24,105,[6] at the beginning of the siege. Dumas denies that Lefebvre had more than 16,000 men at his disposal.[7] The truth lies, perhaps, somewhere between the two.

The troops of the garrison were far from being of the first-class, as is admitted by both sides.[8] Lefebvre gradually completed the investment of the place, occupying the whole of the Nogat island, which was useful to Napoleon as a remount depôt,[9] and disposing his troops in the villages west and south-west of the fortress. Many of his troops, too, were not of the best quality, and Napoleon inculcates on him the necessity, with such troops, for strengthening his front with field works.[10]

On the 6th March, the Schidlitz suburb, in the valley separating the Bischofsberg and Hagelsberg ridges, was stormed and fortified. On the 18th, Danzig was completely invested, except on the north side. On that date Field-Marshal Kalkreuth, commanding the garrison, joined it by the Nehrung, bringing some Russian reinforcements.

Napoleon had already urged the necessity of cutting this last open line, which was of the greatest importance; of occupying the western part of the Nehrung, and of separating Danzig from Weichselmunde and the sea.[11] In execution of this order, General Schramm, with about 2000 men and 6 guns, was sent to Furstenwerder on that branch of the Vistula which falls into the western end of the Frisches-Haff. Crossing silently in the early morning of the 20th March, the French troops reached the northern bank unperceived. Thence they advanced in two columns, driving the Prussian posts partly towards Pillau, partly towards Danzig. The latter only rallied towards Danzig, at Wondelen and Bohnsack. Thence, though reinforced, they were driven along the Nehrung to Weichselmunde. The other French columns, meanwhile, protected Schramm's rear, towards Pillau. About 7 p.m. Kalkreuth attempted, by a sortie on the Nehrung, to prevent Schramm's establishment, but was beaten off. Measures were at once taken to secure

---

5. Hoepfner, iii. 371-380.
6. Ibid., iii. 382-384.
7. Dumas, xviii. 144. See following note.
8. Napoleon, on the 4th March, wrote to Lefebvre that there were only 8000 young troops in Danzig, against 18,000 with him (Corr. 11,921). Again, on the 29th, he says Lefebvre has plenty of troops. There are no good troops in Danzig, and, even if there were, Lefebvre's are their equals (Corr. 12,213).
9. Corr. 12,062, dated 7th March.
10. Corr. 11,162, dated 6th March.
11. Corr. 12,012, dared 12th March.

Schramm's position by field works in all directions: towards Pillau, towards Danzig, and towards Weichselmunde. A bridge over the Vistula was constructed above Danzig.

A general sortie attempted by the garrison, with the object of destroying such works as the besiegers had already constructed, was repulsed. Lefebvre had now collected sufficient troops to warrant him in opening the regular siege.[12]

The question was debated as to the point of attack, and was really decided by Chasseloup, the well-known engineer, to whose counsels Lefebvre was directed to defer in all technical matters. The decision was that the real attack should be on the Hagelsberg front. To divert attention, a false attack was to be made on the Bischofsberg front, and another on the entrenched camp of Neufahrwasser.[13]

It was also very necessary to subdue the works on the left bank of the Lower Vistula, connecting Danzig and Weichselmunde. The ground about them, marshy, and cut up by canals, was extremely unfavourable to the construction of solid works of approach. Schramm was now securely fortified in the Nehrung, his left supported by a village towards the Lower Vistula, his right resting on the sea. His orders were, as far as possible, to intercept communication between Danzig and Weichselmunde.

On the night of the 1st to 2nd April, the first parallel was opened, to a length of 400 yards, on the crest of the Ziganckenberg, at a distance of 1600 yards from the enemy's works of the Hagelsberg. The operation was completely covered from the defenders' observation by a vigorous attack on the village of Aller, to the left. An attempt, next day, by the besieged to establish themselves in rear of the parallel, at Ziganckendorf, failed.

During the 2nd April, the parallel was completed, notwithstanding a heavy fire from the artillery of the Hagelsberg and Bischofsberg. During the following night the French advanced by zigzags from the parallel, and, at the same time, stormed the Kalk redoubt, on the bank of the river in front of the main works. Kalkreuth, however, in the early morning, recaptured this important fort, which for the present the French were unable to take again. On the 3rd April, the first parallel was extended farther to the left, and was supported by various works and batteries, whilst the advance from it

---

12. Napoleon was, so early as the 31st March, urging expedition in the siege on Lefebvre (Corr. 12,245). On the previous day, he had appointed, to command the artillery of the siege, Lariboisière, a trusted officer (Corr. 12,234, dated 30th March).
13. For reasons as to the best point of attack, see note 4.

was pushed forward. On the 9th, the first parallel of the false attack on the Bischofsberg was opened. The besieged, meanwhile, had been working at a counter approach against the left flank of the true attack, and it was necessary to put a stop to them. At 10 p.m., on the 10th, 500 French attempted an assault on the Prussian work, only 80 yards from the enceinte. Overwhelmed by its fire, they were driven off. Renewing the assault at 1 a.m., they succeeded in taking and destroying the work.

During the night of the 11th to 12th, the second parallel was commenced by flying sap. Next day, the batteries and redoubts commanding the river on the left were partially armed. A commencement of the bombardment of the city was made with two howitzers.

But the garrison was commanded by a man of great energy and activity. The works of counter approach were again taken in hand, the French were driven from them, and a new redoubt in front of the Hagelsberg was thrown up. Attacked by the Saxons, this new work was taken and retaken three times, finally remaining in the possession of the besiegers. The French works were still too distant to allow of their maintaining themselves in the counter approach.[14] They were not left undisturbed. On the 13th, so determined an assault was made upon the captured work that, not only were the Saxons ejected from it, but the head of the French trenches was gained, and, for a moment, they were in great peril. The situation was saved by Lefebvre, who, himself heading the 44th regiment,[15] fell, sword in hand, on the Prussians. Once more the tide of victory turned before this vigorous onslaught, supported by the now rallied Saxons. The Prussians were again forced from the redoubt, now strewn with the dead and wounded of this bitter conflict.

On the 14th April, the French second parallel was completed, and two redoubts to support it were begun. During the ensuing night, the works were pushed leftwards, and batteries were constructed to fire upon the Hagelsberg, and the extremity of the Schidlitz suburb.

Another important point was gained on the north bank of the Vistula by Gardanne, who established himself and constructed two works at the north entrance to the canal of Laake, thus interrupting

14. Kirgener, p. 3.

15. This regiment had been at Eylau, part of Augereau's unfortunate corps. It was next to the 14th in the fatal attack, and appears to have lost its eagle. There is, in the *Archives Historiques*, a long correspondence between the two regiments as to which it was that had lost its eagle. The decision was in favour of the 14th, whose eagle was saved by Marbot, according to his own account. In glancing over this correspondence, the author did not observe any mention of Marbot's exploit.

communication by it.[16] On the 16th, a powerful sortie from Weichselmunde was directed on these works. Heavy fighting, lasting seven hours, ended in its repulse, when the works were resumed and completed. They had to be protected from the enemy's fire from Weichselmunde in one direction, and the island of Holm in the other.

At this time, three separate attacks were in progress (1) the true attack on the Hagelsberg; (2) the false attack on the Bischofsberg; (3) another attack on the defender's works on the Lower Vistula.

Using the flying sap, a movement forward from the second parallel was made on the 17th, and a place of arms was constructed on a plateau only 80 yards from the Hagelsberg front. The batteries and redoubts were completed, and their armament advanced. On the 17th, a work on the left bank of the river, designed to cross fire with Gardanne's works on the right bank, was thrown up, and an English corvette, attempting to ascend the river, was forced to desist.

Whilst zigzags on the left of the second parallel were constructed, a great battery was commenced on the Stolzenberg, with a view to bringing a reverse and enfilading fire to bear on the Hagelsberg.

The 19th, 20th, and 21st April were days of rain and snow, which filled the French works, and stopped all progress. The whole of the 10th was spent in clearing the snow from the trenches. On the 21st, a second place of arms in front of the right of the parallel was constructed.[17]

The night of the 22nd-23rd was bright, and the French suffered heavily from the Prussian fire, as they pushed forward in the moonlight, by flying sap, from the right-hand place of arms. By the 24th, the French had 69 guns, howitzers, and mortars firing on the Hagelsberg and the city beyond it. The defenders replied with equal vivacity, but were overmatched. A summons to surrender was refused by Marshal Kalkreuth.

On the 23rd, the sapheads were overthrown by a small sortie. Another battery, against the Bischofsberg was constructed on the southern slope of the Stolzenberg. Artillery and ammunition were now arriving from Warsaw.[18]

The day of the 26th was one of heavy artillery fire on both sides. About 7 p.m., that of the Prussians suddenly ceased, a fact which

---

16. These two redoubts were about 600 yards apart, on the right bank of the canal, and were, on the 17th, connected by a double parapet (Dumas, xviii. p. 154).

17. Kirgener, p. 8.

18. Napoleon, writing to his brother Joseph, on the 24th April, mentions that he has 80 pieces of artillery before Danzig, of which 60 were siege guns. He also indirectly estimates the garrison at 18,000, and the besieging corps at 25,000 (Corr. 12,469).

aroused suspicions that they were about to attempt a sortie, to meet which preparations were made. These suspicions were justified by the event, for, about 10 p.m., the French advanced posts, rushing in, announced the issue of the enemy.

Six hundred Prussian troops, followed by 200 workmen, whose duty it was to destroy the works when captured, fell upon the head of the French trenches. Menard, prepared for the coming storm, met it with the bayonet in front, whilst detachments, which he had placed on his right and left, charged the Prussians in flank. The Prussian loss was heavy, and the sortie completely failed.

A truce of two hours, for the burial of those killed in this sortie, afforded the French an opportunity of surveying the ground in front of them, and selecting sites for new batteries.

On the Lower Vistula, the attack was pushed from the mouth of the Laake canal; the extremity of the Holm island was seized by Sabatier from the left bank of the Vistula, and defended by a channel cut across it from the canal to the river. Communication was thus established, in this direction, between the right and left banks by boat bridges across the river and the canal.

On the 25th, the third parallel in front of the Hagelsberg had been commenced, 40 yards from the covered way on the crest of the rising ground. On the 26th and 27th, it was continued, in the face of sorties on both days. At 10 p.m., on the 28th, the garrison made a fresh sortie in force.[19] Their attack on the left of the third parallel was beaten off, the assailants being pursued to the covered way. A battalion of Prussian grenadiers on the other side was, at first, more successful in penetrating to the head of the trenches, where, however, they met the French reserves. Thrice was the attack renewed before the Prussians were compelled, with heavy loss, to seek again the shelter of their fortress.

On the 29th, the third parallel was extended right and left. On the 30th, the bombardment was continued, and Danzig was fired in several places, though the besieged replied with vigour.

During the night, notwithstanding the illumination by the defenders of the enemy's works by means of fire balls, the communications between the second and third parallels were completed, and the French commenced to approach, by double sap, from two points in the third parallel, towards the capital of the ravelin.

On the earthworks of the place the French artillery was producing but little effect, and the destruction of the palisades became necessary before an assault could be ventured on.

---

19. 2000 men, according to Kirgener (p. 13).

The approaches progressed on the 2nd May, and next night they were united near the parallel. One more sortie against the works was beaten off. Early on the morning of the 4th, the Prussian artillery brought the saps to a standstill, until it was silenced by the batteries of the second parallel. On the 5th and 6th, the saps were continued, though constantly interrupted by the fire of the fortress. They reached to a distance of only 12 yards from the salient of the ravelin.

The Holm island was still held by the garrison, with the exception of the extremity captured on the 26th April. Until the French could get possession of it, they were unable to establish satisfactory batteries taking in reverse the works of the Hagelsberg. Chasseloup insisted on the necessity for seizing it; Lefebvre decided to do so on the night of the 6th–7th. Its garrison consisted of 150 men, 15 guns, a mortar, and a howitzer.[20]

The main attack was to be made by Drouet from the left bank of the Vistula, whilst Gardanne seconded him from the direction of the canal. At 10 p.m., 12 boats, containing 300 men in all, pushed off from the left bank, followed shortly by a second detachment. Landing unperceived, the French stormed two redoubts, driving their defenders to the south end of the island. At the same time, the Kalk redoubt was attacked and taken. The enemy's retreat was cut off by Gardanne, who had crossed the canal The second detachment, from the left bank, was equally successful in capturing a large redoubt. All the works on the island were seized in succession, the garrison being almost entirely destroyed or captured. Surrounded as they were, escape was scarcely possible.

The island was a most valuable prize; it was promptly fortified, and its guns turned against Danzig, the defences of which they took in reverse. A bridge of rafts joining it to the left bank, just below the angle of the river, was hurried on.[21] The flying bridge connecting Danzig with the island was gallantly cut adrift, by a miner named Jacquemart, under a heavy fire.

The works and palisades of the Hagelsberg were at last suffering severely from the heavy fire of the besiegers, and, on the 7th, the crowning of the covered way, opposite the salient of the ravelin, was

20. Hoepfner, iii. 466. Dumas gives only 1000 men besides artillery. He says there were as many howitzers and mortars as guns, but, as only 17 pieces were captured, this seems to be a mistake (Dumas, xviii. 167). The numbers in the text are given by Hoepfner (iii. 446).

21. Kirgener (p. 18) summarises the advantages of the capture of the island and the Kalk redoubt as: (a) the improved reverse fire which was possible from the island; (b) the saving of the necessity far numerous traverses in the trenches to protect the workers from the enfilading fire from the Kalk redoubt.

successfully effected in the face of a storm of grape, which cost the French 100 men. The situation of the mines constructed by the besieged was discovered, and they were occupied.

The defenders of the covered way were forced, by the fire of two batteries, to evacuate the whole of that part of it, except a blockhouse in the re-entrant angle of the right face of the ravelin.

On the 8th, the left sap was advanced to the capital of the bastion.

Lefebvre was now for attempting an assault, for which the place was not yet ripe.[22] Reconnaissances soon satisfied him that this was so. Yet his works of approach had reached a stage when the early surrender of the fortress, unless relief reached it from outside, was a matter of certainty.

The state of affairs was known to Bennigsen, and he had resolved on a supreme effort to save the fortress by an expedition from the sea.

Napoleon, too, had inferred that this must come, and had made his arrangements accordingly.[23] For some days past the presence of Prussian vessels in the Frisches-Haff had been observed. Napoleon had constituted, for the purpose of combating any such attempt at relief, a new reserve corps, of which the command was given to Lannes. It consisted of the picked grenadier division of Oudinot, and of the division of Verdier: altogether, between 15,000 and 16,000 men.

This corps had been detailed for the assistance of Lefebvre, on the distinct understanding that it was to be used only against a relieving force, not for the ordinary work of the siege.[24] Mortier was also ordered to Danzig.[25] Lefebvre had desired Oudinot to send a brigade into the

---

22. This was Napoleon's opinion on the 5th May, when he sent Bertrand to Danzig to inspect the works and bring a personal report (Corr. 12,534). Lefebvre, on the 9th, gave notice to his commanders of his intention to assault (Kirgener, p. 29). It was suspended next day.

23. So early as the 23rd April he warns Lefebvre to be on his guard against a descent from the Frisches-Haff, which the enemy commands (Corr. 12,458). On the 11th May he again writes, indicating the probability of an attempt to relieve the fortress from the sea, but saps he sees no movement in his own front, such as might be expected (Corr. 12,572).

24. Corr. 12,536, dated 5th May, to Berthier, orders the formation of the corps from Oudinot's and Verdier's divisions. The Emperor hopes, by the end of May, to raise its strength to 20,000 by the addition of an Italian division. In Corr. 12,572, dated 11th May, Napoleon tells Lefebvre that Oudinot is available at Marienburg, but is not under Lefebvre's orders. In a letter from Berthier of the same date, Lefebvre is censured for having ordered up Oudinot; and it is remarked that the Emperor does not believe that more than a diversion with a small force will be attempted by the Nehrung. The great effort he expected from the sea. (Printed, Dumas, xix. 288.)

25. Berthier to Mortier, Dumas, xix. 288, dated (continued on next page)

Nogat island from Marienberg, where the corps was assembled. He had also warned Schramm, on the Nehrung, to be on his guard.

On the 10th and 11th May, 57 transports, crowded with Russian troops, appeared off Weichselmunde. They were the relief force, under Kamenskoi, detached from the main army, and sent by sea from Pillau. On the whole, it seems improbable that Kamenskoi commanded more than 7000 or 8000 men,[26] including the garrisons of Weichselmunde and Neufahrwasser. He disembarked, on the 11th, at Neufahrwasser. He was, till he landed, unaware of the loss of the island of Holm, which seriously compromised his plans.

Lannes' leading division (Oudinot) only arrived at Danzig on the 12th, as Kamenskoi landed. The besiegers were in imminent peril had Kamenskoi attacked promptly, before the arrival of the whole. Lefebvre's address to his men shows that he felt his danger. "Comrades," he said, "as long as we live, we will abandon nothing to the enemy; let every man defend his post to the death."

But Kamenskoi was disturbed at finding the island gone, and he hesitated, wasting precious hours and days. The delay gave time for the French reinforcements to arrive, and for arrangements to be completed. With the reserve corps at hand, it was still not so easy for Lefebvre to decide on the best mode of employing it. To Kamenskoi, holding Weichselmunde and Neufahrwasser, with free communication between them across the river, two courses were open. Being safe behind the works, he could elect to act against Schramm in the Nehrung, or against the left flank of the French works on the left bank. In the latter case he could hope for the co-operation of the garrison from the Hagelsberg and Bischofsberg. This was the more promising scheme, as it was the more dangerous to Lefebvre. Attacked in front and flank, there was considerable risk of the besiegers on the left bank being rolled up from their left. If Schramm were attacked, he might be destroyed before he could be succoured; but he was well protected by works, and it was unlikely. It is true that the French had a bridge across the river near its bend; still, a disaster might occur to Lefebvre before Lannes, if he were on the Holm island, could cross. It was de-

<hr />

12th May. On the same date Oudinot is ordered to Danzig, but to leave a battalion at Furstenwerder to construct a bridge (Berthier to Lannes, Dumas, xix. 287). On the 14th, Napoleon writes to Lefebvre that Lannes is only to be used against a relieving force from the sea (*Corr.* 12,881).

26. Dumas (xviii. 174) puts the number as high as 11,000 to 15,000, but seems uncertain. Kirgener (p. 25) only estimates his force at 7000 or 8000. Hoepfner (iii. 483) gives 6600.

cided to keep him on the left bank, whence, if the storm burst on the Nehrung, he might be able to pass in time.

Kamenskoi wasted four days, concerting measures by signal from Weichselmunde, keeping his troops in Neufahrwasser. On the 13th, the besieged force increased the vigour of their fire on the works of approach; a sortie, in the evening, penetrated into the head of the sap before it was repulsed.

Work was continued on the 14th by the French against the bastion on their left, but the difficulties were great. A mine was also started against the blockhouse in the re-entrant angle of the covered way. At last, at 4 a.m. on the 15th May, Kamenskoi issued from Weichselmunde against Schramm and Gardanne, whose troops were drawn up about the redoubts facing Weichselmunde.

The Russian movement was made in four columns:—

1st: 6 battalions, 1 squadron, 200 Cossacks, and 4 guns, on the left, along the seashore against the wood.

2nd: 5 battalions against the work at the head of the wood, in the centre.

3rd: 6 battalions, 120 Cossacks, 4 guns along the Vistula, on the right.

4th: 4 battalions, 100 Cossacks, 6 guns, in reserve in front of the fort.

At the same time, a demonstration with a few hundred men was made, on the opposite bank, by the Neufahrwasser garrison.

In Danzig, 1000 men were ready to cross to the Holm island when it should be attacked from Weichselmunde. The English ships were to endeavour to assist in the river.

On the other side, Schramm had, on his right, the 2nd light infantry; in the centre, a Saxon infantry brigade; on the left, towards the canal, his Polish infantry; in reserve, the Paris infantry regiment.

The first assault was on Schramm's left and centre, about 5 a.m. Seeing them yielding ground, Lefebvre sent over a battalion to his aid. Four times did the Russians attack; on the last occasion they were nearly successful. As they retired, the battle was restored by the use of the reserve.

At this moment, Lannes and Oudinot arrived with the first column of the reserve corps; the engagement became very hot and sanguinary. Oudinot's horse was killed, and, falling against Lannes, the latter also was unhorsed. The two generals continued the fight on foot.

The Russians were now overmatched, and were presently driven back upon Weichselmunde, with a loss of over 1500 killed and wounded. The French lost about equally.[27]

---

27. Hoepfner, iii. 486. He says that the loss (1530) was equal to about one-fourth of Kamenskoi's force.

Kalhreuth had not supported Kamenskoi by a sortie against the works, but had contented himself with a heavy bombardment. He asserted that he was prepared for an attack on the island, when Kamenskoi's advance collapsed, and rendered it useless:[28]

To support the sortie from Weichselmunde, Bulow, with 4 battalions, 2 companies of artillery, and 100 cavalry, sailed on the Frisches-Haff from Pillau. He was late, and Kamenskoi was already defeated when he landed and came upon Schramm's outposts at Kalberg. They fell back on Furstenwerder, whilst the Prussians marched along the south side of the Nehrung to the western extremity of the Haff. Against them, from Furstenwerder, there came the battalion of Oudinot's grenadiers in the Nogat island, with Beaumont's dragoons.[29] Meeting Bulow, they defeated him, and drove him, with heavy loss, 25 miles along the Nehrung.

The attempt to relieve Danzig had failed disastrously, owing largely, as it would appear, to Kamenskoi's delay, as well as to the insufficiency of his force. It was not renewed. The Russians remained in their entrenchments at the mouth of the river.

The besiegers' works against the Hagelsberg had suffered no interruption. On the evening of the 16th, the mine under the blockhouse was fired, but without completely destroying it, though it was much damaged. A fresh mine was commenced from the crater formed, and was continued on the 17th. A small sortie, in the evening, resulted in the spiking of a French howitzer opposite the salient of the bastion, but it was unspiked after the sortie had been repulsed.

On the 18th, 19th, and 20th, a covered descent into the ditch was worked, and endeavours were made, without much success, to destroy the enormous palisades in the ditch.[30]

---

28. Hoepfner, iii. 487.

29. In Berthier's letter to Lannes, of the 12th May (Dumas, xix. 287), he is ordered to leave at Furstenwerder the battalion of grenadiers which had been sent there to construct a bridge and guard the crossing. All the correspondence, about this date, from Berthier, insists that any movement from Pillau along the Nehrung can be nothing but a diversion, and that the real relieving force will come by sea. (See despatches from Berthier to Lefebvre on the 11th, and to Lannes on the 12th, Dumas, xix. 284-288.)

30. The Hagelsberg ditch was found to be 27 feet deep, and the slope of the breach in the left face of the bastion was very steep. Endeavours to make it less so were made from the covered descent (Kirgener, p. 28). The covered descent was made with gabions on either side, roofed in with fascines and earth.

On the 19th, an English corvette, trying to ascend the river, grounded, and was captured.[31] The guns of the fortress were still firing with considerable effect on the works of approach.

Kalkreuth's last sortie was made on the night of the 20th. After succeeding in destroying the work of the preceding day, it was finally driven back with the aid of reinforcements.

On the 21st, Mortier joined Lefebvre with all his corps, except what he had left in front of Colberg. In the night of the 21st, Vallet, a private of the 12th infantry of the line, ventured on a gallant enterprise. On the crest of the breach, in front of the covered descent of the ditch, the Prussians had arranged three great beams, retained by ropes, ready to be rolled down on the assailants issuing from the descent. Vallet alone climbed the breach to cut the cords. He succeeded, though wounded, in his desperate business. The beams rolled into the ditch, and, under the constant fire from the French guns, it was impossible to replace them.

The Hagelsberg was now, or very shortly would be, in a condition to warrant an assault, which was ordered by Lefebvre[32] at Napoleon's instance. Before delivering it, he sent a final summons to Kalkreuth. That officer had made a resistance distinguished by that activity which is essential to every able defence of a fortress, and he now consented to open negotiations.

He declined to treat for the surrender of Neufahrwasser and Weichselmunde, pointing out that, separated as he was from them, he could not control their garrisons.

If he was in a position which compelled him to desire a capitulation on honourable terms, Napoleon was still more inclined to grant them.[33] The summer was now commencing, and the Emperor was anxious to reopen the campaign, which he dared not do with Danzig still holding out in his rear. He wanted, too, the troops besieging it.

---

31. The plan at the end of Kirgener's work shows the scene of this event at a point about halfway between the angle of the river and the northern extremity of the Holm island.

32. Napoleon, at last, thought the time for assault had arrived, and that more men were being lost in the daily bombardments and sorties than would fall in a storm (Berthier to Lefebvre, 13th May, Dumas, xix. 298).

33. *Corr.* 12,629, dated 22nd May, to Lefebvre. The Emperor grudges the loss of the garrison, whom he estimates at 10,000 or 12,000, as prisoners of war; but has clearly weighed with care the considerations in favour of obtaining an immediate surrender. He lays down the terms to he granted, which are practically those accepted by the governor of Danzig. The Emperor still thought it might take another 15 days to compel an unconditional surrender.

After three days of negotiation, the terms of surrender were fixed. The garrison was to march out with all the honours of war, with drums beating, matches lighted, and standards flying, taking two light guns with them. They were to be conducted to the Prussian outposts before Pillau. On the other hand, they engaged not to fight against the French and their allies for a year.

The actual surrender was arranged for the 26th May, on the formal condition that the place was not relieved from outside before then. At noon on that day, the western works were handed over to the French. Next day the garrison marched off along the Nehrung for Pillau, whilst Lefebvre made his formal entry into Danzig.[34]

Kamenskoi had set sail from Weichselmunde, and, shortly after, the garrison of the fort surrendered.

Thus ended this memorable siege, the conduct of which was shortly afterwards acknowledged by the conferment on Lefebvre of the Dukedom of Danzig.[35] The defence had redounded to the credit of Kalkreuth and his garrison, who, contesting almost every inch of the besiegers' progress, had held out over seven weeks against open trenches.

The one blot on the defence would appear to be the failure to support, by sorties, Kamenskoi's relieving force.

The siege is a typical example of the regular approach of a bastioned front with dry ditches; for water, of course, was not available for those of the outer line of works.

The besiegers, too, had many difficulties to contend against; they were, at first, in inferior force, both in men and guns; the perimeter to be guarded was great; there was no proper plan of the defences; the ground on the front of attack was difficult to reconnoitre in advance of the siege works.

The island of Holm was all-important to them, as enabling fire to bear on the reverse of the front of attack. The desirability of its early capture is admitted by Kirgener, the French engineer,[36] but he points out the difficulties of an attack on it, so long as the garrison held the Kalk redoubt, so often taken and retaken, on Lefebvre's left. It was

---

34. The number that marched out is given by Hoepfner (iii. 523) as 335 officers, 12,448 men, 1275 horses. This takes no account of the garrisons of Weichselmunde and Neufahrwasser.

35. Corr. 12,666, dated 28th May, being Napoleon's message to the Senate regarding the creation of a new order of nobility.

36. See Kirgener's conclusions, quoted in Dumas, xviii. 191, etc. They are at pp. 38-47 of Kirgener's précis.

fortunate for the French that they held that island when Kamenskoi fell upon Schramm in the Nehrung. Without it, and the bridge uniting it to the left bank of the Vistula, his relief by Lannes and Oudinot would scarcely have been possible. The capture of Neufahrwasser and Weichselmunde, thus separating Danzig from the sea, was also very desirable. Kirgener, however, points out that all the artillery available was required at the Hagelsberg, and they could only be taken with the aid of siege guns. He also discusses fully the respective merits of an attack on the Hagelsberg and on the Bischofsberg.[37] The reasons in favour of the former are technical, and apparently forcible.

From famine or shortness of supplies or ammunition the garrison had never suffered. Enormous quantities of stores of every description remained in the place, and were of the utmost service to the French. Whether Kalkreuth should not have held out longer is a moot point. The Hagelsberg would probably have been stormed with great slaughter on both sides. It was only an outer defence it is true, but it commanded Danzig, and the main fortress could hardly hope to hold out long against a bombardment from it. Kalkreuth had nothing to hope for from a fresh effort by Kamenskoi to relieve him, nor had he any grounds for believing that Bennigsen would himself be able to do much. On the other hand, the terms offered by Napoleon were such as to indicate his extreme anxiety to terminate the siege which, so long as it lasted, forbade his advance against Bennigsen. Kalkreuth had hardly sufficient grounds for assuming that even a few days' prolongation of the defence would not prove of immense service to the main army, if only in detaining the besieging corps from joining Napoleon's advance. Such considerations tend to throw doubt on the question of whether Kalkreuth did all that was possible.

---

37. *Vide supra*, p. 244, note.

CHAPTER 3

Operations in Silesia and Pomerania, on the Narew and on the Vistula, March to May, 1807

SILESIA

The operations in Silesia were left at the surrender of Breslau on the 7th January.

Brieg, invested by Vandamme with the Wurtemberg division and a few Bavarian battalions towards the end of January, surrendered, with large quantities of artillery and ammunition, on the 8th February.

The Prince of Anhalt-Pless was still in the field. He was attacked and driven into Glatz by the Bavarian cavalry under Lefebvre-Desnouettes, who remained in observation of the fortress, whilst Vandamme laid siege to Kosel, Neisse and Schweidnitz. The last-named surrendered on the 11th April. A vigorous attempt to succour Neisse from Glatz was beaten off, but the fortress held out bravely till the 16th June. Glatz was then attacked, and surrendered on the 28th June.

The army of Silesia had, as already noted, been weakened by a Bavarian division sent to Masséna, in place of which Jerome was directed to recruit 8000 Poles.[1]

It is unnecessary to go farther into the details of the operations in Silesia.[2] As the fortresses fell, the artillery captured in them was utilised for the sieges, not only of the other Silesian fortresses, but also for those of Danzig, Graudenz, and Colberg. The Emperor further drew from Silesia immense resources in kind and in money.[3]

---

1. Corr. 12,305, dated 5th April.
2. Very full details of the sieges will be found in Hoepfner (vol. iv.), who, as a Prussian, was specially interested in them, and who gives throughout much fuller accounts of Prussian than of Russian movements.
3. By June, Jerome's corps had been very much reduced (continues on next page)

In Pomerania, Mortier was last mentioned as holding, up to the end of January, the line of the Peene.

A good deal of trouble was experienced from the enterprise of the Prussian garrison of Colberg, which sent raiding expeditions far and wide.

In the middle of February an Italian division, under Teulié, was sent to blockade the place, which it succeeded in doing after some sharp actions during its advance.

On the 28th January, Mortier, deciding to blockade Stralsund, passed the Peene at Anklam and Demmin, and between them. Granjean on the right, driving the Swedish outposts before him, reached Greifswalde, which he carried with slight loss. Dupas, on the left, advanced parallel to Granjean, without encountering any resistance. The two columns next day, after a slight combat, arrived in front of Stralsund. On the 30th, the blockade of the land side was completed, but the communications by sea with the island of Rugen remained open, and Mortier was much annoyed by fire from gunboats.

For two months he continued before Stralsund, completing the lines of investment, and occasionally engaging in small combats with the garrison, which was no means inactive. During this period 3 French infantry, and 1 cavalry regiment were taken from him to the Vistula, and replaced by Dutch troops.

On the 29th March, he was ordered to leave only Granjean's division[4] before Stralsund, and to proceed, with the rest of his corps, to Colberg. No sooner was he gone than Essen, the Swedish general in command of Stralsund, issued from the place, with greatly superior numbers, against the weak division of Granjean. The latter, attacked in front and threatened on his left, was compelled to fall back by Greifswalde on Anklam across the Peene. Attacked there on the 3rd April, he was again driven on Uckermunde. Once more threatened on both flanks with interruption of his line to Stettin, he retired to that place, reaching it on the 7th April. He now received orders from Mortier to move on Pasewalk. The marshal himself started on the 11th to his assistance at Stettin, which he reached on the 13th with one French

---

by drafts to Masséna, etc. The return for the 15th June (Arch. Hist.) gives his strength as—

Bavarians	2629
Wurtembergers	5640
Total	8269

4. Two French and two Dutch infantry regiments, and one of Dutch cavalry.

and one Italian infantry regiment, and a regiment and a half of cavalry. Granjean was reinforced the same day by a French infantry regiment from Berlin. Mortier, including Granjean's division, now had 12,000 or 13,000 men, about equal to the strength of the Swedes.

Leaving at Pasewalk a provisional regiment which had just arrived, Mortier advanced against the enemy, and, in a series of actions, drove him upon Anklam. The weather was very bad, constant hail and rain, but the Swedes were steadily forced back across the Peene on the 17th April.

Mortier had been authorised to propose to Essen an armistice, and to raise the blockade of Stralsund. The Swedes were discontented at the want of support from England, and the French successes decided Essen, with the consent of his sovereign, to treat.

Between the 18th and the 29th April, the negotiations ended in an armistice terminable only after a month's notice, and confining the Swedes to the line of the Peene. They also made over to the French the islands of Usedom and Wollin, engaging to render no assistance to the beleaguered garrisons in Colberg and Danzig.

This armistice was a great relief to Napoleon, enabling him, as it did, to utilise the greater part of Mortier's corps on the Lower Vistula. No further mention of operations in Swedish Pomerania will be necessary. Mortier may henceforward be considered as forming part of the main army on the Vistula.

On the Vistula and the Narew

When Napoleon, satisfied that the enemy in front of him was at last settling down for the rest which both armies so badly needed, had himself withdrawn his corps to their cantonments, he adhered generally to his original scheme of the 20th February.

He carried on, during this period of rest, some desultory negotiations, not so much, probably, with any hope or desire of success, as with the wish not to irritate Austria by a refusal of her mediation, which had been offered and accepted.[5] He was busy, as ever, directing the siege of Danzig, and ordering the fortification of his line of cantonments[6] so that the position became almost impregnable.

---

5. Corr. 12,391, dated 16th April.
6. Corr. 12,144, dated 24th March, gives detailed orders regarding the entrenched camp at Praga. Corr. 12,321, dated 6th April, again alludes to the strengthening of the front about Osterode. Davout fortified the château at Allenstein (Davout, pp, 187 and 190). Bridge-heads were constructed at Braunsberg and Spanden. Ney fortified Guttstadt. The ground being generally frozen, wood and manure were used for works (Davout, p. 187). Numerous other works on the Alle were constructed (ibid., p, 190)

Supplies, which had been very scarce in February and March,[7] now arrived regularly, as the means of transport were organised and improved. The Imperial headquarters were removed on the 1st April to Finkenstein.[8]

It was only on the 11th May[9] that Napoleon saw indications of an early attempt to relieve Danzig from the sea. The measures which he took to reinforce Lefebvre have already been described in the history of the siege.

Though, on the 11th May, there were no signs visible to Napoleon of a movement in his own front, he was naturally not surprised when they appeared a few days later. It was to be expected that a demonstration at least, if not a serious attack, would be made by Bennigsen to withdraw the Emperor's attention from Danzig, and to prevent him, if possible, from reinforcing Lefebrve. On the same day, 11th May, there were assembled at Heilsberg the Russian 1st, 2nd, 3rd, and 14th divisions, and the cavalry of the left wing; whilst the 7th and 8th divisions, with the right wing cavalry, concentrated at Burgerswalde. On the 13th, a forward movement was made from Heilsberg the Launau, and from Burgerswalde towards Wormditt and Arensdorf; but, as it was reported that Napoleon also was on the point of advancing in great force, the movement was abandoned; on the 14th, the troops returned to their former cantonments.

On the 13th, Platow had successfully attacked a Polish post and had driven in Gazan's outposts in front of Willemburg.[10] A somewhat more decided movement, to be described presently, had been made against Masséna; but, on the whole, the diversion to cover the operations for the relief of Danzig by Kamenskoi was most feeble. Napoleon had expected something much more serious, and was prepared for it.

Had it been more positive in its nature, Ney was to concentrate in a strongly entrenched position about Guttstadt and Wolfsdorf. Davout in similar positions at Hohenstein, Allenstein, and Osterode; Soult at Elditten; Bernadotte on the Lower Passarge. Murat,

---

7. "The Russians appear to be like us, and not to have eaten for several days" (Corr. 11,895 dated 27th February). More complaints of shortness of food (Corr. 11,897, dated 27th February). Ney is told, on the 7th March, that he must be patient in his deficiency of supplies, which are at Osterode, detained by want of transport (Corr. 11,967). Even on the 27th March it is noted that Ney is hard up for food (Corr. 12,194).

8. Corr. 12,263, dated Finkenstein, 2nd April.

9. Corr. 12,572, dated 11th May. Even then Napoleon saw no signs of an advance in front of himself.

10. Masséna, v. 328.

with a great part of his cavalry reserve supported by infantry, would advance through Willemburg and Wurtemberg, followed by Zayonchek from Neidenburg, and with Gazan moving, on his right, from Willemburg on Oertelsberg,[11] thus threatening that left wing which, since the operations before Eylau, had always been a source of anxiety to Bennigsen.

After these futile threats on the part of Bennigsen, both armies settled down again into a tacit cessation of hostilities until the time came, early in June, for the opening of the final campaign.

During the months from the battle of Ostrolenka till June, the course of events on the Narew had not been very active. On the 8th March, the Bavarian division which Napoleon had ordered from Silesia reached Warsaw, between 7000 and 8000 men, under the Crown Prince of Bavaria and General Wrede. Masséna fixed his headquarters at Prasznitz. The Bavarian division he posted with one brigade on the Narew, from Sierock to Pultusk; the other, and the cavalry, partly at Praga, partly at Prasznitz. Suchet's division held the Narew from Pultusk to the Omulew at Zawady. Along the Omulew from Zawady to Willemburg was Gazan's division, with Becker's dragoons between Janow and Chorzel. The link between Gazan's left and Davout's right, at Allenstein, was supplied by Zayonchek's Poles. A third brigade of Bavarians, arriving early in April, remained at Warsaw. On the Russian side, a line of Cossack posts watched the French on the Omulew, and had behind it Wolkonski's troops in support. More Russians, between the Narew and the Bug, watched the course of the former river from Ostrolenka to Sierock. On the 14th April,[12] the Emperor directed Masséna to clear the space in front of the Pultusk and Sierock bridges. This was done by 200 Polish cavalry driving back the Cossacks on Wyszkowo, whilst Lemarrois, from Warsaw, followed in the same direction on the 10th May. Popowo was reached that day, and the Russians concentrated on Wyszkowo. On the 12th they moved out, under General Loewis, against the Bavarians, pushing them back on Nowavics, and, on the following day, to the bridge-head at Sierock.[13]

---

11. Hoepfner, iii. 529.

12. Corr. 12,378, dated 14th April.

13. Masséna's memoirs (Koch) say that, on the 12th May, another attack was made at the mouth of the Omulew, which, though successful at first, was eventually repulsed by Girard. On this day Gazan, as already mentioned, was also attacked at Willemburg. Masséna himself was in front of Chorzel with a Bavarian force, to prevent the turning either of Suchet on his right or of Gazan on his left (Masséna, v. 328)

Masséna, to check this movement, sent troops across the river at Pultusk, towards Poplawy and Psary.[14] Before the superior forces now arrayed against them, the Russians fell back after a sharp fight. After this, Masséna cleared the peninsula between the Bug and the Narew for some distance, and was not seriously molested during the rest of the month of May.[15]

---

14. The date of this action is given in the memoirs of Masséna as the 16th May (Masséna, v. 329).

15. Napoleon's fresh instructions to Masséna are well worthy of study (Corr. 12,596, dated 17th May, 1807). His duties are laid down as: (a) to cover Warsaw; (b) to form the right of the army; (c) to hold an offensive position, alarming the enemy for his left, and preventing him from weakening it to support his centre and right. The enemy could advance on Warsaw either by the Bug or by the Narew. To cover the city, therefore, Sierock would be the best point. The next best position would be astride of the Narew, between Pultusk and Rozan, at the extremity of the great bend which was only 8 or 9 miles from the Bug. The third best would be Pultusk, but it would be inferior owing to its distance from the Bug. Last of all would come Ostrolenka: it, however, would be as far from there to Brok as to Sierock. But there was also to be taken into consideration Masséna's third object, and for that Ostrolenka would be by far the best position. Therefore, Suchet should occupy the right bank in force, with outposts in forts at Ostrolenka. Seven Bavarian battalions should hold Ostrykow, at the angle of the Narew, three should be at Krasnosielsk, two at Pultusk, two at Sierock, a light infantry battalion in Ostrolenka. "Should it be asked why Ostrolenka is to be occupied, the answer is simple; it is, in the first place, that the enemy may not occupy it; next, it is in order to occupy both banks of the Narew, without the navigation of which it is impossible to live; lastly, the occupation of both banks acts as a menace to the enemy."

PART 5

The Final Triumph—
Heilsburg, Friedland & Tilsit

The Renewal of the Campaign and its Progress to the 9th June

THE RUSSIAN ADVANCE

Napoleon had begun to contemplate a renewal of the campaign so early as the 29th April, when he wrote to Soult to send his sick to the rear, preparatory to a general advance.[1] But he did not wish to push on towards Russia so long as Danzig remained untaken on his rear, and he was disappointed as to the progress of the siege. By the 8th May, he was able to judge, approximately, when Danzig would fall. He wrote that he hoped to have it by the 20th, and to commence his general movement in the first half of June. He had fixed on the 10th, thinking that, now Danzig had fallen, it was extremely improbable the enemy would take the initiative.[2] So little did he apprehend this, that he paid a two-days' visit to Danzig so late as the 31st May.[3] Everything was, however, in readiness, whether for an advance or for meeting an attack by the enemy.

Rapp, now appointed Governor of Danzig, had been instructed to put the place in a state to stand a fresh siege from the sea or from the Nehrung.[4] Pile bridges were under construction at Dirschau and Marienburg, which had acquired an entirely new importance as lines

---

1. *Corr.* 12,496.
2. On the afternoon of the 5th June, Napoleon wrote to Soult, "Everything leads to the belief that the enemy is on the move, though it is ridiculous on his part to engage in a general action now that Danzig is taken. . . . I shall be very glad if the enemy spares us the trouble of going to him. My design was to set myself in motion on the 10th" (*Corr.* 12,731).
3. In *Corr.* 12,710, dated 2nd June, the Emperor writes that he had been two days at Danzig; and was returning that evening to Finkenstein.
4. *Corr.* 12,728, dated 5th June. This seems to be merely a written reminder; for the Emperor, during his visit to Danzig, had, no doubt, discussed this question fully.

of communication, since the capture of Danzig.[5] The fullest instructions had been issued for the collection and forwarding of supplies.[6]

All the troops required for the front had arrived, or were on the march, and the corps recently engaged in the siege of Danzig were now available, except in so far as they were required for a garrison for the fortress. Lefebvre's corps was distributed to the garrison and to the corps of Lannes and Mortier.[7]

Facing one another on the line of the Passarge and the Alle, on the Omulew and the Narew, were 220,000 French and auxiliary troops, and 115,000 Russians and Prussians.[8] For the operations north of Masséna's charge there were 190,000 under the Emperor in person, against 100,000 under Bennigsen.

On the 2nd June, Bennigsen, having determined to attack the advanced corps of Ney, had concentrated his army about Heilsberg,

5. *Corr.* 12,662 and 12,663, dated 28th May.

6. These instructions to Daru (*Corr.* 12,689, dated 29th May) are a good example of Napoleon's methods. He states that he wishes to provision his army for eight months. He will require, therefore, for current expenditure and collection of a reserve, a daily supply of 80,000 rations at Warsaw for the right, of 100,000 at Thorn, Wroclavik, and Bromberg for the centre, and of 80,000 for the left at Danzig, Marienburg, Elbing, Marienwerder, etc. The first thing to be done is to settle and mark on a map the areas from which each point is to be supplied. To Warsaw would be assigned a breadth extending from Warsaw to Wroclavik, and a depth including the districts (*arrondissements*) of Warsaw and Kalisch; for the centre, the districts of Posen and Bromberg to a breadth represented by the line Wroclavik-Graudenz; the left would draw from the country between Marienwerder and the sea, with a depth including the whole of Pomerania. Next, the best places for magazines must be selected in each circle. Of supplies there are five sources: (1) what is actually in existence on the 1st June; (2) what can be supplied by each Polish district; (3) what can he demanded from Pomerania; (4) what can be brought up from magazines in rear; (5) what must be brought to supply the existing Polish markets or to start new ones. Before setting up a market, a careful calculation of cost of carriage from Breslau, Custrin, or Magdeburg must be made, and compared with the cost of supplies, if any, procurable in the neighbourhood, the cheapest being chosen. Then follow detailed remarks as to the Lest way of starting markets and searching out the resources of a country.

7. Jomini, Vie de Napoleon, ii. 403.

8. The numbers of the Russians anal Prussians are given in detail by Hoepfner (iii. 555. etc.), and his statement may probably be accepted as fairly correct. It shows these numbers. On the Lower Passarge 15,000 Prussians, exclusive of a detachment on the Nehrung. In support of them was Kamenskoi's division, returned from Danzig, at Lilienthal. The total of this right wing is estimated at 20,000 and 98 guns, including 7500 cavalry. There were, far in rear, the garrison of Koenigsberg and 6000 reserve troops at Gumbinnen. The Russian main army was as follows: (continued on next page)

excepting the advanced guard, Platow's flying column, and the right wing under Lestocq.

His plan for the destruction of Ney was extremely complicated. Whilst Lestocq held the French on the Lower Passarge, 6 columns were to converge on Ney.

1st column—Dochtorow, with 24 battalions and 4 batteries, the 7th and 8th divisions—was to advance from Olbersdorf[9] (Albrechtsdorf), south of Wormditt, driving the French across the Passarge and barring their return with small detachments. He was then to ascend the right bank of the stream, and take up a position between Elditten and Schwendt (Schwenkitten),[10] opposite the bridge of Pithenen. He would thus prevent the junction of Soult and Ney.

Bagration (Launau), advance guard	12,537
Uwarow (cavalry of right wing)	3,836
Dochtorow, 7th division	4,653
Sacken, 3rd division	6,432
Essen III., 8th division	5,670
Osterman Tolstoi, 2nd and 14th divisions	9,615
Galitzin, cavalry of the left wing	2,982
Gortchakow, 6th division and Cossacks	10,873
Guard, Grand Duke Constantine	17,000
Platow's flying column, chiefly Cossacks	6,347
On the Narew, under Tolstoi	15,800

Another 30,000 men, under Lahanov, were on their way, but were still far behind the Russian frontier. Altogether, allowing for sick, straggler, etc., there were about 89,000 regular troops (11,000 of them cavalry), and 8000 Cossacks facing Napoleon. Including the force on the Narew, there were thus about 111,000, not including the Koenigsberg and Graudenz garrisons, the 6000 at Gumbinnen, the detachment on the Nehrung, and the reinforcements under Labanow. (Dumas (xviii. 221) puts the allies at 118,000, including the detachment on the Narew. Danilewski (see note, Hoepfner, iii. 562) gives, as the combined force in the middle of May, 125,000. The discrepancies are not very marked, and it seems safe to take the army at the numbers given in the text. Jomini (Vie de Napoleon, ii. 400) says that the Russians, during the three months after Eylau, had been reinforced by an infantry division and the Guard. Still they were not above 120,000 or 130,000, including Lestocq and the corps on the Narew. The French numbers, according to the table at the end of Dumas, vol. xviii., were, on the Vistula:

Infantry	123,073
Cavalry	30,390
Artillery	4,909
Total	158,372

This does not include officers. Adding for these, and for Dombrowski's division of the 8th corps, the numbers of which are not (continued on next page)

243

2nd column—Sacken, with the 2nd, 3rd, and 14th divisions, and the cavalry of both wings, in all 42 battalions, 140 squadrons, and 9 batteries[11]—was to march by Arensdorf, and attack Ney, supporting the advance guard and the 1st column.

3rd column—Bagration's advance guard, 42 battalions, 10 squadrons, and 6 regiments of Cossacks—leaving its support about Peterswalde, to march by Grünau and Altkirch, so as to cut off the troops which Ney had in Peterswalde. As soon as Altkirch should be taken, the supports to advance and uphold the main body, attacking the enemy between Knopen and Glottau.

4th column—Gortchakow, with the 6th division, 12 battalions, 20 squadrons, and 3 regiments of Cossacks—passing the Alle above Guttstadt, to fall upon Ney's right, detaching a brigade towards Seeburg in support of Platow.

5th column—Platow, 3 battalions, 10 squadrons, 9 regiments of Cossacks, and 12 guns, besides the brigade (Knorring's) above mentioned—masking his movement from Masséna's (Gazan's) outposts about Willemburg, to pass the Alle at Bergfried, and assist in the envelopment of Ney.

6th column—the Grand Duke Constantine, with the 1st division (Guard), 28 battalions, 28 squadrons, 3 batteries—to follow, as reserve, in two columns from Benern, Arensdorf, and Sommerfeld to Petersdorf.

Lestocq, meanwhile, would advance against Bernadotte on the Passarge from Braunsberg to Spanden, holding him there, preventing him from crossing to the right bank, and, at the same time, covering the roads to Zinten and Koenigsberg.

---

stated, it is probable that the army beyond the Lower Vistula was quite 170,000 strong, with about 300 guns. Masséna had about 30,000 on the Narew, and Zayonchek, connecting the two, had perhaps 20,000 Poles. The latter were afterwards used to replace the French at Osterode, Guttstadt, etc., as the Emperor advanced. The exact French numbers at this period are of comparatively little importance, for there can be no doubt that their total beyond the Lower Vistula, excluding the garrison of Danzig and Zayonchek's Poles, exceeded those of Bennigsen by at least 65,000 or 70,000. Rustow (i. 319) gives Napoleon only 158,000, against 101,000 Russians and Prussians on the Vistula, but he, apparently, does not include the troops from Danzig.

9. So the name is written in all the old accounts and maps. In the modern map of 1881, as well as in the copy of the staff map in Moltke's Tactical Problems (Map No. 27), from which the 1881 map is reduced, it is written "Albrechtsdorf.

10. "Schwenkitten" on modern maps.

11. Of 12 to 14 guns each = (say) 120 guns.

The scheme had in its favour the fact that Ney, his front being surrounded by forests, could not see what was going on at any considerable distance. Nevertheless, he obtained sufficient information from his outposts to convince him that some serious movement was in progress before him. He accordingly took measures for the concentration of his corps, with the intention of taking up a position behind Ankendorf, and there holding out till he could receive support from the rest of the army. He also requested Soult to support his left from Elditten, and Davout to strengthen his position at Bergfried on the right.

Bennigsen, originally intending to attack on the 4th of June, had sent orders to Lestocq to alarm the enemy on the Lower Passarge on that day. He now postponed the movement till the 5th, informing Lestocq, but does not seem to have formally cancelled his previous order for the 4th. On that day,[12] therefore, the Prussian outposts and their supports advanced, whilst the main body moved somewhat to its left, so as to be more in touch with the Russians, and available for their assistance in the hour of battle.

Rembow's division was assembled in the night of the 3rd-4th behind Mehlsack, in all about 3000 infantry, 1500 cavalry, and 2 batteries. At 1 a.m. it started for Spanden in four columns. The attack on the bridge-head had already commenced when a message from Dochtorow at Wormditt, inquiring the cause of the cannonade, showed clearly that the attack was premature. Rembow, accordingly, broke off the action and retired, leaving strong outposts watching Spanden. On the same day Dupont had been bombarded at Zagern. These unfortunate premature attacks had no other effect than to put Bernadotte on the alert, and give him time to prepare against a serious advance.

On the 5th June, about 10 a.m., the attack on the Spanden bridgehead was renewed.[13] The works there crossed the neck of a peninsula re-entrant towards the French. A central redoubt, about 1000 paces from the bridge, was connected by parapets with the river on either side. Behind this, immediately in front of the bridge, was another work, open at the gorge, covering the bridge completely.

---

12. Victor (Précis of operations, 1st corps, *Arch. Hist.*) dates these operations the 3rd, which seems to be an error.

13. In a despatch, dated 5th June, to Lannes, Berthier gives the hours at which the various attacks commenced that day on the French corps:

1st corps	Bernadotte	10 a.m.
3rd corps	Davout	9 a.m.
4th corps	Soult	8 a.m.
6th corps	Ney	6 a.m.

The direction of the river facilitated the flanking of the work by troops on the left bank; but as it was, in this neighbourhood, and at this season, fordable in places, its value as a defence was much impaired. In the works beyond the bridge was the 27th light infantry, with 4 guns, and one howitzer. On the left bank, partly above and partly below the bend, was the rest of Villatte's division and artillery.[14]

After two hours' heavy bombardment of the outer work, the Prussians moved to the assault. Waiting till the enemy were at point-blank range, the 27th received them with such a murderous fire that they were driven off with heavy loss,[15] and pursued by the 17th dragoons issuing from the bridge, towards Wusen. In this fight Bernadotte, wounded in the head by a musket ball, had to make over command of the corps to Dupont, who, next day, handed it over to Victor.[16]

Whilst this combat was in progress, Dupont was held fast, at Petelkau and Zagern, by another considerable body of Prussians.[17]

These, of course, were only false attacks; the real one fell upon the advanced corps of Ney, and on that of Soult on his left.

During the night of the 4th-5th Dochtorow had moved on Wormditt. At 6 a.m. he issued from the forest at Albrechtsdorf towards Lomitten, driving in the French outposts. The bridge here was covered by a work, as at Spanden, except that the advanced work consisted of redoubts at either extremity of a breastwork, another work thrown forward on the high ground on the right bank, and another on the corresponding ground of the left bank. On the left front of the bridge, the wood had been fortified by *abattis*. One battalion of the 57th was, with 4 guns, in the bridge-head and works; the other held the wood on the left. A battalion of the 4th light infantry was in the wood on the Liebstadt road, on the left bank. The

---

14. The precise dispositions are thus given by Victor (*Arch. Hist.*):
Girard's brigade (94th and 95th regiments) on the left, in a wood between Spanden and Schlodien.
63rd regiment, on heights behind the bridge.
17th dragoons, with the 63rd infantry.
2 guns, on a height behind the works.
19th dragoons, in front of Deutschendorf.
18th and 20th dragoons, in front of Schlòdien, on the left of Girard's brigade.
15. 500 killed and wounded (Hoepfner, iii. 575). 700 or 800 according to Dumas (xviii. 234).
16. Dumas, xviii. 234. Hoepfner, iii. 575. Victor, *Arch. Hist.* Victor's appointment was ordered in *Corr.* 12,743, dated 9th June, in which the Emperor mentions that he is assembling all his reserves at Mohrungen, and hopes to make an end of the enemy, who seems to be striking a mad blow.
17. Victor (*Arch. Hist.*).

other watched the river from Sporthenen to Alken. The remainder of Carra St. Cyr's division was on the plateau in front of Liebstadt, and from it reinforcements of 3 battalions, and 2 guns, were sent, as soon as the artillery duel began.

The battle was opened, at 8 a.m.,[18] by the Russians advancing against the *abattis* and the works in 3 columns, whilst part of the cavalry forded the river near Sporthenen, and a detachment of infantry with artillery threatened a passage lower down, towards Alken. In the wood, and before the works, a long and sanguinary fight ensued. The *abattis*, carried at the first onslaught, was recaptured from the Russians by French reinforcements. Against the enemy who had passed at Sporthenen, the 24th light infantry charged with the bayonet, driving them again to the right bank, and burning the bridge which they had partially constructed. Meanwhile the *abattis* had once more fallen before the Russian attack, and the victors were about to force the passage at Lomitten when the reinforcements sent by St. Cyr came up. The 2nd battalion of the 57th once more cleared the wood, and for four hours maintained itself behind the *abattis*. At the same time, a battalion of the 46th, and one of the 24th drove on the enemy from in front of the bridge at Lomitten.

Again and again the Russians attempted the storm of the bridgehead. This fierce combat had raged for eight hours when a final effort was made in a single column. Success was almost within its grasp, when a splendid charge, by two French battalions, snatched victory from it.

Dochtorow, during this action, marched off with the greater part of his troops, towards Kalkstein and Elditten, with the intention of seconding the attack on Ney's left. The motive of his movement was correctly appreciated by Soult, who was informed of it by St. Hilaire, standing with his division behind the bridge at Pithenen. Measures were at once taken for defending the passage at this place, which had been protected by earthworks. St. Cyr, at Lomitten, was told to confine himself to the defence of the bridge-head, and even to retire to the left bank, if hard pressed. He evacuated the wood on his left, and was finally forced to leave the earthworks on the right bank, which had become untenable owing to the destruction wrought on them by the enemy's artillery, and by the fires which it had caused in the village of Lomitten. The bridge, protected by the works on the left bank, still remained closed to the Russians. About 8 p.m. the action died out, and the Russians fell back on Albrechtsdorf. According to

18. See note 12.

French accounts, St. Cyr lost about 1200 men, the enemy 2800.[19] Dochtorow does not appear to have made any attempt on Pithenen, finding it too strongly held.

The actions at Spanden and Lomitten were but a cover to the more serious attempt, which was simultaneously made, to cut off Ney's corps in its exposed position about Guttstadt. If the attack had many points in its favour, it had the disadvantage of being opposed by a general who was a consummate master of the art of conducting a rear-guard action, and of delaying, to the last safe moment, the enemy's march.

Ney's positions were—

At Guttstadt: headquarters and Marchand's division, which was also partly in Altkirch and Neuendorf, and had one cavalry and one infantry regiment in front of Schmolainen;

Bisson's division occupied Queetz, Lingnau, Glottau, and Knopen.

Leaving his supports to watch the Schmolainen wood in front, Bagration, with the rest of the advance guard, moved, about 6 a.m.,[20] on Altkirch, which he took without much difficulty, driving its defenders on Guttstadt, where Marchand's division now concentrated. At Altkirch, Bagration halted, waiting for Sacken and Gortchakow, who had started too late to keep in line with him, and without whose help he did not feel strong enough to continue his enveloping movement against Guttstadt. Sacken was only between Dietrichsdorf and Petersdorf when Altkirch was stormed.

Ney, seeing the danger to which his advanced cavalry and infantry at Schmolainen were exposed, seized the opportunity to withdraw them to Guttstadt. To cover the retirement, and his concentration, Ney made a strong counter-attack on Bagration, causing him a loss of about 500 killed and wounded.

As Sacken arrived, the marshal, finding himself greatly outnumbered, fell back in first-rate order on Ankendorf, fighting every step of the way, and holding every fold of the ground with strong swarms of skirmishers; Gortchakow, meanwhile, occupied Guttstadt, which Ney had abandoned.

---

19. Hoepfner, iii. 579. The same authority alleges that Soult admitted that he had been so severely engaged as to be unable to assist Ney. I have been unable to find the letter to Napoleon referred to by Hoepfner (iii. 579, note), but, in a letter to Ney (*Arch. Hist.*), dated June 6th, 3 a.m., the marshal makes the statement referred to.
20. See note 12. Also *Corr.* 12,729, dated 5th June, 2 p.m., in which the Emperor rightly assumes that the attack on Bernadotte was a feint, and that the real assault would be on Ney.

At Ankendorf, and Heiligenthal Ney halted, whilst the Russians took post, towards 3 p.m., about Queetz, with Gortchakow in reserve. Platow, who had crossed the Alle at Bergfried, and arrived nearly in Ney's rear, joined the left of the position at Queetz.

Ney, leaning his right, at Ankendorf, on a wood which he held, was covered by the Queetz lake on his right. His centre and left extended, along a marshy brook, to the Passarge. In front of his left, where the road from Waltersmühl to Deppen crosses the brook, was a small wood. His retreat lay over two bridges, one behind either wing. He had still about 16,000 men; he had lost heavily, some 400 killed and wounded, and 1000 prisoners, besides 2 guns, and a great part of his baggage. The Russian loss had been about 2000 killed and wounded, amongst the latter being Osterman Tolstoi, and Somow.

On the morning of the 6th, the Russian advance guard found Ney still in position. The attack was thus ordered: on the right, a column, under Gallitzin, moved on the small wood in front of Ney's left, seeking to drive it on the bridge at Deppen, and cut off the retreat there. Sacken was sent against the centre, Gortchakow against the right, whilst Bagration and the Grand Duke Constantine served as reserve. Fighting commenced at 5 a.m.

Gortchakow assaulted the wood on the French right front, but was brought to a standstill by Ney's moving forward there also. Steady progress was made by the Russian centre and right columns. Gortchakow, after his failure at the wood, wandered round the further side of the Queetz lake, hoping to turn Ney's right, and avoid the wooded marshy land in front of it. He thus put himself, for several hours, out of action, and left Ney's right in safety. The marshal, who, falling back of necessity before the enemy's immense superiority, had already passed Heiligenthal, at once saw the fault of Gortchakow, and utilised it by returning to Heiligenthal with his right, thus covering the retreat of his centre and left into the valley and across the Passarge. His whole corps got safely across with small loss.

Bennigsen was furious at the ill-success of his plan, and seems to have expressed himself so freely that Sackers left the army temporarily.[21]

The Prussians and Kamenskoi did nothing during this day beyond assembling about Mehlsack. On the evening of the 6th, Bennigsen's advance guard was on the right bank of the Passarge, headquarters at Heiligenthal, the reserve behind it. Gortchakow at Guttstadt and Knopen, with a detachment observing Davout; Dochtorow, leaving; Cossacks to watch the Passarge from Elditten, had joined the Russian right wing.

---

21. Hoepfner, iii. 583.

Bennigsen's offensive had expended its force and come to a standstill. Napoleon had not been idle. He had, as soon as he heard the attack on Ney, on the 5th, directed Murat to assemble his reserve cavalry at Marienburg, Christburg, Elbing, Bischofswerder, Strasburg, and Soldau.[22]

The guard cavalry to assemble at Finkenstein.[23]

Lannes to march at once on Christburg, where he should arrive by 9 a.m. on the 6th.[24]

Mortier to march towards Christburg, halting 5 or 6 miles short of it for orders.[25]

On the 6th, Soult was ordered, if he had been forced to retreat, to cover Mohrungen as long as possible, utilising the defiles between the lakes.[26]

Ney's retreat to Deppen was approved. If he was again attacked, he would defend the defile south of the Narien lake.[27] Davout would support his right.[28]

Similarly, Bernadotte, if forced back, would gain time by a slow retreat on Pr. Holland.[29]

Writing to Davout, at 8 p.m. on the 6th,[30] Napoleon asks whether the enemy will dare to march on Allenstein with the French on their flank at Deppen and Leibstadt. If the enemy advances on Osterode, Davout will choose a position for its defence on the Russian flank. Above all, he must "maintain Alt Ramten, for it is the head of Osterode." In this despatch, the Emperor mentions that his lines of operations are through Marienwerder, Marienburg, and Danzig.

Gazane[31] and Zayonchek[32] had already been ordered to concentrate.

All commanders were required to fill up ammunition and supply wagons, and see that their men had plenty of cartridges. The Emperor himself, sending his heavy baggage to Danzig, went to Saalfeld

22. Berthier to Murat, printed, Dumas, xix. 317.

23. Berthier to Bessières, ibid., xix. 318.

24. Berthier to Lannes, ibid., xix. 318 and 321. In the first despatch the Emperor was uncertain if the enemy meant seriously; in the second, he was certain.

25. Berthier to Mortier, ibid., xix. 323.

26. Berthier to Soult, Dumas, xix. 325.

27. Berthier to Ney, ibid., xix. 326. Also *Corr.* 12,736.

28. *Corr.* 12,730, dated 5th June.

29. Berthier to Bernadotte, ibid., xix. 327.

30. *Corr.* 12,741.

31. Berthier to Gazan, ibid., xix, 321.

32. Berthier to Zayonchek, ibid., xix. 321.

and Seegerswalde, at which latter place he gave up his carriage and mounted his horse.[33]

Davout had been fully alive to the situation. When Platow, on the 5th, had forced the bridge at Bergfried, he had threatened the connexion between Ney and Davout. The latter, anticipating the order received on the 6th from the Emperor, assembled the 1st and 3rd divisions at Allenstein, and sent the 2nd on to the Passarge above Ramten.[34]

On the morning of the 7th, he marched his 1st and 3rd divisions to the left, taking up a position on a small tributary of the right bank of the Passarge, thus effectually threatening the left flank and rear of the Russians in front of Deepen. On the previous evening he had sent a despatch to Ney, saying that, if the enemy continued his movement, he would have Davout with 40,000 men on his rear. This was a considerated exaggeration of numbers for the benefit of Bennigsen. Davout took care to send the despatch by a route on which the luckless bearer was certain to be captured, as he actually was.[35]

Bennigsen had gone to Guttstadt in the night of the 6th-7th, leaving the Grand Duke in command. His lieutenants, thinking the offensive movement was to continue, were preparing to march on the Passarge and on Allenstein, when the commander-in-chief, returning on the evening of the 7th, ordered a retreat.[36]

Napoleon, informed of the hesitation of the enemy to advance against Ney, himself went to Deppen, sending orders to Victor and Soult to force the passage of the Passarge in their front.

The Guard and Mortier were ordered to march on Deepen, as well as the cavalry of Lasalle, Grouchy, and Nansouty. Espagne's and Saint Sulpice's cavalry to Mohrungen.

Latour-Maubourg's cavalry was placed at the disposal of Soult, Milhaud's at that of Davout. Zayonchek's division was ordered to occupy the now deserted Osterode.

---

33. *Corr.* 12,735, dated Finkenstein, 6th June. The movements of the Emperor's headquarters were as follows, up to the 29th June: 6th Finkenstein, 7th Mohrungen, 8th Klein Krickau, 9th Guttstadt, 10th, 11th in front of Heilsberg, 12th, 13th Pr, Eylau, 14th Friedland, 15th near Wehlau, 16th Wehlau, 17th Toplicken, 18th Schwarzlauken, 19th Tilsit. (Itinerary of route of Imperial headquarters kept by Berthier, *Arch. Hist.*).

34. Davout, p. 192, and Friant's report, dated Lochen, 7th June, 1807, at p. 352 of the same volume.

35. Ibid., p. 193. He gives his real strength as 28,891, p. 194.

36. The Emperor at first found it difficult to believe Bennigsen really meant a serious offensive. He says it seems impossible that he should do so, after letting Danzig fall without an attack on the main army (*Corr.* 12,731, dated the 5th June).

On the morning of the 8th, there was no longer any doubt that the Russians were retreating.[37] Napoleon took up the offensive. Soult had his light cavalry at Waltersdorf, where he had sent it after the affair at Lomitten on the 5th.

On the morning of the 8th, his whole corps passed the Passarge at Elditten, and Pithenen, marching on Wolfsdorf, the left covered by Latour-Maubourg's cavalry. To Guyot, commanding his light cavalry, Soult sent orders to confine himself to observing the enemy. That general, however, incautiously involving himself in an action at Kleinenfeld, without making a proper reconnaissance, was surrounded by Cossacks, and his brigade very severely handled, he himself being killed.[38]

Legrand and St. Hilaire (both of Soult's corps), seizing Wolfsdorf, held fast there, with St. Cyr in second line.

This movement against his right flank finally determined Bennigsen to retreat. The news reached him about midday, when he had already seen great masses of French assembling on the farther side of the Passarge. They confined themselves, however, to reconnaissances, and there was no fighting worth mention.

Gortchakow was now ordered direct to the entrenched camp at Heilsberg, by the right bank of the Alle, sending a detachment of two infantry regiments, and one of cavalry, with some Cossacks and 6 guns, under Barasdin, to hold the defile of Launau on the left bank. The rest of the army fell back on Guttstadt, except Bagration with the rear-guard, who only moved in the evening to Queetz.

At noon, orders were sent to Lestocq to watch the Lower Passarge, as well as Soult's movement. At 3 p.m., another order was sent, announcing that Bennigsen meant to fight a battle at Guttstadt next day, and desiring Lestocq to advance against Soult. The bearer of this despatch, passing through Mehlsack, came upon Kamenskoi there. There was a good deal of confusion on this side, with orders and counter-orders, the final result being that Kamenskoi and Lestocq were left behind, intending to attack Soult's left and rear in the battle which they expected next day at Guttstadt.

On the morning of the 9th, Bennigsen drew up his army for battle at Guttstadt. Finding the position not sufficiently satisfactory,

---

37. *Corr.* 12,744, dated 8th June, to Soult. The Emperor says he has forced the enemy to disclose a body of 13,000 infantry and 7000 or 8000 cavalry, and he learns from prisoners that the rest are at Guttstadt.

38. Soult, reporting on this affair, under date 8th June, treats it as a serious reverse. He attributes it entirely to Guyot's carelessness. The losses he puts at 25 killed and 250 prisoners. (Soult to Berthier, 8th June, *Arch. Hist.*).

he changed his mind, and retreated by the right bank of the Alle to Heilsberg, which he reached in the evening. Expecting the French to follow on the right bank, he, at first, only passed over one division to the left bank at Heilsberg, as a support to Barasdin's detachment at Launau. Bagration's rear-guard was left to cover the retreat.

At 3 a.m. on the 9th, Napoleon commenced the passage of the Passarge at Deppen, moving towards Guttstadt. Murat led the way, supported by Ney. Behind him came Lannes and the Guard. Mortier was still a day's march in rear, at Mohrungen. Davout passed the river at and above Hasenburg, for he had fallen back on its left bank on the 8th, one division going so far as Osterode, whilst the others were at the southern extremity of the Schilling lake. He had, on the 8th, received his orders to cross the Passarge next day. Soult, also, was ordered to Guttstadt. Just as he was starting, Kamenskoi appeared, from the direction of Dietrichsdorf, on his left rear. St. Hilaire's division, the nearest, was moved against the enemy, whilst the light cavalry, and Latour-Maubourg, went against Dietrichsdorf.

Kamenskoi's men had already passed the wood of Dietrichsdorf, and were approaching Wolfsdorf. A powerful battery, which he had established in front of the latter village, was quickly silenced by the French guns. St. Hilaire, at this moment, impetuously attacked the Russians with the bayonet, and drove them back, with heavy losses, in confusion. The cavalry continued the pursuit to Wormditt. Soult did not allow himself to be diverted from his march on Guttstadt. Kamenskoi, unmolested beyond Wormditt, after a few hours' rest there behind the Drewenz stream, continued his march to Heilsberg by Migenen, Raunau, and Reimerswalde,[39] arriving there next morning, after a very long march. Meanwhile, Murat was following Bagration, who halted at Glottau to fight an action covering the passage of the rest of the army at Guttstadt. Bravely supporting him, Platow's Cossacks were at first driven back towards the Alle, and began to lose order. Platow, seeing the danger, himself dismounted, and, by his personal example, restored order. Bagration's cavalry, too, made a gallant resistance; it was only when Ney's infantry arrived in support that Murat finally succeeded in driving Bagration into Guttstadt. The Russian general successfully passed the river, covered

---

39. According to Hoepfner (iii. 599), the French victory was hardly so complete here as is alleged by Dumas (xviii. 261). Kamenskoi, he says, retreated in good order to Wormditt, which he reached at 1 p.m. It was only at 2 p.m. that he received a despatch from Bennigsen announcing his abandonment of the intention to stand at Guttstadt.

and followed by Platow's Cossacks, who destroyed the bridges be-hind them.[40]

On the night of the 9th, the French occupied these positions: Soult at Altkirch; Ney, Murat, and the Guard at Guttstadt; Davout held the left bank of the Alle above Guttstadt, and the villages of Knopen and Ankendorf; Mortier was approaching Guttstadt.

Napoleon's design now was, cutting the Russian army from Koenigsberg and its resources, to drive it from the sea and across the Pregel.

While, therefore, he proposed, next day, to attack Bennigsen in front with 50,000 men forming Murat's cavalry, Soult's, Lannes', and Ney's corps, and Savary's grenadiers, he would keep in hand, at Gutts-tadt and Altkirch, the corps of Mortier and Davout, destined to be interposed between Bennigsen's right and Koenigsberg. The Guard in reserve. Victor, on the Lower Passarge, would retain there the Prussians, and presently force them back on Koenigsberg, where they would be hopelessly severed from their allies.

---

40. There were two bridges in the town, and three had been constructed above it (Wilson, p. 141). Platow, who had been on the left on the 5th-7th, passed to the right on the 8th (ibid., p. 140). In the rear-guard action of the 9th, the forces en-gaged on the Russian side were:

Bagration	Infantry	5000
	Cavalry	1500
Platow	Cossacks	2000

During the night, Bagration fell back about halfway to Heilsberg, covered by the Cossacks (ibid., pp, 141-143).

CHAPTER 2

The Battle of Heilsberg and Operations of the 11th - 13th June

The small town of Heilsberg, situated on the left bank of the Alle, was connected by several bridges with a poor suburb on the opposite side. From the hollow in which the town lies, the ground rises to the north, east, and south, to a curved line of heights of—for this generally flat country—fairly commanding elevation. The ridge crosses the river, which divides it about a mile below the town.[1]

On the right bank, the heights curve back rather sharply, till they meet the marshy brook flowing from south to north, through the suburb, to the Alle. On this side, their elevation is greater than that of their northward continuation beyond the river, and they form quite a respectable height. In the brook, with its marshy bed, to the south they find a strong support from the point of view of an army defending them. In this direction they can only be turned with difficulty, by a considerable detour. North of the Alle, the line of hills is less strongly marked; it sweeps away from the river, almost at right angles, for a distance of nearly a mile and a half, before turning back towards the village of Konegen. Two and a quarter miles north of Heilsberg, to the left of the Koenigsberg road, there is a considerable sheet of water on the shore of which is situated the village of Grossendorf. The heights are bare on their outer slope.

It was this line of rising ground which Bennigsen had, during the spring, carefully fortified as a support to his army. The portion on the

---

1. This account of the battle of Heilsberg is based on those of Dumas, Hoepfner, Soult (*Arch. Hist.*), and Savary. Kausler's atlas and text has also been consulted. The text must be accepted with caution, for it commits a glaring error in representing Lannes' corps as consisting of the divisions of Gazan and Suchet. These divisions formed Lannes' old corps, the 5th, which was at this time on the Narew, under Masséna.

right bank was by nature stronger than that on the left. It was also that to which the Russian engineers had devoted most care and attention. Its crest and outer slope were covered with a series of redoubts and other works which, combined with the protection afforded by the marshy stream on its left flank, rendered it almost impregnable to anything but a regular siege.

On the left bank of the river, where it passes through the heights, there was, at the foot of their slope, a work designed for the protection of the bridges above it. Some 500 paces from the river, on a projecting spur, was redoubt No. 1; 900 paces farther in the same line was redoubt No. 2. No. 3 was 1500 paces farther, on the right rear of No. 2. A small earthwork was constructed across the Koenigsberg road, 700 paces south of the Grossendorf lake. These, with two or three interspersed *flèches* or minor works, were all the fortifications on this side of the river. In front of the position on the right bank, the country was thickly wooded along, and to some distance from, the river.

On the north side, an undulating plain stretched in all directions. It was intersected by the semicircular course of the Spuibach, forming the outlet of the Grossendorf lake to the Alle. On the left bank of this brook, rather more than 2 miles north-west of Heilsberg, was the wood of Lawden. Half a mile south-west of the wood was the village of the same name. Continuing the line between the wood and the village, the next point reached is the village of Langwiese, more than half a mile from Lawden; proceeding, always in the same south-westerly direction, another full half-mile, the village of Bewernick is reached; a short distance beyond that the Alle, about three miles below the line of Bennigsen's fortifications. Along the south side of Bewernick passes the road from Guttstadt, by the left bank, on which, at a short distance from the river, it continues to Heilsberg.

On the fortified heights on both banks, Bennigsen, on the 10th June, ranged his army for battle. On the left bank, with its left flank resting on the work near the river, stood the 8th division. Next to it, on the right, the 6th took post. Beyond this the 4th and 5th divisions, and 27 squadrons of Prussian cavalry, continued the line behind the redoubts. From the Mehlsack road the position bent back towards redoubt No. 3, at which point the infantry line ended. It was a continuous double line, in which each regiment had its 1st and 2nd battalions deployed in first line, and the 3rd in column as second line.

Behind the left wing and centre stood, as reserve, 12 battalions, drawn up in three columns. A few more battalions were in front of the left, in and about redoubt No. 1. Kamenskoi's infantry garrisoned redoubts Nos. 2 and 3, the former of which had 16 Russian guns, partly in, and partly near it. No. 3 was held by a 6-pr. battery (14 guns). Behind No. 2, in support of its garrison, was the 2nd battalion Towarzycs regiment (cavalry).

The Russian cavalry extended the infantry line from redoubt No. 3 towards Konegen, ending with the main body of the Cossacks. The rest of the Prussian cavalry was stationed thus: 5 squadrons behind the right of the infantry line; 10 squadrons (Zieten's dragoons) and a horse artillery battery behind the left flank of the Russian cavalry; farther to the rear, 2 squadrons of hussars and the first battalion Towarzycs regiment, in reserve, behind the centre of Kamenskoi's infantry. Beyond the lake, 5 regiments of Cossacks held Grossendorf.

At the commencement, there were, on the right bank, the 1st, 2nd, 3rd, 7th, and 14th divisions. As the day advanced, all these passed to the left bank except a few regiments. The 2nd division held the left of the southern position, resting on the marshes; the fist; on its right, extended to the Alle. The others, at first, were at the three redoubts nearest the river. The Guard hussar regiment was out in front on the Guttstadt road, two more cavalry regiments on that leading to Seeburg,[2] where Knorring, with a flying column, maintained communication with the force on the Narew. To connect the two portions of his position across the river, Bennigsen had a permanent bridge behind his work on the left bank, 3 pontoon bridges a little above it, and 5 permanent bridges in the town.

Between 9 and 10 a.m., the Russian commander-in-chief received information from Barasdin's outposts at Launau, about 6 miles towards Guttstadt on the left bank, that the French were advancing in force in that direction. He at once despatched 2 jäger and 1 musketeer regiments, with a militia battalion, a dragoon regiment, and 2 light guns towards Launau. At the same time, he sent orders to Bagration, who was retiring on the opposite side of the river from Reichenburg, to cross by the pontoon bridges, and to move again up the left bank and fend off the enemy.

At Bewernick, Bagration met Barasdin, and the force sent to his support, retiring before Murat. Rallying them, he posted himself behind the depression in which Bewernick and Langwiese lie. He had three columns of infantry, and one of cavalry, on the near side of the valley, with Cossacks and skirmishers in front, along and behind the Bewernick brook; more cavalry and a battery towards Langwiese. Two batteries occupied the heights behind Bewernick, where the infantry columns were.

---

2. This cavalry was withdrawn to the cavalry reserve, when, towards evening, it became certain that no attack was to be apprehended on the right bank (*Hoepfner*, iii. 605).

Murat, followed by Soult, Savary's grenadiers, and Lannes' corps in the order named, had left Guttstadt early in the morning. As already mentioned, he had driven in Barasdin's outposts, about 8 a.m., at Launau; about 2 p.m., he again drove back on Bewernick the reinforcements which Bennigsen had sent. His further progress was arrested by the batteries which Bagration had posted behind Bewernick. He was compelled to wait for Soult's infantry and artillery to open a road. The latter placed 36 guns, part on a height across the Liebstadt road, part on heights on the left, about 500 yards from Bewernick. The fire of these overpowered and silenced that of the Russian batteries, and cleared the way for an advance on Bewernick, from which the hostile skirmishers had retired.

Shortly after leaving Launau, Legrand's division had borne off to the left, on the direct line to Langwiese; Savary's grenadiers, on the left rear of Legrand, skirted the woods north-west of Bewernick. In front of that village, Soult had St. Cyr's division in 1st, St. Hilaire's in 2nd, line; Murat's cavalry on the left. The objective of Legrand, Savary, and Murat, was Lawden and the wood beyond it. Soult's own cavalry supported St. Cyr and St. Hilaire.

Under the protection of Soult's 36 guns, St. Cyr occupied Bewernick about 3 p.m., and, deploying beyond it, became involved in a long, severe, and slowly advancing conflict with Bagration's infantry, in which he had to seek support from St. Hilaire to enable him to advance. Whilst this combat was proceeding on the Russian side of Bewernick, Murat was moving on Langwiese; Legrand, followed by Savary, on Lawden, which he had nearly reached.

Bagration's cavalry attacked Murat before he reached Langwiese; it was defeated and pursued through the village, losing 2 guns on the left of it. Before he had completely reorganised his cavalry beyond Langwiese, after their passage through it, Murat was attacked by a large force of cavalry. Bennigsen, seeing the French progress towards Langwiese and Lawden, had ordered Uwarow, with 25 squadrons and 3 jäger regiments, to support Bagration.

Crossing the Spuibach in two columns, Uwarow, with the 3 jäger regiments, and a few cavalry, went to the right towards Lawden. He found the village already occupied, and came under artillery fire from a French battery on the Gaberberg. Making a circuit out of range, he occupied the wood with the jägers. The other column, commanded by Koschin, who had so distinguished himself at Pultusk, and Fock crossed the Spuibach at the main road, just as Bagration's men were retreating before St. Cyr. Turning to its right, the column fell upon Murat's cavalry,[3] as it was deploying, and, at the first onset, carried it away in confusion back towards Langwiese. Napoleon, seeing the advance of the Russian cavalry, had sent Savary[4] to support Murat with his two fusilier regiments and 12 guns. In order to reach the plain where Murat was manoeuvring, Savary had to pass a long defile between marshes, and through the village of Langwiese. This defile, he perceived, was also the only line of retreat of the cavalry, should they be defeated. Had he met them in it, the results must have been disastrous; he hurried forward as fast as possible. He had scarcely deployed, two battalions in front and the rest in columns on his flanks, when he was almost carried away by Murat's cavalry, fleeing before the victorious Russians. He opened a steady artillery and infantry fire, refusing to obey Murat's orders to advance with the bayonet. According to his account,[5] the Russian cavalry were supported by infantry and artillery, which he with difficulty beat off, thanks to the excellent service of his own artillery, under Grenier. Murat, rallying behind him, and reinforced by more cavalry, turned the tables. Koschin was killed, Fock wounded, and the Russian cavalry swept back behind the Spuibach.

The final repulse of this cavalry exposed the right flank of Bagration, still on the French side of the Spuibach, and compelled him, pressed in front by St. Cyr, to retreat in some confusion across it. He might have suffered a serious disaster but for the prompt action of the Grand Duke Constantine on the right bank of the Alle. That commander pushed forward a powerful battery to the river below the infall of the brook, the right bank of which he was thus able to sweep, causing heavy loss to St. Cyr and St. Hilaire. St. Cyr, alone, was unable, after several attacks, to cross the brook against Bagration, now drawn up on its farther side. He accordingly gave place to St. Hilaire's

---

3. The "*journaux de marche*" of the cavalry reserve (*Arch. Hist.*) show, as engaged at Heilsberg—2nd and 3rd divisions heavy cavalry, 1st division dragoons; in all, between 6000 and 7000 sabres.

4. Some French writers have endeavoured to ignore the presence of Napoleon on the battlefield. It is, however, proved (*a*) by Savary's statement, as in the text, in his account of his action (iii. 79-81); (*b*) by a statement on p. 162, vol. xvii., of the work, *Victoires, Conquêtes, etc., des Français,* published at Paris in 1818, and certainly not prejudiced against Napoleon; (*c*) by a picture of the battle in the museum at Versailles. Hoepfner (iii. 609) says he arrived at the front at 10 a.m. It is curious that Hoepfner makes no mention of Savary's part in this cavalry action. It is also difficult to believe that he has not (iii. 607) understated the strength of Uwarow's attacking cavalry at 1000. He had most of 25 squadrons, besides the rallied cavalry of Bagration.

5. He probably alludes to the infantry and artillery on Bagration's right.

division, which, after a desperate combat, succeeded in getting to its left bank. Whilst this struggle was going on between Bagration and St. Cyr, Legrand, supported by Savary, moved, under cover of his artillery at and behind Lawden, to the attack of the Lawden wood. In it the French met Uwarow's 3 jäger regiments, who fought fiercely with the bayonet. It was only after a protracted, well-sustained combat that Legrand succeeded in ejecting the enemy, and strongly occupying the wood, which was an invaluable support to the left of the French line.

Bagration and Uwarow had now played to the bitter end their part in warding off, as long as possible, the French troops from the main position. So long as they were on the plain in front of it, they, necessarily, masked the fire of the powerful artillery ranged on the heights before Heilsberg. The curtain, which so far had protected the French from this fire, was now drawn aside. Bagration's infantry, worn out by a long march followed by a severe action, retired by the line of the main road. His jägers stopped to occupy the earthwork on the left bank of the river, the rest passing the Alle, took up their stand in the centre of the southern area. Bagration himself joined Kamenskoi in the northern redoubts. His cavalry, united with that of Uwarow, proceeded to the right wing of the army.

It was at this time that Bennigsen brought over the 7th division, followed by the 3rd and 14th, from the right bank to the left, their place being, to some extent, filled by Bagration's infantry. The 1st and 2nd divisions formed a new reserve on the left bank. Bagration's retreat began between 5 and 6 p.m.; by the latter hour, the plain in front of the Russian entrenchments was cleared of their advanced troops.

The French on the Spuibach plain, at Lawden, and in front of the wood, were now exposed to the full fury of a cannonade from all the guns on the northern heights, as well as from those in many of the works on the south bank, and the battery on the river's edge opposite the mouth of the brook. Their own artillery was not sufficient to reply with great effect to the 150 pieces brought to bear on them. Inaction under such a fire would have been intolerable. St. Hilaire's division on the right, followed by St Cyr's and by the cavalry, pushed on over the plain, towards redoubt No. 1, passing through an ever-increasing storm of artillery fire.

Simultaneously with their advance, Legrand, on the left, and Savary, issued from the Lawden wood, sending forward the 26th light infantry to the storm of redoubt No. 2. Passing through the depression in front of the work, they suffered from a most efficacious grape fire, and from the musketry of the two battalions at the redoubt. Nothing could stop the impetuous charge of the 26th. The redoubt was carried about 7 p.m.,[6] the infantry driven back, and the 1st battalion of the Towarzycs regiment (cavalry), which had attempted to attack the French left, was forced to give way by the musketry fire which it encountered. Grohlmann, who commanded here, finding his troops forced out of the work, the palisades of the gorge of which had been broken to facilitate the withdrawal of the guns, at once sent to Warneck in rear, imploring him to fall upon the intruding French, before they could be supported, or establish themselves firmly in the captured redoubt.

Most readily did Warneck bring forward the Perm and Kaluga regiments. Moving in perfect order, joined by the Sonsk regiment, on their left, they saw the French, in and about the redoubt, not yet firmly settled in it, endeavouring to prepare for its defence. As the Russian regiments marched forward they received a heavy fire of grape from the guns of the work, now turned against them. Warneck, struck by a musket-ball, fell, as he bravely led forward his men. His place was instantly filled by Grohlmann, who was personally well known to the men. With a loud cheer he placed himself at their head. Bravely though the French fought, they could not stand against the bayonets of the Russian infantry. Broken and in disorder, they fled to the rear, pursued by their triumphant conquerors. As Warneck charged, the 1st battalion of the Zieten dragoons, supported by the 1st battalion of the Towarzycs regiment, and the now rallied 2nd battalion, galloped forward on his right. Bringing forward their right shoulders, this body of cavalry fell on the cuirassier division of Espagne halted between the Lawden wood and the infantry. Then ensued a deadly hand-to-hand struggle, ending in the defeat, with great loss, of the cuirassiers. The Prussian horsemen pursued them into the midst of their batteries, hewing down the gunners. It was not until they were met by a heavy infantry fire that the Prussians were forced to retire to their original position.

St. Hilaire, seeing the defeat of the 26th at redoubt No. 2, had sent to support it the 55th regiment from his left.

Charged by more Prussian cavalry, whose approach was concealed by the thick smoke, disordered by the beaten 26th and the Russian infantry, their colonel killed, this regiment, too, was overthrown, and lost its eagle. Not till a fresh French chasseur regiment came to its aid, was it disengaged from the Prussian cavalry, now forced to a rapid retreat through the Russian infantry lines. On this wing there was an indescribable scene of confusion. Legrand's and Savary's infantry—formed in hollow squares, containing the Russian prison-

6. *Wilson*, p. 146.

ers, arranged checkerwise and intermixed with the reserve cavalry—were attacked in all directions by Russian and Prussian cavalry again pushing forward. Slowly they gave way, their squares moving without being broken, again across the Spuibach. But for the timely arrival at this juncture, on their left, of Verdier's division of Lannes' corps, and the support offered by St. Hilaire on their right, they could hardly have avoided total defeat.

As Legrand and Savary were forced back, they necessarily exposed the left flank of St. Hilaire and St. Cyr.

Those generals had arrived close in front of redoubt No. 1, but, met in front by the Russian defenders, and their left flank exposed as above described, they had found themselves unable to go farther. They, too, fell back, suffering appalling losses.

The assault on redoubt No. 2 had occurred soon after 7 p.m.;[7] by 9 p.m. the whole French line was again driven behind the Spuibach, though they still held the Lawden wood beyond it. The Russians had retired, after their victory, to their entrenched positions; the battle seemed over for the night. Not so thought Lannes, who had now reached the field. He resolved on one more attempt. Collecting Verdiers division, he sent it forward once more against redoubt No. 2, from the Lawden wood, about 10 p.m. Warned by a deserter[8] of the impending assault, the Russians were prepared to meet it. As Verdier, supported by the 75th of Legrand's division, moved out across the plain, he was received with such a storm of artillery fire that his division withered before it. The attack collapsed, the troops once more fell back on the wood.

The 18th regiment of Legrand's division had been pushed forward in the afternoon towards Grossendorf, to threaten Bennigsen's communications with Koenigsberg. There it had been set upon by the Cossacks. Formed in battalion squares, it had for hours resisted every attack with success. When the fighting was over on his own front, Legrand sent out two more battalions to its aid. With their help, it was able to rejoin the main French line.

After the failure of Verdier's attempt, a few Russian light infantry were sent in the darkness against the Lawden wood; they found the French too strongly posted there to give any hope of their being

---

7. Napoleon's 78th bulletin (*Corr.* 12,747) says it was 9 p.m. when St. Hilaire was in front of the Russian position. Jomini (*Vie de Napoleon*, ii. 408), apparently following the bulletin, gives the same hour. Wilson (p. 146) says Legrand moved forward "about 7 p.m."

8. *Wilson*, p. 146.

driven out. It was 11 p.m. before the last sounds of fighting died away, and were succeeded by silence, broken only by the shrieks and groans of the many thousand wounded, strewing the plain, between the contending armies.

The honourable warfare of the day gave place to a scene which was equally disgraceful to either army. Swarms of followers, the scum of the armies, skulked out from either side into the plain, not intent upon mutual destruction, but united in a common warfare against the defenceless dead and wounded. The clouds, which had been threatening during the day, discharged a heavy fall of rain, as though Heaven itself wept over this dreadful sight. When morning broke, the soldiers of the two armies, inured as they were to the horrors of war, were yet struck with dismay at the sight which met their eyes on the plain between them. Thousands upon thousands of naked bodies lay upon it; many dead; many still shivering with fever after the night of rain.[9] The dead and wounded alike had been stripped of clothes, and everything they had, by the foul human beasts of prey who, during the hours of darkness, had glutted themselves with the plunder of the sufferers and the dead. So great was the horror inspired by this disgraceful scene, that, by mutual, though unspoken consent, French and Russian met peacefully on the ghastly plain to bury the dead and remove the wounded.

The loss in this great battle was enormous on both sides. Soult's corps alone admittedly lost 6601,[10] the total loss of the French was probably at least 10,000. Yet there were engaged on their side only the corps of Soult, Murat, and one division of Lannes'. The Russians had lost 2000 or 3000 killed, and 5000 or 6000 wounded; in all, not less than 6000 or 8000, besides prisoners.[11] The 1st and 2nd divisions, and the greater part of the Russian cavalry, had not been engaged at all. With such losses, it is easy to judge how fierce was the struggle.

Was this awful loss of life justified by the possible results on either side? It seems doubtful. From Napoleon's point of view, it is certain that his object, in so far as it consisted in compelling the Russian general to evacuate the position he had prepared with such care,

9. At the time of Heilsberg and Friedland the days were oppressively hot, the nights damp and cold (*Larrey*, iii. 85). The weather on the night of the 10th June was bad (*ibid.*, iii. 78).

10. Soult's report, *Arch. Hist.* Hoepfner (iii. 615) gives the number as 8286, and Lannes' losses as 8284. The total loss he puts at 1398 killed, 10,359 wounded, and 864 prisoners. Total, 12,621.

11. *Hoepfner*, iii. 615. Plotho (p. 162) says the Russian loss was 9000. After the battle he gives their strength as still 76,000.

could have been attained with trifling loss on the succeeding day. As Davout and the other corps of the French left appeared beyond Bennigsen's right, there can be no doubt that he would have felt himself bound, as he actually did on the 11th, to seek temporary safety, once more, on the right bank of the Alle. Attacked in front, he was, no doubt, bound to defend himself as he did. But his victory—for such, in a tactical sense it undoubtedly was,—to use Sir Robert Wilson's words, "had not an influence beyond the moment, for the redundant power of the French was still unimpaired, and they could traverse by the right of the position, move on Koenigsberg, or, by throwing bridges over the Alle, surround and blockade the Russian army, who had not two days' bread in their camp, or in those magazines of whose capture Buonaparte vaunts; whilst contagion from the putrid loads that polluted the atmosphere, would have augmented the evils of famine.[12]

Of the tactics of the French in this terrible combat, there is not much that is favourable to be said.

Napoleon attacked a very strong position with very inferior forces, for it was not till too late in the day to save the situation, that Lannes' corps, Ney, and the Guard could reach the battlefield. The two latter took no part in the fighting, and merely served as a support on which the beaten corps in front could fall back.

With Soult's endeavours, in face of an overwhelming enemy, no fault could be found. But for Napoleon's presence on the field, it is not impossible that that cautious marshal would have refrained from pressing his attack much beyond Bewernick, until the turning movement on the Russian right should take effect.

Murat, on this day, appeared to no advantage. Savary relates how the cavalry commander urged him, against his better judgment, to advance with the bayonet, when a steady fire was the only hope for him, as well as for the cavalry.[13] Napoleon was disgusted with the behaviour of his cavalry; " they did nothing I ordered;" he said.[14] Lannes' final

---

12. *Wilson*, p. 149.

nous qu'il fût moins brave, et eût un peu plus de sens commun." The Emperor silenced him, saying he was in a temper, but, nevertheless, remembered the words and the still more unmeasured terms of Lannes.

13. *Savary*, iii. 82, 83. He describes how, in the evening, when every one was out of temper at the ill success of the day, he told the Emperor plainly that his brother-in-law was *"un extravagant qui nous ferait perdre un jour quelque bonne bataille; et qu'enfin il vaudrait mieux pour*

14. See *Wilson*, p. 149, note, who says this remark was made to a "person in high authority," whose name he cannot disclose.

attack, at 10 p.m., was mere waste of life; it could not reasonably be expected to succeed with a single division.[15]

On the other side, Bagration's conduct of his rear-guard action against Soult was as admirable as his fight on the previous evening before Guttstadt. His steadfast resistance wore out the enemy, before they even arrived within striking distance of Bennigsen's line of battle. Similarly, Uwarow, and the Prussian cavalry behaved magnificently towards Lawden against Murat, Savary, and Legrand. The promptitude with which the Grand Duke Constantine supported Bagration, by his battery on the right bank of the Alle, must not be forgotten.

On the morning of the 11th June, the armies again faced one another in order of battle; but, beyond some cannonading of St. Cyr's division, on the French right, by the Russian batteries beyond the river, no fighting occurred. Napoleon had resolved on dislodging Bennigsen by manoeuvring, as he might have done equally well, without making a serious frontal attack on his position, on the previous day.[16]

About noon Bennigsen received information that Davout's corps had been sighted on the Landsberg road.[17] When the marshal presently appeared at Grossendorf, Bennigsen, now seriously alarmed for the safety of his right flank and rear, with supplies running low, and with the prospect of his position becoming untenable, if only from famine, and the terrible odour of the corpses festering in the sun, determined on retreat during the ensuing night, by the right bank of the river.

At 9 p.m., Kamenskoi was ordered to pass the Alle with 9000 men,

---

15. According to Hoepfner (iii. 615, note) the French themselves admit Lannes' loss as 2284 killed, wounded, and prisoners. Most of this must have occurred in the night attack.

16. In renewing the fight next day, I should have risked the destruction of the corps destined for it; there was all the less reason for my exposing myself to this in that, by manoeuvring on Koenigsberg, I was sure to displace the enemy without striking a blow. For a moment I hesitated whether I would march with the corps of Ney and Davout, by my right, to Bischofstein; the motives I have already indicated determined me to take the opposite direction" (Jomini, *Vie de Napoleon*, ii. 408).

17. Bennigsen at first failed to appreciate the true significance of Davout's appearance in this position. He "conceived that the enemy were moving on Koenigsberg, and that General Lestocq, who had been ordered, in the morning, to Zinten from Heiligenbeil, on which he had fallen back, might not be strong enough to resist the advance of the enemy and cover Koenigsberg; he therefore detached General Kamenskoi, with 9000 men, to join him, and ordered General Lestocq to fall back upon Koenigsberg with all expedition and maintain that city, as he (Bennigsen) was moving upon Wehlau with the army to support the line of the Pregel." (*Wilson*, pp. 149, 150). The last words are worthy of special note, as showing that, at this time, Bennigsen had no idea of returning to the left bank of the Alle at Friedland.

to march on Bartenstein, and thence to join Lestocq behind the Frisching. He arrived at Bartenstein (13 miles) early on the morning of the 12th. Starting again at 7 a.m., he made another 13-mile march to Lampasch. Prussian cavalry, reconnoitring on his left flank, found a strong column of the enemy already in Pr. Eylau. Kamenskoi's troops were weary, but, after two hours' rest, they once more set out, more to their right to avoid the enemy, and to seek Lestocq.

Bennigsen, with the rest of the army, crossing the Alle at midnight, unperceived by the French, marched in 4 columns for Bartenstein. Bagration, once more, with Platow's Cossacks, took the post in which he had already shown such marked capacity, the command of the rear-guard. It was not till the morning of the 12th was well advanced that the last troops had passed the river, burning the bridges behind them,[18] as well as the camp on the right bank. Soult presently occupied Heilsberg where he found numbers of Russian wounded and magazines—the latter full according to French accounts,[19] empty according to Wilson.[20] The retreating Russians were followed and watched, not pursued, by only one division of dragoons, and two of light cavalry.[21]

Napoleon, meanwhile, had, on the 11th, again ordered Davout from Grossendorf on Preussisch Eylau, which he reached on the 12th, his advance guard meeting, as has been related, the hussars on Kamenskoi's left. As he left Grossendorf, his rear-guard had a few slight skirmishes with Platow's Cossacks. The 3rd division, in advance, took post on the 12th at Rothenen; the 2nd, delayed by having to make way for the 3rd, as well as for Oudinot's grenadiers, only arrived at Eylau at 8 p.m.; the 1st took up its quarters at Waschkeiten. Marulaz

---

18. Hoepfner (iii. 622) says 11 a.m.; Wilson (p. 151), 7 a.m. The latter authority thinks that the rear of the Russians might well have been involved in a terrible disaster, had the French been more alert, for at sunrise (soon after 3.30 a.m.) there were still three Russian divisions on the left bank. But it must be remembered that Soult's corps alone was at this time facing Heilsberg, and it was no part of Napoleon's programme to draw the Russians on it. "At daybreak on the 11th my army, defiling in two columns, marched for Landsberg and Pr. Eylau. A single corps was left in front of Heilsberg to cover my movement. I did not conceal from myself the possible danger of this course; for in undertaking it I left my own communications in the power of the enemy, who, basing himself on the camp of Heilsberg, could operate on our rear and shut us in between his own army, the Lower Pregel, and the sea" (Jomini, Vie de Napoleon, ii. 409).

19. 78th bulletin (Corr. 12,747).

20. Wilson, p. 149), note.

21. Wilson, p. 151. Latour-Maubourg's dragoon division and the light cavalry divisions of Durosnel and Wattier (Hoepfner, iii. 622; also Dumas, xviii. 283).

made reconnaissances on the Eichorn–Bartenstein road, whilst waiting to act as escort to the reserve park.

Ney, from Launau, marched early on the 12th to Eichorn, halfway between Heilsberg and Eylau.[22]

Napoleon's headquarters were at Eylau on the 12th, and, Bennigsen being now gone from Heilsberg, Soult and Murat were ordered to follow the other corps towards Eylau.[23] Mortier reached Heilsberg from Altkirch, the Guard also was at Heilsberg. Napoleon, with the mass of his army, was now nearer to Koenigsberg than Bennigsen, whom he could, moving on the chord of the arc which the Russians were following, by the right bank of the Alle, intercept at Friedland.

To bring the position up to date, it is necessary to turn back to the movements of Lestocq and Victor on the Lower Passarge.[24]

The latter general, on the 10th, made a general reconnaissance from Spanden, towards Wusen and Baarden. Wusen was abandoned by the Prussians. Heavy artillery fire at Baarden indicated that they were in force towards Mehlsack. On the 11th June, Lestocq intercepted a despatch, from Berthier to Victor, directing the latter to attack the Prussians, to seize Mehlsack, and to be prepared to march either on Drewenz and Landsberg, or direct on Koenigsberg.[25] Seeing the danger to his left flank, Lestocq, at 3 a.m. on the 12th, marched his 1st division from Heiligenbeil to Zinten, where it took position. During the same night, Victor debouched by the Spanden bridge, towards Mehlsack, driving in the Prussian outposts, which retired towards Zinten. Dupont's division, with two regiments of cavalry, marching from Frauenburg and Braunsberg, up the Passarge, followed the rest over the Spanden bridge. One Prussian brigade had

---

22. This, it will be observed, does not quite agree with Jomini's account (*Vie de Napoleon*, ii. 409) just quoted. Hoepfner (iii. 619, note; justly remarks on the extreme difficulty of fixing with certainty the French movements before and after Heilsberg, as well as during the battle itself. In this case, however, there is no room for doubt, as Napoleon's order (*Corr.* 12,745) is dated Heilsberg, 12th June. It directs Ney to march on Eylau, and to be rejoined by two regiments which he had left at Guttstadt. At the same time Zayonchek's Poles were to occupy Guttstadt, now evacuated by the advancing army.

23. To Murat, the Emperor wrote that Soult, passing by Landsberg, was sweeping the Prussians before him. Murat was to reconnoitre the country on his right, by parties, on Bartenstein and Friedland. He was not to disperse his troops, and was to call in the regiment on his left so as to give him more troops for his right.

24. *Dumas*, xviii. 284; *Hoepfner*, iii. 623; Victor, *Arch. Hist.*

25. Berthier to Victor, dated 10th June, Guttstadt, 10 a.m. The despatch is given in full by Hoepfner (iii. 627). Berthier does got seem to have repeated his error of January by sending only one copy, for another reached Victor safely.

been left behind to watch Braunsberg. Victor was compelled to leave the 24th regiment, with 2 guns, at Spanden, to oppose it.[26]

During the night of the 12th-13th, Lestocq received Bennigsen's despatch informing him of his own retreat, and of the detachment of Kamenskoi towards Muhlhausen and the Frisching. Lestocq also heard of the arrival of the French at Eylau. Early on the morning of the 13th he set out on his march to join Kamenskoi behind the Frisching. At 3 p.m. on that day he came upon the head of the Russian column at Gollau, a little way short of Koenigsberg; here, for the moment, he may be left.

Rapp, Governor of Danzig, had received orders to clear the Frische-Nehrung, with a column of 250 men and 4 guns, up to the Pillau channel. Behind this column followed the sailors of the Guard from Elbing. Bennigsen, finding his right more and more outflanked, halted at Bartenstein but a few hours, to rest his troop, before continuing his march to Schippenbeil at midnight of the 12th-13th. He marched in three columns. Kollogribow, with the Russian Guard, marched by the right bank. The second column, of three divisions, and the cavalry of the left wing, took the road along the left bank. The third, of two divisions, acted as support to the rear-guard, composed of one division and the cavalry of the right wing. The Cossacks guarded the flanks.

The head of the column reached Schippenbeil at 4 a.m. on the 13th. As the troops passed through the town, they took position, as if for battle, behind it, between the Alle and its tributary, the Guber. But there was no rest for Bennigsen's troops, wearied though they were with more than a week of constant marching and fighting, for he now learnt that the French were already about Domnau. Trembling for his communications with Lestocq and Koenigsberg, he again resumed his march at midday.

On the 13th, early in the morning, Napoleon directed Murat on Koenigsberg, with St. Sulpice's, and Milhaud's dragoons, and Lasalle's light cavalry. This force, with Davout's corps in support, marched by the direct road; Soult, also in support, to the left, by Kreuzberg. The object of this detachment was to place a strong force between Bennigsen and Koenigsberg in any case. At the same time, Lannes was directed on Friedland through Domnau. Mortier, Ney, and the Guard, following Lannes, took post between Eylau and Domnau. Victor arrived at Eylau.[27] The three cavalry divisions, which had followed Bennigsen to Bartenstein,[28] crossed the river there, and moved on Domnau.

---

26. Operations of 1st corps, by Victor, *Arch. Hist.*

27. At 11 a.m. on the 13th, the Emperor, at Eylau, Summarises the position of his army in a letter to Murat (*Corr.* 12,749). Lannes was advancing on Lampasch, Davout on Wittenburg, Soult had started at 10 a.m. (continued on next page

for Kreuzburg, Victor was at Landsberg, Ney and Mortier just arriving at Eylau. If Murat found himself able to enter Koenigsberg, he was to use Soult for the purpose, as Napoleon wished to have his extreme left in Koenigsberg. If the enemy should arrive to-day at Domnau, Murat would still push Soult on Koenigsberg, placing Davout so as to head the Russians between Domnau and Koenigsberg. In case Bennigsen should march thus by Domnau, it would be necessary for Soult to make sure of the town of Brandenburg, so that there might be no anxiety for the Emperor's communications, which would be by his left. Half an hour later (*Corr.* 12,750) he writes to the same effect to Soult, and expressly states that there are indications of the enemy's intention to concentrate on Domnau. Brandenburg, in these circumstances, would be important, as it would protect the left if the right were exposed. By 3 p.m. (*Corr.* 12,751) the Emperor had heard that Bennigsen was retreating on Schippenbeil, and he tells Lannes to move on Domnau, with cavalry towards Friedland.

28. *Vide supra*, p. 306, note 4.

CHAPTER 3

The Battle of Friedland

LANNES' ACTION—3 A.M. TO NOON

During the last four miles of the route from Domnau to Friedland, the general slope of the country is downwards towards the Alle, on the left bank of which stands the little town of Friedland.[1] Two miles before it is reached, a slight elevation, in rear of Posthenen, affords a clear and uninterrupted view over the whole battlefield, and down to Friedland, lying directly to the spectator's front. On the right front, some 500 paces from the village of Posthenen, is the great wood of Sortlack, extending down to the village of the same name, at the head of a re-entrant angle of the Alle, which here flows between high and steep banks. A mile and a quarter to the left (north) of Posthenen is the village of Heinrichsdorf. Two-thirds of the distance, in a direction but slightly north of east, from Heinrichsdorf to the Alle, is the small wood of Damerau. Behind the line joining Posthenen and Heinrichsdorf are large woods.

The whole space, between the left bank of the river and the points which have just been denoted, is a gently undulating, open plain, with no gradients sufficient to impede the free movement of troops of all arms.

On the 14th June, the whole of this plain was one sheet of crops, rye and wheat.

Open as the plain generally was, there was one feature in it the supreme importance of which was at once recognised by Napoleon. Rising west of Posthenen, a small stream, known as the Millstream, flowing through the village, thence takes a course direct for Friedland. It divides the plain into two portions, the greater extending north-

---

1. The chief materials for this account of the battle of Friedland are the narratives of Dumas, Hoepfner, Savary, Victor (*Arch. Hist.*), Jomini, Wilson, Marbot, Kausler (atlas and text), etc.

wards to the Damerau wood, the lesser southwards to that of Sortlack. In its passage from in front of Posthenen till it reaches the outskirts of Friedland, the brook flows between steep banks, and, though narrow, is a serious military obstacle, entirely obstructing the free passage of troops. At Friedland, it expands into a semicircular pond, covering the greater part of the north side of the town. On the south side is the Alle, flowing at this point from west to east, and then turning north after passing the town. Friedland is thus built at the end of a peninsula, of which the north and south sides, respectively, are closed by the Millstream and by the Alle.

On the opposite bank of the Alle there is a plain similar to that on the left bank, backed by a great wood on the Allenburg road. The large village of Allenau stands back from the river, opposite Sortlack; a smaller village, Kloschenen, is on the brink of the high right bank, 2000 paces below Friedland.

It was 6 p.m. on the 13th June when the head of Bennigsen's army, under Gallitzin, began to reach the neighbourhood of Friedland. Lannes' cavalry had already ejected from the town the few Russian troops guarding the magazines there. A French patrol was surrounded and captured on the right bank of the river. Passing into Friedland, Gallitzin captured 60 cavalry in it; beyond the town, on the west, he found the French 9th Hussars, which he forced back on Lannes' corps at Domnau, taking post with his cavalry at Posthenen.

Kologribow detached small bodies to Wohnsdorf, Allenburg, and Wehlau, to watch the lower passages of the Alle, and to gain communication with Lestocq. There then remained at Friedland, 28 squadrons, and 17 guns.

Towards 8 p.m., Bennigsen himself reached Friedland. Informed of the proximity of Lannes' corps, he ordered the first troops which arrived to cross the river in support of the cavalry, and directed the construction of three pontoon bridges, one above and two below the permanent bridge. It was not till 11 p.m. that the head of the Guard infantry column arrived at Friedland. One battalion was sent over at once to the support of the cavalry, and three more regiments as day dawned (about 3.30), and the French began to appear in force. It was 5 a.m. before the first battalions of the main Russian body came up.

As soon as Lannes had heard, from his retiring cavalry, of the Russian passage at Friedland, he despatched Ruffin's brigade, and part of Oudinot's grenadier division, towards that point. Scarcely had they started, when a despatch from Napoleon warned Lannes that Bennigsen appeared to intend crossing at Friedland, and marching direct on Koenigsberg.[2] The Emperor had promptly ordered Grouchy, from Eylau, with his own dragoon division and Nansouty's cuirassiers, to join Lannes as quickly as possible. Lannes followed shortly, with the rest of Oudinot's and Verdier's divisions.

It was still night when Oudinot, between 2 and 3 a.m., debouched on the Friedland plain, to find Ruffin in front of him, advancing against the Russian cavalry. He pushed forward two battalions into the Sortlack wood, and held his main body in front of Posthenen, on the near bank of a small brook, which issues from the wood towards the Millstream. In front, he placed 2 batteries, and behind them were 5 or 6 battalions, and 1 gun, somewhat to the left, with their backs to the Bothkeim wood. From the Russian side also, skirmishers were sent into the Sortlack wood, where they met the French. Musketry and artillery fire broke out all along the line. The Russian skirmishers were from the Guard infantry, which had been sent over to the left of the cavalry. They were exhausted by a long march without rest, and they were ignorant of the ground.

At 3 a.m., Grouchy arrived with French and Saxon dragoons. At this hour Lannes had on the ground 9000 infantry, and 3000 cavalry.[3] The

2. *Corr.* 12,573. To Lannes, dated Eylau, 13th June, 9 p.m. The Emperor is, he says, uncertain whether it is the whole Russian army or only a detachment that is at Friedland. He promises to send on Ney at 1 a.m., and to have Victor at Domnau by 10 a.m., in case he is required. He presumes Lannes will seize Friedland, if the enemy is not in force there.

3. *Hoepfner*, iii. 653. The numbers engaged at Friedland are, as in the case of every other action in this campaign, most variously stated, thus—Thiers gives 75,000 Russians and 80,000 French; Alison takes the French at 80,000 and the Russians at 55,000, including the detachments to Allenburg, etc.; Dumas puts the Russians at 61,000; Hoepfner gives Bennigsen 46,000 on the left bank of the Alle, besides the 14th division and other troops on the right bank, and the detachments to Allenburg, etc.; Plotho (pp. 162-165), guessing the French force at 70,000 or 80,000, says that, after Heilsberg, Bennigsen still had 76,000. Of these he detached 9000 under Kamenskoi, and 6000 to Allenburg, which would give him 61,000 on both banks of the Alle at Friedland, or, say, 55,000 actually engaged on the left bank. Considerable deductions must, however, be made for stragglers in the long march from Heilsberg. The text of Kausler's *Atlas des Plus Mémorables Batailles*, etc., gives 75,000 Russians and 85,000 French. Marbot allows Napoleon 80,000. There is a close agreement as to the French numbers, and it will not be far wide of the mark to call them 80,000. As for Bennigsen, considering all the authorities, it seems doubtful if his numbers were higher than these:

On the left bank of the Alle	46,000
On right bank	6,000
Detachments to Allenburg, etc.	6,000
Total	58,000

next to arrive were Oudinot's dragoons, who took post behind his right, on the south bank of the Millstream.

This cavalry moved out, between 5 and 6 a.m., across the little brook in front of the guns, against the Russian cavalry. They were not as yet strong enough to beat Kologribow's horsemen. As they were being driven back, they received timely succour by the arrival, at 6 o'clock, of Fresia's Dutch cavalry (of Mortier's corps), who made a fresh addition to the strength of the French right, and forced Kologribow to retire. Whilst these cavalry combats were in progress, Grouchy had observed that the Russians, who were now rapidly crossing the river, were advancing in force on Heinrichsdorf by the road to Koenigsberg. From the village they would be in a position to gain the French rear through the Georgenau wood.

Sending Nansouty forward from the Domnau road, Grouchy followed towards Heinrichsdorf, direct from Posthenen. Nansouty, passing through the Georgenau wood, drove out of it, through Heinrichsdorf, the advanced troops of the Russians, until he was stopped by infantry and artillery. Ordering Nansouty to form front towards the enemy at the village, Grouchy himself charged their guns as they entered it; whilst Nansouty, aided by Albert's dragoons, now sent up by Lannes, attacked in front. Disordered by a successful onslaught, the French were, in turn, charged by Russian cavalry, who, however, only succeeded in facilitating the withdrawal of most of their own guns before they were beaten off. Grouchy then drew up his men on either side of Heinrichsdorf at its eastern entrance.

All this time a desultory combat, without any decisive result on either side, had been in progress along Lannes' whole front. That marshal found himself in a position in some ways similar to that which he had held at Pultusk. As at Pultusk, he was facing a very superior force, for the Russians were now hurrying across the Friedland bridges, Bennigsen hoping and believing that only Lannes was at hand. But there was this great difference between the two cases, that, at Pultusk, Lannes felt he had nothing to fall back on, whilst, at Friedland, he knew that the Emperor was hurrying up an overwhelming force to his aid.

It was now 9 a.m., and there were on the field 9000 French infantry and 8000 cavalry. Lannes had made the most of his small force. He covered the whole of his front with an unusually dense line of skirmishers; the troops behind them were able to give the impression of larger numbers, owing to the detached groups of trees, the inequalities of the ground, and the high crops. Lannes also, by moving them about and deploying them in different positions, conveyed the impression of the arrival of more troops. Their business was to fight a delaying action, to keep Bennigsen occupied, and to induce him to bring across the river his whole army, very inferior in numbers to the corps which Napoleon, in a few hours, would be able to collect against it. By 9 o'clock, Bennigsen had passed across the river 46,000 men, a force amply sufficient to overwhelm Lannes, with whom alone he still believed he would have to deal.[4] Six divisions of infantry, and most of the cavalry, had crossed. As his troops arrived, the Russian commander drew them up on the plain between Sortlack and the Damerau wood. On the northern half of this space, between Damerau and the Millstream, the 8th, 7th, 6th, and 3rd divisions, under Gortchakow, stood, whilst the smaller southern portion, from the Millstream to Sortlack, was occupied by the 1st and 2nd divisions, the advance guard, and part of the cavalry under Kologribow. The greater part of the cavalry was in the northern portion, under Uwarow and Gallitzin. The infantry were drawn up in two lines; in the first the regiments stood with their first and third battalions deployed, the end battalion in column behind. The second line consisted of entire regiments in columns of battalions, behind the 3rd battalions of the front line. The greater part of the Cossacks were about the Damerau wood. In the Sortlack wood were about 3000 picked jägers, who had been driven back into it, and were fighting there. In support of them, at Sortlack, stood two battalions, five squadrons, and four guns.

To obliterate, as far at possible, the separation of the left from his centre and right, Bennigsen threw four small bridges across the Millstream. On the right bank of the Alle remained the 14th division and 20 squadrons, on the Schippenbeil road, as well as Platow's flying column, and a large part of the artillery. The detachments which Kologribow had made to Wohnsdorf and Allenburg, were reinforced by a Guard infantry regiment, 3 cavalry regiments, some Cossacks, and a part of the Guard artillery.[5] Some of the guns covered the pontoon bridges, a battery at Kloschenen supported the right wing across the river, another fired on the French issuing, from Sortlack wood, against the left flank.

The fight in that wood had oscillated backwards and forwards: at

---

4. At 9 a. m. all the divisions had passed except one. The 6000 men detached towards Allenburg were sent back from the left bank (*Wilson*, p. 155).

5. *Hoepfner*, iii. 656. Wilson (p. 155) says Bennigsen detached 6000 men to guard the lower passages of the Alle at Allenburg, This number may perhaps fairly represent the detachments made and thus reinforced.

one moment the Russian jägers had driven the French out of it; a few moments later the latter had returned, and again made their way deep into the covert, only once more to be driven back to its edge. So the fight swayed backwards and forwards.

About 9 o'clock, the whole Russian army moved forward, bringing its left into line with the front then held by the jägers in Sortlack wood, whilst the right wing stood 500 or 600 paces short of Heinrichsdorf.

The Cossacks, pushing into and through that village, arrived on the rear of the French line towards Schwonau, as the Russian cavalry of the right wing attacked it in front. Beaumont and Colbert, with 2500 cavalry of the 1st and 6th corps, quickly drove off the Cossacks, and then, joining in the severe cavalry fight which was in progress, they turned the balance in favour of the French.

Mortier's corps[6] was now beginning to appear on the scene, Dupas' division of it reaching Heinrichsdorf just in time to arrest the progress of the Russian infantry. Dupas then took his stand on the right of the village, which was still occupied by 3 battalions of grenadiers. The remainder of the grenadiers returned to their own division, on the right, whilst 3 Polish regiments, of Dombrowski's division, placed themselves behind the battery in front of Posthenen. The French now had 23,000 infantry and 10,500 cavalry present when, at 10 a.m., Verdier's division, the rear of Lannes' corps, at last put in an appearance, raising the French to 40,000 against 46,000 Russians. Bennigsen at last began to see that he was likely to have more on his hands than be could manage. He could only hope that Napoleon would not be able to overwhelm him before night should afford him an opportunity of retrieving the error which he had committed in crossing the river. Meanwhile, officer after officer had been despatched to inform Napoleon of the position of affairs.

NAPOLEON'S ARRIVAL ON THE SCENE

He reached the field about noon,[7] and, from the height in rear of Posthenen, scanned the battlefield. A very different sight was before him on this bright summer morning from that which he had witnessed under the wintry sky of Eylau, and he was in very different spirits. To his staff he had remarked at Domnau, "The enemy appears to wish to

---

6. The return for the 15th June (*Arch. Hist.*) shows this corps as comprising only one weak French division of 3976 men, besides cavalry and artillery. The other two divisions, the numbers of which are not stated, were Poles.

7. *Hoepfner*, iii. 659. Marbot (i. 282) says 11 a.m. Jomini (*Vie de Napoleon*, ii. 413) gives 1 p.m. as the hour.

give battle to-day; so much the better, it is the anniversary of Marengo." His wonderful power of grasping the points of a battlefield at once showed him the faultiness of Bennigsen's position, split in two by the Millstream, with his left wing across the opening of the triangular peninsular ending at Friedland, bounded on one side by the Millstream, on the other by the Alle. He saw that this wing was cut off from the support of the rest of the army by the stream, and that the four bridges, by which Bennigsen had attempted to remedy this fatal defect, were almost useless. He saw that, as the left wing was forced back, it would be driven closer and closer together, until it was enclosed in Friedland, where its defeat, with the capture of the town, must infallibly bring disaster upon the centre and right, if they attempted to maintain their position, with the river, unfordable as he believed it to be, close behind them. He felt that Bennigsen had lost his only chance of escape by neglecting to fall upon Lannes with far greater vigour, and to destroy him before the rest of the army could arrive.

By this time, Napoleon had sufficient strength to hold back the wearied Russians until the arrival of Ney, Victor, and the Guard. Till then, he was not anxious to press the fight, in which a lull now occurred. By 2 p.m. the orders for the battle were dictated and issued. They were as follows:[8]

Marshal Ney will take the right from Posthenen towards Sortlack, and will rest on the present position of General Oudinot.

Marshal Lannes will form the centre, which will commence at the left of Marshal Ney, from Heinrichsdorf, up to about opposite the village of Posthenen; the grenadiers of Oudinot, at present forming the right of Marshal Lannes, will lean insensibly to the left, in order to draw upon themselves the attention of the enemy.

Marshal Lannes will close in his divisions as much as possible, by this closure enabling himself to form two lines.

The left will be formed by Marshal Mortier, holding Heinrichsdorf and the Koenigsberg road, and thence extending opposite the Russian right wing. Marshal Mortier will never advance, as the movement will be by our right, pivoting on the left.

The cavalry of General Espagne, and General Grouchy's dragoons, united to the cavalry of the left wing, will manoeuvre so as to cause as much harm as possible to the enemy when he, pressed by the vigorous attack of our right, shall feel the neces-

---

8. *Corr.* 12,756, dated "Bivouac behind Posthenen, 14th June."

sity of retreat. General Victor and the Imperial Guard, horse and foot, will form the reserve, and will be placed at Grünhof, Bothkeim, and behind Posthenen.

Lahoussaye's division of dragoons will be under the orders of General Victor; that of General Latour-Maubourg will obey Marshal Ney. Nansouty's division of heavy cavalry will be at the disposal of Marshal Lannes, and will fight alongside the cavalry of the reserve, in the centre.

I shall be with the reserve in the centre.

The advance must be always from the right, and the initiative of the movement must be left to Marshal Ney, who will await my orders to begin.

As soon as the right advances against the enemy, all the artillery of the line will redouble its fire in the direction most useful for the protection of the attack on the right.

But the Emperor was still in some doubt as to what force was in front of him. On the previous evening, his cavalry had not been able to give him any precise information as to the enemy's movements.[9] Murat, according to Savary,[10] had informed him, on the morning of the 13th, that the bulk of the Russian army was marching direct on Koenigsberg. The cavalry had, apparently, over-estimated Kamenskoi's 9000 men. The fact of his detaching two entire corps and three cavalry divisions to deal with the enemy at Koenigsberg shows that Napoleon believed the Russians to be in much greater strength in that direction than they really were. When he reached the front, at Posthenen, Oudinot had told him there were 80,000 men in front of him. Savary, sent out to see if the enemy were, as Napoleon could hardly believe possible, determined to fight a great battle with the river close behind them, reported that they were still crossing the bridges in great numbers.[11] The Emperor's doubts are clearly exhibited by a despatch dated, "Before Friedland, 3 p.m., June 14th,"[12] which is worth quoting in full.

The cannonade has been in progress since 3 a.m.; the enemy appears to be here in order of battle with his army; at first he wished to debouch towards Koenigsberg; now he appears to be seriously meditating the battle which is about to commence. His Majesty hopes that you are already in Koenigsberg (a divi-

---

9. *Savary*, iii. 84. "Our cavalry could give no precise account of the enemy's march."
10. *Loc. cit.*
11. *Savary*, iii. 87.
12. *Dumas*, xix. 327.

sion of dragoons and Marshal Soult are sufficient to enter that town), and that, with two cuirassier divisions and Marshal Davout, you will have marched for Friedland; for it is possible the battle may last over to-morrow. Endeavour, therefore, to arrive by 1 a.m. We have not, as yet, any news of you to-day. Should the Emperor be led to suppose that the enemy is in very great force, it is possible he may rest satisfied to-day with bombarding him, and wait for you. Communicate part of this letter to Marshals Soult and Davout."

From noon till 5 p.m. the action was maintained in a desultory fashion, chiefly by the artillery of both sides. The Russians who had been marching all night, and most of the previous day, were exhausted. At 4 p.m., Victor's corps and the French Guard arrived.

As Bennigsen saw column upon column arriving on the edge of the woods behind Posthenen, moving into line, and forming a "deep girdle of glittering steel,"[13] on the horizon, he bitterly repented his passage of the river, and had already given orders to attempt a retreat. They had scarcely been issued when they had to be cancelled.

THE RENEWED BATTLE

At 5 o'clock,[14] the comparative silence was broken by three salvoes of 20 guns, the signal for the advance. The echo of the last had not died away before, from the whole line of French artillery, there burst forth a furious fire. At the ame moment, Ney's corps, already collected in the clearings of the nearer portion of the Sortlack wood,[15] dashed forward with loud cheers, driving the jägers slowly back. By 6 o'clock the wood was cleared, and Ney's columns began to debouch on the farther side. The supporting Russian troops, at Sortlack, were powerless to stop their movement, but a battery on the farther bank of the Alle caused them some annoyance.

In mass of divisions, Marchand leading on the right, Bisson on the left, Latour-Maubourg behind, Ney pushed on. Marchand, overwhelming the retiring Russians at Sortlack, drove them in wild confusion into the Alle below the village. To accomplish this he had to

---

13. *Wilson*, p. 157.
14. 5.30 according to *Wilson*, p. 159.
15. Ney formed his columns in the wood. Only the artillery were on the roads through it; but, fortunately, there were three broad clearings, each sufficiently wide to allow of a column of infantry and one of cavalry, as well as the artillery, standing in them (*Savary*, iii. 87-88).

diverge to his right, into the eastward bend of the river, thus leaving an open space between himself and Bisson. Into this space dashed Kologribow at the head of his cavalry but he was promptly met by Latour-Maubourg, moving up to fill the gap. Charged by this force in front, fired into by Marchand and Bisson on his flanks, Kologribow's attempt to split Ney's infantry failed. Marchand, as the Russians retired again, moving westwards along the river, effected, once more, his union with Bisson, and the two ranged themselves across the neck of the Friedland peninsula, from the re-entrant angle of the Alle to the Millstream. The Russians in the peninsula, now bent back at an obtuse angle from the line north of the brook, were gradually being compressed by the narrowing space into compact masses on which the French artillery wrought fearful havoc.

As Ney advanced, Napoleon had moved up Victor's corps, on the right of the Eylau road, in two lines, with Lahoussaye's dragoons in 3rd line. Durosnel's cavalry followed. Ney's corps, with a cloud of skirmishers in front, again moved forward towards Friedland, Latour-Maubourg following some way behind. Marchand, on the ground sloping towards Friedland and the Alle, was suffering heavily by case from the Russian batteries beyond it, to silence which Ney moved his corps artillery to the bank. Bisson, protected by the slope towards the Millstream, was less exposed.

Both divisions, however, lost heavily from this artillery fire, as well as from the infantry and artillery fire, against their front. They were already wavering when Bennigsen's reserve cavalry, standing beyond the brook, crossed it and fell upon their left flank. It wanted but this blow to complete the repulse of Ney. His troops were retreating in considerable disorder when help reached them. Dupont, with his division of Victor's corps, had pushed forward his guns, which had barely time to fire a round of case before the Russian cavalry was upon them. Dupont, with great promptitude, for which he earned the special approval of Napoleon,[16] changing direction to the right, hurried up his infantry at the double into the gap, on Ney's left, cut by the cavalry. This division was specially enthusiastic in its attack, for, up to the surrender of Ulm, it had belonged to Ney's command.[17] The men felt, therefore, that on them depended the safety of old friends and comrades in the glorious fields of 1805. Latour-Maubourg and Durosnel also galloped forward against the Russian cavalry, which was now carried back on the infantry across

---

16. *Savary*, iii. 89.
17. Jomini, *Vie de Napoleon*, ii. 419.

the neck of the peninsula, spreading disorder in its ranks. The confusion was still further increased by the fire of 38 guns, which Senarmont, holding 6 more in reserve,[18] and escorted by Lahoussaye's cavalry and a battalion of infantry, moved steadily forward, opening fire first at 600 paces, then at 300, at 150, and, finally, at 60. The Russian cavalry made a desperate effort against this battery, but the French gunners, calmly awaiting their approach, mowed them down with a volley of grape.[19]

The Russian left, in the peninsula, was now, in hopeless confusion, making the best of its way into Friedland, pursued hotly by Ney's rallied troops, as well as by Dupont and the fire of Senarmont's guns.[20]

Dupont, having restored the fight here and completed the Russian disaster, wheeled to his left, across the Millstream, a movement which brought him upon the left flank and rear of the Russian centre, still maintaining its forward position.

Ney, pressing on into Friedland, and engaging in a fierce fight in the streets, was in possession of the town by 8 p.m. The Russian cavalry and infantry in front of him streamed towards the now burning bridges. At 7.30, the Russian artillery, beyond the river, had set fire to the houses nearest the bridges, and the flames had spread to the bridges themselves.[21] The river was too deep to ford with safety; great numbers of the Russians, failing to reach the bridges whilst they were still passable, were drowned in the attempt to cross by swimming. Their heavy accoutrements dragged down the infantry.[22]

The battle, as designed by Napoleon, was as good as won when Friedland was captured. Lannes and Mortier had intelligently carried out their orders by fighting a waiting action,[23] merely detaining Gortchakow north of the Millstream, though harassing him with a ter-

---

18. Victor, *Arch. Hist.* At 60 yards Senarmont used nothing but grape, which told with awful effect on the crowded Russians.

19. *Ibid.* He says that when Senarmont had dispersed this cavalry, he was supported by a battalion of Frère's brigade and the 4th division of dragoons. Dupont lost 649 killed and wounded altogether.

20. "Senarmont's and Ney's artillery sowed terror and death amongst the battalions and squadrons of the enemy, which, with their backs to the town, to the river, or to the brook, knew not by which way to escape front destruction" (Jomini, *Vie de Napoleon*, ii. 419).

21. Hoepfner, iii. 667. Jomini says, "Bagration, having withdrawn, fired the bridges to stop our pursuit" (*Vie de Napoleon*, ii. 419). "During this contest the bridges were ordered to he fired" (*Wilson*, p. 160).

22. Savary, iii. 91.

23. Lannes and Mortier had even allowed Gortchakow to gain some success, to draw him farther into the trap (Jomini, *Vie de Napoleon*, ii. 420).

rible artillery fire, to which he could but feebly respond.[24] It was only when he saw the thick smoke rising from the houses and the bridges of Friedland, that he realised that his retreat in that direction was cut off. He had already fallen back to the position of the early morning before the overwhelming fire of the artillery of the 1st and 6th corps. Dupont was north of the pond, at Friedland, on his left flank.

Leaving his cavalry to hold in check, as far as possible, the corps of Lannes and Mortier, he sent his two nearest divisions of infantry to the recapture of Friedland. These brave men, charging with the bayonet Dupont's and Ney's troops, carried them back into the town, and re-occupied the part of it nearest the lower pontoon bridge, only to find the bridge burning and impossible to cross. Some sought to cross to the right bank there, the majority wended their way, still fighting, down the river to Kloschenen, where, fortunately for Bennigsen, late in the evening, there had been discovered a deep ford, the existence of which had previously been unknown. Bad, and deep, as it was, it proved the salvation of the Russian army; for it not only gave a chance of crossing to its infantry and cavalry, but also enabled Bennigsen, with infinite difficulty, to get back many of his guns. These he managed to get up the steep right bank, and range there as a cover to the retreat, though it was for long impossible for them to fire on the confused throng of friends and foes. Much of the ammunition was rendered useless by water in the deep ford.[25]

Instant retreat was now the only course open to Gortchakow, with his remaining two divisions of infantry, his artillery, and his cavalry. The last he still left, to cover him against Mortier and Lannes. First he withdrew his guns, then his infantry. The latter slowly retired in great masses, through which the French artillery tore wide lanes, marking every halting-place with heaps and lines of dead and wounded.

It was now the moment for Napoleon to slip the leash in which he had, so far, held his centre and left. Rejoicing to be at last allowed to take an active part, the infantry of Lannes and Mortier poured over the plain towards the Alle, to complete the destruction which the artillery

---

24. The fire was tremendous. Victor alone had 48 guns in one great battery. Bennigsen, trying to make the best of his bad position, formed squares flanking one another; in doing so, he lost a great part of his front of infantry fire (*Savory*, iii. 90). The French, until the battle recommenced in the evening, had been concealed from the view and the fire of the Russians by the trees, the high crops and grass, and the inequalities of the ground, of which they took every advantage. The Russians, on the contrary, were fully exposed, standing in lines and column, on the open plain (*Wilson*, p. 150).

25. *Wilson*, p. 161.

had begun. They found their enemy in no mood for surrender; the brave Russian infantry preferred death by the bayonets of their opponents, or to take their chance of drowning in the river, to yielding themselves prisoners; few were taken. Part of the cavalry crossed with the broken infantry near Kloschenen; the majority retreated down the left bank, to Allenburg. Had Napoleon's cavalry, beyond Heinrichsdorf, shown the energy which might have been expected from them, this retreat by the left should have been impossible. There were 40 French squadrons in this direction, opposed to but 22 Russian. Even Savary, no friend of Murat, deplores his absence.[26] He would have seen the opportunity and have rolled up the Russian right, so that scarcely a man could have escaped. As it was, the French squadrons remained dismounted during the greater part of the renewed battle, content with what they had accomplished in the morning, doing nothing. The reason given, forsooth, was that they had no orders.[27] Murat at least would not have waited for orders with such a chance before him.

The defeated Russians who succeeded in crossing the river, united with the reserve in the Gnatten wood. Thence, in two columns, they marched for Wehlau, their rear covered by Platow's flying column, which, during the day, had made a futile attempt to cross the river behind Ney's right, but had been easily beaten off.[28]

At Allenburg, the retreat was joined by the cavalry, which had followed the left bank. At noon, on the 15th, Bennigsen had got together, at Wehlau, his broken army. Pursuit, there was none worth mentioning. A French general is said to have remarked that Friedland was "a battle gained and a victory lost."[29]

During the night, the French corps occupied the following positions when the battle at last, about 11 p.m., ceased. Lannes on the Koenigsberg road, between Friedland and Heinrichsdorf. Mortier beyond Friedland, on both banks of the river. Victor at Posthenen. Ney in and behind Friedland. The Guard, surrounding their victorious Emperor, slept on the plain where had stood the Russian centre.

---

26. *Savary*, iii. 92.

27. This was not even correct, for Napoleon's orders had directed Grouchy, Espagne, and the cavalry of the left wing, to "manoeuvre so as to cause as much harm as possible to the enemy when he, pressed by the vigorous attack of our right, shall feel the necessity of retreat." Their inaction was certainly no compliance with this order. The cavalry reserve engaged at Friedland, according to Murat (*Arch. Hist.*), consisted of the 1st, 2nd, and 3rd heavy divisions, the 1st, 2nd, and 4th dragoon divisions. The last-named was with Victor.

28. *Wilson*, p. 159, note.

29. *Wilson*, p. 162.

The permanent bridge at Friedland was quickly rendered service-able; for the flames had failed to destroy the strong buttresses built to protect it against floating ice in the winter. Over it, early on the 15th, part of the cavalry set out to follow the Russians, whilst the rest went down the left bank. Before it could reach Bennigsen, he had passed his troops across the Pregel at Wehlau, and was, for the time being, safe.

The battlefield of Friedland[30] presented, on the morning of the 15th, a ghastly spectacle. The French had lost considerably, though less than they had at Heilsberg. On the Russian side the destruction had been fearful. Friedland was filled with dead and wounded; but the most terrible spectacle was on the plain, north of the Millstream. There, long lines of corpses marked where the troops had been mown down by artillery fire, as they patiently stood for hours, unable to advance, unwilling to retire. Farther to their rear, the positions where their squares had halted in their retreat, to resist the pursuing French, were outlined by dead; between these places a broad trail of blood and bodies marked their line of movement.[31]

Before Friedland, about the Eylau road, the dead, lying thick and close, marked where Senarmont's and Ney's batteries had ploughed great furrows through the masses of fleeing Russians, crowded togeth-er in the narrow peninsula, or where Bennigsen's cavalry had tempo-rarily arrested Ney's victorious advance.

Tactics at Friedland & Strategy of the Campaign

Bennigsen's object in crossing the Alle at Friedland is the first point requiring notice in dealing with this battle. It has been said that he proposed to attempt a direct march on Koenigsberg, instead of, as he certainly intended when he wrote to Lestocq on the 11th June,[32] after Heilsberg, crossing the Pregel first. Napoleon himself was evidently un-der this impression, when he wrote from Posthenen, at 3 p.m. on the 14th, to Murat.[33] This view seems to be erroneous. What Bennigsen really appears to have meant was to crush Lannes, whom alone he be-lieved to be within reach of Friedland, and then to continue his march

---

30. The respective losses of the armies in this battle are, as usual, very variously stated, and it is only possible, by a comparison of the different authorities, to arrive at an approximation to the truth. The French losses were probably about 7000 or 8000. Plotho (p. 168) puts that of the Russians at 18,000 to 20,000. The French claim that it was 25,000.

31. See Savary's description of the field (iii. 92).

32. *Wilson*, p. 150.

33. *Vide supra*, p. 321.

on Wehlau. A general action on a favourable field was what Napoleon desired above all things. At Friedland, Bennigsen gave him precisely what he wanted.[34] Though it was absolutely necessary for Bennigsen to stop any French passage of the Alle in force at Friedland, he would have been wiser to content himself with holding that point strongly, whilst his army defiled past it, en route for Wehlau. To stop and attack Lannes, even had he alone been there, was to waste valuable time. Moreover, Bennigsen's men, exhausted by a march of 34 miles[35] in 48 hours, in oppressively hot weather,[36] were hardly fit to undertake a day of fighting.

If Bennigsen was badly informed as to the French movements, Napoleon was equally in doubt as to the distribution of the two Russian forces, towards Koenigsberg, and on the Alle.

Bennigsen's position at Friedland, with a considerable river close behind his back, with his only line of retreat, so far as he knew, behind

34. Bennigsen himself wrote: "I freely admit that I should have done better not to undertake the affair of Friedland; I had the power, and I should have been safer to maintain my resolution not to undertake a serious battle, since it was not necessary for the safety of the march of my army; but false reports, with which every general is often beset, had raised in me the erroneous view, which was confirmed by all my intelligence, that Napoleon had, with the greater part of his army, taken the road towards Koenigsberg" (*Hoepfner*, iii. 656). Wilson fairly describes the action as "a battle undertaken from an error of information, persevered in from an apprehension of retreat, but whose catastrophe was alleviated by the extraordinary valour of the officers and troops" (pp. 161, 162). "The weakness of the French column suggested to Bennigsen the idea of fighting a fortunate battle en passant" (*Rustow*; i. 322). Adams (Great Campaigns, p. 154) puts very clearly the object of Napoleon. "Hoepfner blames him (Napoleon) for not continuing the battle of Heilsberg on the 11th June instead of manoeuvring; but his abstention is a proof of his sense of the precarious nature of his position, and he was, moreover, anxious to economise force. "Without Bennigsen's blunder, the Russians would have arrived safely on the Pregel, whilst Napoleon's line, already extended, would have been still further stretched. The point had been reached when the occupation of territory was of no further value, but in this poor district rather the contrary, and a general action was the sole object worth striving for. This object was attained at Friedland by good fortune, which, according to Bennigsen, was owing to his misinformation as to Napoleon's movements on Koenigsberg." It may be said Napoleon had his chance of a general action at Heilsberg. True! but Heilsberg was a very unfavourable field for him. Friedland was all that he could desire.

35. Left Heilsberg midnight, 11th–12th—

	Miles
Reached Bartenstein noon 12th	13
Reached Schippenbeil	8
Schippenbeil to Friedland	13
Total	34

36. The day of Friedland was oppressively hot (*Marbot*, i. 279).

his left wing, and with his front split in two by a serious obstacle to the free movement of troops, was as bad as it could be.[37] It is true he had another line of escape by the Allenburg road, on the left bank of the Alle; but that, again, led from a wing parallel to his line, and was close against the river. His one chance was to overpower Lannes, whilst that officer was still in very inferior force in the early morning, and thus clear for himself space for a less unfavourable field of battle.

Napoleon had, perhaps, rarely been more happy in appreciating, at the first glance, the features of a battlefield. His orders for the renewal of the attack show, by their reiteration of the caution to his left not to press forward, how completely he had estimated the vital importance to Bennigsen of Friedland, and the tongue of land on which it stood. Yet he failed at first, as is shown by his letter to Murat, to value correctly the strength of the force to which he was opposed. It was not till the action recommenced that he saw that Bennigsen had delivered himself into his hands. Could he have been certain of the Russians remaining another 24 hours on the hither side of the river, he might, even as it was, have preferred waiting till the arrival of Murat and Davout gave him a still greater Preponderance of numbers,[38] and until his own troops, many of whom (Victor's corps especially) had had much fatiguing marching, were rested. But he had too often experienced the Russian general's capacity for slipping away during the night from the most dangerous positions to risk a repetition of these tactics. When, therefore, Ney's advance had shown him his great superiority of force, he had no longer any hesitation in pressing home his assault.

Dupont's action in support of Ney, without any orders from Victor,[39] reflected credit on that unfortunate general, whose great reputation was afterwards destroyed at Baylen.

---

37. Wilson (p. 153,) says of it: "His (Bennigsen's) own feeble army was lodged in a position that was untenable, from which progress could not be made against an equal force, nor retreat be effected without great hazard, and where no military object would be attained for the interests or reputation of the Russian army, whose courage had been sufficiently established, without tilting for fame as adventurers who have nothing to lose and everything to win." "There was in his (Bennigsen's) conduct a mixture of rash imprudence and of irresolution quite irreconcilable" (Jomini, *Vie de Napoleon*, ii. 421). "Bennigsen, ill at the time, seemed to have forgotten that he had come to the left bank to fight" (*Rustow*, i. 323).

38. "Perhaps I should have done better to wait for Davout and Murat. I should not have hesitated had I thought Bennigsen would dare to continue his march towards Koenigsberg *viâ* Abschwang. Reinforced by 40,000 men, including my cavalry, I should have driven him on the marshy forests of Zehlau and Frischind, from which he could never have emerged" (Jomini, *Vie de Napoleon*, ii. 413).

39. *Savary*, iii. 89.

The inaction of the French cavalry at Heinrichsdorf, in the evening, is almost inexplicable. All that can be said is that Napoleon seems to have been so busy with the operations of his infantry, as to neglect to insist on compliance with his orders. Murat would have acted even without orders. Grouchy, possibly, did not consider he was in a position to warrant his doing so; though, as already pointed out, he had orders.

The failure to pursue during the night is, on the face of it, still more difficult of explanation. No general ever was more alive than Napoleon to the advantages of pursuing a defeated enemy, "*l'epée dans les reins*," to use the forcible French expression. If his infantry were tired, his cavalry had no reason for being so. They had neither marched an excessive distance, nor had any very heavy fighting.

Is it possible that the Emperor's slackness, in this respect, was due to political considerations? He felt that Bennigsen was badly beaten, and could not again face him short of the Niemen. The Russian army was worn out by marching and fighting. A pursuit, such as that of the Prussians after Jena, must have caused the enemy much loss, and given rise to very bitter feelings towards the French in the breasts of the leader, as well as of the Russian soldiery. At this period Napoleon did not yet contemplate the invasion which he attempted in 1812, with such disastrous results. He still had doubts as to Austria, and it would have ill suited him to be involved in a fresh campaign beyond the Niemen. A murderous pursuit might have so incensed the Czar as to induce him to continue the struggle which, he must have known, would eventually be stopped by winter, and to adopt the Fabian tactics, afterwards so successfully employed in 1812.

Napoleon did not wish to make a permanent enemy of Russia. He had already written to Talleyrand[40] that he would prefer the Russian to the Austrian alliance, if he had to choose between the two. He wanted Russia, as a sea power with a large seaboard and a great trade with England, to join him in his campaign against the commerce of his detested enemy. In these conditions, is it not probable that the Emperor thought that the destruction of a few thousand Russians, in a night pursuit, was not worth the risk of a continuation of the war?

The strategy of the first few days of the campaign requires but little comment. Napoleon had left Ney in a somewhat exposed position, according to some authorities,[41] as a bait to the Russians. That marshal was the best man to be placed thus; for he could always be relied on to make the most of a rear-guard action, to hold the enemy and delay

---

40. *Corr.* 12,028, dated 14th March, 1807.
41. Jomini, *Vie de Napoleon*, ii. 406.

him to the utmost, without compromising himself. He showed his mastery of such tactics on the 5th and 6th of June. Davout's position enabled him to support Ney's right, and to threaten the left flank and rear of the Russians as they advanced to the Passarge.

Napoleon did not expect Bennigsen to assume the offensive. The Russian general had, he considered, lost his opportunity, if he ever had one, in failing to make a general advance in support of Kamenskoi's attempt to relieve Danzig. If he was going to attempt the offensive at all, then was his chance. He was, but for the absence of Kamenskoi's 7000 or 8000 men, as strong on the 15th May as he was on the 5th June. Napoleon, on the other hand, was weaker by the corps of Lannes, Mortier, and all of Lefebvre's except what was required for the garrison of Danzig after its fall—quite 40,000 men in all. In June, Napoleon had an enormous preponderance of numbers over his adversary, and if he began to concentrate rearwards towards Osterode, "*il ne reculait que pour mieux sauter.*" If Bennigsen's forward move had not stopped at the Passarge, it must inevitably have done so before the lakes at Osterode.

When the tide turned, Napoleon's movement was a simple one to the front with the bulk of his army, whilst he endeavoured, by holding Lestocq and Kamenskoi on the Lower Passarge with the 1st corps, to separate them from the rest of Bennigsen's army. Lestocq had been dealt with in a precisely similar manner in the two earlier phases of the campaign, before Pultusk and before Eylau.[42]

When the French reached the bend of the Alle at Guttstadt, there were, according to Jomini, two courses open to the emperor, between which he hesitated for a moment. Napoleon himself has nowhere indicated that he had any such doubts. He might, says Jomini, have pushed forward, establishing his line with its left at Guttstadt, and his right towards Bischofstein. "It would have been absolutely the same movement as that of Jena and Naumburg against the Prussians, with better chances of success; for the Russian army, beaten on its left and driven back on the Lower Passarge and the Frisches-Haff, would have been thrown into the sea. Koenigsberg, no doubt, offered it a ref-

---

42. Adams (*Great Campaigns*, p. 153, 154.) says, "It is difficult to see, moreover, the object the allies had in assigning a detached sphere of action to the Prussian contingents. The German authorities agree that, in spite of constant defeat, the individual German soldier retained the confident feeling of physical superiority; but the cause may probably be found in a superannuated system, by which the Prussian leaders were first of all punctiliously unwilling to serve other than independently, fearful lest such a course would imply inferiority; and next, showed a reluctance to adopt anything new after a long period of peace."

uge; but that place itself, with the Baltic behind it on the west, and the Curisches-Haff on the north, would have offered no issue to this beaten army; for I should have forestalled it at Wehlau, as soon as it began to retreat.

"The second course to take was to advance direct against the entrenched camp of Heilsberg, whilst 50,000 men manoeuvred by my left on Eylau, to menace the line of operations of the allies, to force them to abandon their redoubts without fighting, to press them vigorously in their retreat, and to strike them heavily at the passages of the Pregel and the Niemen. This last course was less advantageous; it was even contrary to the rules of strategy, which do not allow of compromising a considerable corps by passing it between the enemy and the sea. I preferred it, because my left was already in that direction, and, in order to manoeuvre by my right, I should have to describe a long circle round the Russian army, to uncover the roads which served for communication with Thorn and Warsaw, and to threw myself into the wooded country on the right bank of the Alle. However, I must admit I should have acted in a better military spirit in adopting the first course.

"One of the motives which contributed most to determine me in favour of the second was that I had already remarked, at the time of the battle of Eylau, that Bennigsen showed a pusillanimous anxiety for Koenigsberg; but, as it was not a military point, I thought that he had special motives, whether of policy towards Prussia, or of consideration for the great magazines. In depriving the enemy of his magazines, I should procure them for my own troops, which, in a distant country, is essential; I should overturn the enemy's system of operations. On the other hand, it was possible that the march of Soult on Koenigsberg might decide the Russians to retreat to their right, to cover that city, and I was always master of the power to throw forces on their left flank, threatening to cut them from Tilsit. For these subsidiary reasons I disregarded strategical principles, and decided to advance on Heilsberg by the left bank of the Alle.[43]

The arguments in favour of the course actually adopted are, no doubt, valid; but it may be doubted if Napoleon ever hesitated in his choice, or if the first course really was the best strategically. His lines of communication were not at this period with Warsaw primarily, or even with Thorn. They were by Marienwerder, Marienburg, and Danzig. The proposed movement to the right would have laid them all open, that to the left covered completely the Marienwerder, Marienburg, and Danzig lines.

---

43. Jomini, *Vie de Napoleon*, pp. 406-408.

Moreover, Bennigsen, if he were not bold enough to attack the lines of communication, would probably have taken fright and retreated down the Alle long before the extended movement round his left could have been completed. He would then have had the advantage of the shorter line to the Pregel, and would have been joined on it by the Prussians. As has already been said, Bennigsen could probably have been manoeuvred out of Heilsberg, without the bloody battle of the 10th June.

When Napoleon divided his army at Eylau, marching partly on Koenigsberg, partly on Friedland, it seems almost impossible to doubt that, as before at Pultusk, he was under an entirely erroneous impression as to the distribution of the two portions of the enemy. His cavalry could give no precise account of the enemy's march,[44] and probably exaggerated the strength of Kamenskoi's 9000 men marching past Eylau on the 12th. It is difficult to believe that the Emperor would have deliberately detached 60,000 men to deal with less than half their number. His despatch to Murat from Posthenen seems to show that he recognised his mistake. With Murat, and half the cavalry he had at Koenigsberg, on the field at Friedland, it is likely that that battle would have resulted in a still greater disaster for the Russians. Soult's corps, with a cavalry division, and, perhaps, the addition of one division of Davout's infantry, could easily have dealt with Lestocq and Kamenskoi, had the Emperor known how small their force was. Had he detached 30,000 or 35,000, under Soult or Davout, against Koenigsberg, he would have been quite safe in that direction, and would have disposed of an additional 25,000 or 30,000 men at Friedland, not to mention the advantage of having Murat to lead the cavalry of the left wing.

---

44. *Savary*, iii. 84.

CHAPTER 4

Koenigsberg and Tilsit

A glace back must now be given to the movements of the detached forces in the direction of Koenigsberg. Lestocq and Kamenskoi were last mentioned when, about 3 p.m. on the 13th, they met at Gollau. Between them they mustered about 25,000 men, all that were available to oppose 9000 of Murat's cavalry, 22,000 of Soult's corps,[1] and 29,000 of Davout's; in all 60,000. Of the allied forces, Lestocq took command. They had been in touch with Murat's cavalry, and fighting with them, on the evening of the 13th, on the direct road from Eylau to Koenigsberg.

On the 14th, Soult's advanced guard, moving on the Kreuzburg-Koenigsberg road, first encountered the enemy at Bergau. Lestocq was at Gollau, opposing the progress of Murat, when Soult's arrival on his right flank forced him to retreat on the city. A battalion of his infantry was cut off and captured by Milhaud's dragoons with Soult.

Another attempt to make a stand against the now united corps of Soult and Murat, 1000 paces from the works of Koenigsberg, was found to be hopeless. Outflanked and severely pressed, the allies shut themselves into Koenigsberg. The French force was now supplemented by the arrival of Davout. Gudin's division joined Must's right, and extended towards the Pregel, above the city. A battery, which Davout established in this direction to test the possibility of an assault, was

---

1. Soult, at the opening of the campaign, had 30,000 men; but he had lost 6600 at Heilsberg alone, and, including the losses on the Passarge, he cannot have lost less than 8000 since the 5th June. The cavalry employed began the campaign at the following strength:

Lasalle	5703
St. Sulpice	1967
Milhaud 1859	
Total	9529

Davout, at the same time, had 29,560.

silenced by the superior fire of the defenders. Davout then ordered Friant, supported by Morand, to make preparations for the passage of the river, but only passed over one regiment.

About mid-day, a brigade of about 1200 men, which Lestocq had left behind to watch the direction of Brandenburg, appeared behind Soult's left, attempting to rejoin the Prussians. It made a brave struggle for liberty, but, surrounded in a village, it was forced to lay down its arms.

All this time, Lestocq and Kamenskoi, ignorant of Bennigsen's movements, were buoyed by the hope that a bold defence of the city could not fail to be supported by him in the course of a few hours. Setting fire to the Brandenburg suburb, on the left bank of the river, Lestocq withdrew most of his troops within the fortifications. Those which remained were attacked in the suburb by Legrand's division, which inflicted heavy loss on them, and took a number of prisoners. The works of the place were strong enough to render an assault out of the question. Soult refused to listen to the rash counsels of Murat in favour of it.

In the evening, Murat receiving Napoleon's order, dated 3 p.m. on the same afternoon before Friedland, at once started with Davout's corps in the direction of Friedland. Soult, now left alone before Koenigsberg, was in strength inferior to that of the enemy. He therefore contented himself with taking up a position of observation in front of the fortress. Lestocq endeavoured to send, through Soult's lines, a small body of cavalry with a despatch for Bennigsen, of whom he had still heard no news. The party was surrounded and the despatch captured, as was the cavalry belonging to the brigade which had been cut off in the afternoon.

On the 5th, Soult began preparations for an attack on the fortress, which he bombarded. At 10 p.m., it was ascertained, from deserters, that Kamenskoi's corps had left as soon as the news of the battle of Friedland had arrived, and that the Prussians were preparing to follow. On the morning of the 16th, Soult entered the fortress, where he captured the single battalion which Lestocq had left to cover his evacuation. A large number of wounded Russians and Prussians were found in the town, and very large magazines and stores of every sort, as well as of artillery.[2]

To return to Bennigsen and Napoleon: the former, passing the Pregel, at Wehlau, on the 15th, by a single bridge, burnt it behind him, and, at Petersdorf, on the farther bank opposite the mouth of the

---

2. Soult's report (*Arch. Hist.*) says he took, in Koenigsberg, 3600 sick and wounded Russians, and 4000 Prussians.

Alle, gave his troops a few hours of much-needed rest. On the 16th, he marched 18 miles to a position between Mehlauken and Popliken. On the 17th he made another march of 18 miles, across the little river Schillup, where he was rejoined by Lestocq and Kamenskoi. On the 18th, the allied army, passing through Tilsit, crossed the Niemen on boat bridges, which were immediately afterwards burnt by Bagration, who, as before, commanded the rear-guard in this last retreat.

Napoleon, meanwhile, had moved thus:

After the victory of Friedland, the march of Murat and Davout, towards that point, ceased to be necessary. They were diverted, therefore, from Abschwangen, across the Pregel, at Tapiau. Murat, sending his light cavalry to Wehlau, reached Tapiau with St. Sulpice's dragoons and Davout's corps, on the morning of the 16th.

It was not till 24 hours later that Davout succeeded in getting across the river. With his light cavalry he set out in pursuit of the enemy in the directions of Koenígsberg and Labiau, whilst Napoleon also manoeuvred to his left, in the hope of driving the Prussians on the Curisches-Haff. It was too late. Marulaz alone reached the Prussian rear-guard, with which he engaged in small combats. Murat, after passing the Pregel on the 16th, rejoined the main army, with St. Sulpice's dragoons, at Wehlau.

The army which had fought at Friedland marched, on the 15th, to Wehlau, except the corps of Ney, which remained at Friedland.

On the 16th and 17th, Victor, followed by Lannes, Mortier, and the Guard, in the order named, passed the Pregel. He was at Petersdorf on the evening of the 16th. On the 17th the cavalry, supported by part of Victor's corps, had a slight engagement with Bagration at Mehlauken. He was again seen on the 8th near the Niemen.

On the morning of the 19th, Murat entered Tilsit; Victor was halted on the left bank of the river below Tilsit, Davout above it.

Ney, meanwhile, moved, on the 17th and 18th, to Gumbinnen, covering the right flank of the army. Soult remained on the left, at Koenigsberg, sending St. Hilaire to invest Pillau on the east, whilst Rapp's detachment, on the Nehrung, invested it on that side and from the sea. It shortly capitulated.

****

There remain to be narrated the operations of Masséna on the Narew. On the 11th June, the Russians, having advanced between the Narew and the Bug, attacked, with 6000 or 8000 men, Drenzewo and the French entrenched camp at Borki, a little below Ostrolenka on the right bank of the Narew. Claparède, defending it, was at the same time bombarded by batteries on the left bank.[3] He was finally forced out,[4] and the Russians entrenched themselves in it.

Suchet had reached Rozan with the rest of his division. On the 12th, at 10 a.m., Masséna in person directed an attack on the Russian lines. Overwhelmed by superior numbers, they were forced, under the protection of their batteries, partly across the Omulew, and partly across the Narew, at Ostrolenka.

No further movement of importance took place till the 22nd, when Masséna, already informed of the result of the battle of Friedland, marched on Ostrolenka which he reached on the evening of the 23rd, to find the Russians gone in the direction of Tykoczin. He followed them by Nowogrod, Lomza, and Sniadow towards Bialystok, as ordered by the Emperor.

On the 19th June, Bennigsen, now on the right bank of the Niemen, received orders from the allied sovereigns to demand an armistice. About mid-day the demand[5] was transmitted to Murat in Tilsit, and was passed on to Napoleon, who shortly afterwards reached the town, and who at once accepted the proposal to negotiate.

On the 21st, the armistice was signed on the following conditions:

(*a*) Armistice to be for the purpose of negotiating a peace.

(*b*) Either party proposing to terminate it to give one month's notice of his intention.

(*c*) A separate armistice to be concluded between the French and Prussian armies.

(*d*) The line of delimitation between the armies was fixed.

(*e*) Plenipotentiaries, for the negotiation of peace, to be at once appointed, and commissions for the exchange of prisoners.

---

3. According to the memoirs of Masséna (v. 331), there were 8000 Russians, and Tutchkow had covered his real attack by threatening a passage at Rozan. An attack by cavalry was also made on Gazan at Zawady on the Omulew.

4. Back to Nozewo (*Masséna*, v. 331).

5. The terms of Bennigsen's letter to Bagration for communication to Murat were as follows: "After the torrents of blood which have lately flowed in battles as sanguinary as frequent, I should desire to assuage the evils of this destructive war, by proposing an armistice before we enter upon a conflict, a fresh war, perhaps more terrible than the first. I request you, Prince, to convey to the chiefs of the French army this my intention, of which the consequences may produce all the more salutary results, seeing that there is already question of a general congress, and which may prevent an useless effusion of blood. Kindly inform me of the result of your action" (*Wilson*, p. 170, note).

Napoleon had spoken the prologue to the great drama in his proclamation of the 2nd December, 1806; on the 22nd June, he delivered the epilogue. "Soldiers, on the 5th June, we were attacked in our cantonments by the Russian army, which misconstrued the causes of our inactivity. It perceived, too late, that our repose was that of the lion; now it does penance for its mistake. In the days of Guttstadt, of Heilsberg, in the ever-memorable day of Friedland, in 10 days campaigning we have taken 120 guns, and seven standards; we have killed, wounded, or captured 60,000 Russians; torn from the enemy's army all its magazines, its hospitals, its ambulances, the fortress of Koenigsberg, the 300 vessels which were in the port, laden with every kind of supplies, and 160,000 muskets,[6] which England was sending to arm our enemies.

"From the shores of the Vistula, we have reached those of the Niemen, with the rapidity of the eagle. At Austerlitz you celebrated the anniversary of the coronation; you have this year worthily celebrated that of the battle of Marengo, which put an end to the war of the second coalition. Frenchmen, you have been worthy of yourselves, and of me; you will return to France covered with laurels, after having acquired a peace which guarantees its own durability. It is time for our country to live in repose, sheltered from the malign influence of England.

" My rewards will prove to you my gratitude and the greatness of the love I bear you."

The positions taken by the armies, pending the completion of the peace negotiations, of the result of which there could be no doubt, were the following:

French:

Headquarters of Guard at Koenigsberg, with detachments at Tilsit guarding the Emperor's person. Soult at Labiau.

Davout, Lahoussaye, and Lasalle at Tilsit.

Ney, and Latour-Maubourg at Marienpol, east of Gumbinnen.

Mortier and the Polish divisions at Augustowo, Olitta, and Nsobra, on Ney's right.

Victor at Wehlau. Lannes at Koenigsberg, Tapiau & Brandenburg.

---

6. Wilson (p. 166, note) denies the capture of these muskets, which, he says, were landed at Riga. He also affirms that there was very little left in Koenigsberg of supplies or artillery, most of them having been removed by Lestocq. It is hardly probable that that officer had time to make considerable removals.

Espagne, Saint Sulpice, Nansouty, Grouchy, and Milhaud, the cavalry reserve, in cantonments on the Pregel and Alle.

Murat, fixing his headquarters at Koenigsberg, himself remained with the Emperor at Tilsit. Masséna's corps was at Nowogrod.

Russians and Prussians:

Imperial headquarters at Pickupponen, opposite Tilsit.

Gortchakow, with two divisions, the cavalry of the right wing, that of the advanced guard, and all the Cossacks and Bashkirs, at Willkischken, Limspohnen, and Bennigskeiten.

Essen, with four divisions and the cavalry of the left wing, at and about Georgenburg.

Lestocq and Kamenskoi's two divisions, in cantonments, between the Gilge and Russ rivers.

Labanow, with two divisions, about Kanen.

Tolstoi, with three divisions, near Bialystock, with outposts on the upper Narew, facing Masséna.

Kologribow, with the Guard, except one battalion, one cavalry regiment, and one squadron of another, the Czars personal guard, retired to cantonments in Lithuania.[7]

With the armies thus posted, Napoleon proceeded to enact the transformation scene which was to mark his new position as the arbiter of the destinies of Europe.

Prussia he had crushed, and was determined to humiliate to the lowest depths. Russia he had defeated, not conquered. He required her aid in the struggle with the one enemy whom he had been unable to cripple. He proposed a personal meeting, to settle the bases of peace, between himself and the Czar Alexander. There was no mention of the King of Prussia. Alexander, flattered by the recognition of the pre-eminence of his own power, accepted the proposal.

An enormous raft was constructed by the French engineers, and moored in midstream. It bore a magnificently decorated pavilion, worthy of the memorable scene which was to take place within it.

On the 25th June, towards 1 p.m., Napoleon accompanied by Berthier, Bessières, Duroc, and Caulaincourt, left the southern bank at the same moment as Alexander, with the Grand Duke Constantine, Bennigsen, Labanow, Uvarow, and Count Lieven, set out from the northern. Reaching the raft simultaneously, the two Emperors

---

7. Some of the places named above are not marked on the map, being beyond its limits.

embraced, and then, alone, entered on a discussion lasting two hours, the purport of which can be guessed only from its results. It has been said that Alexander's first words were, "I hate the English as much as you do yourself." To which Napoleon replied, "If that is the case, peace is already made." It is unnecessary to put any great faith in this story. The Czar may have thought he had not received so much support, in men and money, as he had a right to expect from Great Britain; but her conduct had certainly not been such as to warrant so complete a revulsion of feeling towards her.

The King of Prussia was contemptuously left out of this meeting, at which, presumably, his spoliation was decided on. He was only admitted to the second interview, on the succeeding day, after which the Czar and the King occupied quarters in Tilsit, which had been neutralised for their accommodation. It was only on this day that the armistice with the Prussians was signed and ratified.

The beautiful and noble Queen of Prussia accompanied her husband. She it was who had been the spirit of the war. Napoleon had not the magnanimity to forgive her conduct, now that her power had been broken. His whole treatment of her and the King was such as to show that he regarded them, and Prussia, as unworthy of his consideration. With the unpleasant history of these days we need not deal fully.

Napoleon, determined to treat entirely separately with Russia and Prussia, insisted on distinct treaties. That between Russia and France was executed on the 7th July, and ratified two days later. The Prussian treaty was executed only on the day on which that with Russia was ratified, and it was not ratified till the 12th July.

Of the complicated provisions of the treaties a short resumé is all that seems necessary. Napoleon, bent on passing every possible insult upon the unfortunate Prussians, attributed such poor terms as he granted them to the intercession of Alexander. Of the conquered territories, he restored to Prussia that part of the Duchy of Magdeburg which was situated on the right bank of the Elbe, thereby excluding the fortress itself, which he knew the Queen specially cherished. Also he surrendered Pomerania, Silesia, and other territories constituting approximately the kingdom as it was before the 1st January, 1772. From that portion of the ancient kingdom of Poland which had been acquired by Prussia in and after 1772 he constituted the Grand Duchy of Warsaw, which he presented to the King of Saxony, together with a military right of way across the intervening Prussian territory. He excepted a considerable area in the direction of Bialystock, which was made over to Russia. Danzig he made a free city, under the protection of Prussia and Saxony. The recognition of the Napoleonic Kings of Naples and Holland, of the Confederation of the Rhine, of the new kingdom of Westphalia, now carved out of Prussian territory west of the Elbe and bestowed on Jerome Bonaparte, was stipulated for.

Turkey, which had so materially helped him, was abandoned by Napoleon, anxious in every way to conciliate Russia. He merely offered his mediation between the two powers, whilst agreeing to accept that of the Czar between England and himself. Prussia, as well as Russia, was bound to aid his campaign against the commerce of Great Britain.

Such were the more important provisions of the treaties, the full details of which can be studied in the documents themselves.[8] Their result was aggrandisement of the power of Napoleon to an enormous, of Russia to a small extent, at the expense of Prussia.

Prussia was hedged round with states subservient to French interests—the Rhenish Confederation, Saxony, Westphalia, the Grand Duchy of Warsaw, Holland, and Danzig. England's last allies on the Continent, with the exception of Sweden, which was soon to follow, were torn from her.

With the gradual withdrawal of the French armies it is not proposed to deal. Napoleon's grasp on continental Europe was now assured, and it was not till his own action in the Peninsula of Spain sowed the germs of the "Spanish ulcer," and until Austria, in 1809, made another struggle for liberty, that his almost universal power was challenged.

---

8. Printed in full by Wilson (pp. 263-271).

Maps & Plans

EXPLANATION OF PLANS.

PLAN 1.

Passages of the Bug and the Ukra.

(1) French bridge and bridge head at Okunin.
(2) Batteries on left bank of Bug, flanking bridge head.
(3) Triangular island at mouth of Ukra.
(4) (4) French bridges across left branch of Ukra.
(5) (5) Osterman Tolstoi's position at Czarnowo.

PLAN 2.

Battle of Pultusk.

French.

(1) Lannes and Suchet in Mosin wood.
(2) Gazan's division.
(3) Wedell.
(4) Claparède, and Treilhard's cavalry.
(5) d'Aultanne's (Gudin's) division of III. Corps.

Russians.

(6) Barclay de Tolly.
(7) Bagavout.
(8) 1st main line.
(9) 2nd main line.
(10) Reserves.
(11) Cavalry—20 squadrons preparing to support Barclay.
(12) Great battery directed on French in wood.
(13) Battalion on left bank of Narew.
(14) Polish cavalry and Cossacks, driven in by d'Aultanne.

PLAN 3.

Battle of Golymin.

French.

(1) Durosnel's cavalry } VII. Corps
(2) Heudelet's division } (Augereau).
(3) Desjardins' division }
(4) Morand's division (1 brigade) } III. Corps
(5) Friant's division } (Davout).
(6) Reserve cavalry and Marulaz's (III. Corps).
(7) d'Honniere's brigade (Morand's division).
(8) Rapp's dragoons.

Russians.

(9) Sacken's troops from Ciechanow.
(10) Tcherbatow.
(11) Infantry defending wood against Morand.
(12) Infantry defending Osiek wood, and in marshes bordering Pultusk road.
(13) Cavalry on Pultusk road, about to be charged by Rapp.
(14) Reserves about Golymin.

PLAN 4.

Battle of Eylau.

Russians.

(1) (1) 1st, 2nd, and 3rd main lines.
(2) The two great reserve columns.
(3) Archangel regiment.
(4) Horse artillery (60 guns).
(5) Bagavout and Barclay.

French.

(6) Guard infantry and artillery.
(7) VII. Corps (Augereau).
(8) St. Hilaire's division, III. Corps (Soult's).
(9) Part of Legrand's and Leval's divisions (Soult's Corps).
(10) Schinner's and Vivier's brigades (Soult's Corps).
(11) D'Hautpoult's cuirassiers.
(12) Guard cavalry.
(13) Grouchy's dragoons.
(14) Klein's dragoons.
(15) Milhaud's heavy cavalry.
(16) Lasalle's light cavalry.
(17) Bruyère, Guyot, Colbert, Durosnel — light cavalry.
(18) Reserve (one regiment Guard infantry, 18th of line, and 2 guns).
(19) Advance guard of Friant's division of III. Corps (Davout).

A —— A French left after Ney's evacuation of Schloditten.
B — — B French right at close of battle.
B' + + + B' Extreme line reached by Davout before Prussians arrived.
C — -- — C Russian front at close of battle.
D ———— D Direction of Augereau's advance at 10.30 a.m.

PLAN 5.

Siege of Danzig.

(Besiegers' works marked by heavy line.)
(1) (1) Works protecting Schramm's camp on Nehrung.
(2) (2) Two redoubts, and connecting parapet, constructed by Schramm on April 15–17.
(3) Channel cut on April 26, by French, across the extremity of Holm Island.
(4) French work constructed, on April 17, to cross fire with (2) (2).
(5) First battery constructed on Stolzenberg on April 17.
(6) Second battery on Stolzenberg, constructed April 23.
(7) First parallel against Bischofsberg, opened April 9.

PLAN 6.

Battle of Heilsberg.

Russians.

(1) (1) Main infantry lines on left bank of Alle.
(2) (2) Russian cavalry.
(3) (3) Prussian cavalry.
(4) (4) Kamenskoi's division defending redoubts Nos. 2 and 3.
(5) (5) Bagration, &c., on right bank.
(6) Bagration's jägers left in work by river.
(7) Grand Duke Constantine's battery on right bank.
(8) Cossacks at Grossendorf attacking French 18th of line.
(9) 1st and 2nd divisions, in reserve.

French.

(10) St. Hilaire's division } III. (Soult's)
(11) St. Cyr's division } Corps.
(12) Light cavalry division }
(13) 26th light infantry advancing against redoubt No. 2
(14) (14) Legrand's division (Soult's Corps), Savary and Murat.
(15) Verdier's division (Lannes' reserve Corps).
(16) 18th infantry in squares at Grossendorf.
(17) Remainder of Lannes' Corps, VI. Corps (Ney) and Guard on the march.

PLAN 7.

Battle of Friedland.

Russians.

(1) Cavalry of right wing and Cossacks.
(2) Main lines of infantry centre and right.
(3) Guard.
(4) 1st and 2nd division (left wing).
(5) Troops from Sortlack driven on river by Marchand.
(6) (6) Reserves—14th division and Platow's flying column on right bank.
(7) Kologribow's cavalry about to charge Marchant's left.

French.

(8) Cavalry of Grouchy, Espagne, and left wing.
(9) (9) VIII. Corps (Mortier).
(10) (10) Lannes' reserve corps (Verdier and Oudinot).
(11) (11) I. Corps (Victor).
(12) (12) Guard infantry and cavalry.
(13) Bisson's division. } VI. Corps (Ney) advan-
(14) Marchand's division } cing against Friedland.
(15) Latour Maubourg's cavalry advancing to meet Kologribow's attack on Marchand.
(16) Direction of advance of Dupont's division and Senarmont's battery.
(17) Bridges over Alle, of boats.
(18) Permanent bridge.

French Infantry ■ Russian & Prussian Infantry ◆ Artillery ✦✦✦✦
    Cavalry ◻   "   Cavalry ◆

(1) Enlarged map for passages of Bug & Ukra.

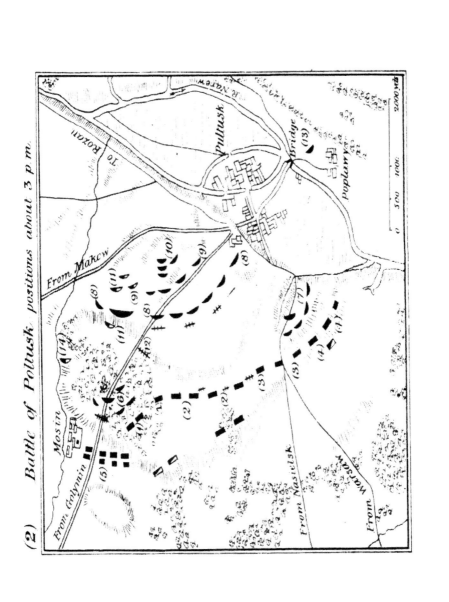

(2)   *Battle of Pultusk: positions about 3 p.m.*

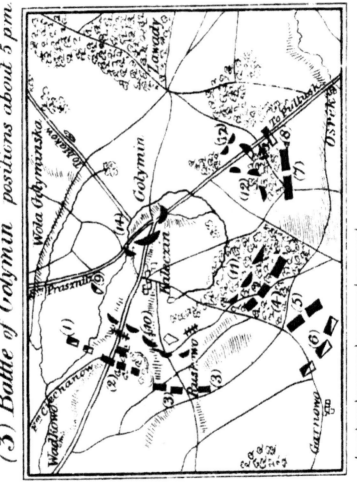

(3) Battle of Golymin   positions about 5 pm.

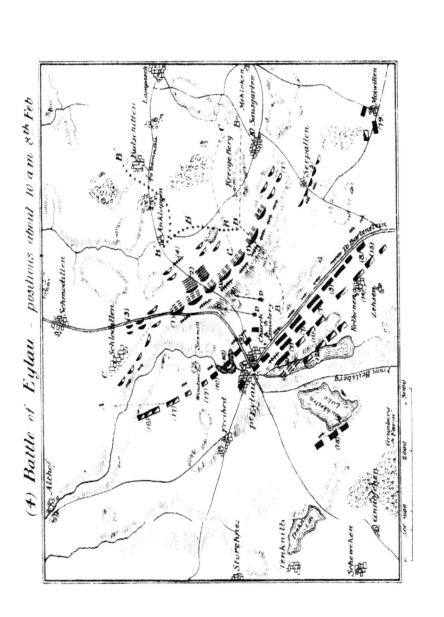

(4) *Battle of Eylau – positions about 10 a.m. 8th Feb*

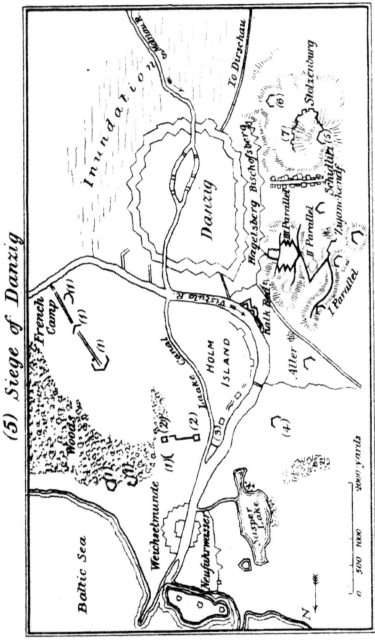

(5) Siege of Danzig

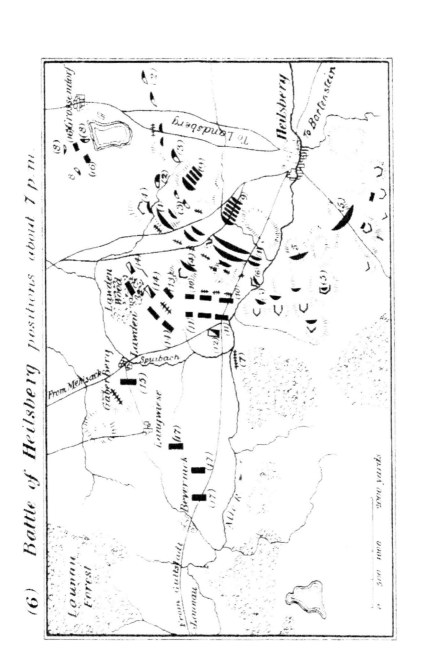

(6) *Battle of Heilsberg* positions about 7 p.m.

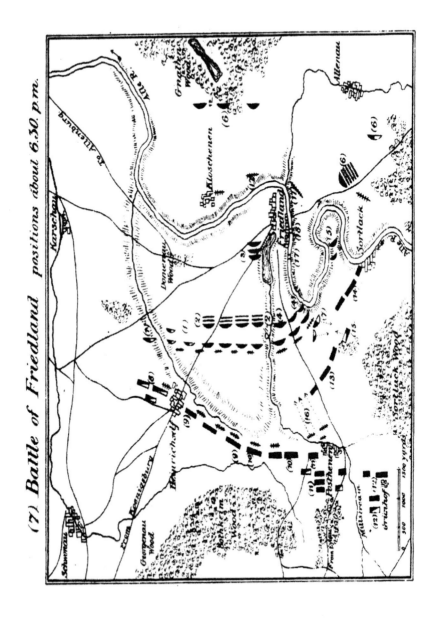

(7) Battle of Friedland positions about 6.30 p.m.

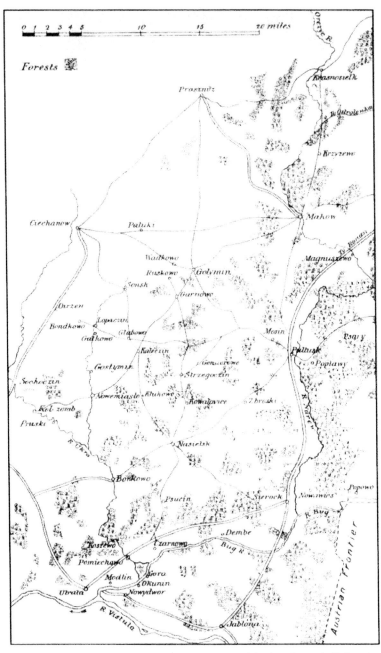

Campaign of Pultusk and Golymin

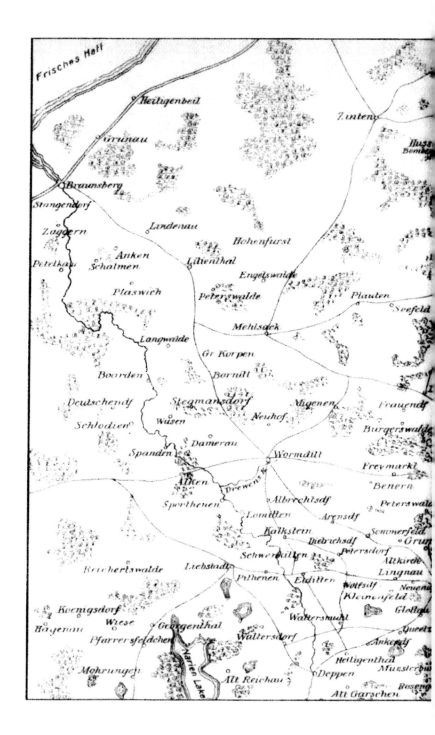

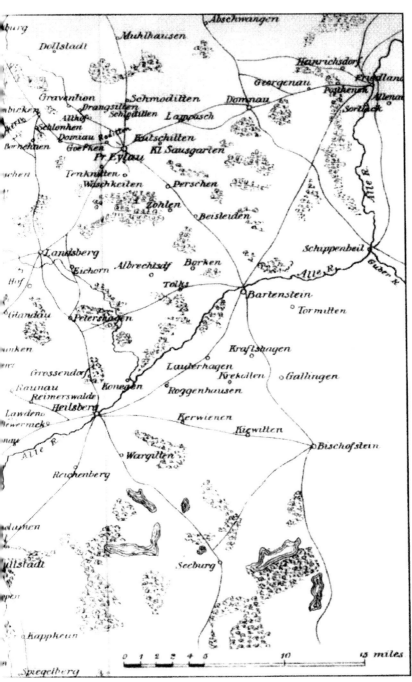

Operations, February to July

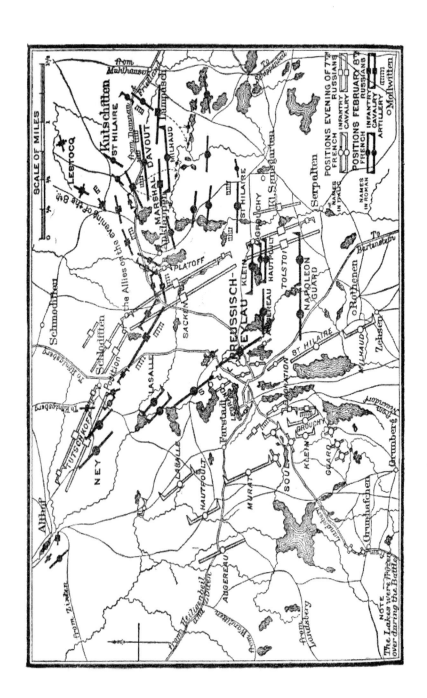

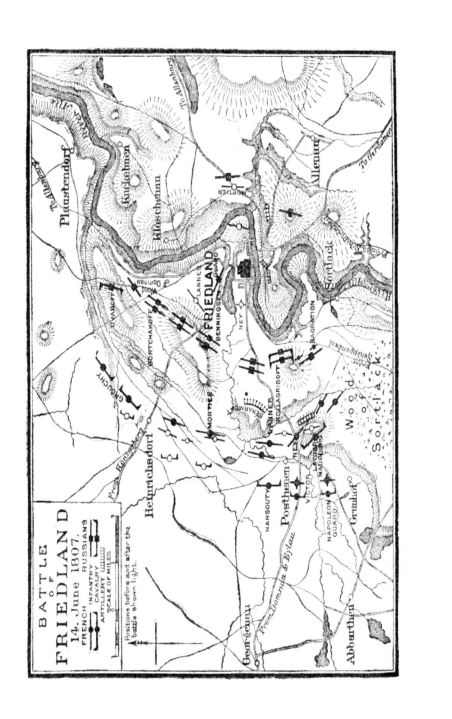

BATTLE
OF
FRIEDLAND
14. June 1807.
FRENCH   RUSSIANS
INFANTRY
CAVALRY
ARTILLERY
SCALE OF MILES

Positions before and after the
battle shown light.

LEONAUR

ALSO FROM LEONAUR

AVAILABLE IN SOFTCOVER OR HARDCOVER WITH DUST JACKET

BUGEAUD: A PACK WITH A BATON *by Thomas Robert Bugeaud*—The Early Campaigns of a Soldier of Napoleon's Army Who Would Become a Marshal of France.

WATERLOO RECOLLECTIONS *by Frederick Llewellyn*—Rare First Hand Accounts, Letters, Reports and Retellings from the Campaign of 1815.

SERGEANT NICOL *by Daniel Nicol*—The Experiences of a Gordon Highlander During the Napoleonic Wars in Egypt, the Peninsula and France.

THE JENA CAMPAIGN: 1806 *by F. N. Maude*—The Twin Battles of Jena & Auerstadt Between Napoleon's French and the Prussian Army.

PRIVATE O'NEIL *by Charles O'Neil*—The recollections of an Irish Rogue of H. M. 28th Regt.—The Slashers—during the Peninsula & Waterloo campaigns of the Napoleonic war.

ROYAL HIGHLANDER *by James Anton*—A soldier of H.M 42nd (Royal) Highlanders during the Peninsular, South of France & Waterloo Campaigns of the Napoleonic Wars.

CAPTAIN BLAZE *by Elzéar Blaze*—Life in Napoleons Army.

LEJEUNE VOLUME 1 *by Louis-François Lejeune*—The Napoleonic Wars through the Experiences of an Officer on Berthier's Staff.

LEJEUNE VOLUME 2 *by Louis-François Lejeune*—The Napoleonic Wars through the Experiences of an Officer on Berthier's Staff.

CAPTAIN COIGNET *by Jean-Roch Coignet*—A Soldier of Napoleon's Imperial Guard from the Italian Campaign to Russia and Waterloo.

FUSILIER COOPER *by John S. Cooper*—Experiences in the 7th (Royal) Fusiliers During the Peninsular Campaign of the Napoleonic Wars and the American Campaign to New Orleans.

FIGHTING NAPOLEON'S EMPIRE *by Joseph Anderson*—The Campaigns of a British Infantryman in Italy, Egypt, the Peninsular & the West Indies During the Napoleonic Wars.

CHASSEUR BARRES *by Jean-Baptiste Barres*—The experiences of a French Infantryman of the Imperial Guard at Austerlitz, Jena, Eylau, Friedland, in the Peninsular, Lutzen, Bautzen, Zinnwald and Hanau during the Napoleonic Wars.

CPSIA information can be obtained at www.ICGtesting.com
Printed in the USA
LVOW07s1030240215

428132LV00001B/16/P